SOCIAL WELFARE

HELP OR HINDRANCE?

ISSN 1532-1177

SOCIAL WELFARE
HELP OR HINDRANCE?

Eileen Kaplan

INFORMATION PLUS® REFERENCE SERIES
Formerly published by Information Plus, Wylie, Texas

GALE®

THOMSON
™
GALE

Detroit • New York • San Diego • San Francisco • Cleveland • New Haven, Conn. • Waterville, Maine • London • Munich

Social Welfare: Help or Hindrance?

Eileen Kaplan

Project Editor
Ellice Engdahl

Editorial
Paula Cutcher-Jackson, Kathleen Edgar, Christy Justice, Debra Kirby, Prindle LaBarge, Elizabeth Manar, Kathleen Meek, Charles B. Montney, Heather Price

Permissions
Lori Hines, Shalice Shah-Caldwell

Product Design
Michael Logusz

Composition and Electronic Prepress
Evi Seoud

Manufacturing
Keith Helmling

LIBRARY OF CONGRESS CATALOGING-IN-PUBLICATION DATA

ISBN 0-7876-5103-6 (set)
ISBN 0-7876-6067-1
ISSN 1532-1177

Printed in the United States of America
10 9 8 7 6 5 4 3 2 1

TABLE OF CONTENTS

Federal, state, and local governments, as well as private institutions, share in the expenditures on social welfare services. This chapter examines the costs and types of programs available to those in need.

The summer of 1996 saw the passage of a new welfare bill which brought about profound changes in the way America handles its welfare programs. This chapter discusses the 1996 welfare law as well as changes that have been made since its passage.

Millions of Americans suffer from poverty. This chapter includes a discussion of how poverty is defined and examines poverty statistics across a number of societal characteristics. Income, tax relief, and hunger are also explored.

The wealth and earnings gap between the rich and poor continues to increase. Studies of household incomes and household net worth illustrate this fact. For most poor Americans, poverty is not a static condition; some stay poor, others manage to improve their economic conditions.

Poor families are more likely to need government assistance to survive than non-poor families. The structure of the family usually indicates how much that family needs to rely on welfare. Other factors such as child support payments, unemployment compensation, and the minimum wage affect the poverty status of America's families.

This chapter explores the types of households that participate in welfare programs. Characteristics such as gender, race and ethnicity, age, education level, employment status, and regional differences all factor into who participates and who doesn't. Not surprisingly, individuals who receive one form of welfare may likely qualify for and receive others.

The welfare-reform law enacted in 1996 ended the entitlement welfare program and replaced it with a block grant program. This chapter provides background on the two programs and examines their similarities and differences. Also examined are the effects of these programs on welfare recipients.

Benefit programs provide cash and/or non-cash aid to individuals who meet certain low-income qualifications. This chapter explores Supplemental Security Income, the Food Stamp Program, National School Lunch and School Breakfast Programs, Medicaid, and other major programs designed to assist low-income Americans.

Since the Great Depression of the 1930s, the federal government has created work programs designed to combat unemployment. The passage of the 1996 welfare law laid the foundation for a work-based welfare system. Welfare recipients are now expected to participate in work activities while receiving benefits.

This chapter discusses the successes and failures of welfare since its 1996 reform. A discussion about who left welfare and who remains, employment and earnings, welfare spending, and support services reveals the cautious optimism concerning welfare reform.

PREFACE

Social Welfare: Help or Hindrance? is one of the latest volumes in the Information Plus Reference Series. Previously published by the Information Plus company of Wylie, Texas, the Information Plus Reference Series (and its companion set, the Information Plus Compact Series) became a Gale Group product when Gale and Information Plus merged in early 2000. Those of you familiar with the series as published by Information Plus will notice a few changes from the 2000 edition. Gale has adopted a new layout and style that we hope you will find easy to use. Other improvements include greatly expanded indexes in each book, and more descriptive tables of contents.

While some changes have been made to the design, the purpose of the Information Plus Reference Series remains the same. Each volume of the series presents the latest facts on a topic of pressing concern in modern American life. These topics include today's most controversial and most studied social issues: abortion, capital punishment, care for the elderly, crime, health care, the environment, immigration, minorities, social welfare, women, youth, and many more. Although written especially for the high school and undergraduate student, this series is an excellent resource for anyone in need of factual information on current affairs.

By presenting the facts, it is Gale's intention to provide its readers with everything they need to reach an informed opinion on current issues. To that end, there is a particular emphasis in this series on the presentation of scientific studies, surveys, and statistics. These data are generally presented in the form of tables, charts, and other graphics placed within the text of each book. Every graphic is directly referred to and carefully explained in the text. The source of each graphic is presented within the graphic itself. The data used in these graphics are drawn from the most reputable and reliable sources, in particular from the various branches of the U.S. government and from major independent polling organizations. Every effort has been made to secure the most recent information available. The reader should bear in mind that many major studies take years to conduct, and that additional years often pass before the data from these studies are made available to the public. Therefore, in many cases the most recent information available in 2002 dated from 1999 or 2000. Older statistics are sometimes presented as well, if they are of particular interest and no more-recent information exists.

Although statistics are a major focus of the Information Plus Reference Series, they are by no means its only content. Each book also presents the widely held positions and important ideas that shape how the book's subject is discussed in the United States. These positions are explained in detail and, where possible, in the words of their proponents. Some of the other material to be found in these books includes: historical background; descriptions of major events related to the subject; relevant laws and court cases; and examples of how these issues play out in American life. Some books also feature primary documents, or have pro and con debate sections giving the words and opinions of prominent Americans on both sides of a controversial topic. All material is presented in an even-handed and unbiased manner; the reader will never be encouraged to accept one view of an issue over another.

HOW TO USE THIS BOOK

Aid for the poor has long been a controversial topic in the United States. Most Americans agree that society should help those who have fallen on hard times, but there are many different opinions as to how this is best accomplished. The 1990s were a time of particularly heavy debate about this issue, resulting in major changes to the U.S. welfare system in 1996 with the introduction of the Personal Responsibility and Work Opportunity Reconciliation Act, requiring recipients to work in exchange for time-limited assistance. In this book, both the old and the new welfare systems are examined, and their differences are highlighted. The volume also describes those who make use of the welfare system, why they use it, and what they get out of it.

Social Welfare: Help or Hindrance? consists of ten chapters and three appendices. Each chapter is devoted to a particular aspect of social welfare. For a summary of the information covered in each chapter, please see the synopses provided in the Table of Contents at the front of the book. Chapters generally begin with an overview of the basic facts and background information on the chapter's topic, then proceed to examine sub-topics of particular interest. For example, Chapter 2: Recent Welfare-Reform Legislation begins with an overview of mid-1990s changes in welfare reform law, including the formation of the Temporary Assistance for Needy Families (TANF) program. The chapter then moves on to examine the Personal Responsibility and Work Opportunity Reconciliation Act of 1996 in great detail. Areas covered include block grants, Supplemental Social Security (SSI), child support, child care, welfare restrictions, child nutrition programs, and food stamps. The chapter concludes with a discussion of state flexibility in regard to waivers and the 1997 Balanced Budget Reconciliation Act. Readers can find their way through a chapter by looking for the section and sub-section headings, which are clearly set off from the text. Or, they can refer to the book's extensive index if they already know what they are looking for.

Statistical Information

The tables and figures featured throughout *Social Welfare: Help or Hindrance?* will be of particular use to the reader in learning about this issue. The tables and figures represent an extensive collection of the most recent and important statistics on social welfare, as well as related issues—for example, graphics in the book cover the amount of money spent each year for various government welfare programs; the demographics of poverty; the role of child support payments in preventing poverty; and the number of people who use welfare-to-work programs to escape poverty. Gale believes that making this information available to the reader is the most important way in which we fulfill the goal of this book: to help readers understand the issues and controversies surrounding social welfare and reach their own conclusions about them.

Each table or figure has a unique identifier appearing above it, for ease of identification and reference. Titles for the tables and figures explain their purpose. At the end of each table or figure, the original source of the data is provided.

In order to help readers understand these often complicated statistics, all tables and figures are explained in the text. References in the text direct the reader to the relevant statistics. Furthermore, the contents of all tables and figures are fully indexed. Please see the opening section of the index at the back of this volume for a description of how to find tables and figures within it.

Appendices

In addition to the main body text and images, *Social Welfare: Help or Hindrance?* has three appendices. The first is the Important Names and Addresses directory. Here the reader will find contact information for a number of government and private organizations that can provide further information on aspects of social welfare. The second appendix is the Resources section, which can also assist the reader in conducting his or her own research. In this section, the author and editors of *Social Welfare: Help or Hindrance?* describe some of the sources that were most useful during the compilation of this book. The final appendix is the index. It has been greatly expanded from previous editions, and should make it even easier to find specific topics in this book.

ADVISORY BOARD CONTRIBUTIONS

The staff of Information Plus would like to extend their heartfelt appreciation to the Information Plus Advisory Board. This dedicated group of media professionals provides feedback on the series on an ongoing basis. Their comments allow the editorial staff who work on the project to continually make the series better and more user-friendly. Our top priorities are to produce the highest-quality and most useful books possible, and the Advisory Board's contributions to this process are invaluable.

The members of the Information Plus Advisory Board are:

- Kathleen R. Bonn, Librarian, Newbury Park High School, Newbury Park, California

- Madelyn Garner, Librarian, San Jacinto College—North Campus, Houston, Texas

- Anne Oxenrider, Media Specialist, Dundee High School, Dundee, Michigan

- Charles R. Rodgers, Director of Libraries, Pasco-Hernando Community College, Dade City, Florida

- James N. Zitzelsberger, Library Media Department Chairman, Oshkosh West High School, Oshkosh, Wisconsin

COMMENTS AND SUGGESTIONS

The editors of the Information Plus Reference Series welcome your feedback on *Social Welfare: Help or Hindrance?* Please direct all correspondence to:

Editors
Information Plus Reference Series
27500 Drake Rd.
Farmington Hills, MI 48331-3535

ACKNOWLEDGMENTS

The editors wish to thank the copyright holders of material included in this volume and the permissions managers of many book and magazine publishing companies for assisting us in securing reproduction rights. We are also grateful to the staffs of the Detroit Public Library, the Library of Congress, the University of Detroit Mercy Library, Wayne State University Purdy/Kresge Library Complex, and the University of Michigan Libraries for making their resources available to us.

Following is a list of the copyright holders who have granted us permission to reproduce material in Information Plus: Social Welfare. *Every effort has been made to trace copyright, but if omissions have been made, please let us know.*

For more detailed source citations, please see the sources listed under each individual table and figure.

Center on Budget and Policy Priorities: Figure 3.3, Figure 3.4, Figure 8.2

Centers for Disease Control and Prevention: Figure 7.3

Economic Policy Institute, Center on Budget and Policy Priorities, and National Employment Law Project: Table 5.6

The Gallup Organization: Table 7.1

The Library of Congress Congressional Research Service: Figure 2.1, Figure 7.1, Figure 7.2, Table 7.2, Table 7.3, Table 7.4, Table 7.5, Table 9.4, Table 9.5

Mathematica Policy Research, Inc.: Figure 3.7, Figure 3.8, Figure 3.9, Figure 3.10, Figure 9.1

National Association of State Budget Officers: Figure 1.1, Figure 1.2, Figure 1.3, Figure 1.4

Social Security Administration: Table 1.3, Table 1.6, Table 1.7, Table 3.1, Figure 8.1, Table 8.2, Table 8.3, Table 8.4, Table 8.13, Table 8.14

The Urban Institute. Weil, Alan. From "Figure 2. Distribution of Federal and State TANF Spending, 1996 and 2000 (in 2000 Dollars)," in *Ten Things Everyone Should Know about Welfare Reform,* New Federalism: Issues and Options for States, Series A, no. A-52. The Urban Institute, Washington, DC. Reproduced by permission: Figure 10.2

U.S. Census Bureau: Table 1.1, Table 1.2, Table 1.4, Table 1.5, Figure 3.1, Figure 3.2, Table 3.2, Table 3.3, Table 3.4, Table 3.5, Table 3.7, Table 3.8, Table 3.9, Figure 4.1, Figure 4.2, Figure 4.3, Figure 4.4, Figure 4.5, Figure 4.6, Figure 4.7, Table 4.1, Table 4.2, Table 4.3, Table 4.4, Table 4.5, Table 4.6, Figure 5.2, Figure 5.3, Figure 5.4, Table 5.1, Table 5.2, Table 5.3, Table 5.4, Table 5.12, Figure 6.1, Table 6.1, Table 6.2, Table 6.3, Table 6.4, Table 8.10, Table 8.15, Table 8.16, Table 8.17

U.S. Department of Agriculture: Figure 3.5, Figure 3.6, Table 3.10, Table 8.5, Table 8.6, Table 8.7, Table 8.9, Table 8.11, Table 8.12

U.S. Department of Health and Human Services: Figure 5.1, Table 5.11, Table 7.10, Table 7.11, Table 7.12, Table 7.13, Figure 10.1, Figure 10.3, Table 10.1, Table 10.2

U.S. Department of Health and Human Services, Family Support Administration, and Library of Congress Congressional Research Service: Table 7.6

U.S. Department of Labor: Table 3.6, Figure 5.5, Table 5.9, Table 5.10, Table 5.13, Table 5.14, Table 5.15

U.S. General Accounting Office: Figure 8.4, Figure 8.5

U.S. House of Representatives: Figure 2.2, Table 5.5, Table 5.7, Table 5.8, Table 6.5, Table 6.6, Table 6.7, Table 7.7, Table 7.8, Table 7.9, Table 8.1, Table 8.18, Table 8.19, Table 9.1, Table 9.2, Table 9.3

U.S. National Archives & Records Administration and U.S. Government Printing Office: Table 8.8

The White House, Office of Management and Budget: Figure 8.3

CHAPTER 1

HOW MUCH DOES THE NATION SPEND ON WELFARE?

The U.S. Social Security Administration defines social welfare expenditures as the cost of "cash benefits, services, and the administration of public programs that directly benefit individuals and families." This broad definition includes expenditures for social security (Old-Age, Survivor's, Disability, and Health Insurance, or OASDHI), health and medical programs, education, housing, veterans' programs, and public aid programs.

In fiscal year 1995 (the last year for which information on social welfare expenditures is available) federal, state, and local governments spent about $1.5 trillion on social welfare programs. Table 1.1 breaks down all social welfare spending by specific categories and by state and federal spending. The 1995 total expenditure for social welfare was almost 21 percent of the gross domestic product (GDP, the monetary total of the domestic goods and services produced by a country) of the United States. This reflects an increase of 2.4 percentage points in social welfare spending as a percentage of GDP over the previous five years. (See Table 1.2.)

The federal government accounted for about 59 percent of total spending on social welfare, while state and local governments spent the remaining 41 percent. But the proportion of expenditures at the federal and state level in each category of spending was very different. For example, social insurance outlays made up about two-thirds (65 percent) of federal welfare spending (primarily in social security) and one-fifth (20 percent) of state and local welfare spending. On the other hand, expenditures on education accounted for very little (less than 3 percent) of the total federal welfare spending, while over half (55 percent) of state and local welfare costs were spent for education. (See Table 1.1.)

Federal social welfare expenditures remained relatively stable in the 1980s and 1990s, making up between 50 and 60 percent of all federal spending. However, expenditures on social welfare have been increasing as a percentage of

state and local government costs. State and local spending for social welfare grew from 69 percent of total spending in 1985 to 84 percent in 1995. (See Table 1.2.) This continual increase was a major reason for the severe budget problems faced by local and state governments during the early 1990s. However, the strong economy of the mid-1990s made it easier for the states to absorb these costs.

PUBLIC AID

While the Social Security Administration uses a broad definition of social welfare to categorize public expenditures, public welfare or public aid is generally taken to refer to cash or noncash assistance for low-income persons. This more narrow definition excludes social insurance programs such as Social Security and Medicare, which are considered entitlement programs, that is, programs to which people have a right because of contributions they have made from their earnings. This volume focuses on welfare programs that provide benefits or services to persons who are determined to be eligible based on a test of their income or "means."

Public assistance has usually included such programs as Aid to Families with Dependent Children/Temporary Assistance for Needy Families (AFDC/TANF), General Assistance, and Medicaid. Virtually all the programs are included in Table 1.1 under "Public aid." In 1995 public aid accounted for 16.9 percent of all social welfare spending. More than half of this went for Medicaid and other medical expenses. Costs for social services increased moderately (in constant dollars, which account for inflation) from 1980 to 1995, compared to the cost of specific programs such as AFDC/TANF, Supplemental Security Income (SSI), and food stamps, which had grown significantly by 1995.

The portion of the GDP spent on social welfare increased only moderately between 1975 and 1995 (from

TABLE 1.1

Social welfare expenditures under public programs, 1980–95

[In billions of dollars (493 represents $493,000,000,000), except percent.]

Year	Total	Social insur-ance	Public aid	Health and medical programs[1]	Veterans pro-grams	Educa-tion	Housing	Other social welfare	All health and medical care[2]
Total:									
1980	493	230	73	27	21	121	7	14	100
1985	732	370	98	39	27	172	13	14	171
1990	1,049	514	147	61	31	258	19	18	274
1992	1,267	619	208	70	36	292	21	22	353
1993	1,367	659	221	75	36	332	21	23	382
1994	1,436	684	238	80	38	344	27	25	409
1995	1,505	705	254	86	39	366	29	27	435
Federal:									
1980	303	191	49	13	21	13	6	9	69
1985	451	310	63	18	27	14	11	8	122
1990	617	422	93	27	30	18	17	9	190
1992	750	496	139	32	35	20	17	11	250
1993	805	534	152	33	36	20	19	11	276
1994	853	557	163	35	37	24	25	12	295
1995	888	580	170	37	38	23	27	12	308
State and local:									
1980	190	39	23	14	(Z)	108	1	5	31
1985	281	59	35	21	(Z)	158	2	6	49
1990	432	92	54	34	(Z)	240	3	9	84
1992	517	123	69	38	1	272	3	11	103
1993	561	125	69	42	1	312	2	12	106
1994	583	126	75	45	1	320	2	13	114
1995	617	126	83	49	1	342	2	14	127
Percent Federal:									
1980	62	83	68	47	99	11	91	65	69
1985	62	84	64	46	99	8	88	56	71
1990	59	82	63	44	98	7	85	50	69
1993	59	81	69	44	98	6	91	48	72
1994	59	82	68	43	98	7	92	48	72
1995	59	82	67	43	98	6	93	47	71
Per capita (current dollars):									
1980	2,126	990	314	118	92	523	30	59	434
1985	3,009	1,516	405	161	111	708	52	56	705
1990	4,123	2,017	579	243	120	1,018	77	71	1,081
1993	5,238	2,523	849	287	137	1,275	80	87	1,466
1994	5,446	2,591	905	305	141	1,308	103	94	1,554
1995	5,622	2,632	949	320	144	1,368	109	99	1,628
Per capita (constant (1995) dollars):[3][4]									
1980	3,788	1,764	560	210	164	932	53	105	764
1985	4,131	2,081	556	223	152	972	71	77	969
1990	4,741	2,319	665	279	138	1,170	89	81	1,243
1993	5,487	2,644	889	301	144	1,335	84	91	1,536
1994	5,570	2,650	925	312	144	1,338	105	96	1,589
1995	5,622	2,632	949	320	144	1,368	109	99	1,628

Z Less than $500 million.

[1] Excludes program parts of social insurance, public aid, veterans, and other social welfare.

[2] Combines "health and medical programs" with medical services included in social insurance, public aid, veterans, vocational rehabilitation, and antipoverty programs.

[3] Excludes payments within foreign countries for education, veterans, OASDHI (old-age, survivors, disability, and health insurance), and civil service retirement.

[4] Constant dollar figures are based on implicit price deflators for personal consumption expenditures published by U.S. Bureau of Economic Analysis in *Survey of Current Business*.

SOURCE: "No. 598. Social Welfare Expenditures Under Public Programs: 1980 to 1995," in *Statistical Abstract of the United States, 2000,* U.S. Census Bureau, Washington, DC, 2000

18.2 percent to 20.9 percent). In 1995 public aid account-ed for 3.5 percent of the nation's GDP, an increase of approximately one percentage point from expenditures in the late 1970s and 1980s. However public health and medical costs nearly doubled, from 3.2 percent of the GDP in 1975 to 6.1 percent of the GDP in 1995. (See Table 1.3.) This increase reflects, among many factors,

the growing number of older Americans, who have greater need of medical services, as well as the increasing cost of medical care in general.

A rapid increase occurred in public spending on health and medical care between 1980 and 1998. (See Table 1.4.) In 1980 the government spent $104.8 billion

TABLE 1.2

Social welfare expenditures under public programs as percent of GDP and total government outlays, 1980–95

[493 represents $493,000,000,000]

Year	Total expenditures				Federal				State and local government			
			Percent of —				Percent of —				Percent of —	
	Total (bil. dol.)	Percent change[1]	Total GDP[2]	Total govt. outlays	Total (bil. dol.)	Percent change[1]	Total GDP[2]	Total federal outlays	Total (bil. dol.)	Percent change[1]	Total GDP[2]	Total state and local outlays
1980	493	14.7	18.6	57.2	303	15.2	11.4	54.4	190	13.8	7.2	62.9
1985	732	8.0	18.4	54.4	451	7.1	11.3	48.7	281	9.3	7.1	68.8
1990	1,049	9.6	18.5	58.2	617	9.1	10.9	51.4	432	10.3	7.6	74.0
1992	1,267	9.2	20.6	63.7	750	10.8	12.2	57.4	517	7.0	8.4	77.6
1993	1,367	7.8	21.1	66.6	805	7.2	12.4	60.0	561	8.5	8.7	80.7
1994	1,436	5.1	21.0	64.5	853	6.1	12.5	57.4	583	3.7	8.5	80.4
1995	1,505	4.8	20.9	67.5	888	4.1	12.4	60.2	617	5.8	8.6	83.6

[1] Percent change from immediate prior year.
[2] Gross domestic product.

SOURCE: "No. 599. Social Welfare Expenditures Under Public Programs as Percent of GDP and Total Government Outlays: 1980 to 1995," in *Statistical Abstract of the United States, 2000*, U.S. Census Bureau, Washington, DC, 2000

on health care. A decade later, not accounting for inflation, government spending on health and medical care rose to $283.2 billion, and by 1998 it reached $522.7 billion. Three-fourths (75 percent) of all this spending was on two programs—Medicare and public assistance payments (primarily Medicaid). In 1980 the government paid about $37.5 billion for Medicare; less than two decades later, in 1998, it spent $216.6 billion. Similarly, spending on public assistance medical payments (Medicaid) in 1980 barely exceeded $28 billion, but by 1998 Medicaid accounted for over $175 billion. These are huge changes involving enormous sums of money over a relatively short time. This situation helps to explain some of the problems governments face in trying to control their budgets and why health care has become a major national issue.

Welfare Payments

According to the U.S. Bureau of the Census, in 1999 the two major categories of public cash benefit payments paid out about $48.8 billion. Family assistance payments (primarily AFDC/TANF, not including Medicaid) totaled $17.8 billion, while $31 billion was paid out for SSI. Spending for SSI increased by 18 percent between 1994 and 1999, from $26.3 billion to $31 billion. Much of this growth reflects the increase in the number of retired Americans, many of whom need Supplemental Security Income in order to live. By contrast, expenditures for family assistance declined by 23 percent, from $23.2 billion in 1994 to $17.8 billion in 1999. (See Table 1.5.)

PER CAPITA SPENDING

Another way to look at social welfare spending is to consider per capita spending, or how much would theoretically be spent on each person in the United States if the total expenditures were equally divided among the population. In 1995 per capita spending for all government social welfare expenditures reached $5,622. About one-half (47 percent) went for social insurance, mainly social security, and one-fourth (24 percent) went for education. Seventeen percent went for public aid, about 6 percent for health care costs, 2.6 percent for Veteran programs, and 2 percent toward other programs. (See Table 1.6.)

The lower section of Table 1.6 presents per capita spending in constant 1995 dollars that account for increases caused by inflation. From 1980 to 1995 social welfare expenditures per capita, under public programs, rose 48 percent in constant dollars. The largest increases occurred in total health care costs (113 percent), public aid (69 percent), and social insurance (49 percent). Expenditures for education rose 47 percent, while veterans' programs and other welfare programs dropped.

STATE EXPENDITURES FOR SOCIAL WELFARE

In fiscal year 2000 state governments spent a total of approximately $945.3 billion, an increase of 7 percent over 1999. The largest expenditures were on elementary and secondary education (22.5 percent) and Medicaid (19.5 percent), followed by higher education (10.9 percent) and transportation (8.8 percent). (See Figure 1.1.) About 2.4 percent went for public assistance to the needy, which totaled $23 billion.

As increased demands were made on state and local funding, much of the impetus for welfare reform came from the states before federal welfare programs were overhauled in 1996. Furthermore, welfare reform became a key goal for President Bill Clinton. In August 1996 he signed into law the Personal Responsibility and Work Opportunity Reconciliation Act of 1996 (PL 104-193). This controversial law repealed the 60-year-old AFDC (Aid to Families with Dependent Children) program and

TABLE 1.3

Gross domestic product and social welfare expenditures under public programs, fiscal years 1965–95[1]

Item	1965	1970	1975	1980	1985	1990[2]	1992[2]	1993[2]	1994[2]	1995
					Amount (in millions)					
Gross domestic product	$701,000	$1,023,100	$1,590,800	$2,718,900	$4,108,000	$5,682,900	$6,149,300	$6,476,600	$6,837,100	$7,186,900
Total social welfare expenditures[3]	77,084	145,979	288,967	492,213	731,840	1,048,951	1,266,504	1,366,743	1,435,714	1,505,136
Social insurance	28,123	54,691	123,013	229,754	369,595	513,822	618,938	659,210	683,779	705,483
Public aid	6,283	16,488	41,447	72,703	98,362	146,811	207,953	221,000	238,025	253,530
Health and medical programs	6,155	10,030	16,535	26,762	38,643	61,684	70,143	74,706	80,130	85,507
Veterans' programs	6,031	9,078	17,019	21,466	27,042	30,916	35,642	36,378	37,895	39,072
Education	28,108	50,846	80,834	121,050	172,048	258,332	292,145	331,997	344,091	365,625
Housing	318	701	3,172	6,879	12,598	19,468	20,151	20,782	27,032	29,361
Other social welfare	2,066	4,145	6,947	13,599	13,552	17,918	21,532	22,670	24,762	26,558
All health and medical care[4]	9,302	24,801	51,022	99,145	170,665	274,472	353,174	381,710	408,780	435,075
					As percent of gross domestic product					
Gross domestic product	100.0	100.0	100.0	100.0	100.0	100.0	100.0	100.0	100.0	100.0
Total social welfare expenditures	11.0	14.3	18.2	18.1	17.8	18.5	20.6	21.1	21.0	20.9
Social insurance	4.0	5.3	7.7	8.5	9.0	9.0	10.1	10.2	10.0	9.8
Public aid	.9	1.6	2.6	2.7	2.4	2.6	3.4	3.4	3.5	3.5
Health and medical programs	.9	1.0	1.0	1.0	.9	1.1	1.1	1.2	1.2	1.2
Veterans' programs	.9	.9	1.1	.8	.7	.5	.6	.6	.6	.5
Education	4.0	5.0	5.1	4.5	4.2	4.5	4.8	5.1	5.0	5.1
Housing	[5]	.1	.2	.3	.3	.3	.3	.3	.4	.4
Other social welfare	.3	.4	.4	.5	.3	.3	.4	.4	.4	.4
All health and medical care	1.3	2.4	3.2	3.6	4.2	4.8	5.7	5.9	6.0	6.1

[1] Through 1976, fiscal year ended June 30 for federal government, most states, and some localities. Beginning in 1977, federal fiscal year ended Sept. 30.

[2] Revised data.

[3] Represents program and administrative expenditures from federal, state and local public revenues and trust funds under public law. Includes workers' compensation and temporary disability insurance payments made through private carriers and self-insurers. Includes capital outlay and some expenditures abroad.

[4] Combines "health and medical programs" with medical services provided in connection with social insurance, public aid, veterans', and "other social welfare" categories.

[5] Less than 0.05 percent.

Note: Gross domestic product data from Department of Commerce, *Survey of Current Business*. GDP figures revised in 1996 to reflect changes in the source data. Social welfare expenditures data taken or estimated from *Federal Budgets, Census of Governments,* and reports of administering agencies.

SOURCE: "Table 3.A.1. Gross domestic product and social welfare expenditures under public programs, fiscal years 1965–95[1]," in *Social Security Bulletin, Annual Statistical Supplement, 2000,* Social Security Administration, Washington, DC, 2000

created the Temporary Assistance for Needy Families (TANF) block grant program. Though states must comply with time limits, work requirements, and child protection guidelines, they were given the flexibility to design their own welfare programs. Each state was required to submit a complete plan of implementation no later than July 1, 1997.

Prior to the passage of Public Law 104-193, 43 states were granted federal waivers to set aside federal regulations and guidelines to introduce their own reform proposals. For example, in March 1996 a Texas plan was approved limiting benefits to a maximum of three years but allowing the recipients to hold more assets, including up to $2,000 in savings, without reducing welfare benefits.

The state and federal governments jointly fund cash assistance. In 2000 the federal government provided almost half (42.8 percent) of the funding while the states funded the rest, mostly from general funds. (See Figure 1.2.) Spending for cash assistance took 2.4 percent of total state expenditures: 1.5 percent was for cash assistance under TANF and the remainder was for other cash assistance programs. The federal government paid a larger portion of TANF (56.6 percent) than it did for all of state welfare. State spending on cash assistance under TANF and other cash welfare programs dropped following the enactment of welfare reform legislation in 1996.

Medicaid

The National Association of State Budget Officers observed in the *2000 State Expenditure Report* (Washington, D.C., 2001), "Medicaid expenditures have escalated and are consuming a greater portion of states' budgets." As a percent of total state expenditures, Medicaid spending increased from 10 percent in 1987 to 14 percent in 1991 and 19.5 percent in 2000. Two factors that help explain this dramatic increase are the rate of inflation for medical goods and services and the increased number of persons eligible for Medicaid.

In 2000 total spending on Medicaid, not including administrative costs, reached $205 billion, up 31.4 percent from 1995. Of the $205 billion total, the federal government paid 57 percent, and the states paid the remaining 43 percent. (See Figure 1.3.) In 2000 the states spent $88 billion on Medicaid, almost triple the $32 billion spent in 1990. (See Figure 1.4.)

TABLE 1.4

National health expenditures by type, 1980–98

[In billions of dollars (247.3 represents $247,300,000,000), except percent. Includes Puerto Rico and outlying areas]

Type of expenditure	1980	1985	1990	1993	1994	1995	1996	1997	1998
Total	**247.3**	**428.7**	**699.4**	**898.5**	**947.7**	**993.3**	**1,039.4**	**1,088.2**	**1,149.1**
Annual percent change[1]	14.9	9.9	12.2	7.4	5.5	4.8	4.6	4.7	5.6
Percent of gross domestic product	8.9	10.3	12.2	13.7	13.6	13.7	13.6	13.4	13.5
Private expenditures	**142.5**	**254.5**	**416.2**	**513.2**	**524.7**	**537.3**	**559.0**	**586.0**	**626.4**
Health services and supplies	138.0	248.0	405.9	501.3	513.0	526.3	547.5	572.7	613.4
Out-of-pocket payments	60.3	100.7	145.0	167.1	168.2	170.5	178.1	189.1	199.5
Insurance premiums[2]	69.8	132.8	239.6	306.8	315.3	324.0	334.9	346.7	375.0
Other	8.0	14.5	21.4	27.4	29.5	31.8	34.5	37.0	38.8
Medical research	0.3	0.5	1.0	1.2	1.3	1.3	1.4	1.5	1.6
Medical facilities construction	4.2	6.0	9.3	10.7	10.5	9.6	10.1	11.8	11.5
Public expenditures	**104.8**	**174.2**	**283.2**	**385.3**	**423.0**	**456.0**	**480.4**	**502.2**	**522.7**
Percent federal of public	68.7	70.7	68.9	71.5	71.2	71.5	72.3	72.3	72.1
Health services and supplies	97.6	164.3	268.9	368.2	404.3	436.2	460.0	480.7	500.4
Medicare[3]	37.5	72.1	111.5	148.7	166.9	185.3	199.4	211.3	216.6
Public assistance medical payments[4]	28.0	44.4	80.4	126.8	140.1	151.6	159.5	165.2	175.5
Temporary disability insurance[5]	0.1	0.1	0.1	0.1	0.1	0.1	0.1	0.1	0.1
Workers' compensation (medical)[5]	5.1	8.0	16.1	18.5	18.6	17.9	17.7	17.5	17.0
Defense Dept. hospital, medical	4.4	7.5	11.6	13.3	13.2	13.4	13.3	13.4	13.6
Maternal, child health programs	0.9	1.3	1.9	2.2	2.3	2.4	2.4	2.5	2.6
Public health activities	6.7	11.6	19.6	25.3	28.2	29.8	31.3	34.6	36.6
Veterans' hospital, medical care	5.9	8.7	11.4	14.3	15.3	15.6	16.5	16.5	17.1
Medical vocational rehabilitation	0.3	0.4	0.6	0.6	0.7	0.7	0.7	0.8	0.8
State and local hospitals[6]	5.6	7.0	10.8	11.8	12.0	11.9	11.5	11.2	11.8
Other[7]	3.1	3.3	5.0	6.6	7.1	7.5	7.5	7.7	8.7
Medical research	5.2	7.3	11.3	13.3	14.6	15.4	15.7	16.4	18.3
Medical facilities construction	2.0	2.6	3.0	3.8	4.1	4.4	4.7	5.2	4.0

[1] Change from immediate prior year.
[2] Covers insurance benefits and amount retained by insurance companies for expenses, additions to reserves, and profits (net cost of insurance).
[3] Represents expenditures for benefits and administrative cost from federal hospital and medical insurance trust funds under old-age, survivors, disability, and health insurance programs; see text, of this section.
[4] Payments made directly to suppliers of medical care (primarily medicaid).
[5] Includes medical benefits paid under public law by private insurance carriers, state governments, and self-insurers.
[6] Expenditures not offset by other revenues.
[7] Covers expenditures for Substance Abuse and Mental Health Services Administration, Indian Health Service; school health and other programs.

SOURCE: "No. 151. National Health Expenditures by Type: 1980–1998," in *Statistical Abstract of the United States: 2000,* U.S. Census Bureau, Washington, DC, 2001

PRIVATE WELFARE EXPENDITURES

The private sector is an important source of social welfare funding. These expenditures can be grouped into four program categories: health and medical care, welfare services, education, and income maintenance. In 1994 private spending for welfare services reached $86 billion, more than 3.5 times the almost $23 billion spent in 1980 (in current dollars, which do not account for inflation). As a fraction of total private outlays, spending on social welfare services increased from 7.9 percent in 1972 to 9.4 percent in 1994. (See Table 1.7.) Welfare services funded by private sources include:

- Individual and family services (counseling and referral services for families and children, family service agencies, adoption services, emergency and disaster services, child day-care services, and senior citizen services).

- Residential care (group foster homes, halfway homes, and housing and shelter for the homeless).

- Recreation and group work (YMCA, YWCA, Boy Scouts, and Girl Scouts).

- Civic, social, and fraternal organizations.

- Job training and vocational rehabilitation, such as sheltered workshops, vocational rehabilitation agencies, and skill-training centers.

EFFECTS OF NEW WELFARE-REFORM LEGISLATION

The intent of the Personal Responsibility and Work Opportunity Reconciliation Act of August 1996 (PL 104-193) was to reduce future welfare expenditures by changing provisions and requiring work from welfare recipients. The 1997 Balanced Budget Reconciliation Act modified some provisions of PL 104-193 and restored and even added funding for certain programs. Both pieces of legislation brought about sweeping changes in the welfare system, and their "work first" emphasis has resulted in a significant reduction in welfare caseloads. While welfare

TABLE 1.5

Government transfer payments to individuals, by type, 1990–99

[In millions of dollars (561,399 represents $561,399,000,000)]

Item	1990	1994	1995	1996	1997	1998	1999
Total	561,399	792,815	841,041	883,042	914,942	933,394	964,173
Retirement & disability insurance benefit payments	263,854	334,773	350,027	364,623	379,415	391,873	402,844
Old age, survivors, & disability insurance	244,135	312,145	327,667	341,987	356,602	369,291	379,905
Railroad retirement and disability	7,221	7,963	8,028	8,085	8,193	8,225	8,203
Worker's compensation payments (federal & state)	8,618	10,734	10,530	10,795	10,606	10,313	10,374
Other government disability insurance & retirement [1]	3,880	3,931	3,802	3,756	4,014	4,044	4,362
Medical payments	189,099	308,292	337,532	361,342	379,557	384,877	399,060
Medicare	107,929	160,891	180,283	195,581	209,198	208,755	208,081
Public assistance medical care [2]	78,176	144,886	155,017	163,629	168,288	174,079	188,972
Military medical insurance [3]	2,994	2,515	2,232	2,132	2,071	2,043	2,007
Income maintenance benefit payments	63,481	95,642	100,444	102,494	100,288	100,475	104,137
Supplemental Security Income (SSI)	16,670	26,269	27,726	28,903	29,154	30,322	31,024
Family assistance [4]	19,187	23,163	22,637	20,325	17,717	17,012	17,760
Food stamps	14,741	22,842	22,447	21,955	18,732	16,463	15,492
Other income maintenance [5]	12,883	23,368	27,634	31,311	34,685	36,678	39,861
Unemployment insurance benefit payments	18,208	24,055	21,864	22,480	20,299	19,934	20,765
State unemployment insurance compensation	17,644	23,072	20,975	21,614	19,469	19,183	20,016
Unemployment compensation for federal civilian employees	215	378	339	326	281	252	223
Unemployment compensation for railroad employees	89	63	62	65	72	61	65
Unemployment compensation for veterans	144	398	320	279	259	241	231
Other unemployment compensation [6]	116	144	168	196	218	197	230
Veterans benefit payments	17,687	19,705	20,545	21,430	22,233	23,170	24,076
Veterans pension and disability	15,550	16,936	17,565	18,286	19,061	20,068	20,887
Veterans readjustment [7]	257	853	1,086	1,138	1,234	1,203	1,358
Veterans life insurance benefits	1,868	1,904	1,883	1,997	1,929	1,891	1,823
Other assistance to veterans [8]	12	12	11	9	9	8	8
Federal education & training assistance payments [9]	7,300	8,562	9,007	8,568	11,481	11,189	11,264
Other payments to individuals [10]	1,770	1,786	1,622	2,105	1,669	1,876	2,027

[1]Consists largely of temporary disability payments and black lung payments.
[2]Consists of medicaid and other medical vendor payments.
[3]Consists of payments made under the TriCare Management Program (formerly called CHAMPUS) for the medical care of dependents of active duty military personnel and of retired military personnel and their dependents at nonmilitary medical facilities.
[4]Through 1995, consists of Emergency Assistance and Aid to Families With Dependent Children. Beginning with 1998, consists of benefits—generally known as Temporary Assistance for Needy Families—provided under the Personal Responsibility and Work Opportunity Reconciliation Act of 1996. For 1996-97, consists of payments under all three of these programs.
[5]Consists largely of general assistance, refugee assistance, foster home care and adoption assistance, earned income tax credits, and energy assistance.
[6]Consists of trade readjustment allowance payments, Redwood Park benefit payments, public service employment benefit payments, and transitional benefit payments.
[7]Consists largely of veterans' readjustment benefit payments, educational assistance to spouses and children of disabled or deceased veterans, payments to paraplegics, and payments for autos and conveyances for disabled veterans.
[8]Consists largely of state and local government payments to veterans.
[9]Excludes veterans. Consists largely of federal fellowship payments (National Science Foundation fellowships and traineeships, subsistence payments to state maritime academy cadets, and other federal fellowships), interest subsidy on higher education loans, basic educational opportunity grants, and Job Corps payments.
[10]Consists largely of Bureau of Indian Affairs payments, education exchange payments, Alaska Permanent Fund dividend payments, compensation of survivors of public safety officers, compensation of victims of crime, disaster relief payments, compensation for Japanese internment, and other special payments to individuals.

SOURCE: "No. 519. Government Transfer Payments to Individuals by Type: 1990 to 1999," in *Statistical Abstract of the United States: 2001*, U.S. Census Bureau, Washington, DC, 2001

reform advocates claim that the new system has lifted former welfare recipients out of poverty and into gainful employment, critics argue that changes have pushed those who left welfare for work deeper into poverty.

TABLE 1.6

Social welfare expenditures under public programs, selected years 1965–95

Fiscal year	Total expenditures		Per capita expenditures for—						
	Amount (in millions)[1]	Per capita[2]	Social insurance	Public aid	Health and medical programs	Veterans' programs	Education	Other social welfare	Total health care costs[3]
					Current dollars				
1965	$76,837.00	$390.69	$142.29	$31.95	$31.30	$30.30	$142.73	$10.50	$47.30
1970	145,183.20	697.91	261.75	79.26	46.18	43.16	244.27	19.93	119.22
1975	288,457.60	1,315.73	558.66	189.05	76.36	76.95	368.56	31.69	232.73
1980	491,597.80	2,126.35	989.95	314.47	117.92	92.02	523.41	58.82	428.84
1985	730,896.70	3,009.79	1,515.98	405.05	162.14	110.53	708.41	55.81	705.81
1990[4]	1,046,498.30	4,124.03	2,017.31	578.55	243.08	119.79	1,017.96	70.61	1,081.64
1991[4]	1,157,039.40	4,520.44	2,184.52	708.48	257.11	126.13	1,082.84	77.28	1,227.66
1992[4]	1,263,322.90	4,868.30	2,376.93	801.36	270.30	133.35	1,125.73	82.97	1,360.98
1993[4]	1,364,067.80	5,237.51	2,523.19	848.56	286.84	137.40	1,274.67	87.04	1,465.62
1994[4]	1,432,756.70	5,446.19	2,590.96	904.78	304.59	141.10	1,307.88	94.13	1,553.85
1995	1,502,234.40	5,622.39	2,631.98	948.88	320.03	143.86	1,368.34	99.40	1,628.35
					Percentage increase to 1995				
1965	1,855.09	1,339.10	1,749.73	2,870.01	922.58	374.72	858.71	846.38	3,342.80
1970	934.72	705.60	905.53	1,097.20	593.04	233.36	460.17	398.81	1,265.82
1975	420.78	327.32	371.13	401.92	319.07	86.96	271.27	213.70	599.69
1980	205.58	164.41	165.87	201.74	171.38	56.33	161.43	68.98	279.71
1985	105.53	86.80	73.62	134.26	97.38	30.16	93.16	78.11	130.71
1990	43.55	36.33	30.47	64.01	31.65	20.10	34.42	40.77	50.54
1991	29.83	24.38	20.48	33.93	24.47	14.06	26.37	28.62	32.64
1992	18.91	15.49	10.73	18.41	18.40	7.89	21.55	19.79	19.65
1993	10.13	7.35	4.31	11.82	11.57	4.70	7.35	14.19	11.10
1994	4.85	3.24	1.58	4.87	5.07	1.96	4.62	5.60	4.79
					Constant (1995) dollars				
1965	330,706.45	1,681.52	612.42	137.51	134.70	130.43	614.30	45.20	203.57
1970	510,513.47	2,454.10	920.40	278.70	162.37	151.75	858.94	70.07	419.22
1975	735,498.53	3,354.81	1,424.44	482.03	194.71	196.21	939.74	80.79	593.39
1980	875,760.32	3,788.01	1,763.56	560.21	210.07	163.94	932.43	104.79	763.96
1985	1,003,118.43	4,130.78	2,080.61	555.91	222.52	151.70	972.25	76.59	968.69
1990	1,203,025.82	4,740.88	2,319.05	665.09	279.44	137.70	1,170.22	81.17	1,243.42
1991	1,286,130.57	5,024.79	2,428.25	787.52	285.80	140.20	1,203.65	85.90	1,364.63
1992	1,359,335.44	5,238.29	2,557.58	862.26	290.84	143.48	1,211.28	89.28	1,464.41
1993	1,429,149.91	5,487.40	2,643.58	889.04	300.53	143.96	1,335.49	91.20	1,535.55
1994	1,465,443.16	5,570.44	2,650.07	925.42	311.54	144.32	1,337.72	96.27	1,589.30
1995	1,502,234.40	5,622.39	2,631.98	948.88	320.03	143.86	1,368.34	99.40	1,628.61
					Percentage increase to 1995				
1965	354	234	330	590	138	10	123	120	700
1970	194	129	186	240	97	-5	59	42	288
1975	104	68	85	97	64	-27	46	23	174
1980	72	48	49	69	52	-12	47	-5	113
1985	50	36	27	71	44	-5	41	30	68
1990	25	19	13	43	15	4	17	22	31
1991	17	12	8	20	12	3	14	16	19
1992	11	7	3	10	10	0	13	11	11
1993	5	2	0	7	6	0	2	9	6
1994	3	1	-1	3	3	0	2	3	2

[1] Excludes expenditures in foreign countries for Old Age, Survivors, Disability, and Health Insurance (OASDHI) benefits, civil service retirement benefits, veterans' programs, and education.

[2] Includes housing, not shown separately.

[3] Combines "health and medical" programs with medical services provided in connection with social insurance, public aid, veterans', and "other social welfare" programs.

[4] Revised data

SOURCE: Ann Kallman Bixby, "Total and Per Capita Social Welfare Expenditures Under Public Programs, in Current and Constant (1995) Dollars, Selected Years 1965–95," in "Public Social Welfare Expenditures, Fiscal Year 1995," *Social Security Bulletin*, vol. 62, no. 2, 1999

FIGURE 1.1

Total state government expenditures by function, fiscal 2000

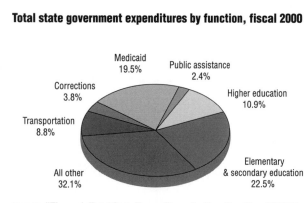

SOURCE: "Figure 4. Total State Expenditures by Function, Fiscal 2000," in *2000 State Expenditure Report,* National Association of State Budget Officers, Washington, DC, Summer 2001

FIGURE 1.2

State expenditures for total public assistance by fund source, fiscal 2000

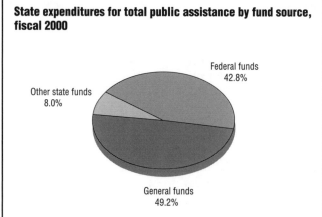

SOURCE: "Figure 12. State Expenditures for Total Public Assistance by Fund Source, Fiscal 2000," in *2000 State Expenditure Report,* National Association of State Budget Officers, Washington, DC, Summer 2001

FIGURE 1.3

State expenditures for Medicaid by fund source, fiscal 2000

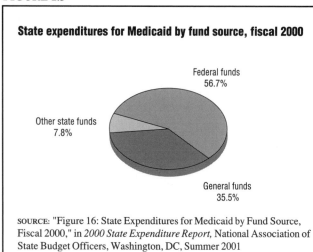

SOURCE: "Figure 16: State Expenditures for Medicaid by Fund Source, Fiscal 2000," in *2000 State Expenditure Report,* National Association of State Budget Officers, Washington, DC, Summer 2001

FIGURE 1.4

Actual and projected state Medicaid spending, 1970–2000

(In billions)

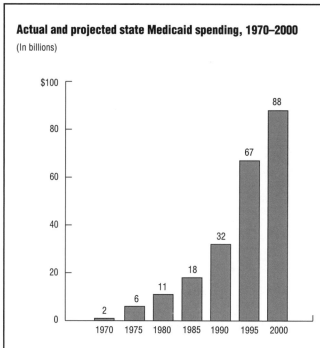

Based on projections by the Congressional Budget Office in January 2001, assumes a 57 percent federal share of total Medicaid costs.

SOURCE: "Figure 15. Actual and Projected State Medicaid Spending, 1970–2000 (In Billions)," in *2000 State Expenditure Report,* National Association of State Budget Officers, Washington, DC, 2001

TABLE 1.7

Welfare services—private expenditures as a percent of total private outlays, 1972–94

[Amounts in millions]

Year	Expenditure	Percent of total private outlays
1972	$ 7,545	7.9
1973	8,297	8.0
1974	8,970	7.9
1975	10,067	7.8
1976	11,748	8.1
1977	13,535	8.1
1978	16,590	8.8
1979	19,540	9.0
1980	22,776	9.1
1981	25,728	9.0
1982	28,067	8.6
1983	31,392	8.6
1984	34,749	8.5
1985	38,999	8.4
1986	43,211	8.4
1987	47,601	8.7
1988	52,579	8.8
1989	59,312	8.9
1990	64,583	9.0
1991	68,998	9.0
1992	76,022	9.2
1993	80,899	9.3
1994	86,297	9.4

SOURCE: Wilmer L. Kerns, "Welfare Services: Private Expenditures as a Percent of Total Private Outlays: National Income and Product Accounts Data, 1972–94," in "Public Social Welfare Expenditures, 1972–1994," *Social Security Bulletin,* vol. 60, no. 1, 1997

CHAPTER 2

RECENT WELFARE-REFORM LEGISLATION

A TIME OF RADICAL CHANGE

The summer of 1996 brought about profound and controversial changes in the way America handles its welfare programs. Much criticism had been directed toward the previous welfare system, based mainly on Aid to Families with Dependent Children (AFDC). This criticism centered on claims that the system produced welfare dependency rather than temporary assistance to help recipients move into a job and off welfare. According to the testimony of LaDonna Pavetti of the Urban Institute before the U.S. House of Representatives Ways and Means Committee in May 1996, about 70 percent of AFDC recipients had received AFDC for more than 24 months and 48 percent had received assistance for more than 60 months. In addition to limiting the length of time spent on welfare and requiring participation in work activities, issues addressed under welfare reform included: child care; child support; young, unmarried women with children; assistance to immigrants; and welfare costs.

When earlier welfare-reform efforts stalled in the federal government, many states began to explore ways to modify their welfare programs. In President Bill Clinton's first term, 43 states were granted federal waivers, allowing them to experiment with different approaches to welfare and work. State plans generally included stiffer work requirements and time limits as well as greater demands of parental responsibility. Many of the programs that developed from those waivers helped to lay the foundation for the new welfare-reform law.

After many proposals, much congressional discussion, and several presidential vetoes, a massive welfare-reform bill, the Personal Responsibility and Work Opportunity Reconciliation Act (PL 104-193), was signed into law in August 1996. Replacing AFDC with Temporary Assistance for Needy Families (TANF), the law requires that a welfare recipient work in exchange for time-limited assistance. It provides $1 billion over five years for performance bonuses to reward states for moving welfare recipients into jobs. PL 104-193 also requires a state "maintenance of effort," a continuation of welfare spending at a level that is at least 80 percent of its 1994 expenditures. The law contains comprehensive child support enforcement and support for families moving from welfare to work, including increased funding for child care and guaranteed medical coverage.

Overall the welfare caseload fell from a high of 5.1 million families in March 1994 to 2.1 million families in September 2001, a drop of 58.8 percent. This represents the largest welfare caseload decline in history. Caseloads have fallen by 56 percent since 1996, the last year of operation of AFDC. (See Figure 2.1.) Observers agree that some of the decline was the result of a strong economy in which unemployment was around 4 percent, an unprecedented low, rather than welfare reform. A study conducted by the City University of New York and cited by the U.S. Department of Health and Human Services in its 2001 *TANF Annual Report to Congress,* attributed 60 percent of the reductions in caseloads to welfare reform and 20 percent to the effects of a robust economy. The Council of Economic Advisers estimated that about one-third of the reduction in caseloads between 1996 and 1998 was due to changes in federal and state policies, approximately 10 percent to the strong economy, 10 percent to the higher minimum wage, and from 1 percent to 5 percent to the lower real value of welfare benefits.

Some wonder whether the new welfare system is recession-proof. Other critics of the new system question whether it is fair to everyone. Some are concerned that the new system leads to former welfare recipients—without adequate health care, child care, and affordable housing—slipping through the cracks of the welfare system into destitution and homelessness. Under the new system, states that are unable to provide jobs with a

FIGURE 2.1

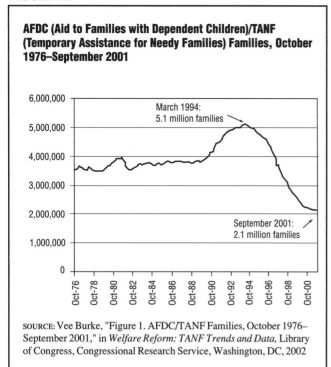

AFDC (Aid to Families with Dependent Children)/TANF (Temporary Assistance for Needy Families) Families, October 1976–September 2001

SOURCE: Vee Burke, "Figure 1. AFDC/TANF Families, October 1976–September 2001," in *Welfare Reform: TANF Trends and Data,* Library of Congress, Congressional Research Service, Washington, DC, 2002

living wage may merely move the poor population from welfare into low-wage work and deeper into poverty. As a result, modifications to welfare legislation continue to be proposed.

The Balanced Budget Act of 1997 (PL 105-33) made many modifications and additions to the 1996 welfare-reform law, including changes to the TANF block grant and funding for additional grants. A U.S. Senate agriculture bill, which passed the Senate overwhelmingly in May 1998, included a provision to restore food stamps to 250,000 legal immigrants who were cut from the rolls under the 1996 law. Following passage by the House of Representatives, President Clinton signed the bill into law on June 23, 1998.

THE PERSONAL RESPONSIBILITY AND WORK OPPORTUNITY RECONCILIATION ACT OF 1996 (PRWORA)

Signed into law on August 22, 1996, PL 104-193 gives states broad flexibility to design and operate their own welfare programs while at the same time holding them accountable to the proposed regulations. States were required to implement their block grant programs by July 1, 1997. The Congressional Budget Office (CBO) predicted that though welfare spending would continue to grow about 50 percent through the beginning of the 21st century, the rate of growth would be reduced. The CBO claimed that this drop in the growth of welfare spending would reduce the federal budget deficit by nearly $55 billion. (See Figure 2.2.)

A brief summary of the welfare-reform law, based primarily on information prepared by the U.S. Department of Health and Human Services, follows.

Title I: Block Grants

The law combines AFDC, Emergency Assistance, and the JOBS program into a single block grant (a lump sum of money) for each state. Federal funding for this TANF block grant is capped at an estimated $16.4 billion per fiscal year 1996 through 2002. Each state's allotment is based on previous years' federal funding for AFDC benefits and administration, Emergency Assistance, and JOBS.

States have considerable control over how they will implement the programs covered by the block grant, but the act requires that:

- Families on welfare for five cumulative years no longer receive further cash assistance. States can set shorter time limits and can exempt up to 20 percent of their caseload from the time limits.

- To count toward meeting the work requirement, a state must require individuals to participate in employment (public or private), on-the-job training, community service, work experience, vocational training (up to 12 months), or child care for other workers for at least 20 hours per week. State and local communities are responsible for the development of work, whether by creating community service jobs or by providing income subsidies or hiring incentives for potential employers.

- As part of their state plans, states must require parents to work after two years of receiving benefits. In 2000 states were required to have 40 percent of all parents, and at least one adult in 90 percent of all two-parent families, engaged in a work activity for a minimum of 20 hours per week for single parents and 35 hours a week for at least one adult in two-parent families. The rates for all families started at 25 percent in 1997 and increased five percentage points each year to 50 percent in 2002. For two-parent families the rates started at 75 percent and increased in 1999 to 90 percent. In 2000 all states met the overall participation rate for all families, but eight states failed to meet the goal for two-parent families.

- Each state must maintain at least 80 percent of its fiscal year 1994 level of spending on these programs. If a state meets the work requirement percentages, the maintenance-of-effort level may be reduced to 75 percent of 1994 spending. States must maintain spending at 100 percent of 1994 levels for access to the $2 billion federal contingency fund. This contingency fund was designed to assist states affected by high population growth or severe economic conditions, such as increases in food stamp caseloads or high unemployment rates.

- Unmarried teenage parents (under age 18) must live with an adult or with adult supervision and must participate in educational or job training to receive benefits. In addition, the law encourages "second chance homes" to provide teen parents with the skills and support they need and provides $50 million a year in new funding for state abstinence education activities.

None of the block grant funds can be used for adults who have been on welfare for over five years or who do not work after receiving benefits for two years. However, states are offered some flexibility in how to spend their TANF funds.

Title II: Supplemental Social Security (SSI)

The act redefines "disability" for children who receive SSI. A child will be considered disabled if he or she has a medically determinable physical or mental impairment that results in marked and severe functional limitations that can be expected to cause death or has lasted or can be expected to last at least 12 months. Reference to "maladaptive behavior" as a medical criterion was removed from the listing of impairments used for evaluating mental disabilities in children.

Title III: Child Support

To be eligible for federal funds, each state must operate a Child Support Enforcement program that meets federal guidelines. The state must establish centralized registries of child-support orders and centers for collection and disbursement of child-support payments, and parents must sign their child-support rights over to the state in order to be eligible for TANF benefits. The state must also establish enforcement methods, such as revoking the driver's and professional licenses of delinquent parents. In 2000 the Child Support Enforcement program collected almost $18 billion, up 49 percent since 1996.

To receive full benefits, a mother must cooperate with state efforts to establish paternity. She may be denied assistance if she refuses to disclose the father. Paternity establishments rose to more than 1.6 million in 2000, an increase of over 47 percent since 1996.

Title IV: Restricting Welfare and Public Benefits for Noncitizens

The original law severely limited or banned benefits to most legal immigrants who entered the country on or after the date on which the bill became law. Ineligibility continued for a five-year period or until they attained citizenship. In addition, states had the option of withholding eligibility for Medicaid, TANF, and other social services from legal immigrants already residing in the United States. Refugees/asylees (those who have come for political or other asylum or sanctuary), veterans, and Cuban/Haitian immigrants were exempted from the five-year ban.

FIGURE 2.2

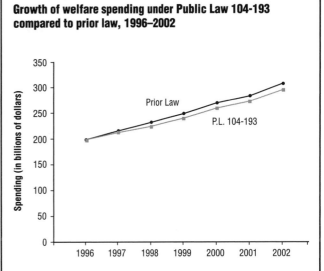

Growth of welfare spending under Public Law 104-193 compared to prior law, 1996–2002

SOURCE: U.S. House of Representatives, Committee on Ways and Means, "Public Law 104-193 Moderates the Growth of Welfare Spending While Saving $54.6 Billion (1996–2002)" in *Summary of Welfare Reforms Made by Public Law 104–193, The Personal Responsibility and Work Opportunity Reconciliation Act and Associated Legislation,* 10th Cong. 2d Sess., 1996

Illegal immigrants have no entitlement to benefit programs, such as TANF or Medicaid. They can receive emergency medical care, short-term disaster relief, immunizations, and treatment for communicable diseases (in the interest of public health). They can also get community services such as soup kitchens and shelters, some housing programs, and school lunches/breakfasts if their children are eligible for free public education. States have established programs to verify the legality of an immigrant before paying benefits and may elect to deny Women, Infants, and Children (WIC) benefits and other child nutrition programs to illegal aliens.

The Balanced Budget Act of 1997 and the Noncitizen Technical Amendment Act of 1998 invested $11.5 billion to restore disability and health benefits to 380,000 legal immigrants who were in the United States before welfare reform became law on August 22, 1996. The Balanced Budget Act also extended the SSI and Medicaid eligibility period for refugees and people seeking asylum from five years after entry to seven years to give these residents more time to naturalize.

Title V: Child Protection

The law gives states the authority to use current federal funds to pay for foster care for children in child-care institutions. It extended the enhanced federal match for statewide automated child-welfare information systems through 1997 and appropriated $6 million per year (fiscal years 1996–2002) for a national random sample study of abused and neglected children.

Title VI: Child Care

The law requires that states maintain spending for child care for low-income families at the level of fiscal years 1994 or 1995, whichever is greater, in order to be eligible for federally-matched funds. Mandatory funding is set at $13.9 billion for fiscal years 1997 through 2002, with states receiving an estimated $1.2 billion per year before matching begins. The remainder of the funds are available for state matching at the Medicaid rate. Total federal and state expenditures on child care totaled $3.2 billion in 2000, an increase of 60 percent over 1999 ($2 billion).

As under prior law, states must establish standards for prevention and control of infectious diseases, such as immunization programs, and for building codes and physical safety in child-care institutions. Child-care workers must also receive minimal training in health and safety. However, many low-income persons rely on informal sources of child care, including relatives and friends.

As a result of more parents working while still on welfare or leaving welfare to work, the critical need for child care has become more pronounced. The Urban Institute reported that more than 1.9 million children received childcare each month in 2000, compared to approximately 1 million per month in 1996. The child-care support system gives priority to families leaving welfare for work over other low-income families. However, a study conducted by Abt Associates in 1999, *National Study of Child Care for Low-Income Families: State and Community Substudy Interim Report* (Ann Collins, Jean Layzer, J. Lee Kreader, Alan Werner, and Fred B. Glantz, Cambridge, MA, 2000), found that none of the 16 states examined in the study served more than 25 percent of the children eligible under federal guidelines. Some have expressed the view that the current system penalizes low-income families who are already working, who are less likely to receive child care than welfare-leavers (those making the transition from welfare to work).

Title VII: Child Nutrition Programs

The law continues the existing child nutrition programs, such as the school lunch and breakfast programs. Maximum reimbursement is reduced, however, for the Summer Food Service Program and for some institutional food programs. States may decide whether to include or exclude legal immigrants from these programs.

Title VIII: Food Stamps and Commodities

The new law reduces maximum benefits to the level of the "Thrifty Food Plan," an index set by the U.S. Department of Agriculture that reflects the amount of money needed to purchase food to meet minimal nutrition requirements. Benefits are indexed to the rate of inflation so that they increase as inflation rises.

The law also restructures the way certain expenses and earnings are counted in establishing eligibility for food stamps. When recipients' benefits are calculated, their countable monthly income is reduced by several "deductions," including a "standard deduction" and a deduction for excessively high shelter expenses. These deductions raise food stamp allotments. The standard deduction is frozen at the current level, $134 (in the contiguous 48 states and Washington, D.C.). The cap (limit) on shelter expense deductions gradually increased from $247 per month in 1996 to $300 in 2001 and will be frozen at $300 per month thereafter. State and local energy assistance is counted as income.

By law, all food stamp recipients who are 18 to 50 years old and without children (Able-Bodied Adults Without Dependents) must work at least part-time or be limited to 3 months of assistance in a 36-month period. Recipients who were in a workfare program (subsidized jobs) for 30 days but lost their placement may qualify for an additional three months of food stamps. (This provision was revised to allow states to exempt 15 percent of ABAWD recipients from this restriction.

The law increases the penalties for recipients and retailers convicted of fraud or trafficking in food stamps. It also allows states to convert food stamp benefits to wage subsidies for employers who hire food stamp recipients; the workers then receive salaries rather than food stamps.

STATE FLEXIBILITY REGARDING WAIVERS

Under the welfare-reform law, states that had received approval for waivers prior to July 1, 1997, were given the option to continue those cash assistance programs under some or all of those waivers. States were allowed to retain provisions that were inconsistent with the new law until their waivers expired if they accepted the option of continuing cash assistance programs covered by the waivers. However, the law limited the extent to which inconsistencies apply so as to maintain the law's strong work requirements.

The most common inconsistencies with the law's provisions for which waivers were claimed included the law's work and participation requirements. For instance, the law states that individuals must be engaged in work within 24 months without expressly providing for any exemptions. Vermont is operating under a waiver that requires individuals to obtain employment within 30 months.

Another inconsistency between the welfare-reform law and state waivers concerns time limits. The law requires the termination of assistance after five years but includes a 20 percent hardship exemption. As of June 2002, eight states were operating under waivers from the time-limit requirements. Most of these waivers are due to expire in 2003.

Other areas inconsistent with the welfare law's provisions include those related to penalties for noncompliance with work requirements, transitional assistance, teen-parent school attendance, teen-parent living-arrangement requirements, and child-support cooperation penalties. The Department of Health and Human Services must review the state plans and approve the inconsistencies due to waivers.

1997 BALANCED BUDGET RECONCILIATION ACT

The 1997 Balanced Budget Reconciliation Act (PL 105-33) made a number of changes affecting state programs funded under TANF block grants, including partially restoring funding for some of the program cuts made in the 1996 welfare law. SSI benefits were restored to legal elderly or disabled immigrants who were receiving assistance as of August 22, 1996. These benefits were also restored to immigrants who were legally residing in the United States as of that date and subsequently became disabled. Legal immigrants who arrived after the passage of the welfare reform law are not eligible for assistance.

Funding for the food stamp employment and training program was increased so that states could create workfare, or subsidized job slots, for food stamp recipients. Eighty percent of the funds must be spent on food stamp recipients who are 18 to 50 years old and without children (Able-Bodied Adults Without Dependents, or ABAWD). With the 1996 law, this group was limited to three months of food stamp assistance during each 36-month period unless the recipient was working at least half-time or engaged in employment and training. The balanced budget act allows states to exempt 15 percent of the ABAWD population from the three-month limit.

This act set a new mandatory penalty for failure to reduce assistance for TANF recipients who refuse to work. This penalty, to be imposed by the Secretary of Health and Human Services, may not be less than 1 percent, or more than 5 percent, of the TANF grant. The act also specified a mandatory 5 percent penalty if a state failed to meet work participation rates. Under the 1996 law, the HHS secretary had the option to penalize states.

Formulas were changed and the cap raised to allow a larger number of individuals participating in vocational education training to count toward the state's TANF work participation rate. Several changes were made in work definitions for the mandatory work requirements.

The 1997 balanced budget act also created two additional grants to aid state welfare programs. A welfare-to-work grant provided $3 billion over two years (1998 and 1999) to be used for job-related activities directed mainly at individuals with significant work barriers, such as lack of education and low skills in reading or mathematics, substance abuse, or a poor work history. In addition, the act created a $20.3 billion child health block grant, the State Children's Health Insurance Program. This money was targeted for assistance to uninsured, low-income children. States could use the new funds to make more children eligible for Medicaid or to purchase other health coverage, or both.

On April 12, 1999, the Department of Health and Human Services (HHS) issued the final TANF regulations. They include many provisions, some of which reflect significant changes from the proposed regulations, which affirm and enhance the flexibility of states to determine how best to use TANF funds to assist low-income families. The regulations, together with the already-existing substantial TANF financial reserves in many states that resulted from the decreasing number of welfare cases, provide strong support for states to improve their welfare reform approaches. The federal welfare law restricts HHS's authority to regulate state conduct or enforce any TANF provision except to the extent expressly provided in the law. The federal law expressly provides that HHS will impose penalties if a state fails to comply with requirements of the law in a number of areas. For example, a state can be subject to penalties if it uses federal TANF funds improperly, if it fails to expend the amount of state funds required under maintenance-of-effort provisions, if it fails to meet work participation rates, or if it fails to comply with time limits applicable to federal TANF funds.

There still is concern, however, that if states do not use their TANF funds, they may be taken away by the federal government for other purposes. In 1999 several proposals in the U.S. Congress sought to divert unused TANF funds to offset other legislative initiatives. While maintaining a surplus is tempting, opponents have urged states to spend more of their allotted money in order to avoid such an occurrence.

TANF REAUTHORIZATION

Authorization for the Personal Responsibility and Work Opportunity Reconciliation Act of 1996 was scheduled to end on September 30, 2002. A number of bills related to reauthorization were put forward and a number of issues were debated in Congress, including changes in work requirements, funding levels, the role of education and training, and income support for those leaving the welfare rolls. New legislation passed by the House in May 2002 would limit the flexibility granted to the states under the original act.

CHAPTER 3

POVERTY

BACKGROUND

The federal government began measuring poverty in 1959. During the 1960s President Lyndon Baines Johnson declared a national war on poverty. Researchers realized that very few statistical tools were available to measure the number of Americans who continued to live in poverty in the most affluent nation in the world. In order to fight this "war," it had to be determined who was poor and why.

During the early 1960s Mollie Orshansky of the Social Security Administration suggested that the poverty income level be defined as the income sufficient to purchase a minimally adequate amount of goods and services. The necessary data for defining and pricing a full "market basket" of goods were not available then, nor are they available now. Orshansky noted, however, that in 1955 the U.S. Department of Agriculture (USDA) had published a "Household Food Consumption Survey," which showed that the average family of three or more persons spent approximately one-third of its after-tax income on food. She multiplied the USDA's 1961 economy food plan (a no-frills food basket meeting the then-recommended dietary allowances) by three.

Basically this defined a poor family as any family or person whose after-tax income was not sufficient to purchase a minimally adequate diet if one-third of the income was spent on food. Differences were allowed for size of family, gender of the head of the household, and whether it was a farm or nonfarm family. The threshold (the level at which poverty begins) for a farm family was set at 70 percent of a nonfarm household. (The difference between farm and nonfarm households was eliminated in 1982.)

Poverty Thresholds

The poverty guidelines set by the U.S. Department of Health and Human Services (HHS) are based on the poverty thresholds as established by the U.S. Bureau of the Census. The poverty thresholds, used for statistical purposes, are updated each year to reflect inflation. People with incomes below the applicable threshold are classified as living below the poverty level.

The poverty guidelines vary by family size and composition. For a family of four in 2000 the poverty guideline was $17,050 in annual income. A person living alone who earned less than $8,350 was considered poor, as was a family of eight members making less than $28,650. Notice, in Table 3.1, that the poverty level is considerably higher in Alaska and Hawaii, where the cost of living is higher than in the contiguous 48 states and the District of Columbia.

The poverty guidelines set by HHS are very important because various government agencies use them as the basis for eligibility to key assistance programs. HHS uses the poverty guidelines to determine Community Services Block Grants, Low-Income Home Energy Assistance Block Grants, and Head Start allotments. The guidelines are also the basis for funding the USDA's Food Stamp Program, National School Lunch Program, and Special Supplemental Food Program for Women, Infants, and Children (WIC). The U.S. Department of Labor uses the guidelines to determine funding for the Job Corps and other employment and training programs under the Workforce Investment Act. Some state and local governments choose to use the federal poverty guidelines for some of their own programs, such as state health insurance programs and financial guidelines for child support enforcement.

POVERTY—THEN AND NOW

Race and Ethnicity

Table 3.2 gives the nation's poverty rates from 1959 through 2000 for all people and by subcategories of types of family and race and ethnic background. Figure 3.1 gives a graphic depiction of the number of poor people and the poverty rates for the same years. In 1959, 22.4

TABLE 3.1

Poverty guidelines for families of specified size, 1965–2000

Date of issuance[1]	1 person	2 persons	3 persons	4 persons	5 persons	6 persons	7 persons	8 persons	Increment[2]
December 1965	$1,540	$1,990	$2,440	$3,130	$3,685	$4,135	$4,635	$5,135	$500
August 1967	1,600	2,000	2,500	3,200	3,800	4,200	4,700	5,300	500
September 1968	1,600	2,100	2,600	3,300	3,900	4,400	4,900	5,400	500
September 1969	1,800	2,400	3,000	3,600	4,200	4,800	5,400	6,000	600
December 1970	1,900	2,500	3,100	3,800	4,400	5,000	5,600	6,200	600
November 1971	2,000	2,600	3,300	4,000	4,700	5,300	5,900	6,500	600
October 1972	2,100	2,725	3,450	4,200	4,925	5,550	6,200	6,850	650
March 1973	2,200	2,900	3,600	4,300	5,000	5,700	6,400	7,100	700
May 1974	2,330	3,070	3,810	4,550	5,290	6,030	6,770	7,510	740
March 1975	2,590	3,410	4,230	5,050	5,870	6,690	7,510	8,330	820
April 1976	2,800	3,700	4,600	5,500	6,400	7,300	8,200	9,100	900
April 1977	2,970	3,930	4,890	5,850	6,810	7,770	8,730	9,690	960
April 1978	3,140	4,160	5,180	6,200	7,220	8,240	9,260	10,280	1,020
May 1979	3,400	4,500	5,600	6,700	7,800	8,900	10,000	11,100	1,100
April 1980	3,790	5,010	6,230	7,450	8,670	9,890	11,110	12,330	1,220
March 1981	4,310	5,690	7,070	8,450	9,830	11,210	12,590	13,970	1,380
April 1982	4,680	6,220	7,760	9,300	10,840	12,380	13,920	15,460	1,540
February 1983	4,860	6,540	8,220	9,900	11,580	13,260	14,940	16,620	1,680
February 1984	4,980	6,720	8,460	10,200	11,940	13,680	15,420	17,160	1,740
March 1985	5,250	7,050	8,850	10,650	12,450	14,250	16,050	17,850	1,800
February 1986	5,360	7,240	9,120	11,000	12,880	14,760	16,640	18,520	1,880
February 1987	5,500	7,400	9,300	11,200	13,100	15,000	16,900	18,800	1,900
February 1988	5,770	7,730	9,690	11,650	13,610	15,570	17,530	19,490	1,960
February 1989	5,980	8,020	10,060	12,100	14,140	16,180	18,220	20,260	2,040
February 1990	6,280	8,420	10,560	12,700	14,840	16,980	18,120	21,260	2,140
February 1991	6,620	8,880	11,140	13,400	15,660	17,920	20,180	22,440	2,260
February 1992	6,810	9,190	11,570	13,950	16,330	18,710	21,090	23,470	2,380
February 1993	6,970	9,430	11,890	14,350	16,810	19,270	21,730	24,190	2,460
February 1994	7,360	9,840	12,320	14,800	17,280	19,760	22,240	24,720	2,480
February 1995	7,470	10,030	12,590	15,150	17,710	20,270	22,830	25,390	2,560
March 1996	7,740	10,360	12,980	15,600	18,220	20,840	23,460	26,080	2,620
March 1997	7,890	10,610	13,330	16,050	18,770	21,490	24,210	26,960	2,720
February 1998	8,050	10,850	13,650	16,450	19,250	22,050	24,850	27,650	2,800
March 1999	8,240	11,060	13,880	16,700	19,520	22,340	25,160	27,980	2,820
February 2000	8,350	11,250	14,150	17,050	19,950	22,850	25,750	28,650	2,900

Note: Guidelines for Alaska and Hawaii differ. They are:

Year	Alaska 1 person	Alaska Increment	Hawaii 1 person	Hawaii Increment
1980	$4,760	$1,520	$4,370	$1,400
1981	5,410	1,720	4,980	1,580
1982	5,870	1,920	5,390	1,770
1983	6,080	2,100	5,600	1,930
1984	6,240	2,170	5,730	2,000
1985	6,560	2,250	6,040	2,070
1986	6,700	2,350	6,170	2,160
1987	6,860	2,380	6,310	2,190
1988	7,210	2,450	6,650	2,250
1989	7,480	2,550	6,870	2,350
1990	7,840	2,680	7,230	2,460
1991	8,290	2,820	7,610	2,600
1992	8,500	2,980	7,830	2,740
1993	8,700	3,080	8,040	2,820
1994	9,200	3,100	8,470	2,850
1995	9,340	3,200	8,610	2,940
1996	9,660	3,280	8,910	3,010
1997	9,870	3,400	9,070	3,130
1998	10,070	3,500	9,260	3,220
1999	10,320	3,520	9,490	3,240
2000	10,430	3,630	9,590	3,340

Separate figures for Alaska and Hawaii reflect Office of Economic Opportunity administrative practice beginning in the 1966–70 period. The U.S. Census Bureau, producer of the primary version of the poverty measure (the poverty thresholds), does not produce separate figures for Alaska and Hawaii.

[1]The guidelines are effective from the date of issuance (unless otherwise specified by a particular program using them). Before 1983, the guidelines shown are for nonfarm families only.

[2]Add this amount for each additional family member. Before 1973, increments between some of the smaller family sizes differed from the increment shown in the table. Beginning in 1973, the increment has been the same between all family sizes in each year's set of guidelines.

SOURCE: "Table 3.E8.—Poverty guidelines for families of specified size, 1965–2000," in *Annual Statistical Supplement, 2000 to the Social Security Bulletin,* Social Security Administration, Office of Policy, Office of Research, Evaluation, and Statistics

TABLE 3.2

Poverty status of people by family relationship, race, and Hispanic origin, 1959–2000

[Numbers in thousands. People as of March of the following year]

Year and characteristic	All people			People in families						Unrelated individuals		
				All families			Families with female householder, no husband present					
	Total	Below poverty level		Total	Below poverty level		Total	Below poverty level		Total	Below poverty level	
		Number	Percent		Number	Percent		Number	Percent		Number	Percent
ALL RACES												
2000	275,917	31,139	11.3	229,476	22,088	9.6	37,428	10,436	27.9	45,120	8,530	18.9
1999	273,493	32,258	11.8	228,633	23,396	10.2	38,223	11,607	30.4	43,432	8,305	19.1
1998	271,059	34,476	12.7	227,229	25,370	11.2	39,000	12,907	33.1	42,539	8,478	19.9
1997	268,480	35,574	13.3	225,369	26,217	11.6	38,412	13,494	35.1	41,672	8,687	20.8
1996	266,218	36,529	13.7	223,955	27,376	12.2	38,584	13,796	35.8	40,727	8,452	20.8
1995	263,733	36,425	13.8	222,792	27,501	12.3	38,908	14,205	36.5	39,484	8,247	20.9
1994	261,616	38,059	14.5	221,430	28,985	13.1	37,253	14,380	38.6	38,538	8,287	21.5
1993	259,278	39,265	15.1	219,489	29,927	13.6	37,861	14,636	38.7	38,038	8,388	22.1
1992[2]	256,549	38,014	14.8	217,936	28,961	13.3	36,446	14,205	39.0	36,842	8,075	21.9
1991[2]	251,192	35,708	14.2	212,723	27,143	12.8	34,795	13,824	39.7	36,845	7,773	21.1
1990	248,644	33,585	13.5	210,967	25,232	12.0	33,795	12,578	37.2	36,056	7,446	20.7
1989	245,992	31,528	12.8	209,515	24,066	11.5	32,525	11,668	35.9	35,185	6,760	19.2
1988[2]	243,530	31,745	13.0	208,056	24,048	11.6	32,164	11,972	37.2	34,340	7,070	20.6
1987[2]	240,982	32,221	13.4	206,877	24,725	12.0	31,893	12,148	38.1	32,992	6,857	20.8
1986	238,554	32,370	13.6	205,459	24,754	12.0	31,152	11,944	38.3	31,679	6,846	21.6
1985	236,594	33,064	14.0	203,963	25,729	12.6	30,878	11,600	37.6	31,351	6,725	21.5
1984	233,816	33,700	14.4	202,288	26,458	13.1	30,844	11,831	38.4	30,268	6,609	21.8
1983	231,700	35,303	15.2	201,338	27,933	13.9	30,049	12,072	40.2	29,158	6,740	23.1
1982	229,412	34,398	15.0	200,385	27,349	13.6	28,834	11,701	40.6	27,908	6,458	23.1
1981	227,157	31,822	14.0	198,541	24,850	12.5	28,587	11,051	38.7	27,714	6,490	23.4
1980	225,027	29,272	13.0	196,963	22,601	11.5	27,565	10,120	36.7	27,133	6,227	22.9
1979	222,903	26,072	11.7	195,860	19,964	10.2	26,927	9,400	34.9	26,170	5,743	21.9
1978	215,656	24,497	11.4	191,071	19,062	10.0	26,032	9,269	35.6	24,585	5,435	22.1
1977	213,867	24,720	11.6	190,757	19,505	10.2	25,404	9,205	36.2	23,110	5,216	22.6
1976	212,303	24,975	11.8	190,844	19,632	10.3	24,204	9,029	37.3	21,459	5,344	24.9
1975	210,864	25,877	12.3	190,630	20,789	10.9	23,580	8,846	37.5	20,234	5,088	25.1
1974	209,362	23,370	11.2	190,436	18,817	9.9	23,165	8,462	36.5	18,926	4,553	24.1
1973	207,621	22,973	11.1	189,361	18,299	9.7	21,823	8,178	37.5	18,260	4,674	25.6
1972	206,004	24,460	11.9	189,193	19,577	10.3	21,264	8,114	38.2	16,811	4,883	29.0
1971	204,554	25,559	12.5	188,242	20,405	10.8	20,153	7,797	38.7	16,311	5,154	31.6
1970	202,183	25,420	12.6	186,692	20,330	10.9	19,673	7,503	38.1	15,491	5,090	32.9
1969	199,517	24,147	12.1	184,891	19,175	10.4	17,995	6,879	38.2	14,626	4,972	34.0
1968	197,628	25,389	12.8	183,825	20,695	11.3	18,048	6,990	38.7	13,803	4,694	34.0
1967	195,672	27,769	14.2	182,558	22,771	12.5	17,788	6,898	38.8	13,114	4,998	38.1
1966	193,388	28,510	14.7	181,117	23,809	13.1	17,240	6,861	39.8	12,271	4,701	38.3
1965	191,413	33,185	17.3	179,281	28,358	15.8	16,371	7,524	46.0	12,132	4,827	39.8
1964	189,710	36,055	19.0	177,653	30,912	17.4	(NA)	7,297	44.4	12,057	5,143	42.7
1963	187,258	36,436	19.5	176,076	31,498	17.9	(NA)	7,646	47.7	11,182	4,938	44.2
1962	184,276	38,625	21.0	173,263	33,623	19.4	(NA)	7,781	50.3	11,013	5,002	45.4
1961	181,277	39,628	21.9	170,131	34,509	20.3	(NA)	7,252	48.1	11,146	5,119	45.9
1960	179,503	39,851	22.2	168,615	34,925	20.7	(NA)	7,247	48.9	10,888	4,926	45.2
1959	176,557	39,490	22.4	165,858	34,562	20.8	(NA)	7,014	49.4	10,699	4,928	46.1
WHITE												
2000	225,993	21,291	9.4	187,670	14,430	7.7	23,606	5,210	22.1	37,217	6,404	17.2
1999	224,373	21,922	9.8	187,139	15,141	8.1	23,895	5,891	24.7	36,151	6,375	17.6
1998	222,837	23,454	10.5	186,184	16,549	8.9	24,211	6,674	27.6	35,563	6,386	18.0
1997	221,200	24,396	11.0	185,147	17,258	9.3	23,773	7,296	30.7	34,858	6,593	18.9
1996	219,656	24,650	11.2	184,119	17,621	9.6	23,744	7,073	29.8	34,247	6,463	18.9
1995	218,028	24,423	11.2	183,450	17,593	9.6	23,732	7,047	29.7	33,399	6,336	19.0
1994	216,460	25,379	11.7	182,546	18,474	10.1	22,713	7,228	31.8	32,569	6,292	19.3
1993	214,899	26,226	12.2	181,330	18,968	10.5	23,224	7,199	31.0	32,112	6,443	20.1
1992[2]	213,060	25,259	11.9	180,409	18,294	10.1	22,453	6,907	30.8	31,170	6,147	19.7
1991[2]	210,133	23,747	11.3	177,619	17,268	9.7	21,608	6,806	31.5	31,207	5,872	18.8
1990	208,611	22,326	10.7	176,504	15,916	9.0	20,845	6,210	29.8	30,833	5,739	18.6
1989	206,853	20,785	10.0	175,857	15,179	8.6	20,362	5,723	28.1	29,993	5,063	16.9
1988[2]	205,235	20,715	10.1	175,111	15,001	8.6	20,396	5,950	29.2	29,315	5,314	18.1
1987[2]	203,605	21,195	10.4	174,488	15,593	8.9	20,244	5,989	29.6	28,290	5,174	18.3
1986	202,282	22,183	11.0	174,024	16,393	9.4	20,163	6,171	30.6	27,143	5,198	19.2

TABLE 3.2

Poverty status of people by family relationship, race, and Hispanic origin, 1959–2000 [CONTINUED]

[Numbers in thousands. People as of March of the following year]

Year and characteristic	All people			People in families						Unrelated individuals		
				All families			Families with female householder, no husband present					
		Below poverty level			Below poverty level			Below poverty level			Below poverty level	
	Total	Number	Percent	Total	Number	Percent	Total	Number	Percent	Total	Number	Percent
WHITE [continued]												
1985	200,918	22,860	11.4	172,863	17,125	9.9	20,105	5,990	29.8	27,067	5,299	19.6
1984	198,941	22,955	11.5	171,839	17,299	10.1	19,727	5,866	29.7	26,094	5,181	19.9
1983	197,496	23,984	12.1	171,407	18,377	10.7	19,256	6,017	31.2	25,206	5,189	20.6
1982	195,919	23,517	12.0	170,748	18,015	10.6	18,374	5,686	30.9	24,300	5,041	20.7
1981	194,504	21,553	11.1	169,868	16,127	9.5	18,795	5,600	29.8	23,913	5,061	21.2
1980	192,912	19,699	10.2	168,756	14,587	8.6	17,642	4,940	28.0	23,370	4,760	20.4
1979	191,742	17,214	9.0	168,461	12,495	7.4	17,349	4,375	25.2	22,587	4,452	19.7
1978	186,450	16,259	8.7	165,193	12,050	7.3	16,877	4,371	25.9	21,257	4,209	19.8
1977	185,254	16,416	8.9	165,385	12,364	7.5	16,721	4,474	26.8	19,869	4,051	20.4
1976	184,165	16,713	9.1	165,571	12,500	7.5	15,941	4,463	28.0	18,594	4,213	22.7
1975	183,164	17,770	9.7	165,661	13,799	8.3	15,577	4,577	29.4	17,503	3,972	22.7
1974	182,376	15,736	8.6	166,081	12,181	7.3	15,433	4,278	27.7	16,295	3,555	21.8
1973	181,185	15,142	8.4	165,424	11,412	6.9	14,303	4,003	28.0	15,761	3,730	23.7
1972	180,125	16,203	9.0	165,630	12,268	7.4	13,739	3,770	27.4	14,495	3,935	27.1
1971	179,398	17,780	9.9	165,184	13,566	8.2	13,502	4,099	30.4	14,214	4,214	29.6
1970	177,376	17,484	9.9	163,875	13,323	8.1	13,226	3,761	28.4	13,500	4,161	30.8
1969	175,349	16,659	9.5	162,779	12,623	7.8	12,285	3,577	29.1	12,570	4,036	32.1
1968	173,732	17,395	10.0	161,777	13,546	8.4	12,190	3,551	29.1	11,955	3,849	32.2
1967	172,038	18,983	11.0	160,720	14,851	9.2	12,131	3,453	28.5	11,318	4,132	36.5
1966	170,247	19,290	11.3	159,561	15,430	9.7	12,261	3,646	29.7	10,686	3,860	36.1
1965	168,732	22,496	13.3	158,255	18,508	11.7	11,573	4,092	35.4	10,477	3,988	38.1
1964	167,313	24,957	14.9	156,898	20,716	13.2	(NA)	3,911	33.4	10,415	4,241	40.7
1963	165,309	25,238	15.3	155,584	21,149	13.6	(NA)	4,051	35.6	9,725	4,089	42.0
1962	162,842	26,672	16.4	153,348	22,613	14.7	(NA)	4,089	37.9	9,494	4,059	42.7
1961	160,306	27,890	17.4	150,717	23,747	15.8	(NA)	4,062	37.6	9,589	4,143	43.2
1960	158,863	28,309	17.8	149,458	24,262	16.2	(NA)	4,296	39.0	9,405	4,047	43.0
1959	156,956	28,484	18.1	147,802	24,443	16.5	(NA)	4,232	40.2	9,154	4,041	44.1
WHITE NON-HISPANIC												
2000	193,878	14,572	7.5	159,100	8,783	5.5	18,028	3,250	18.0	33,887	5,447	16.1
1999	193,334	14,875	7.7	159,362	9,118	5.7	18,233	3,618	19.8	33,136	5,440	16.4
1998	192,754	15,799	8.2	159,301	10,061	6.3	18,547	4,074	22.0	32,573	5,352	16.4
1997	191,859	16,491	8.6	158,796	10,401	6.5	18,474	4,604	24.9	32,049	5,632	17.6
1996	191,459	16,462	8.6	159,044	10,553	6.6	18,597	4,339	23.3	31,410	5,455	17.4
1995	190,951	16,267	8.5	159,402	10,599	6.6	18,340	4,183	22.8	30,586	5,303	17.3
1994	192,543	18,110	9.4	161,254	12,118	7.5	18,186	4,743	26.1	30,157	5,500	18.2
1993	190,843	18,882	9.9	160,062	12,756	8.0	18,508	4,724	25.5	29,681	5,570	18.8
1992[2]	189,001	18,202	9.6	159,102	12,277	7.7	18,016	4,640	25.8	28,775	5,350	18.6
1991[2]	189,116	17,741	9.4	158,850	11,998	7.6	17,609	4,710	26.7	29,215	5,261	18.0
1990	188,129	16,622	8.8	158,394	11,086	7.0	17,160	4,284	25.0	28,688	5,002	17.4
1989	186,979	15,599	8.3	158,127	10,723	6.8	16,827	3,922	23.3	28,055	4,466	15.9
1988[2]	185,961	15,565	8.4	157,687	10,467	6.6	16,828	3,988	23.7	27,552	4,746	17.2
1987[2]	184,936	16,029	8.7	157,785	11,051	7.0	16,787	4,075	24.3	26,439	4,613	17.4
1986	184,119	17,244	9.4	157,665	12,078	7.7	16,739	4,350	26.0	25,525	4,668	18.3
1985	183,455	17,839	9.7	157,106	12,706	8.1	16,749	4,136	24.7	25,544	4,789	18.7
1984	182,469	18,300	10.0	156,930	13,234	8.4	16,742	4,193	25.0	24,671	4,659	18.9
1983	181,393	19,538	10.8	156,719	14,437	9.2	16,369	4,448	27.2	23,894	4,746	19.9
1982	181,903	19,362	10.6	157,818	14,271	9.0	15,830	4,161	26.3	23,329	4,701	20.2
1981	180,909	17,987	9.9	157,330	12,903	8.2	16,323	4,222	25.9	22,950	4,769	20.8
1980	179,798	16,365	9.1	156,633	11,568	7.4	15,358	3,699	24.1	22,455	4,474	19.9
1979	178,814	14,419	8.1	156,567	10,009	6.4	15,410	3,371	21.9	21,638	4,179	19.3
1978	174,731	13,755	7.9	154,321	9,798	6.3	15,132	3,390	22.4	20,410	3,957	19.4
1977	173,563	13,802	8.0	154,449	9,977	6.5	14,888	3,429	23.0	19,114	3,825	20.0
1976	173,235	14,025	8.1	155,324	10,066	6.5	14,261	3,516	24.7	17,912	3,959	22.1
1975	172,417	14,883	8.6	155,539	11,137	7.2	13,809	3,570	25.9	16,879	3,746	22.2
1974	171,463	13,217	7.7	155,764	9,854	6.3	13,763	3,379	24.6	15,699	3,364	21.4
1973	170,488	12,864	7.5	155,330	9,262	6.0	12,731	3,185	25.0	15,158	3,602	23.8

TABLE 3.2

Poverty status of people by family relationship, race, and Hispanic origin, 1959–2000 [CONTINUED]

[Numbers in thousands. People as of March of the following year]

Year and characteristic	All people			People in families						Unrelated individuals		
				All families			Families with female householder, no husband present					
		Below poverty level			Below poverty level			Below poverty level			Below poverty level	
	Total	Number	Percent	Total	Number	Percent	Total	Number	Percent	Total	Number	Percent
BLACK												
2000	35,748	7,901	22.1	29,495	6,147	20.8	12,184	4,720	38.7	6,098	1,708	28.0
1999	35,373	8,360	23.6	29,488	6,688	22.7	12,644	5,179	41.0	5,619	1,552	27.6
1998	34,877	9,091	26.1	29,333	7,259	24.7	13,156	5,629	42.8	5,390	1,752	32.5
1997	34,458	9,116	26.5	28,962	7,386	25.5	13,218	5,654	42.8	5,316	1,645	31.0
1996	34,110	9,694	28.4	28,933	7,993	27.6	13,193	6,123	46.4	4,989	1,606	32.2
1995	33,740	9,872	29.3	28,777	8,189	28.5	13,604	6,553	48.2	4,756	1,551	32.6
1994	33,353	10,196	30.6	28,499	8,447	29.6	12,926	6,489	50.2	4,649	1,617	34.8
1993	32,910	10,877	33.1	28,106	9,242	32.9	13,132	6,955	53.0	4,608	1,541	33.4
1992[2]	32,411	10,827	33.4	27,790	9,134	32.9	12,591	6,799	54.0	4,410	1,569	35.6
1991[2]	31,313	10,242	32.7	26,565	8,504	32.0	11,960	6,557	54.8	4,505	1,590	35.3
1990	30,806	9,837	31.9	26,296	8,160	31.0	11,866	6,005	50.6	4,244	1,491	35.1
1989	30,332	9,302	30.7	25,931	7,704	29.7	11,190	5,530	49.4	4,180	1,471	35.2
1988[2]	29,849	9,356	31.3	25,484	7,650	30.0	10,794	5,601	51.9	4,095	1,509	36.8
1987[2]	29,362	9,520	32.4	25,128	7,848	31.2	10,701	5,789	54.1	3,977	1,471	37.0
1986	28,871	8,983	31.1	24,910	7,410	29.7	10,175	5,473	53.8	3,714	1,431	38.5
1985	28,485	8,926	31.3	24,620	7,504	30.5	10,041	5,342	53.2	3,641	1,264	34.7
1984	28,087	9,490	33.8	24,387	8,104	33.2	10,384	5,666	54.6	3,501	1,255	35.8
1983	27,678	9,882	35.7	24,138	8,376	34.7	10,059	5,736	57.0	3,287	1,338	40.7
1982	27,216	9,697	35.6	23,948	8,355	34.9	9,699	5,698	58.8	3,051	1,229	40.3
1981	26,834	9,173	34.2	23,423	7,780	33.2	9,214	5,222	56.7	3,277	1,296	39.6
1980	26,408	8,579	32.5	23,084	7,190	31.1	9,338	4,984	53.4	3,208	1,314	41.0
1979	25,944	8,050	31.0	22,666	6,800	30.0	9,065	4,816	53.1	3,127	1,168	37.3
1978	24,956	7,625	30.6	22,027	6,493	29.5	8,689	4,712	54.2	2,929	1,132	38.6
1977	24,710	7,726	31.3	21,850	6,667	30.5	8,315	4,595	55.3	2,860	1,059	37.0
1976	24,399	7,595	31.1	21,840	6,576	30.1	7,926	4,415	55.7	2,559	1,019	39.8
1975	24,089	7,545	31.3	21,687	6,533	30.1	7,679	4,168	54.3	2,402	1,011	42.1
1974	23,699	7,182	30.3	21,341	6,255	29.3	7,483	4,116	55.0	2,359	927	39.3
1973	23,512	7,388	31.4	21,328	6,560	30.8	7,188	4,064	56.5	2,183	828	37.9
1972	23,144	7,710	33.3	21,116	6,841	32.4	7,125	4,139	58.1	2,028	870	42.9
1971	22,784	7,396	32.5	20,900	6,530	31.2	6,398	3,587	56.1	1,884	866	46.0
1970	22,515	7,548	33.5	20,724	6,683	32.2	6,225	3,656	58.7	1,791	865	48.3
1969	22,011	7,095	32.2	20,192	6,245	30.9	5,537	3,225	58.2	1,819	850	46.7
1968	21,944	7,616	34.7	(NA)	6,839	33.7	(NA)	3,312	58.9	(NA)	777	46.3
1967	21,590	8,486	39.3	(NA)	7,677	38.4	(NA)	3,362	61.6	(NA)	809	49.3
1966	21,206	8,867	41.8	(NA)	8,090	40.9	(NA)	3,160	65.3	(NA)	777	54.4
1959	18,013	9,927	55.1	(NA)	9,112	54.9	(NA)	2,416	70.6	1,430	815	57.0
HISPANIC[1]												
2000	33,719	7,155	21.2	29,981	6,026	20.1	6,032	2,204	36.5	3,520	1,012	28.7
1999	32,669	7,439	22.8	29,198	6,349	21.7	6,113	2,488	40.7	3,207	991	30.9
1998	31,515	8,070	25.6	28,055	6,814	24.3	6,074	2,837	46.7	3,218	1,097	34.1
1997	30,637	8,308	27.1	27,467	7,198	26.2	5,718	2,911	50.9	2,976	1,017	34.2
1996	29,614	8,697	29.4	26,340	7,515	28.5	5,641	3,020	53.5	2,985	1,066	35.7
1995	28,344	8,574	30.3	25,165	7,341	29.2	5,785	3,053	52.8	2,947	1,092	37.0
1994	27,442	8,416	30.7	24,390	7,357	30.2	5,328	2,920	54.8	2,798	926	33.1
1993	26,559	8,126	30.6	23,439	6,876	29.3	5,333	2,837	53.2	2,717	972	35.8
1992[2]	25,646	7,592	29.6	22,695	6,455	28.4	4,806	2,474	51.5	2,577	881	34.2
1991[2]	22,070	6,339	28.7	19,658	5,541	28.2	4,326	2,282	52.7	2,146	667	31.1
1990	21,405	6,006	28.1	18,912	5,091	26.9	3,993	2,115	53.0	2,254	774	34.3
1989	20,746	5,430	26.2	18,488	4,659	25.2	3,763	1,902	50.6	2,045	634	31.0
1988[2]	20,064	5,357	26.7	18,102	4,700	26.0	3,734	2,052	55.0	1,864	597	32.0
1987[2]	19,395	5,422	28.0	17,342	4,761	27.5	3,678	2,045	55.6	1,933	598	31.0
1986	18,758	5,117	27.3	16,880	4,469	26.5	3,631	1,921	52.9	1,685	553	32.8
1985	18,075	5,236	29.0	16,276	4,605	28.3	3,561	1,983	55.7	1,602	532	33.2
1984	16,916	4,806	28.4	15,293	4,192	27.4	3,139	1,764	56.2	1,481	545	36.8
1983	16,544	4,633	28.0	15,075	4,113	27.3	3,032	1,670	55.1	1,364	457	33.5
1982	14,385	4,301	29.9	13,242	3,865	29.2	2,664	1,601	60.1	1,018	358	35.1
1981	14,021	3,713	26.5	12,922	3,349	25.9	2,622	1,465	55.9	1,005	313	31.1

TABLE 3.2

Poverty status of people by family relationship, race, and Hispanic origin, 1959–2000 [CONTINUED]

[Numbers in thousands. People as of March of the following year]

Year and characteristic	All people			People in families						Unrelated individuals		
				All families			Families with female householder, no husband present					
		Below poverty level			Below poverty level			Below poverty level			Below poverty level	
	Total	Number	Percent	Total	Number	Percent	Total	Number	Percent	Total	Number	Percent
HISPANIC[1] [continued]												
1980	13,600	3,491	25.7	12,547	3,143	25.1	2,421	1,319	54.5	970	312	32.2
1979	13,371	2,921	21.8	12,291	2,599	21.1	2,058	1,053	51.2	991	286	28.8
1978	12,079	2,607	21.6	11,193	2,343	20.9	1,817	1,024	56.4	886	264	29.8
1977	12,046	2,700	22.4	11,249	2,463	21.9	1,901	1,077	56.7	797	237	29.8
1976	11,269	2,783	24.7	10,552	2,516	23.8	1,766	1,000	56.6	716	266	37.2
1975	11,117	2,991	26.9	10,472	2,755	26.3	1,842	1,053	57.2	645	236	36.6
1974	11,201	2,575	23.0	10,584	2,374	22.4	1,723	915	53.1	617	201	32.6
1973	10,795	2,366	21.9	10,269	2,209	21.5	1,534	881	57.4	526	157	29.9
1972	10,588	2,414	22.8	10,099	2,252	22.3	1,370	733	53.5	488	162	33.2
ASIAN AND PACIFIC ISLANDER												
2000	11,357	1,226	10.8	9,948	946	9.5	1,049	204	19.5	1,375	271	19.7
1999	10,916	1,163	10.7	9,618	919	9.6	1,097	253	23.0	1,267	238	18.8
1998	10,873	1,360	12.5	9,576	1,087	11.4	1,123	373	33.2	1,266	257	20.3
1997	10,482	1,468	14.0	9,312	1,116	12.0	932	313	33.6	1,134	327	28.9
1996	10,054	1,454	14.5	8,900	1,172	13.2	1,018	300	29.5	1,120	255	22.8
1995	9,644	1,411	14.6	8,582	1,112	13.0	919	266	28.9	1,013	260	25.6
1994	6,654	974	14.6	5,915	776	13.1	582	137	23.6	696	179	25.7
1993	7,434	1,134	15.3	6,609	898	13.6	725	126	17.4	791	228	28.8
1992[2]	7,779	985	12.7	6,922	787	11.4	729	183	25.0	828	193	23.3
1991[2]	7,192	996	13.8	6,367	773	12.1	721	177	24.6	785	209	26.6
1990	7,014	858	12.2	6,300	712	11.3	638	132	20.7	668	124	18.5
1989	6,673	939	14.1	5,917	779	13.2	614	212	34.6	712	144	20.2
1988[2]	6,447	1,117	17.3	5,767	942	16.3	650	263	40.5	651	160	24.5
1987[2]	6,322	1,021	16.1	5,785	875	15.1	584	187	32.0	516	138	26.8

NA Not available.

[1]Hispanics may be of any race.

[2]For 1992, figures are based on 1990 census population controls. For 1991, figures are revised. For 1988 and 1987, figures are based on new processing procedures and are also revised.

Note: Prior to 1979, people in unrelated subfamilies were included in people in families. Beginning in 1979, people in unrelated subfamilies are included in all people but are excluded from people in families.

SOURCE: Joseph Dalaker, "Table A-1. Poverty Status of People by Family Relationship, Race, and Hispanic Origin: 1959 to 2000," in *Poverty in the United States: 2000,* U.S. Census Bureau, Washington, DC, September 2001

percent of the nation's population, or 39.5 million persons, lived below the poverty level. By 1973 the U.S. poverty rate had been halved, to 11.1 percent. The numbers and percentages were reduced for both African Americans and whites, but African Americans (23.7 percent) saw greater percentage gains than whites (9.7 percent). Analysts believe this decline was due both to the growth in the economy and to the success of some of the antipoverty programs instituted in the late 1960s.

The poverty rate began to increase in the early 1980s, coinciding with a downturn in household and family incomes for all Americans. The poverty rate rose steadily until it reached an 18-year high of 15.2 percent in 1983, a year during which the country was climbing out of a serious economic recession. The percentage of Americans living in poverty then began dropping, falling to 12.8 percent in 1989. After that, however, the percentage increased

again, reaching 15.1 percent in 1993 (39.3 million people). It then dropped to 12.7 percent in 1998 (34.5 million) and continued to drop to 11.3 percent (31.1 million) in 2000. (See Table 3.2 and Figure 3.1.)

Poverty rates have been consistently lower for whites than for minorities. In 1959, 18.1 percent of all whites, or 28.5 million people, lived below the poverty level. By 1970 the rate declined to 9.9 percent, about where it remained for the next 10 years. In 1983 the percentage of whites living in poverty reached an 18-year high of 12.1 percent. By 2000 it had dropped to 9.4 percent (21.3 million people). (See Table 3.2.)

By contrast, poverty rates for African Americans declined from 55.1 percent (9.9 million) in 1959 to 33.5 percent (7.5 million) in 1970. In 1983 rates for African Americans were 35.7 percent, still almost triple the rate for whites. In 2000, a year in which the American economy

FIGURE 3.1

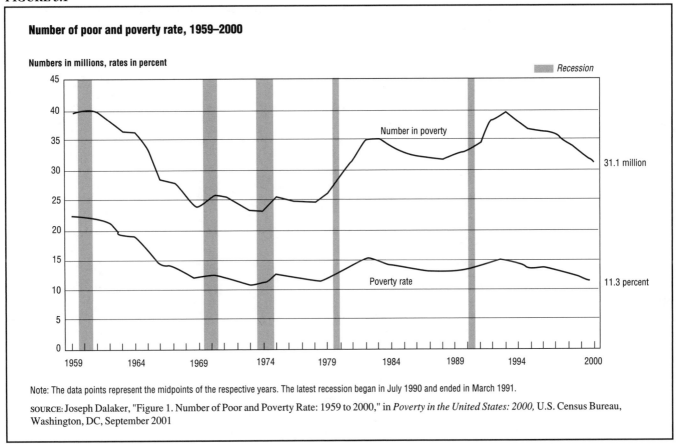

Number of poor and poverty rate, 1959–2000

Numbers in millions, rates in percent

Recession

Number in poverty

31.1 million

Poverty rate

11.3 percent

Note: The data points represent the midpoints of the respective years. The latest recession began in July 1990 and ended in March 1991.

SOURCE: Joseph Dalaker, "Figure 1. Number of Poor and Poverty Rate: 1959 to 2000," in *Poverty in the United States: 2000,* U.S. Census Bureau, Washington, DC, September 2001

was very strong, over one-fifth (22.1 percent, or 7.9 million) of all African Americans were poor. This percentage is the lowest recorded poverty rate ever for African Americans. (See Table 3.2.) African American children and older persons have been particularly affected by poverty. In 2000, 30.9 percent of African Americans under 18 years of age and 22.3 percent of African Americans 65 years or over (as opposed to 17.4 percent of African Americans aged 18 to 64 years) were poor.

Among those of Hispanic origin, in 1972 (the first year for which statistics were recorded by the U.S. Census Bureau for the Hispanic ethnicity), 22.8 percent lived below the poverty level. Between 1972 and 1985, the number of Hispanics living below the poverty level more than doubled, from 2.4 million to 5.2 million. Over this same period, the total Hispanic population rose from 10.6 million to 18.1 million. (Persons of Hispanic origin can be of any race.) The poverty rate among Hispanics reached 29.9 percent in 1982 and then dropped to 26.2 percent in 1989. The poverty rate reached 30.7 percent, its highest recorded point, in 1994, then dropped to 29.4 in 1996 and 21.2 (or 7.2 million) in 2000. (See Table 3.2.) A large proportion (28 percent) of young Hispanics under 18 years of age and about one-fifth (18.8 percent) of those 65 years and older were poor.

The poverty rate in 2000 for Asian and Pacific Islanders was 10.8 percent (or 1.2 million), only slightly higher than the rate for whites (9.4 percent). The rate was lower than it was in 1987, the first year that the Census Bureau kept statistics on Asian and Pacific Islanders, when 16.1 percent lived below the poverty level. (See Table 3.2.)

Although a far higher percentage of African Americans and Hispanics than whites were poor, almost half of the 31.1 million people who were poor in 2000 were non-Hispanic whites. In that year, 46.8 percent of poor Americans were non-Hispanic whites, 25.4 percent were African Americans, 23 percent were Hispanics, and 3.9 percent were Asians and Pacific Islanders. (See Table 3.3.)

Age

In 2000, 16.2 percent of children under 18 years old were poor; this was a decline of 6.5 percentage points from 22.7 percent in 1993. The percent of those age 65 and older below the poverty line declined from 12.2 percent in 1993 to 10.2 percent in 2000. (See Table 3.3.) From 1959 to 2000 the number of people 65 years and older living in poverty dropped significantly, from about 35 percent to 10.2 percent. (See Figure 3.2.)

In 2000 more than one-fourth of the nation's poor were either under 18 years of age (16.2 percent) or 65 years of age and older (10.2 percent). In comparison to the nonpoor, children are overrepresented among the

TABLE 3.3

People and families in poverty by selected characteristics, 1993–2000

[Numbers in thousands.]

Characteristic	2000 below poverty				1993 below poverty				Change[1] 1993 to 2000			
	Number	90-pct. C.I. (±)	Percent	90-pct. C.I. (±)	Number	90-pct. C.I. (±)	Percent	90-pct. C.I. (±)	Number	90-pct. C.I. (±)	Percent	90-pct. C.I. (±)
PEOPLE												
Total	31,139	880	11.3	0.3	39,260	933	15.1	0.4	*−8,122	1,281	*−3.9	0.5
Family status												
In families	22,088	755	9.6	0.3	29,927	829	13.6	0.4	*−7,839	1,122	*−4.0	0.5
Householder	6,226	227	8.6	0.3	8,393	263	12.3	0.4	*−2,167	347	*−3.7	0.5
Related children under 18	11,086	451	15.7	0.7	14,961	487	22.0	0.8	*−3,875	663	*−6.3	1.0
Related children under 6	3,931	283	16.9	1.3	6,097	331	25.6	1.5	*−2,166	434	*−8.7	2.0
In unrelated subfamilies	520	59	39.4	5.2	945	77	54.3	5.3	*−425	97	*−14.9	7.4
Reference person	198	36	37.5	7.9	367	48	51.6	8.0	*−168	59	*−14.1	11.2
Children under 18	314	82	41.8	12.3	554	105	57.2	12.7	*−239	133	−15.4	17.7
Unrelated individual	8,530	276	18.9	0.6	8,388	263	22.1	0.7	142	382	*−3.1	1.0
Male	3,458	161	16.0	0.8	3,281	151	18.1	0.9	176	220	*−2.1	1.2
Female	5,073	202	21.6	0.9	5,107	194	25.7	1.1	−34	280	*−4.1	1.4
Race[2] and Hispanic origin												
White	21,291	742	9.4	0.3	26,226	783	12.2	0.4	*−4,935	1,079	*−2.8	0.5
Non-Hispanic	14,572	622	7.5	0.3	18,882	674	9.9	0.4	*−4,311	918	*−2.4	0.5
Black	7,901	416	22.1	1.2	10,877	443	33.1	1.3	*−2,975	607	*−10.9	1.8
Asian and Pacific Islander	1,226	178	10.8	1.6	1,134	165	15.3	2.2	92	242	*−4.5	2.7
Hispanic[3]	7,155	398	21.2	1.2	8,126	400	30.6	1.5	*−971	564	*−9.4	1.9
Age												
Under 18 years	11,633	461	16.2	0.6	15,727	495	22.7	0.7	*−4,095	676	*−6.5	1.0
18 to 64 years	16,146	648	9.4	0.4	19,783	681	12.4	0.4	*−3,637	941	*−3.0	0.6
18 to 24 years	3,893	192	14.4	0.7	4,854	204	19.1	0.8	*−961	281	*−4.6	1.1
25 to 34 years	3,892	199	10.4	0.5	5,804	230	13.8	0.5	*−1,912	303	*−3.4	0.8
35 to 44 years	3,678	192	8.2	0.4	4,415	202	10.6	0.5	*−737	280	*−2.4	0.6
45 to 54 years	2,441	158	6.4	0.4	2,522	155	8.5	0.5	−81	220	*−2.1	0.7
55 to 59 years	1,175	110	8.8	0.8	1,057	100	9.9	0.9	118	150	−1.0	1.3
60 to 64 years	1,066	105	10.2	1.0	1,129	105	11.3	1.0	−63	148	−1.1	1.5
65 years and over	3,360	179	10.2	0.5	3,755	181	12.2	0.6	*−395	253	*−2.0	0.8
Nativity												
Native	26,442	816	10.7	0.3	34,086	875	14.4	0.4	*−7,644	1,198	*−3.7	0.5
Foreign born	4,697	411	15.7	1.4	5,179	413	23.0	1.8	−482	582	*−7.3	2.3
Naturalized citizen	1,107	201	9.7	1.8	707	155	10.1	2.2	*400	253	−0.4	2.8
Not a citizen	3,590	360	19.4	1.9	4,472	385	28.7	2.5	*−882	526	*−9.3	3.1
Region												
Northeast	5,433	357	10.3	0.7	6,839	383	13.3	0.8	*−1,405	523	*−3.0	1.0
Midwest	5,971	411	9.5	0.7	8,172	459	13.4	0.8	*−2,201	617	*−3.9	1.0
South	12,205	595	12.5	0.6	15,375	637	17.1	0.7	*−3,170	870	*−4.6	0.9
West	7,530	474	11.9	0.8	8,879	492	15.6	0.9	*−1,349	683	*−3.7	1.2
Residence												
Inside metropolitan areas	24,296	788	10.8	0.4	29,615	826	14.6	0.4	*−5,319	1,142	*−3.8	0.5
Inside central cities	12,967	589	16.1	0.7	16,805	638	21.5	0.8	*−3,838	869	*−5.3	1.1
Outside central cities	11,329	553	7.8	0.4	12,810	561	10.3	0.5	*−1,481	788	*−2.4	0.6
Outside metropolitan areas	6,843	530	13.4	1.1	9,650	600	17.2	1.1	*−2,807	801	*−3.8	1.5

poor, while the elderly are underrepresented. Children make up about 37.4 percent of the poor even though they represent only a little more than one-fourth (26.1 percent) of the total population. People over 65 years old made up 12 percent of the total population in 2000 but only 10.2 percent of the poor. (See Figure 3.2 and Table 3.4.) Most observers credit Social Security for the sharp decline in poverty among the elderly.

CHILD POVERTY. The child poverty rate, at 16.2 percent of the nation's children under the age of 18, was nearly twice the poverty rate for adults (9.4 percent) in 2000. Very young children are at the greatest risk of being poor. According to the National Center for Children in Poverty, the United States has the highest rate of young child poverty of all Western industrialized nations.

In 2000 nearly 18 percent of children under the age of three lived in poverty, a decline from 27 percent in 1993. Nearly 45 percent of very young children living with a female householder (with no spouse present) were poor, compared to 9 percent of children under three years old living with families headed by a married couple. Poverty rates for African American children under age three (35 percent) and Hispanic children under three (30 percent) are three times higher than the rates for white children (10 percent).

Childhood poverty is a matter of great concern because strong evidence exists that poverty can limit a

TABLE 3.3

People and families in poverty by selected characteristics, 1993–2000 [CONTINUED]

[Numbers in thousands.]

Characteristic	2000 below poverty				1993 below poverty				Change[1] 1993 to 2000			
	Number	90-pct. C.I. (±)	Percent	90-pct. C.I. (±)	Number	90-pct. C.I. (±)	Percent	90-pct. C.I. (±)	Number	90-pct. C.I. (±)	Percent	90-pct. C.I. (±)
FAMILIES												
Total	**6,226**	**227**	**8.6**	**0.3**	**8,393**	**263**	**12.3**	**0.4**	***−2,167**	**347**	***−3.7**	**0.5**
White	4,153	179	6.9	0.3	5,452	202	9.4	0.4	*−1,299	270	*−2.5	0.5
Non-Hispanic	2,820	145	5.3	0.3	3,988	168	7.6	0.3	*−1,168	222	*−2.3	0.4
Black	1,686	109	19.1	1.3	2,499	130	31.3	1.7	*−813	169	*−12.1	2.2
Asian and Pacific Islander	235	39	8.8	1.5	235	378	13.5	2.3	–	54	*−4.7	2.7
Hispanic[3]	1,431	100	18.5	1.4	1,625	102	27.3	1.8	*−194	143	*−8.8	2.3
Type of Family												
Married-couple	2,638	140	4.7	0.3	3,481	156	6.5	0.3	*−843	209	*−1.8	0.4
White	2,163	125	4.4	0.3	2,757	137	5.8	0.3	*−595	186	*−1.4	0.4
Non-Hispanic	1,447	100	3.3	0.2	2,042	117	4.7	0.3	*−595	153	*−1.4	0.4
Black	260	41	6.1	1.0	458	53	12.3	1.5	*−199	67	*−6.3	1.8
Asian and Pacific Islander	169	33	7.7	1.6	177	33	12.4	2.4	−8	47	*−4.8	2.9
Hispanic[3]	742	71	14.1	1.4	770	69	19.1	1.8	−28	99	*−4.9	2.3
Female householder, no husband present	3,099	151	24.7	1.3	4,424	179	35.6	1.6	*−1,325	235	*−10.9	2.1
White	1,656	109	20.0	1.4	2,376	127	29.2	1.7	*−720	166	*−9.2	2.2
Non-Hispanic	1,127	89	16.9	1.4	1,699	105	25.0	1.7	*−571	137	*−8.1	2.2
Black	1,303	95	34.6	2.8	1,908	112	49.9	3.3	*−605	146	*−15.2	4.4
Asian and Pacific Islander	60	20	19.9	7.1	43	16	18.6	7.4	17	26	1.3	10.3
Hispanic[3]	597	64	34.2	4.0	772	69	51.6	5.4	*−175	94	*−17.4	6.8

C.I. = Confidence interval.
– Represents zero. *Statistically significant at the 90-percent confidence level.
[1]As a result of rounding, some differences may appear to be slightly higher or lower than the differences of the reported rates.
[2]Data for American Indians and Alaska Natives are not shown separately.
[3]Hispanics may be of any race.

SOURCE: Joseph Dalaker, "Table A-4. People and Families in Poverty by Selected Characteristics: 1993 and 2000," in *Poverty in the United States: 2000,* U.S. Census Bureau, Washington, DC, September 2001

---

child's physical and cognitive development. According to the Children's Defense Fund report *The High Price of Poverty for Children of the South* (May 1998):

- Poverty is a greater risk to children's overall health status than is living in a single-parent family.

- Poor children are twice as likely as nonpoor children to be born weighing too little or to suffer stunted growth.

- Poor children suffer more mental and physical disabilities.

- Poverty makes children hungry. Hungry children are more likely to be hyperactive and to have serious behavior problems. They are four times more likely to have difficulty concentrating in school.

- Poor children score lower on reading and math tests and are twice as likely to repeat a year of school as nonpoor children.

- Poor children earn 25 percent lower wages when they become young adults.

Regions

In 2000 the Midwest had the lowest poverty rate (9.5 percent) among the nation's four regions, followed by the Northeast with 10.3 percent. Poverty rates were highest in the West (11.9 percent) and the South (12.5 percent). (See Table 3.3.)

Family Status

Almost 1 in every 10 families (9.6 percent) in the United States was living in poverty in 2000. Families headed by married couples had the lowest poverty rate (4.7 percent). Almost one-fourth (24.7 percent) of all families with a female householder (with no husband present) were living in poverty, a 10.9 percent decline since 1993. (See Table 3.3.)

BY RACE. In 2000 non-Hispanic white (5.3 percent) and Asian and Pacific Islander (8.8 percent) families had much lower poverty rates than African American (19.1 percent) or Hispanic (18.5 percent) families. However, rates had declined considerably after 1993 for African Americans (12.1) and Hispanics (8.8 percent) in comparison to non-Hispanic whites (2.3 percent) and Asian and Pacific Islanders (4.7 percent). Non-Hispanic white married-couple families (3.3 percent) were less likely to live in poverty than African American (6.1 percent), Asian and Pacific Islander (7.7 percent), or Hispanic (14.1 percent) families headed by married couples. (See Table 3.3.)

FIGURE 3.2

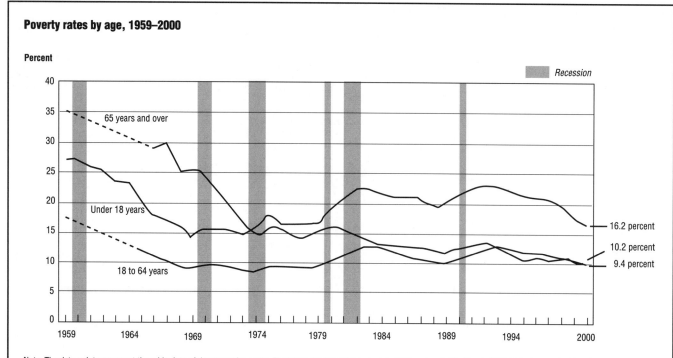

Poverty rates by age, 1959–2000

Percent

Recession

65 years and over

Under 18 years

18 to 64 years

16.2 percent

10.2 percent

9.4 percent

1959   1964   1969   1974   1979   1984   1989   1994   2000

Note: The data points represent the midpoints of the respective years. The latest recession began in July 1990 and ended in March 1991. Data for people 18 to 64 and 65 and older are not available from 1960 to 1965.

SOURCE: Joseph Dalaker, "Figure 2. Poverty Rates by Age: 1959 to 2000," in *Poverty in the United States: 2000,* Current Population Reports P60-214, U.S. Census Bureau, Washington, DC, September 2001

Hispanic and African American female heads of household are at particularly high risk of poverty. While less than one-fifth (16.9) of non-Hispanic white families headed by a female with no husband present were living in poverty in 2000, 34.6 percent of female-headed African American families, 34.2 percent of female-headed Hispanic families, and 19.9 percent of female-headed Asian and Pacific Islander families were poor. (See Table 3.3.)

States

State poverty rates vary widely from year to year and should be used with caution when ranking the states for statistical purposes. However, on average, over the years 1998, 1999, and 2000, Connecticut, Iowa, Maryland, Minnesota, and New Hampshire had the lowest poverty rates, while Arkansas, the District of Columbia, Louisiana, Mississippi, Montana, New Mexico, and West Virginia had the highest rates. (See Table 3.5.)

Work Experience

The probability of a family living in poverty is influenced by three primary factors: the size of the family, the number of workers, and the characteristics of the wage earners. As the number of wage earners in a family increases, the probability of poverty declines. The likelihood of a second wage earner is greatest in families headed by married couples.

About 6.5 percent of all Americans who worked in 1999 lived in poverty, compared to 19.5 percent of those who did not work that year. Less than half (45.3 percent) of poor persons 16 years old and over worked at least some of the year, with only 31.8 percent working 27 weeks or more. This compares to 71.3 percent of all people 16 years old and over who worked at least some of the year, with 63.9 percent working 27 weeks or more. (See Table 3.6.)

Most poor children live in families where one or more adults work. However, millions of working parents are not able to earn enough to lift their families out of poverty, even those who work full-time all year. In the report *A Hand Up: How State Earned Income Tax Credits Help Working Families Escape Poverty in 2001* (Center on Budget and Policy Priorities, 2001), Nicholas Johnson reported that in 2000 approximately 4.4 million families with children in which the parents were not elderly or disabled had incomes below the federal poverty line. Of these families, 3 million (69 percent) had a working parent. (See Figure 3.3.)

Education

Not surprisingly, poverty rates drop sharply as years of schooling rise. The U.S. Bureau of the Census reported that in 1999 the poverty rate was 22.4 percent for persons who had not completed high school, 9.2 percent for those

TABLE 3.4

Ratio of family income to poverty threshold for people by selected characteristics, 2000

(Numbers in thousands.)

Characteristic	Total	Under 0.50		Under 1.00		Under 1.25	
		Number	Percent of total	Number	Percent of total	Number	Percent of total
PEOPLE							
Total	275,917	12,158	4.4	31,139	11.3	43,465	15.8
Age							
Under 18 years	71,932	4,693	6.5	11,633	16.2	15,671	21.8
18 to 24 years	26,962	1,760	6.5	3,893	14.4	5,259	19.5
25 to 34 years	37,440	1,793	4.8	3,892	10.4	5,320	14.2
35 to 44 years	44,780	1,404	3.1	3,678	8.2	5,159	11.5
45 to 54 years	38,040	971	2.6	2,441	6.4	3,433	9.0
55 to 59 years	13,338	456	3.4	1,175	8.8	1,586	11.9
60 to 64 years	10,446	353	3.4	1,066	10.2	1,451	13.9
65 years and over	32,979	727	2.2	3,360	10.2	5,587	16.9
Race[1] and Hispanic Origin							
White	225,993	8,002	3.5	21,291	9.4	30,828	13.6
Non-Hispanic	193,878	5,725	3.0	14,572	7.5	21,306	11.0
Black	35,748	3,363	9.4	7,901	22.1	10,154	28.4
Other races	14,176	793	5.6	1,946	13.7	2,483	17.5
Asian and Pacific Islander	11,357	449	4.0	1,226	10.8	1,590	14.0
Hispanic[2]	33,719	2,460	7.3	7,155	21.2	10,072	29.9
FAMILY STATUS							
In families	229,476	8,197	3.6	22,088	9.6	31,353	13.7
Householder	72,383	2,412	3.3	6,226	8.6	8,889	12.3
Related children under 18	70,769	4,306	6.1	11,086	15.7	15,039	21.3
Related children under 6	23,261	1,730	7.4	3,931	16.9	5,373	23.1
Unrelated individual	45,120	3,651	8.1	8,530	18.9	11,496	25.5
Male	21,629	1,639	7.6	3,458	16.0	4,594	21.2
Female	23,491	2,012	8.6	5,073	21.6	6,902	29.4

[1]Data for American Indians and Alaska Natives are not shown separately.
[2]Hispanics may be of any race.

SOURCE: Joseph Dalaker, "Table E. Ratio of Family Income to Poverty Threshold for People by Selected Characteristics: 2000," in *Poverty in the United States: 2000,* Current Population Reports P60-214, U.S. Census Bureau, Washington, DC, September 2001

who had graduated from high school but had not gone to college, and 6.1 percent for those with some college but less than a bachelor's degree.

The general relationship between education and welfare applied for all races. But there were some large differences among the races. For example, the 1999 poverty rates for African American and Hispanic high school graduates age 25 and over who had not gone to college were 17.9 percent and 14.2 percent, respectively, while white graduates had a much lower poverty rate (7.9 percent).

MEDIAN INCOME

In its surveys, the U.S. Bureau of the Census differentiates between households and families. A household is an individual living alone or a group of persons living together who may or may not be related, while a family is composed of two or more related individuals. All families are households, but not all households are families. In 2000 there were 106.4 million households in the United States but only 72.4 million families. (See Table 3.7.)

Household Income

The median income (half the population earns less than this amount, and half earn more) for all households in 2000 was $42,148. African American ($30,439) and Hispanic ($33,447) households had much lower median incomes than did non-Hispanic white households ($45,904) and Asian and Pacific Islander households ($55,521). (See Table 3.7.)

Family Income

In 2000 the median income for all families was $51,751. The median family income is almost three times the 2000 average poverty threshold of $17,500 for a family of four. Families headed by married couples of all racial and ethnic backgrounds enjoyed the greatest financial success (a median income of $59,346), with incomes more than twice that of female-headed households ($28,116). (See Table 3.7.)

Per Capita Income

In its annual *Current Population Survey*, the U.S. Census Bureau determines the per capita income in the

TABLE 3.5

Percent of people in poverty by state, 1998–2000

State	3-year average 1998–2000 Percent	3-year average 1998–2000 90-pct. C.I. (±)	Average 1999–2000 Percent	Average 1999–2000 90-pct. C.I. (±)	Average 1998–99 Percent	Average 1998–99 90-pct. C.I. (±)	Difference in 2-year moving averages Percent	Difference in 2-year moving averages 90-pct. C.I. (±)
United States	**11.9**	**0.2**	**11.5**	**0.3**	**12.3**	**0.3**	***−0.7**	**0.2**
Alabama	14.6	2.1	14.6	2.4	14.8	2.5	−0.2	2.0
Alaska	8.3	1.6	7.8	1.9	8.5	1.9	−0.7	1.6
Arizona	13.6	1.8	12.0	2.1	14.3	2.2	*−2.2	1.8
Arkansas	15.8	2.1	16.4	2.5	14.7	2.4	1.6	2.1
California	14.0	0.8	13.3	0.9	14.6	1.0	*−1.2	0.8
Colorado	8.5	1.6	8.1	1.9	8.7	1.9	−0.6	1.6
Connecticut	7.6	1.8	6.7	2.0	8.3	2.2	−1.6	1.8
Delaware	9.8	2.0	9.5	2.3	10.3	2.3	−0.8	1.9
District of Columbia	17.3	2.6	14.8	2.8	18.6	3.1	*−3.7	2.6
Florida	12.1	1.0	11.5	1.2	12.8	1.2	*−1.2	1.0
Georgia	12.6	1.7	12.1	2.0	13.2	2.1	−1.1	1.7
Hawaii	10.5	2.1	10.3	2.4	10.9	2.4	−0.6	2.0
Idaho	13.3	1.9	13.5	2.2	13.5	2.3	−	1.8
Illinois	10.5	1.1	10.8	1.3	10.0	1.2	0.8	1.1
Indiana	8.2	1.6	7.6	1.9	8.0	1.9	−0.5	1.7
Iowa	7.9	1.7	7.3	1.9	8.3	2.0	−1.0	1.6
Kansas	10.4	1.9	10.8	2.2	10.9	2.2	−	1.8
Kentucky	12.5	2.0	11.9	2.3	12.8	2.3	−0.9	1.9
Louisiana	18.6	2.2	18.3	2.6	19.1	2.6	−0.8	2.2
Maine	9.8	2.0	9.5	2.3	10.5	2.4	−1.0	1.9
Maryland	7.3	1.7	7.4	2.0	7.2	1.9	0.2	1.6
Massachusetts	10.2	1.3	10.9	1.6	10.2	1.6	0.7	1.3
Michigan	10.2	1.1	9.9	1.3	10.3	1.3	−0.4	1.1
Minnesota	7.8	1.6	6.6	1.7	8.8	1.9	*−2.2	1.6
Mississippi	15.5	2.1	14.5	2.4	16.9	2.6	*−2.4	2.0
Missouri	9.7	1.8	9.7	2.1	10.7	2.2	−1.0	1.7
Montana	16.0	2.1	15.8	2.5	16.1	2.5	−0.3	2.1
Nebraska	10.6	1.9	9.8	2.2	11.6	2.3	−1.8	1.8
Nevada	10.0	1.8	9.7	2.0	10.9	2.2	−1.2	1.7
New Hampshire	7.4	1.8	6.3	1.9	8.8	2.2	*−2.5	1.7
New Jersey	8.1	1.1	7.9	1.2	8.2	1.3	−0.3	1.0
New Mexico	19.3	2.3	18.7	2.6	20.5	2.7	−1.8	2.2
New York	14.7	1.0	13.8	1.1	15.4	1.1	*−1.6	0.9
North Carolina	13.2	1.5	12.9	1.7	13.8	1.7	−0.9	1.4
North Dakota	12.7	2.1	11.5	2.3	14.1	2.5	*−2.6	2.0
Ohio	11.1	1.2	11.1	1.3	11.6	1.4	−0.5	1.1
Oklahoma	14.1	2.0	14.0	2.3	13.4	2.3	0.6	2.0
Oregon	12.8	2.1	11.6	2.3	13.8	2.5	*−2.1	2.0
Pennsylvania	9.9	1.0	9.2	1.2	10.3	1.2	*−1.2	1.0
Rhode Island	10.0	2.1	9.2	2.4	10.7	2.5	−1.5	2.0
South Carolina	11.9	2.1	11.0	2.3	12.7	2.4	−1.7	2.0
South Dakota	9.3	1.7	8.6	2.0	9.3	2.0	−0.7	1.8
Tennessee	13.3	2.0	13.3	2.4	12.7	2.3	0.6	2.0
Texas	14.9	1.1	14.9	1.2	15.0	1.3	−0.2	1.0
Utah	8.1	1.5	7.6	1.7	7.3	1.7	0.3	1.5
Vermont	10.1	2.0	10.2	2.4	9.8	2.3	0.4	2.0
Virginia	8.1	1.6	7.8	1.8	8.4	1.9	−0.6	1.5
Washington	9.4	1.8	9.6	2.2	9.2	2.1	0.4	1.8
West Virginia	15.8	2.1	14.8	2.4	16.8	2.5	−2.0	2.0
Wisconsin	8.8	1.7	8.9	2.0	8.7	1.9	0.2	1.7
Wyoming	11.0	1.9	11.2	2.3	11.1	2.2	0.1	1.8

− Represents zero.

* Statistically significant at the 90–percent confidence level (C.I.).

SOURCE: Joseph Dalaker, "Table D. Percent of People in Poverty by State: 1998, 1999, and 2000," in *Poverty in the United States: 2000,* Current Population Reports P60-214, U.S. Census Bureau, Washington, DC, 2001

United States. Per capita income is computed by dividing the total money income by the total population. In other words, it represents the amount of income that every man, woman, and child would receive if the nation's total earnings were divided equally among them. In 2000 the per capita income for all Americans was $22,199. The 2000 per capita incomes for different racial and ethnic groups were: non-Hispanic whites, $25,278; Asian and Pacific Islanders, $22,352; African Americans, $15,197; and Hispanics, $12,306. (See Table 3.7.) Comparing the per capita income with the poverty level for a family of four in 2000 ($17,050) reveals that the poverty level for four people is less than the per capita income.

TABLE 3.6

Poverty status and work experience of persons in families and unrelated individuals, 1999

(Numbers in thousands)

Poverty status and work experience	Total persons	In married-couple families				In families maintained by women			In families maintained by men			Unrelated individuals
		Husbands	Wives	Related children under 18	Other relatives	Householder	Related children under 18	Other relatives	Householder	Related children under 18	Other relatives	
TOTAL												
All persons[1]	209,067	54,714	55,247	5,475	17,180	12,669	1,760	9,763	4,003	429	3,832	43,996
With labor force activity	149,042	43,850	36,715	2,576	12,719	9,370	767	6,712	3,224	168	2,740	30,200
1 to 26 weeks	15,391	1,574	3,774	1,560	3,001	941	498	1,104	194	82	308	2,355
27 weeks or more	133,651	42,276	32,941	1,016	9,718	8,429	269	5,607	3,030	87	2,432	27,845
With no labor force activity	60,025	10,864	18,532	2,900	4,461	3,298	993	3,051	779	261	1,091	13,796
At or above poverty level												
All persons[1]	187,707	52,059	52,575	5,063	16,402	9,144	1,218	8,289	3,531	371	3,548	35,508
With labor force activity	139,376	42,304	35,842	2,488	12,414	7,153	608	6,087	2,944	152	2,614	26,770
1 to 26 weeks	12,521	1,396	3,493	1,513	2,896	342	380	856	124	73	252	1,197
27 weeks or more	126,855	40,909	32,349	975	9,519	6,811	228	5,231	2,820	79	2,362	25,573
With no labor force activity	48,331	9,754	16,733	2,575	3,987	1,991	610	2,202	588	219	934	8,738
Below poverty level												
All persons[1]	21,360	2,655	2,672	413	778	3,525	542	1,474	472	58	284	8,488
With labor force activity	9,666	1,546	873	88	305	2,218	159	625	280	16	126	3,430
1 to 26 weeks	2,871	179	282	47	105	599	118	248	70	9	56	1,159
27 weeks or more	6,796	1,367	592	41	200	1,618	41	377	211	7	69	2,272
With no labor force activity	11,694	1,110	1,798	325	474	1,307	383	849	191	42	158	5,058
Poverty rate[2]												
All persons[1]	10.2	4.9	4.8	7.5	4.5	27.8	30.8	15.1	11.8	13.5	7.4	19.3
With labor force activity	6.5	3.5	2.4	3.4	2.4	23.7	20.7	9.3	8.7	9.5	4.6	11.4
1 to 26 weeks	18.7	11.3	7.5	3.0	3.5	63.7	23.7	22.5	35.9	10.6	18.3	49.2
27 weeks or more	5.1	3.2	1.8	4.1	2.1	19.2	15.3	6.7	7.0	8.4	2.9	8.2
With no labor force activity	19.5	10.2	9.7	11.2	10.6	39.6	38.6	27.8	24.6	16.1	14.5	36.7

[1] Data on families include persons in primary families and unrelated subfamilies.
[2] Number below the poverty level as a percent of the total.
Note: Data refer to persons 16 years and older. Data for 1999, which were collected in the March 2000 supplement to the Current Population Survey, are not strictly comparable with data for 1998 and earlier years because of the introduction in January 2000 of revised population controls used in the survey.

SOURCE: Thomas M. Beers, "Table 5. Persons in families and unrelated individuals: Poverty status and work experience, 1999," in *A Profile of the Working Poor, 1999*, U.S. Department of Labor, Bureau of Labor Statistics, Washington, DC, February 2001

TAX RELIEF FOR THE POOR

Both conservatives and liberals hailed the Tax Reform Act of 1986 (PL 99-514) as a major step toward relieving the tax burden of low-income families, one group of Americans whose wages and benefits have been eroding since 1979. The law enlarged and "inflation-proofed" the Earned Income Tax Credit (EITC), which provides a refundable tax credit that both offsets taxes and often operates as a wage supplement. Only those who work can qualify. The amount is determined, in part, by how much each qualified individual or family earned. It is also adjusted to the size of the family. To be eligible for the family EITC, workers must live with their children, who must be under 19 years old or full-time students under 24 years old.

The maximum credit for 2001 was $2,428 for tax-payers with one child, $4,008 for taxpayers with more than one child, and $364 for persons with no children. Families get less if their income is very low because they are also eligible for public assistance. Working families receive the maximum benefit if their earnings are at least $7,140 (for families with one child) or $10,020 (for families with more than one child), up to an adjusted gross income of no more than $13,090. Benefits phase down gradually when income surpasses $13,090 and phase out entirely for families with two or more children at $32,121. (See Figure 3.4.)

The largest EITC benefits go to families that are getting off welfare. The gradual phaseout and the availability of the EITC at above-poverty income levels help to stabilize a parent's employment by providing additional money to cover expenses associated with working, such as child care and transportation. Research has found that the EITC has been an effective work incentive and has significantly increased work participation among single mothers.

Those who do not owe income tax, or who owe an amount smaller than the credit, receive a check directly from the Internal Revenue Service (IRS) for the credit due them. Most recipients claim the credit when they file an income tax form. The EITC lifted more than 4.8 million people, including 2.6 million children, out of poverty in 1999.

FIGURE 3.3

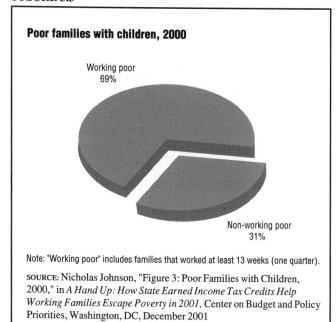

Poor families with children, 2000

Working poor
69%

Non-working poor
31%

Note: "Working poor" includes families that worked at least 13 weeks (one quarter).

SOURCE: Nicholas Johnson, "Figure 3: Poor Families with Children, 2000," in *A Hand Up: How State Earned Income Tax Credits Help Working Families Escape Poverty in 2001,* Center on Budget and Policy Priorities, Washington, DC, December 2001

Although the Tax Reform Act of 1986 has helped ease the burden of federal taxes, most of the poor still pay a substantial share of their income in state and local taxes. To relieve this tax burden, 10 states have enacted a state EITC, and 16 others offer state EITCs based on the federal credit. These state programs boost the income of families that move from welfare to work and prevent states from taxing poor families deeper into poverty.

HOW ACCURATE IS THE "POVERTY LEVEL"?

Almost every year since the U.S. Bureau of the Census first defined the poverty level, observers have been concerned about the accuracy of the estimated poverty level. The figure had been based on the finding that the average family in the mid-1950s spent about one-third of its income on food. That figure was multiplied by three to allow for expenditures on all other goods and services. This represented the after-tax money income of an average family relative to the amount it spent on food. Since 1965 the poverty threshold has been adjusted each year only for inflation.

Since that time, living patterns have changed, and food costs have become a smaller percentage of family spending. For example, the U.S. Bureau of Labor Statistics, in its *Consumer Expenditures in 2000* (Washington, DC, 2001), reported that in 2000 the average family spent 13.6 percent of its total expenditures on food, while housing accounted for about one-third (32.4 percent) of family spending. Based on these changes in buying patterns, should the amount spent on food be multiplied by a factor of seven instead of three? Or should the poverty level be based on housing or other factors? What about geographical differences in the cost of living?

The proportion of family income spent on food is not the only change in family living since the 1950s. Both parents in a family are far more likely to be working than they were a generation ago. There is also a much greater likelihood that a single parent, most likely a mother, will be heading the family. Child-care costs, which were of little concern during the 1950s, have become a major issue for working mothers and single parents at the beginning of the 21st century.

Critics of the current poverty calculations tend to believe that the poverty levels have been too low, since they are based on a 50-year-old concept of American life that does not reflect today's economic and social realities. Most feel the poverty level should be raised, probably to about 130 to 150 percent of the current levels. A 1989 study prepared by the Joint Economic Committee of Congress cited the example of a working mother with two children earning an income at the poverty level, who spends $50 per week on child care and no more than 30 percent of her earnings on housing. (This is the proportion that the U.S. Department of Housing and Urban Development [HUD] has established as the basic affordability standard.) In this particular example, 30 percent of her income would equal about $226 a month for rent and utilities. Unless this woman lived in public or subsidized housing (more than two-thirds of the poor do not live in public or subsidized housing), finding an apartment for her family for this amount would be very hard. If she spent a bare minimum on food, she would have about $30 left after taxes. This $30 would have to cover medical care, clothing, personal care items, and an occasional ice cream cone for her two children.

Some are concerned because the poverty threshold is different for elderly and nonelderly Americans. When the poverty threshold was first established, it was thought that older people did not need as much food. Therefore, the value of their basic food needs was lower. Consequently, when this figure was multiplied by three to get the poverty rate, it was naturally lower than the rate for nonelderly people. (The U.S. government, however, uses the poverty rate for nonelderly Americans when determining the eligibility for welfare services for all people, including the elderly.) Critics point out that while the elderly might eat less than younger people, they have greater needs in other areas, which are not considered when their food needs are simply multiplied by three. Probably the most notable difference between the needs of the elderly and nonelderly is in the area of health care. The Bureau of Labor Statistics, in *Consumer Expenditures in 2000*, found that while the total population interviewed spent about 5.4 percent of their income on health care, those over 65 years of age spent 12.2 percent. These critics feel that the poverty level should be the same for everyone, no matter what their age.

TABLE 3.7

Comparison of summary measures of income by selected characteristics, 1993, 1999, and 2000

[Households and people as of March of the following year.]

Characteristic	2000 Median income — Number (1,000)	Value (dollars)	90-percent confidence interval (±) (dollars)	Median income in 1999 (in 2000 dollars) — Value (dollars)	90-percent confidence interval (±) (dollars)	Median income in 1993 (in 2000 dollars) — Value (dollars)	90-percent confidence interval (±) (dollars)	Percent change in real income 1999 to 2000 — Percent change	90-percent confidence interval (±)	Percent change in real income 1993 to 2000 — Percent change	90-percent confidence interval (±)
HOUSEHOLDS											
All households	106,417	42,148	324	42,187	325	36,746	282	−0.1	0.9	*14.7	1.2
Type of Household											
Family households	72,375	51,751	390	51,618	464	44,090	402	0.3	1.0	*17.4	1.4
Married-couple families	55,598	59,346	620	58,736	519	50,729	505	1.0	1.1	*17.0	1.7
Female householder, no husband present	12,525	28,116	650	27,043	614	21,813	551	*4.0	2.7	*28.9	4.4
Male householder, no wife present	4,252	42,129	1,346	43,243	1,355	35,109	1,383	−2.6	3.5	*20.0	6.1
Nonfamily households	34,042	25,438	380	25,391	459	22,207	431	0.2	1.9	*14.5	2.8
Female householder	18,824	20,929	424	20,586	469	17,506	441	1.7	2.5	*19.6	3.9
Male householder	15,218	31,267	525	31,786	587	29,086	642	−1.6	2.0	*7.5	3.0
Race and Hispanic Origin of Householder											
All races[1]	106,417	42,148	324	42,187	325	36,746	282	−0.1	0.9	*14.7	1.2
White	88,545	44,226	452	43,932	406	38,768	371	0.7	1.1	*14.1	1.6
Non-Hispanic	79,376	45,904	434	45,856	474	40,195	387	0.1	1.1	*14.2	1.5
Black	13,352	30,439	757	28,848	882	22,974	747	*5.5	3.4	*32.5	5.4
Asian and Pacific Islander	3,527	55,521	2,443	52,925	3,191	45,105	3,649	4.9	6.4	*23.1	11.3
Hispanic origin[2]	9,663	33,447	1,114	31,767	772	26,919	890	*5.3	3.0	*24.3	5.8
Age of Householder											
15 to 24 years	6,392	27,689	827	26,017	712	22,740	784	*6.4	3.5	*21.8	5.6
25 to 34 years	18,554	44,473	1,022	43,591	684	36,793	567	2.0	2.3	*20.9	3.3
35 to 44 years	23,904	53,240	906	52,582	675	48,063	588	1.3	1.8	*10.8	2.3
45 to 54 years	21,797	58,218	1,277	58,829	905	54,350	979	−1.0	2.2	*7.1	3.0
55 to 64 years	13,943	44,992	1,002	46,095	1,098	39,373	1,002	−2.4	2.6	*14.3	3.9
65 years and over	21,828	23,048	423	23,578	388	20,879	416	*−2.2	1.9	*10.4	3.0
Nativity of the Householder											
Native	94,059	42,586	410	42,773	347	37,332	298	−0.4	1.0	*14.1	1.4
Foreign born	12,359	38,929	1,206	37,259	981	31,017	938	*4.5	3.4	*25.5	5.4
Naturalized citizen.	5,740	44,456	1,969	45,423	2,499	37,357	1,556	−2.1	5.6	*19.0	7.2
Not a citizen	6,618	35,413	1,313	32,247	1,066	27,592	1,117	*9.8	4.4	*28.3	7.0
Region											
Northeast	20,212	45,106	926	43,394	723	39,694	716	*3.9	2.2	*13.6	3.1
Midwest	24,497	44,646	814	44,113	860	36,933	563	1.2	2.2	*20.9	2.9
South	38,525	38,410	614	38,700	566	33,453	524	−0.7	1.7	*14.8	2.6
West	23,183	44,744	834	44,155	809	39,685	758	1.3	2.1	*12.7	3.0
Residence											
Inside metropolitan areas	85,737	44,984	449	44,222	471	39,074	406	*1.7	1.2	*15.1	1.7
Inside central cities	32,030	36,987	503	36,768	522	31,221	443	0.6	1.6	*18.5	2.3
Outside central cities	53,706	50,262	472	49,311	646	44,945	522	*1.9	1.3	*11.8	1.7
Outside metropolitan areas	20,681	32,837	795	34,130	962	29,769	604	*−3.8	2.9	*10.3	3.5
EARNINGS OF FULL-TIME, YEAR-ROUND WORKERS											
Male	58,731	37,339	225	37,701	231	35,765	226	*−1.0	0.7	*4.4	0.9
Female	41,567	27,355	176	27,208	192	25,579	184	0.5	0.8	*6.9	1.0
PER CAPITA INCOME											
All races[1]	276,540	22,199	230	21,893	217	18,319	166	*1.4	1.2	*21.2	1.7
White	226,401	23,415	271	23,127	255	19,497	194	1.2	1.4	*20.1	1.8
Non-Hispanic	194,161	25,278	313	24,919	299	20,941	214	1.4	1.5	*20.7	1.9
Black	35,919	15,197	444	14,881	396	11,534	322	2.1	3.4	*31.8	5.3
Asian and Pacific Islander	11,384	22,352	1,221	21,844	1,221	18,456	1,247	2.3	6.7	*21.1	10.5
Hispanic origin[2]	33,863	12,306	377	12,011	416	10,317	354	2.5	3.5	*19.3	5.5

*Statistically significant change at the 90-percent confidence level.

NA = Not available.

[1] Data for American Indians and Alaska Natives are not shown separately in this table.

[2] Hispanics may be of any race.

SOURCE: Carmen DeNavas-Watt, Robert W. Cleveland, and Mark I. Roemer, "Table A. Comparision of Summary Measures of Income by Selected Characteristics: 1993, 1999, and 2000," in *Money Income in the United States: 2000,* Current Population Reports P60-213, U.S. Census Bureau, Washington, DC, September 2001

FIGURE 3.4

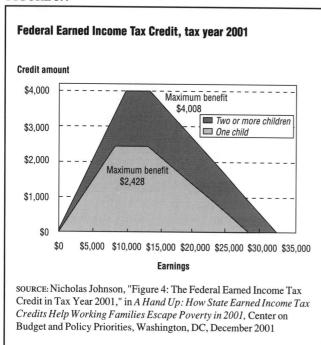

Federal Earned Income Tax Credit, tax year 2001

SOURCE: Nicholas Johnson, "Figure 4: The Federal Earned Income Tax Credit in Tax Year 2001," in *A Hand Up: How State Earned Income Tax Credits Help Working Families Escape Poverty in 2001,* Center on Budget and Policy Priorities, Washington, DC, December 2001

A 1995 report prepared by the National Research Council's Panel on Poverty and Family Assistance raised several important issues regarding poverty thresholds or measurement of need. The panel recommended that new thresholds be developed, using consumer expenditure data to represent a budget for basic needs: food, clothing, shelter (including utilities), and a small allowance for miscellaneous needs. This budget would be adjusted to reflect the needs of different family types and geographic differences in costs. Research and discussion continue on these issues.

How Should Income Be Defined?

The Panel on Poverty and Family Assistance also recommended that family resources be redefined to reflect the net amount available to buy goods and services in that budget for basic needs. Critics have pointed out that the definition of income used to set the poverty figure is not accurate because it does not include the value of all welfare services as income. If the value of these services were counted as income, they believe the proportion of Americans considered to be living in poverty would be lower.

In the 1990s the Census Bureau developed several experimental methods of estimating income for evaluating poverty levels, but the bureau has had considerable difficulty determining the value of many of these subsidies. For example, the bureau first tried to consider Medicare and Medicaid at full market value (this meant taking the total amount of money that the government spent on medical care for a particular group and then dividing it by the number of people in that group). The value often was greater than the actual earnings of the low-income family, which meant that, although the family's total earnings may not have been enough to cover food and housing, adding the market value of Medicare or Medicaid to its earnings put the family above the poverty threshold.

This did not make much sense, so the Census Bureau began trying a "fungible value" (giving equivalent value to units) for Medicare and Medicaid. When the bureau measures a household's income, if the earners cannot cover the cost of housing and food, Medicare and Medicaid are given no value. However, if the family can cover the cost of food and shelter, the Census Bureau figures the difference between the household income and the amount needed to meet basic housing and food costs. It then values the health services at this difference (up to the amount of the market value of the medical benefits). This is very complicated, but the Bureau of the Census believes it gives a fair value to these services. Similar problems have developed in trying to determine the value of housing subsidies, school lunches, and other benefits.

Still other observers point out that most income definitions do not include assets and liabilities. Perhaps the poor household has some assets, including a home or car, that could be converted into income. One experimental definition of income includes capital gains on earnings, although it seems to make little difference—about 90 percent of all capital gains are earned by those in the upper fifth of the earnings scale. Including assets generally means little, since the overwhelming majority of poor families have few financial assets. The Bureau of the Census reports that more than half the poor have no assets at all and about four-fifths have assets of less than $1,000, a relatively insignificant amount from which to earn income.

Another major issue is the question of income before and after income taxes. While the Tax Reform Act of 1986 (PL 99-514) removed most poor households from the federal income tax rolls, many poor households still pay state and local taxes. Naturally, some critics claim, the taxes paid to local and state governments are funds that are no longer available for feeding and housing the family and, therefore, should not be counted as income.

Table 3.8 lists the various experimental definitions for income that the Bureau of the Census has considered. Table 3.9 shows the effects of selected definitions on the poverty rate.

HUNGER IN AMERICA

When thinking of the consequences of poverty, people often visualize the poor being badly housed, or in the worst case, homeless, instead of people not having enough to eat. While it may be hard to imagine some Americans not having enough to eat, many Americans go to bed hungry or experience times when there is not enough food for the family.

During the 1980s a growing number of studies found that Americans, especially children, were suffering from hunger. Many observers did not believe these reports or thought they had been exaggerated. In 1984 a Task Force on Food Assistance appointed by President Ronald Reagan found that it could not "report definitive evidence on the extent of hunger" because there was no agreed-upon way to measure hunger.

To determine the extent of hunger in the United States, the Food Research and Action Center (FRAC) in Washington, D.C., an advocacy group for the poor, released the findings of the Community Childhood Hunger Identification Project (CCHIP). In this first FRAC survey, interviews were conducted of 2,335 households with incomes at or below 185 percent of poverty and with at least one child under 12 years of age. The results of this survey, released in 1991, indicated that 32 percent of U.S. households with incomes at or below 185 percent of the poverty level were hungry. At least one child out of every eight under 12 years of age suffered from hunger. Another 40 percent of low-income children were at risk for hunger.

Between 1992 and 1994 FRAC sponsored the second round of CCHIP surveys in nine states and the District of Columbia (5,282 low-income families with at least one child age 12 or under). For the purposes of its report, FRAC defined hunger as food insufficiency—skipping meals, eating less, running out of food—that occurs because of limited household resources. The results were reported in *Community Childhood Hunger Identification Project: A Survey of Childhood Hunger in the United States* (Washington, DC, 1995).

Based on the findings of the second CCHIP surveys, FRAC concluded that about 4 million children age 12 and under experienced hunger in some part of one or more months during the previous year. Another 9.6 million children were at risk of becoming hungry.

The CCHIP survey studied one child in each household (the child with the most recent birthday) and found that, in comparison with nonhungry children, hungry children were:

- More than three times as likely to suffer from unwanted weight loss.

- More than four times as likely to suffer from fatigue.

- Almost three times as likely to suffer from irritability.

- More than three times as likely to have frequent headaches.

- Almost one and a half times as likely to have frequent ear infections.

- Four times as likely to suffer from concentration problems.

- Almost twice as likely to have frequent colds.

Based on the findings from CCHIP, FRAC concluded that although federal food programs are targeted to households most in need, a common barrier to program participation is a lack of information, particularly about eligibility guidelines. FRAC believes that if federal, state, and local governments made a greater effort to ensure that possible recipients were aware of their eligibility for food programs, such as Women, Infants, and Children (WIC) and the School Breakfast Program, there would be a large drop in hunger in the United States.

In 1997 the Urban Institute conducted the National Survey of American Families (NSAF). Nearly half of low-income families (those with family incomes up to 200 percent of the federal poverty line) who were interviewed in 1997 reported that the food they purchased ran out before they got money to buy more or they worried they would run out of food. Four out of five of these families with food problems reported suffering actual food shortages, and one out of five worried about food shortages. More children than adults lived in families that worried about or had trouble affording food, so that 54 percent of low-income children experienced the problem. The NSAF was repeated in 1999, and families reported fewer problems affording food than in 1997. Four in 10 low-income families were either concerned about or had difficulty affording food, down 10 percent from 1997. However, approximately half of all low-income children still lived in families with difficulties affording food or concern about lack of food.

Since 1995 the Food and Nutrition Service of the U.S. Department of Agriculture (USDA) and the U.S. Census Bureau have conducted annual surveys of food security, food insecurity, and hunger. (Food-secure households are those that have access at all times to enough food for an active, healthy life. Food-insecure households are uncertain of having, or unable to acquire, enough food to meet basic needs at all times during the year.) The survey is based on an 18-item scale:

1. Worried food would run out before (I/we) got money to buy more

2. Food bought didn't last and (I/we) didn't have money to get more

3. Couldn't afford to eat balanced meals

4. Adult(s) cut size of meals or skipped meals

5. Respondent ate less than felt he/she should

6. Adult(s) cut size or skipped meals in 3 or more months

7. Respondent hungry but didn't eat because couldn't afford

TABLE 3.8

Median household income by definition, 1999 and 2000

[Income in 2000 dollars]

Definition of income	Median income		Percent change 1999–2000 [2]
	2000	1999	
Income before taxes:			
1. Money income excluding capital gains (official measure)	42,148	42,187	−0.1
2. Definition 1 less government cash transfers	38,912	38,536	1.0
3. Definition 2 plus capital gains	39,430	39,107	0.8
4. Definition 3 plus health insurance supplements to wage or salary income	41,196	41,128	0.2
Income after taxes:			
5. Definition 4 less social security payroll taxes	38,557	38,462	0.2
6. Definition 5 less federal income taxes (excluding the EIC)	35,596	35,552	0.1
7. Definition 6 plus the earned income credit (EIC)[1]	35,769	35,731	0.2
8. Definition 7 less state income taxes	34,642	34,647	–
9. Definition 8 plus nonmeans-tested government cash transfers	38,157	38,132	0.1
10. Definition 9 plus the value of medicare	39,876	39,923	−0.1
11. Definition 10 plus the value of regular-price school lunches	39,887	39,988	−0.3
12. Definition 11 plus means-tested government cash transfers	40,068	40,189	−0.3
13. Definition 12 plus the value of medicaid	40,435	40,530	−0.2
14. Definition 13 plus the value of other means-tested government noncash transfers	40,574	40,645	−0.2
15. Definition 14 plus net imputed return on equity in own home	42,812	42,538	0.6

– Represents zero or rounds to zero.

[1]Includes EIC for 13 states (Colorado, Illinois, Iowa, Kansas, Maine, Maryland, Massachusetts, New Jersey, New York, Oregon, Rhode Island, Vermont, and Wisconsin) and the District of Columbia that use federal eligibility rules to compute the state credit as a percentage of the federal EIC.
[2]There were no statistically significant changes between 1999 and 2000 for any of the income definitions.

SOURCE: Carmen DeNavas-Watt, Robert W. Cleveland, and Mark I. Roemer, "Table F. Median Household Income by Definition: 1999 and 2000," in *Money Income in the United States: 2000,* Current Population Reports P60-213, U.S. Census Bureau, Washington, DC, 2001

TABLE 3.9

Cumulative effect of taxes and transfers on poverty estimates, 1999–2000

(Numbers in thousands)

Selected income definitions	2000		1999		2000-1999 Difference	
	Number below poverty	Poverty Rate	Number below poverty	Poverty Rate	Number below poverty	Poverty Rate
Definition 1 (current measure)	31,139	11.3	32,258	11.8	*-1,119	*-0.5
Definition 2 (definition 1 less government cash transfers)	51,335	18.6	52,542	19.2	*-1,207	*-0.6
Definition 4 (definition 2 plus capital gains and employee health benefits)	49,115	17.8	50,628	18.5	*-1,513	*-0.7
Definition 6 (definition 4 less social security payroll and federal income taxes[1])	52,602	19.1	53,556	19.6	-954	*-0.5
Definition 7 (definition 6 plus the earned income credit (EIC))	48,331	17.5	49,523	18.1	*-1,192	*-0.6
Definition 8 (definition 7 less state income taxes)	48,755	17.7	49,954	18.3	*-1,199	*-0.6
Definition 9 (definition 8 plus nonmeans-tested government cash transfers)	30,736	11.1	31,961	11.7	*-1,225	*-0.6
Definition 11 (definition 9 plus the value of Medicare and regular-price school lunch)	29,753	10.8	30,800	11.3	*-1,047	*-0.5
Definition 14 (definition 12 plus the value of Medicaid and other means-tested government noncash transfers)	23,911	8.7	24,161	8.8	-250	-0.1

*Statistically significant at the 90 percent confidence level.
[1]This definition refers to social security and federal income tax liabilities before taking into account refundable credits i.e. EIC.

SOURCE: "The Cumulative Effect of Taxes and Transfers on Poverty Estimates: 1999–2000," in *Poverty 2000,* U.S. Census Bureau, Washington, DC, September 2001 [Online] http://www.census.gov/hhes/poverty/poverty00/tablee.html [accessed August 6, 2002]

8. Respondent lost weight

9. Adult(s) did not eat for whole day

10. Adult(s) did not eat for whole day in 3 or more months

11. Relied on few kinds of low-cost food to feed child(ren)

12. Couldn't feed child(ren) balanced meals

13. Child(ren) were not eating enough

14. Cut size of child(ren)'s meals

15. Child(ren) were hungry

16. Child(ren) skipped meals

17. Child(ren) skipped meals in 3 or more months

18. Child(ren) did not eat for whole day

Figure 3.5 shows that both the extent of food insecurity and hunger declined somewhat after 1995. The number of food-insecure households fell 12 percent and the prevalence of hunger fell by 24 percent from 1995 through 1999. In 1999, 8.7 percent of households reported food insecurity at some time during the year, and 2.8 percent reported being hungry.

Low-income households were more likely to experience food insecurity and hunger during the year. More than 12 percent of households below the poverty line reported being hungry at some time during 1999, more than four times the rate in the general population. (See Figure 3.6 and Table 3.10.)

Families headed by married couples are much less likely to experience food insecurity (9.6 percent) than families headed by single females (29.7 percent). Food insecurity is also more prevalent among non-Hispanic African American families (21.2 percent) and Hispanic families (20.8 percent) than among non-Hispanic whites (7 percent). (See Table 3.10).

GROWING DEMAND FOR EMERGENCY FOOD ASSISTANCE

Second Harvest National Research Study

America's Second Harvest is the nation's largest charitable hunger-relief organization, serving 23.3 million persons per year. In 2001 Mathematica Policy Research conducted a study of the Second Harvest network by means of interviews with 32,000 clients and 24,000 questionnaires from local agencies. The findings are reported in *Hunger in America, 2001 National Report* (Myoung Kim, Jim Ohls, and Rhoda Cohen, Princeton, NJ, 2001). The study found the following characteristics of recipients of emergency food assistance:

- More than 23.3 million people sought emergency food assistance in 2001: 21.3 million at food pantries, 1.3 million at kitchens, and 0.7 million at shelters. Of the adult clients who visited emergency food programs in 2001, approximately 61.6 percent were female, 38.3 percent male.

- More than a third (38.9 percent) of all emergency client households had at least one member working.

- Sixty-four percent of the households have incomes at or below the poverty level.

- Assistance from government welfare programs (TANF, general assistance, and Supplemental Security Income) was the main source of income for 15.9 percent of all clients. Other government assistance (social security, workers' compensation, and unemployment compensation) was the main source of income for 30.5 percent of clients.(See Figure 3.7.)

- Some 44.9 percent of recipients at all program sites were white; 35.4 percent, African American; 16.7 percent, Hispanic; and 4.8 percent, Native American/Alaskan Native. Figure 3.8 shows the percentage of adults of various racial backgrounds who picked up food at a pantry, were clients at a kitchen, or were clients at a shelter.

- Almost two-thirds (62.8 percent) of clients are high school graduates.

- Almost two-thirds (63.9 percent) of clients have applied for and 29.8 percent currently receive food stamps. See Figure 3.9 for an analysis of the use of food stamps by type of food program.

- Ten percent of all clients are homeless. Thirty-six percent reported having to choose between paying for food and paying their rent or mortgage. Figure 3.10 shows the housing situation for pantry, kitchen, and shelter clients.

- Twenty-nine percent reported that at least one household member was in poor health.

Over half of the agencies surveyed reported an increase in the number of clients serviced at program sites since 1998.

U.S. Conference of Mayors Status Report

Since 1982 the U.S. Conference of Mayors has conducted an annual survey of hunger and homelessness in U.S. cities. In 2001 a survey of 27 cities indicated a growing demand for emergency food assistance. The *Status Report on Hunger and Homelessness in America's Cities: 2001* (United States Conference of Mayors, Washington, DC, 2001) reported that demand for emergency food assistance had increased by an average of 23 percent from the previous year in 93 percent of the cities

FIGURE 3.5

FIGURE 3.6

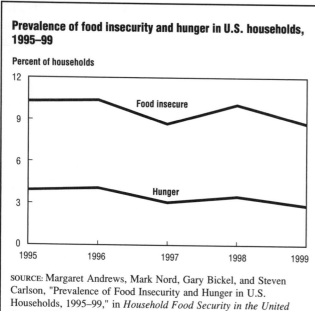

Prevalence of food insecurity and hunger in U.S. households, 1995–99

SOURCE: Margaret Andrews, Mark Nord, Gary Bickel, and Steven Carlson, "Prevalence of Food Insecurity and Hunger in U.S. Households, 1995–99," in *Household Food Security in the United States, 1999,* U.S. Department of Agriculture, Economic Research Service, Food and Rural Economics Division, Washington, DC, September 2000.

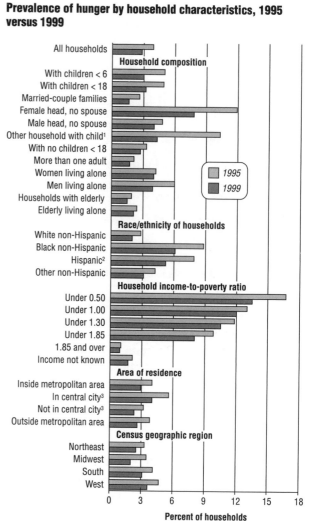

Prevalence of hunger by household characteristics, 1995 versus 1999

[1]Households with children in complex living arrangements, e.g., children of other relatives or unrelated roommate or border.
[2]Hispanics may be of any race.
[3]Subtotals do not add to metropolitan totals because central-city residence is not identified for about 17 percent of households in metropolitan statistical areas.

SOURCE: Margaret Andrews, Mark Nord, Gary Bickel, and Steven Carlson, "Prevalence of Hunger, 1995 versus 1999," in *Household Food Security in the United States, 1999,* U.S. Department of Agriculture, Economic Research Service, Food and Rural Economics Division, Washington, DC, September 2000.

surveyed. Ninety-two percent of cities surveyed reported increased demand for emergency food among families with children. Thirty-seven percent of persons requesting emergency food assistance were employed. The causes of hunger, according to officials in the surveyed cities, included low-paying jobs, unemployment, food stamp cuts, high housing costs, poverty or lack of income, weakening of the economy, utility costs, and welfare reform.

TABLE 3.10

Prevalence of food security, food insecurity, and hunger by selected characteristics of households, 1999

(Based on unadjusted data)

| Category | Total* | Food secure | | Food insecure: | | | | | |
| | | | | All | | Without hunger | | With hunger | |
	1,000	1,000	Percent	1,000	Percent	1,000	Percent	1,000	Percent
All households	104,684	94,154	89.9	10,529	10.1	7,420	7.1	3,109	3.0
All persons in households	270,318	239,304	88.5	31,015	11.5	23,237	8.6	7,779	2.9
Adults in households	198,900	179,960	90.5	18,941	9.5	13,869	7.0	5,072	2.5
Children in households	71,418	59,344	83.1	12,074	16.9	9,368	13.1	2,707	3.8
Household composition:									
With children < 6	17,231	14,439	83.8	2,792	16.2	2,265	13.1	527	3.1
With children < 18	37,884	32,290	85.2	5,594	14.8	4,340	11.5	1,254	3.3
Married couple families	26,303	23,771	90.4	2,532	9.6	2,105	8.0	428	1.6
Female head, no spouse	8,744	6,146	70.3	2,598	29.7	1,890	21.6	709	8.1
Male head, no spouse	2,187	1,817	83.1	370	16.9	280	12.8	89	4.1
Other household with child[1]	650	556	85.6	94	14.4	66	10.1	28	4.3
With no children < 18	66,800	61,865	92.6	4,935	7.4	3,080	4.6	1,855	2.8
More than one adult	39,568	37,380	94.5	2,188	5.5	1,470	3.7	718	1.8
Women living alone	16,046	14,473	90.2	1,573	9.8	908	5.7	665	4.1
Men living alone	11,187	10,013	89.5	1,174	10.5	701	6.3	473	4.2
Households with elderly	24,704	23,265	94.2	1,439	5.8	1,055	4.3	385	1.6
Elderly living alone	10,049	9,413	93.7	636	6.3	423	4.2	214	2.1
Race/ethnicity of households:									
White non-Hispanic	78,998	73,451	93.0	5,546	7.0	3,873	4.9	1,673	2.1
Black non-Hispanic	12,616	9,936	78.8	2,680	21.2	1,866	14.8	814	6.4
Hispanic[2]	9,192	7,285	79.2	1,907	20.8	1,406	15.3	502	5.5
Other non-Hispanic	3,878	3,482	89.8	396	10.2	275	7.1	121	3.1
Household income-to-poverty ratio:									
Under 0.50	4,563	2,774	60.8	1,789	39.2	1,164	25.5	625	13.7
Under 1.00	11,319	7,169	63.3	4,150	36.7	2,767	24.5	1,383	12.2
Under 1.30	17,432	11,799	67.7	5,633	32.3	3,767	21.6	1,866	10.7
Under 1.85	27,261	20,145	73.9	7,116	26.1	4,907	18.0	2,210	8.1
1.85 and over	63,909	61,299	95.9	2,610	4.1	1,969	3.1	641	1.0
Income not known	13,513	12,710	94.1	803	5.9	545	4.0	258	1.9
Area of residence:									
Inside metropolitan area	84,304	75,844	90.0	8,460	10.0	5903	7.0	2558	3.0
In central city[3]	26,718	23,027	86.2	3,691	13.8	2,578	9.6	1113	4.2
Not in central city[3]	43,103	39,793	92.3	3,310	7.7	2,290	5.3	1,020	2.4
Outside metropolitan area	20,379	18,311	89.9	2,069	10.1	1,517	7.4	552	2.7
Census geographic region:									
Northeast	19,960	18,301	91.7	1,659	8.3	1,147	5.7	512	2.6
Midwest	24,592	22,554	91.7	2,038	8.3	1,514	6.2	524	2.1
South	37,598	33,431	88.9	4,166	11.1	2,945	7.8	1,221	3.3
West	22,533	19,868	88.2	2,665	11.8	1,813	8.0	852	3.8

[1]Households with children in complex living arrangements, e.g., children of other relatives or unrelated roommate or border.
[2]Hispanics may be of any race.
[3]Subtotals do not add to metropolitan totals because central-city residence is not identified for about 17 percent of households in metropolitan statistical areas.

SOURCE: Margaret Andrews, Mark Nord, Gary Bickel, and Steven Carlson, "Table 2—1999: Prevalence of Food Security, Food Insecurity, and Hunger by Selected Characteristics of Households," in *Household Food Security in the United States, 1999,* U.S. Department of Agriculture, Economic Research Service Food and Rural Economics Division, Washington, DC, September 2000.

FIGURE 3.7

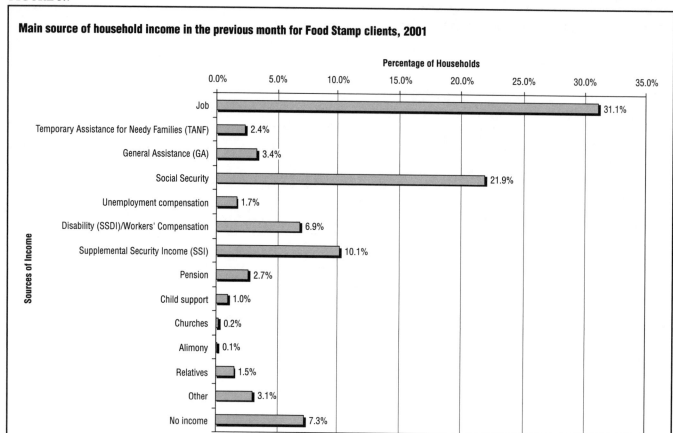

Main source of household income in the previous month for Food Stamp clients, 2001

SOURCE: Myoung Kim, Jim Ohls and Rhoda Cohen, "Chart 5.8.3.1. Main Source of Household Income for Previous Month," in *Hunger in America, 2001, National Report Prepared for America's Second Harvest,* Mathematica Policy Research, Inc., Princeton, NJ, 2001

FIGURE 3.8

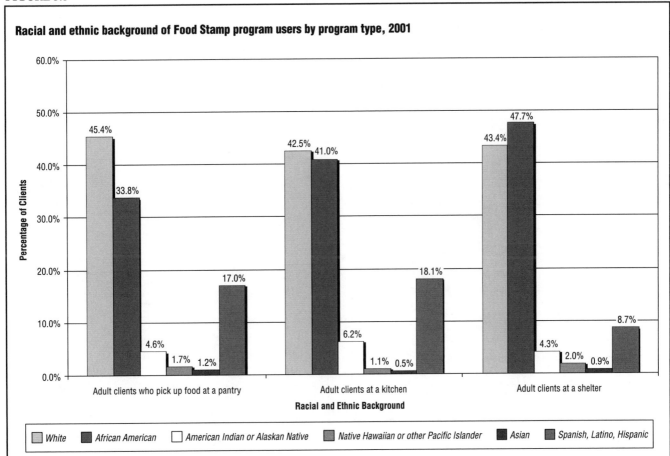

Racial and ethnic background of Food Stamp program users by program type, 2001

SOURCE: Myoung Kim, Jim Ohls and Rhoda Cohen, "Chart 5.6.1. Racial and Ethnic Background, By Program Type," in *Hunger in America, 2001, National Report Prepared for America's Second Harvest,* Mathematica Policy Research, Inc., Princeton, NJ, 2001

FIGURE 3.9

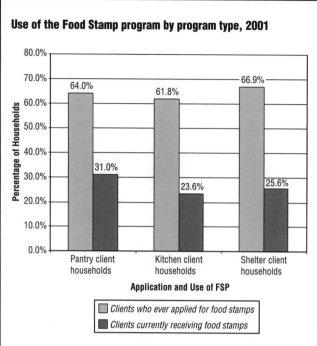

Use of the Food Stamp program by program type, 2001

SOURCE: Myoung Kim, Jim Ohls and Rhoda Cohen, "Chart 7.1.1. Use of Food Stamp Program, By Program Type," in *Hunger in America, 2001, National Report Prepared for America's Second Harvest,* Mathematica Policy Research, Inc., Princeton, NJ, 2001

FIGURE 3.10

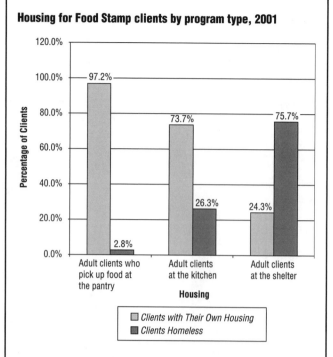

Housing for Food Stamp clients by program type, 2001

SOURCE: Myoung Kim, Jim Ohls and Rhoda Cohen, "Chart 5.9.1. Housing, by Program Type," in *Hunger in America, 2001, National Report Prepared for America's Second Harvest,* Mathematica Policy Research, Inc., Princeton, NJ, 2001

CHAPTER 4

A CHANGING NATION—WEALTH AND INCOME DISTRIBUTION

The U.S. Census Bureau has released a number of studies showing a change in the distribution of wealth and earnings in the United States. This change has resulted in an increase in the gap between the rich and the poor. Unlike many short-term economic changes that are often the product of normal economic cycles of growth and recession, these changes seem to indicate fundamental changes in American society.

GROWING INCOME INEQUALITY

In the 1980s, 1990s, and 2000, the Census Bureau tracked a growing inequality in income in the United States. For comparison purposes, the bureau divides the population into five income groups (quintiles). In 2000 the income differences were close to record highs, with only the top fifth having increased its percentage of the nation's income since the 1980s. The average income of the top fifth of households, after adjusting for inflation, was 26.6 percent higher than in 1990. In contrast, the average income of the poorest fifth of households was only 10.3 percent higher than in 1990. Census data show that in 2000 the quintile of households with the highest incomes received 50 percent of the national income, about the same as that received by the other 80 percent of the population combined. (See Table 4.1.)

Why Is the "Income Gap" Growing?

Many reasons exist to explain the growing inequality, although observers disagree about which are more important. One reason is that the proportion of the elderly population, who are likely to earn less, is growing. In 2000, 20.5 percent of all households were headed by a householder 65 years of age or older. (A "household" may consist of a single individual or a group of related or unrelated people living together, while a "family" is made up of related individuals.) In addition, more people are living in nonfamily situations (either alone or with nonrel-

atives). In 2000, 32 percent lived in nonfamily households, which tend to earn about half that of family households. (See Table 4.2 for the characteristics of households by income in 2000.)

Also contributing to growing income inequality is the increase in the number of households headed by females with no husband as well as the increase in labor force participation of women. In 2000 the proportion of female-headed households with no husband present was 17.3 percent of all family households, and female householders (either in family or nonfamily living arrangements or living alone) constituted 29.5 percent of all households in the nation. Female-headed households typically earn significantly less than other types of households. (On average, women earn 70 percent of what men earn.)

Other factors that contribute to the growing income gap include the decline in the influence of unions and the changing occupational structure, in general, from better-paying manufacturing positions to lower-paying service jobs. The average wage paid to less-educated workers (after adjusting for inflation) has actually dropped since the 1980s. In 2000 the annual income of male workers with one to three years of high school who had not graduated was 21.5 percent lower than in 1980. High-school graduates experienced an 18 percent wage decline. In addition, the proportion of low-wage workers who receive employer-based health insurance and pension benefits dropped significantly between 1979 and 2000.

MEDIAN HOUSEHOLD INCOMES

Table 4.3 shows the distribution of median income for households from 1967 to 2000. ("Median" means that half the measured values are above the specified value and half are below.) In 2000 dollars, adjusted for inflation, the median income of American households declined 4.4 percent from 1990 to 1993, but bounced back slightly by

TABLE 4.1

Selected measures of household income dispersion, 1980, 1990, and 2000

(Households as of March of the following year. Income in current and 2000 CPI-U-RS adjusted dollars 28/)

Measures of Income Dispersion	2000 29/	1990	1980
Household Income at Selected Percentiles			
In Current Dollars:			
20th percentile upper limit	17,955	12,500	7,556
50th (median)	42,000	29,943	17,710
80th percentile upper limit	81,960	55,205	31,700
95th percentile lower limit	145,526	94,748	51,500
In 2000 Dollars:			
20th percentile upper limit	17,955	16,050	15,035
50th (median)	42,000	38,446	35,238
80th percentile upper limit	81,960	70,882	63,075
95th percentile lower limit	145,526	121,654	102,472
Household Income Ratios of Selected Percentiles			
95th/20th	8.11	7.58	6.82
95th/50th	3.46	3.16	2.91
80th/50th	1.95	1.84	1.79
80th/20th	4.56	4.42	4.20
20th/50th	0.43	0.42	0.43
Mean Household Income of Quintiles			
In Current Dollars:			
Lowest quintile	10,190	7,195	4,483
Second quintile	25,334	18,030	10,819
Third quintile	42,361	29,781	17,807
Fourth quintile	65,729	44,901	26,219
Highest quintile	141,620	87,137	46,053
In 2000 Dollars:			
Lowest quintile	10,190	9,238	8,920
Second quintile	25,334	23,150	21,527
Third quintile	42,361	38,238	35,431
Fourth quintile	65,729	57,652	52,169
Highest quintile	141,620	111,881	91,634
Shares of Household Income of Quintiles			
Lowest quintile	3.6	3.9	4.3
Second quintile	8.9	9.6	10.3
Third quintile	14.9	15.9	16.9
Fourth quintile	23.0	24.0	24.9
Highest quintile	49.6	46.6	43.7
Gini coefficient of income inequality	0.460	0.428	0.403

SOURCE: Adapted from "Table IE-1. Selected Measures of Household Income Dispersion: 1967–2000," in *Historical Income Tables—Income Equality,* U.S. Census Bureau, Washington, DC, April 16, 2002 [Online] http://www.census.gov/hhes/income/histinc/ie1.html [accessed May 6, 2002]

1996. By 2000 median income rose to $42,148, 9.6 percent above the 1990 level. In 1967, 22.9 percent of households earned less than $15,000 per year, and 21.8 percent earned $50,000 or more. By 2000, 16 percent earned less than $15,000 while 42.7 percent earned $50,000 or more.

Types of Households

In 2000 family households made up nearly 68 percent of all households in the United States. Their median income was $51,751. The type of household, however, made a big difference in income level. The median income of families headed by married couples was $59,343. But male householders with no wife present made only $42,143, and female householders with no husband present earned only $28,126. Nonfamily households showed consistently lower median incomes. Females living alone earned only $18,163, the lowest median income. (See Table 4.2.)

Race and Hispanic Origin

The level of income also varied widely by race and ethnicity. In 2000 the median income for non-Hispanic white households was $45,910; for African Americans, $30,436; and for Hispanics, $33,455. African American and Hispanic households tend to have lower earnings than non-Hispanic white households. Twenty-six percent of African American households earned less than $15,000 per year, compared to 18.8 percent of Hispanic households and 14 percent of non-Hispanic white households. Minorities were also less likely to have high incomes. While 15.2 percent of non-Hispanic white households earned $100,000 or more, only 6.1 percent of African American households and 5.8 percent of Hispanic households earned that much. (See Table 4.2.)

Age

The age of the householder was also a factor in the level of income. In 2000 householders age 65 and older, who are usually past their peak earning years, had a median income of only $23,047, while householders under age 65 had a median income of $48,770. Those from 45 to 54, the highest-earning age group, had a median income of $58,217. (See Table 4.2.)

Work Experience

Although working is an important factor in avoiding poverty, working in itself may not be enough to save a household from poverty. Of the 76 million households with a working householder in 2000, 7.4 percent earned less than $15,000, which is below the poverty threshold for a family of four ($17,050). While the majority of working householders (86.8 percent) worked full-time, a significant proportion (13.2 percent) held part-time jobs. As expected, the wages of part-time working householders were lower; 20.3 percent earned less than $15,000 in 2000. (See Table 4.2.)

Education

Not surprisingly, the more education a person has, the more likely he or she is to earn a higher income. For example, according to Census Bureau data for 2000, for men with doctoral degrees, the median personal income was $70,961, and for women with doctoral degrees, the median personal income was $50,430. For those with less than a ninth-grade education, men earned a median income of $17,658, and women earned a median income of $11,370. High-school graduates (including those with general equivalency diplomas) fared better, with men earning $30,665 and women earning $18,393.

TABLE 4.2

Household income by selected characteristics, 2000

[Numbers in thousands. Based on a November 2001 weighting correction. Households as of March of the following year.]

	Total	Less than $5,000	$5,000 to $9,999	$10,000 to $14,999	$15,000 to $24,999	$25,000 to $34,999	$35,000 to $49,999	$50,000 to $74,999	$75,000 to $99,999	$100,000 and over	Median income Value (dollars)	Median income Standard Error (dollars)	Mean income Value (dollars)	Mean income Standard Error (dollars)
ALL RACES														
ALL HOUSEHOLDS	106,418	3,065	6,475	7,412	14,269	13,315	16,471	20,099	11,051	14,262	42,151	197	57,047	319
TYPE OF RESIDENCE														
Inside metropolitan areas	85,737	2,414	4,663	5,543	10,821	10,185	13,147	16,488	9,430	13,046	44,986	272	60,292	371
Inside central cities	32,018	1,334	2,461	2,483	4,684	4,178	4,935	5,421	2,871	3,650	36,984	306	51,590	522
1 million or more	20,325	846	1,552	1,486	2,869	2,498	3,147	3,478	1,919	2,530	38,428	537	54,010	710
Under 1 million	11,693	488	909	997	1,815	1,679	1,788	1,943	952	1,121	34,655	622	47,385	716
Outside central cities	53,719	1,080	2,202	3,060	6,137	6,008	8,211	11,067	6,559	9,396	50,264	287	65,479	501
1 million or more	37,005	704	1,289	1,952	3,850	3,967	5,393	7,524	4,848	7,478	53,679	530	70,675	663
Under 1 million	16,714	376	913	1,108	2,287	2,040	2,818	3,542	1,711	1,919	42,471	536	53,975	641
Outside metropolitan areas	20,681	650	1,811	1,869	3,448	3,130	3,324	3,611	1,622	1,216	32,844	484	43,593	679
REGION														
Northeast	20,212	630	1,301	1,427	2,460	2,314	2,844	3,808	2,244	3,184	45,118	561	60,517	679
Midwest	24,496	648	1,329	1,579	3,222	3,025	3,755	5,012	2,787	3,138	44,647	495	56,989	623
South	38,526	1,204	2,735	2,962	5,541	5,100	6,213	6,910	3,426	4,434	38,402	373	53,007	533
West	23,185	583	1,109	1,444	3,045	2,875	3,659	4,369	2,594	3,506	44,759	508	60,796	796
TYPE OF HOUSEHOLD														
Family households	72,380	1,343	1,915	3,097	8,108	8,538	11,702	15,845	9,332	12,499	51,751	237	66,502	405
Married-couple families	55,603	581	745	1,611	4,913	5,920	8,749	13,227	8,272	11,586	59,343	377	74,290	495
Male householder, no wife present	4,252	90	177	217	596	569	838	955	401	410	42,143	827	53,960	1,361
Female householder, no husband present	12,525	671	994	1,269	2,600	2,049	2,116	1,663	660	503	28,126	395	36,188	472
Nonfamily households	34,039	1,722	4,559	4,315	6,160	4,777	4,769	4,254	1,719	1,763	25,439	231	36,941	463
Male householder	15,218	668	1,405	1,404	2,531	2,333	2,402	2,414	1,032	1,029	31,269	320	44,108	871
Living alone	11,536	591	1,305	1,294	2,159	1,863	1,761	1,508	583	473	26,723	329	37,343	848
Female householder	18,821	1,054	3,154	2,911	3,629	2,444	2,367	1,840	687	734	20,929	258	31,147	442
Living alone	16,283	1,010	3,097	2,816	3,370	2,133	1,892	1,201	387	377	18,163	298	26,061	324
AGE OF HOUSEHOLDER														
Under 65 years	84,591	2,479	3,561	4,030	9,396	9,990	13,768	18,035	10,227	13,106	48,770	289	62,869	380
15 to 24 years	6,393	442	481	583	1,319	1,126	1,044	878	272	248	27,711	505	36,784	946
25 to 34 years	18,554	556	667	875	2,305	2,576	3,437	4,285	1,913	1,940	44,477	620	54,905	645
35 to 44 years	23,904	475	747	941	2,307	2,614	3,947	5,614	3,297	3,962	53,243	551	67,038	740
45 to 54 years	21,797	511	745	826	1,839	2,079	3,172	4,651	3,245	4,730	58,217	777	73,145	827
55 to 64 years	13,944	495	921	804	1,626	1,595	2,168	2,605	1,501	2,227	44,993	609	62,216	1,008
65 years and over	21,827	586	2,914	3,382	4,873	3,325	2,703	2,064	824	1,156	23,047	257	34,484	431
65 to 74 years	11,211	223	1,213	1,320	2,207	1,863	1,673	1,361	581	770	28,147	427	40,696	716
75 years and over	10,616	363	1,701	2,061	2,666	1,461	1,030	703	244	386	18,873	279	27,924	443
Mean age of householder	48.64	47.10	58.02	57.31	52.20	48.69	46.33	44.84	45.44	47.06	(X)	(X)	(X)	(X)
SIZE OF HOUSEHOLD														
One person	27,820	1,600	4,402	4,110	5,528	3,996	3,653	2,709	970	850	21,468	208	30,739	403
Two people	35,388	758	1,080	1,878	4,920	5,067	5,953	7,075	3,769	4,888	44,530	396	59,207	545
Three people	17,259	343	517	670	1,662	1,763	2,886	4,036	2,367	3,015	54,196	617	67,186	782
Four people	15,430	214	269	421	1,209	1,405	2,272	3,801	2,487	3,353	61,847	473	76,799	1,036
Five people	6,686	71	136	218	541	698	1,048	1,549	1,007	1,417	60,295	954	76,017	1,563
Six people	2,396	40	42	72	263	239	421	579	298	442	54,841	1,456	71,443	2,318
Seven people or more	1,439	37	29	42	146	147	239	350	153	296	54,663	1,763	67,023	2,289

TABLE 4.2

Household income by selected characteristics, 2000 [CONTINUED]

[Numbers in thousands. Based on a November 2001 weighting correction. Households as of March of the following year.]

	Total	Less than $5,000	$5,000 to $9,999	$10,000 to $14,999	$15,000 to $24,999	$25,000 to $34,999	$35,000 to $49,999	$50,000 to $74,999	$75,000 to $99,999	$100,000 and over	Median income Value (dollars)	Median income Standard Error (dollars)	Mean income Value (dollars)	Mean income Standard Error (dollars)
Mean size of household	2.60	1.94	1.61	1.84	2.17	2.37	2.65	2.95	3.11	3.25	(X)	(X)	(X)	(X)
NUMBER OF EARNERS														
No earners	21,161	2,003	4,547	3,933	4,806	2,586	1,633	993	329	331	15,171	188	21,600	232
One earner	37,467	940	1,677	2,954	7,076	6,811	7,077	5,899	2,211	2,821	33,399	320	46,585	485
Two earners or more	47,791	121	251	525	2,386	3,918	7,761	13,208	8,511	11,110	66,069	332	80,945	541
Two earners	37,600	117	228	479	2,171	3,531	6,622	10,512	6,214	7,727	62,112	279	77,530	624
Three earners	7,570	4	23	46	203	338	952	2,113	1,630	2,261	76,263	779	90,043	1,255
Four earners or more	2,620	—	—	—	13	49	188	583	667	1,122	91,218	1,230	103,657	1,841
Mean number of earners	1.41	0.39	0.34	0.55	0.86	1.15	1.48	1.82	2.07	2.15	(X)	(X)	(X)	(X)
WORK EXPERIENCE OF HOUSEHOLDER														
Total	106,418	3,065	6,475	7,412	14,269	13,315	16,471	20,099	11,051	14,262	42,151	197	57,047	319
Worked	76,040	927	1,666	3,012	8,106	9,240	12,911	17,278	10,014	12,886	52,147	205	67,039	410
Worked at full-time jobs	66,002	480	993	2,093	6,625	7,936	11,420	15,648	9,139	11,667	54,398	319	69,110	446
50 weeks or more	56,479	226	389	1,361	5,072	6,624	9,801	13,989	8,358	10,659	57,149	278	72,308	498
27 to 49 weeks	6,234	55	242	426	917	872	1,138	1,166	643	775	42,234	729	54,981	966
26 weeks or less	3,289	200	362	306	637	439	481	494	137	233	27,465	892	40,978	1,555
Worked at part-time jobs	10,038	446	672	918	1,481	1,305	1,491	1,629	876	1,219	36,898	727	53,420	1,005
50 weeks or more	5,338	81	269	476	772	664	845	969	511	750	42,088	955	60,648	1,609
27 to 49 weeks	2,104	71	140	233	328	283	306	310	192	241	34,877	1,286	49,381	1,622
26 weeks or less	2,596	294	263	209	381	358	340	350	173	228	28,435	828	41,832	1,486
Did not work	30,379	2,138	4,809	4,400	6,162	4,075	3,559	2,822	1,037	1,376	20,821	217	32,036	364
EDUCATIONAL ATTAINMENT														
Total	100,026	2,623	5,994	6,829	12,950	12,189	15,427	19,221	10,780	14,014	43,556	259	58,342	333
Less than 9th grade	6,753	357	1,417	1,124	1,434	868	710	534	196	112	17,557	413	25,940	545
9th to 12th grade (no diploma)	9,111	473	1,272	1,278	1,930	1,294	1,221	1,055	345	242	22,753	403	32,011	751
High school graduate (includes equivalency)	30,785	876	1,934	2,438	4,902	4,461	5,360	6,050	2,737	2,028	36,722	289	45,372	363
Some college, no degree	18,165	368	730	1,057	2,280	2,554	3,171	3,916	2,067	2,022	44,449	587	55,984	688
Associate degree	8,214	144	239	347	846	1,042	1,454	1,897	1,148	1,098	50,356	741	60,287	958
Bachelor's degree or more	26,997	405	402	585	1,558	1,970	3,512	5,767	4,286	8,512	71,437	465	91,118	908
Bachelor's degree	17,521	283	285	438	1,132	1,475	2,510	3,952	2,698	4,748	65,922	602	84,032	1,042
Master's degree	6,435	81	86	98	306	379	738	1,338	1,137	2,273	77,935	1,131	96,722	2,072
Professional degree	1,641	19	19	32	69	76	135	207	235	850	100,000	(X)	125,387	4,376
Doctorate degree	1,400	21	13	17	52	41	128	270	217	642	93,361	3,756	113,866	3,908
TENURE														
Owner occupied	72,048	1,277	2,776	3,849	7,894	8,105	11,110	15,203	9,200	12,635	51,215	241	66,462	432
Renter occupied	32,748	1,659	3,516	3,359	5,999	4,946	5,192	4,714	1,793	1,569	27,959	304	37,540	352
Occupier paid no cash rent	1,622	129	183	204	376	264	169	182	58	58	22,798	798	32,692	1,565
WHITE														
ALL HOUSEHOLDS	88,543	2,066	4,885	5,867	11,522	11,120	13,595	17,193	9,712	12,583	44,232	275	59,280	363
TYPE OF RESIDENCE														
Inside metropolitan areas	69,971	1,552	3,400	4,250	8,514	8,259	10,560	13,829	8,175	11,433	47,356	297	63,149	430
Inside central cities	23,004	704	1,546	1,635	3,227	3,002	3,449	4,193	2,251	2,998	40,433	459	55,919	676
1 million or more	13,757	409	919	912	1,821	1,670	2,058	2,517	1,447	2,003	42,472	684	59,572	970
Under 1 million	9,247	295	626	723	1,406	1,332	1,391	1,676	803	994	37,155	695	50,484	856

TABLE 4.2

Household income by selected characteristics, 2000 [CONTINUED]

[Numbers in thousands. Based on a November 2001 weighting correction. Households as of March of the following year.]

	Total	Less than $5,000	$5,000 to $9,999	$10,000 to $14,999	$15,000 to $24,999	$25,000 to $34,999	$35,000 to $49,999	$50,000 to $74,999	$75,000 to $99,999	$100,000 and over	Median income Value (dollars)	Median income Standard Error (dollars)	Mean income Value (dollars)	Mean income Standard Error (dollars)
Outside central cities	46,967	848	1,854	2,615	5,287	5,257	7,111	9,636	5,925	8,435	51,001	317	66,691	547
1 million or more	31,911	541	1,079	1,669	3,267	3,381	4,591	6,397	4,330	6,655	55,106	496	72,267	738
Under 1 million	15,056	307	775	946	2,019	1,877	2,520	3,239	1,594	1,780	43,589	639	54,872	664
Outside metropolitan areas	18,571	514	1,485	1,617	3,008	2,861	3,035	3,364	1,537	1,151	34,160	527	44,703	701
REGION														
Northeast	17,172	419	1,032	1,126	2,075	1,908	2,419	3,366	1,967	2,859	47,205	569	62,895	766
Midwest	21,472	459	1,018	1,314	2,745	2,662	3,268	4,522	2,580	2,905	46,617	493	58,839	673
South	30,221	744	1,909	2,192	4,116	4,032	4,753	5,656	2,938	3,882	40,879	371	56,241	627
West	19,678	444	925	1,235	2,586	2,518	3,154	3,649	2,228	2,938	44,592	544	61,275	904
TYPE OF HOUSEHOLD														
Family households	60,214	851	1,283	2,229	6,315	7,001	9,704	13,611	8,233	10,987	54,293	343	69,193	457
Married-couple families	48,647	480	606	1,356	4,242	5,167	7,567	11,562	7,415	10,252	60,080	327	75,080	535
Male householder, no wife present	3,274	51	122	151	456	436	631	777	299	350	44,020	1,352	56,870	1,702
Female householder, no husband present	8,293	320	555	721	1,616	1,398	1,507	1,272	519	385	31,230	490	39,530	628
Nonfamily households	28,329	1,215	3,602	3,638	5,207	4,119	3,890	3,582	1,479	1,597	25,985	247	38,209	539
Male householder	12,581	477	1,087	1,118	2,077	2,012	1,985	2,023	868	934	31,873	336	45,993	1,033
Living alone	9,488	436	1,014	1,040	1,762	1,595	1,449	1,264	485	443	27,326	410	38,955	1,010
Female householder	15,748	738	2,515	2,520	3,130	2,107	1,906	1,558	611	663	21,287	282	31,990	497
Living alone	13,681	705	2,481	2,445	2,928	1,855	1,544	1,030	342	352	18,695	299	26,776	366
AGE OF HOUSEHOLDER														
Under 65 years	69,152	1,611	2,490	2,905	7,091	8,080	11,139	15,330	8,980	11,526	51,422	222	66,047	438
15 to 24 years	4,955	256	342	432	986	929	841	720	225	224	29,414	563	38,520	989
25 to 34 years	14,652	335	429	564	1,688	2,018	2,759	3,606	1,628	1,625	47,028	447	57,314	742
35 to 44 years	19,473	315	531	670	1,727	2,031	3,110	4,724	2,922	3,444	56,498	511	70,301	864
45 to 54 years	18,169	331	521	591	1,358	1,702	2,586	3,982	2,863	4,235	61,682	533	76,888	946
55 to 64 years	11,903	375	667	647	1,333	1,401	1,843	2,297	1,342	1,998	47,075	745	64,744	1,124
65 years and over	19,391	455	2,395	2,962	4,431	3,040	2,455	1,863	733	1,057	23,620	263	35,150	469
65 to 74 years	9,846	152	968	1,128	1,980	1,661	1,523	1,211	516	705	28,889	455	41,695	788
75 years and over	9,545	303	1,427	1,834	2,450	1,378	932	652	216	352	19,431	282	28,399	473
Mean age of householder	49.40	49.32	59.67	59.51	54.00	49.81	47.06	45.20	45.63	47.32	(X)	(X)	(X)	(X)
SIZE OF HOUSEHOLD														
One person	23,169	1,141	3,495	3,485	4,690	3,450	2,993	2,295	827	794	21,969	229	31,763	470
Two people	30,373	530	755	1,463	4,051	4,408	5,155	6,214	3,352	4,446	46,251	409	61,189	602
Three people	13,854	181	325	402	1,221	1,328	2,272	3,465	2,076	2,583	58,027	694	71,021	911
Four people	12,725	127	184	281	864	1,105	1,828	3,193	2,224	2,920	64,665	707	80,268	1,185
Five people	5,467	46	93	152	403	532	870	1,272	859	1,240	62,134	946	79,027	1,753
Six people	1,846	15	17	58	191	188	303	458	254	363	56,915	1,339	75,777	2,856
Seven people or more	1,109	28	15	26	102	108	173	297	121	238	57,433	2,275	69,592	2,736
Mean size of household	2.56	1.83	1.52	1.73	2.09	2.30	2.61	2.92	3.09	3.20	(X)	(X)	(X)	(X)
NUMBER OF EARNERS														
No earners	17,901	1,337	3,501	3,337	4,277	2,388	1,525	908	310	318	16,578	204	23,033	260
One earner	30,056	624	1,187	2,114	5,365	5,532	5,725	5,023	1,910	2,575	35,389	245	49,528	584
Two earners or more	40,586	105	197	416	1,880	3,199	6,345	11,261	7,492	9,691	67,482	359	82,489	600
Two earners	31,999	102	185	380	1,716	2,898	5,472	8,981	5,496	6,769	63,428	406	79,004	689
Three earners	6,302	2	11	36	154	259	717	1,760	1,408	1,953	77,895	1,000	92,549	1,428

TABLE 4.2

Household income by selected characteristics, 2000 [CONTINUED]

[Numbers in thousands. Based on a November 2001 weighting correction. Households as of March of the following year.]

	Total	Less than $5,000	$5,000 to $9,999	$10,000 to $14,999	$15,000 to $24,999	$25,000 to $34,999	$35,000 to $49,999	$50,000 to $74,999	$75,000 to $99,999	$100,000 and over	Median income Value (dollars)	Median income Standard Error (dollars)	Mean income Value (dollars)	Mean income Standard Error (dollars)
Four earners or more	2,285	—	—	—	10	41	156	519	588	970	90,891	1,257	103,545	2,010
Mean number of earners	1.41	0.41	0.33	0.51	0.82	1.12	1.46	1.80	2.07	2.13	(X)	(X)	(X)	(X)
WORK EXPERIENCE OF HOUSEHOLDER														
Total	88,543	2,066	4,885	5,867	11,522	11,120	13,595	17,193	9,712	12,583	44,232	275	59,280	363
Worked	63,032	646	1,202	2,203	6,161	7,545	10,468	14,703	8,775	11,329	54,579	321	69,607	467
Worked at full-time jobs	54,431	321	720	1,509	4,925	6,423	9,155	13,232	7,981	10,164	56,547	293	71,609	509
50 weeks or more	46,733	156	298	949	3,715	5,351	7,868	11,823	7,280	9,293	59,721	398	74,774	570
27 to 49 weeks	5,137	46	158	334	720	701	928	1,007	570	672	44,357	978	57,113	1,102
26 weeks or less	2,560	119	264	227	491	371	359	401	131	198	29,081	1,017	42,937	1,670
Worked at part-time jobs	8,601	324	482	694	1,236	1,122	1,313	1,471	794	1,165	40,002	728	56,935	1,128
50 weeks or more	4,592	53	195	360	635	556	742	875	452	723	45,348	1,070	64,881	1,837
27 to 49 weeks	1,811	55	106	176	273	252	266	275	180	229	37,110	1,544	52,146	1,817
26 weeks or less	2,199	217	180	158	328	314	305	322	161	213	30,594	1,095	44,286	1,481
Did not work	25,511	1,420	3,683	3,664	5,361	3,575	3,126	2,490	938	1,255	22,123	224	33,765	417
EDUCATIONAL ATTAINMENT														
Total	83,588	1,810	4,542	5,435	10,536	10,191	12,754	16,473	9,488	12,359	45,553	254	60,511	379
Less than 9th grade	5,663	269	1,125	941	1,221	740	640	475	164	88	18,707	495	26,514	607
9th to 12th grade (no diploma)	6,942	238	893	936	1,453	1,077	1,010	858	273	204	24,649	445	34,016	943
High school graduate (includes equivalency)	25,765	626	1,450	1,963	4,007	3,771	4,389	5,289	2,454	1,817	38,014	390	46,726	386
Some college, no degree	15,219	275	552	845	1,871	2,101	2,622	3,345	1,830	1,778	45,891	498	57,786	788
Associate degree	6,868	94	190	283	658	851	1,182	1,593	1,041	976	52,136	796	62,531	1,102
Bachelor's degree or more	23,131	309	332	466	1,326	1,652	2,911	4,913	3,726	7,496	72,728	668	93,333	1,018
Bachelor's degree	14,921	221	231	348	955	1,243	2,055	3,339	2,365	4,163	67,223	694	86,125	1,174
Master's degree	5,562	61	73	72	265	312	619	1,167	986	2,008	79,120	1,271	98,642	2,297
Professional degree	1,462	12	18	30	62	64	122	190	203	760	100,000	(X)	126,659	4,773
Doctorate degree	1,185	14	10	15	43	34	115	217	172	565	97,854	3,427	118,033	4,476
TENURE														
Owner occupied	63,231	1,026	2,298	3,330	6,888	7,116	9,607	13,377	8,265	11,325	51,864	260	67,519	472
Renter occupied	24,030	954	2,465	2,384	4,328	3,760	3,860	3,661	1,399	1,219	29,365	340	38,979	421
Occupier paid no cash rent	1,281	86	121	153	306	244	128	156	48	40	24,146	903	33,420	1,749
BLACK														
ALL HOUSEHOLDS	13,355	815	1,394	1,263	2,199	1,728	2,244	2,030	868	815	30,436	460	40,067	643
TYPE OF RESIDENCE														
Inside metropolitan areas	11,732	709	1,110	1,060	1,856	1,526	2,014	1,867	808	781	31,805	474	41,166	637
Inside central cities	7,096	536	832	707	1,210	961	1,210	888	438	313	27,535	658	35,794	665
1 million or more	5,133	368	569	479	879	681	894	686	334	243	28,551	778	37,156	826
Under 1 million	1,963	168	263	228	331	281	316	202	104	70	24,731	1,193	32,229	1,045
Outside central cities	4,637	173	278	354	646	564	804	979	370	468	39,652	839	49,387	1,227
1 million or more	3,391	109	163	210	431	436	585	769	299	390	42,394	1,200	52,891	1,482
Under 1 million	1,245	65	115	143	215	129	219	210	72	78	31,290	2,335	39,846	2,084
Outside metropolitan areas	1,623	105	284	203	343	202	230	162	59	34	20,569	1,059	32,120	3,158
REGION														
Northeast	2,347	169	242	249	318	341	345	310	192	179	30,426	1,014	41,429	1,230
Midwest	2,461	169	276	233	408	305	403	389	155	124	30,053	1,232	38,275	1,301

TABLE 4.2

Household income by selected characteristics, 2000 [CONTINUED]

[Numbers in thousands. Based on a November 2001 weighting correction. Households as of March of the following year.]

	Total	Less than $5,000	$5,000 to $9,999	$10,000 to $14,999	$15,000 to $24,999	$25,000 to $34,999	$35,000 to $49,999	$50,000 to $74,999	$75,000 to $99,999	$100,000 and over	Median income Value (dollars)	Median income Standard Error (dollars)	Mean income Value (dollars)	Mean income Standard Error (dollars)
South	7,354	425	792	696	1,277	945	1,307	1,098	409	406	29,778	708	39,191	966
West	1,193	51	84	85	196	137	189	232	112	106	36,975	1,666	46,476	2,322
TYPE OF HOUSEHOLD														
Family households	8,814	406	545	701	1,430	1,199	1,553	1,525	726	729	36,063	620	46,267	882
Married-couple families	4,290	56	86	151	445	502	852	1,056	537	605	50,729	708	62,513	1,593
Male householder, no wife present	762	28	51	50	114	107	173	135	70	33	37,015	1,617	41,151	1,560
Female householder, no husband present	3,762	321	409	500	870	590	528	334	119	91	21,698	524	28,774	687
Nonfamily households	4,541	409	849	562	770	529	691	504	142	86	20,551	545	28,033	723
Male householder	2,007	139	282	235	353	244	321	302	89	42	24,811	1,213	31,842	952
Living alone	1,603	113	265	211	317	206	247	190	47	7	21,286	849	26,908	839
Female householder	2,534	270	566	327	417	285	369	202	53	44	16,807	688	25,016	1,045
Living alone	2,209	261	545	308	376	248	287	130	41	13	14,825	654	21,417	670
AGE OF HOUSEHOLDER														
Under 65 years	11,416	703	957	914	1,857	1,510	2,040	1,870	798	767	32,915	684	42,355	728
15 to 24 years	1,087	158	126	121	251	146	140	112	21	12	20,486	796	29,155	3,296
25 to 34 years	2,796	155	213	255	496	434	511	461	158	113	31,347	847	39,077	1,242
35 to 44 years	3,273	142	200	213	472	466	665	624	240	253	37,546	827	45,700	1,217
45 to 54 years	2,707	150	190	195	381	304	474	465	267	281	38,450	1,330	47,802	1,314
55 to 64 years	1,553	98	228	130	257	159	250	208	113	108	28,446	1,973	40,952	2,478
65 years and over	1,939	112	437	349	343	218	204	160	69	48	16,481	710	26,593	979
65 to 74 years	1,083	60	200	159	175	158	131	119	46	35	21,005	1,818	30,799	1,446
75 years and over	856	52	236	190	168	60	73	41	23	12	13,358	739	21,268	1,194
Mean age of householder	45.33	43.03	52.46	49.28	44.82	43.17	43.40	43.04	45.56	46.04	(X)	(X)	(X)	(X)
SIZE OF HOUSEHOLD														
One person	3,811	374	811	520	693	454	534	320	88	20	17,626	691	23,726	529
Two people	3,752	182	268	340	701	536	622	594	273	236	31,626	770	42,385	1,299
Three people	2,491	140	170	215	353	343	444	411	201	213	35,950	1,583	45,307	1,546
Four people	1,881	69	78	118	268	221	351	391	171	214	42,311	1,530	53,548	2,398
Five people	824	19	33	54	103	113	132	196	87	88	43,494	2,411	53,865	2,747
Six people	394	23	23	11	56	30	109	82	31	28	41,896	1,411	46,002	2,551
Seven people or more	201	7	11	6	25	31	52	36	17	17	40,062	3,330	47,279	3,647
Mean size of household	2.67	2.16	1.87	2.22	2.46	2.66	2.88	3.13	3.20	3.51	(X)	(X)	(X)	(X)
NUMBER OF EARNERS														
No earners	2,697	544	917	496	427	144	88	62	12	8	9,233	276	13,146	450
One earner	5,742	260	436	696	1,420	1,061	1,052	551	179	86	25,421	431	30,353	498
Two earners or more	4,916	10	41	71	353	523	1,103	1,417	677	720	55,160	973	66,183	1,434
Two earners	3,884	10	32	64	317	463	911	1,125	469	494	51,765	590	63,537	1,669
Three earners	881	—	9	8	34	57	170	252	172	180	65,081	2,023	74,263	2,923
Four earners or more	151	—	—	1	4	3	22	40	36	46	76,298	4,541	87,148	5,495
Mean number of earners	1.31	0.35	0.39	0.69	1.02	1.30	1.61	1.92	2.16	2.31	(X)	(X)	(X)	(X)
WORK EXPERIENCE OF HOUSEHOLDER														
Total	13,355	815	1,394	1,263	2,199	1,728	2,244	2,030	868	815	30,436	460	40,067	643
Worked	9,493	239	416	661	1,574	1,357	1,904	1,789	795	758	38,234	526	47,883	840
Worked at full-time jobs	8,413	130	250	480	1,400	1,222	1,779	1,689	736	727	40,114	531	50,197	898
50 weeks or more	7,063	59	82	346	1,141	1,054	1,538	1,522	684	636	42,037	535	52,774	1,024

TABLE 4.2

Household income by selected characteristics, 2000 [CONTINUED]

[Numbers in thousands. Based on a November 2001 weighting correction. Households as of March of the following year.]

	Total	Less than $5,000	$5,000 to $9,999	$10,000 to $14,999	$15,000 to $24,999	$25,000 to $34,999	$35,000 to $49,999	$50,000 to $74,999	$75,000 to $99,999	$100,000 and over	Median income Value (dollars)	Median income Standard Error (dollars)	Mean income Value (dollars)	Mean income Standard Error (dollars)
27 to 49 weeks	803	7	79	67	151	118	153	102	47	80	32,424	1,937	43,491	2,165
26 weeks or less	547	64	90	66	108	50	87	65	5	12	17,722	1,900	26,764	1,605
Worked at part-time jobs	1,080	108	166	181	174	136	126	100	60	31	18,647	1,428	29,862	2,181
50 weeks or more	549	25	61	95	94	70	73	65	50	15	24,861	3,208	33,426	1,887
27 to 49 weeks	215	13	29	43	43	26	25	24	4	7	19,087	3,344	28,454	2,597
26 weeks or less	317	71	75	43	37	39	27	10	5	9	11,350	1,493	24,649	6,410
Did not work	3,862	576	978	602	626	371	339	241	72	57	13,043	422	20,853	590
EDUCATIONAL ATTAINMENT														
Total	12,268	657	1,268	1,142	1,948	1,582	2,104	1,918	847	803	31,594	477	41,034	634
Less than 9th grade	817	72	244	142	137	88	55	46	24	10	13,172	828	21,135	1,239
9th to 12th grade (no diploma)	1,873	211	361	303	407	177	181	155	57	23	16,351	730	24,069	943
High school graduate (includes equivalency)	4,147	217	428	411	759	569	811	603	211	139	29,390	1,031	36,770	1,179
Some college, no degree	2,423	81	150	182	349	378	464	470	188	161	36,749	948	44,205	1,270
Associate degree	1,017	39	39	44	153	167	216	206	76	78	37,930	958	45,922	1,660
Bachelor's degree or more	1,990	38	45	60	143	204	376	438	292	392	55,906	2,718	67,706	1,896
Bachelor's degree	1,367	28	34	43	119	145	286	315	169	227	50,897	933	64,832	2,428
Master's degree	477	10	11	18	17	49	75	100	81	116	66,215	3,690	69,403	2,988
Professional degree	89	—	—	—	—	6	10	9	24	40	88,724	40,273	100,558	9,434
Doctorate degree	57	—	—	—	7	4	5	15	17	9	(B)	(B)	(B)	(B)
TENURE														
Owner occupied	6,401	210	408	429	819	791	1,188	1,280	625	650	41,431	639	51,146	1,058
Renter occupied	6,685	571	927	792	1,332	920	1,018	729	236	161	22,133	443	30,157	729
Occupier paid no cash rent	269	34	59	42	48	17	38	21	6	4	15,007	2,394	22,748	2,114
HISPANIC														
ALL HOUSEHOLDS	9,663	320	702	798	1,764	1,422	1,707	1,682	711	556	33,455	678	42,411	659
TYPE OF RESIDENCE														
Inside metropolitan areas	8,854	288	631	715	1,566	1,296	1,562	1,573	673	551	34,347	697	43,379	708
Inside central cities	4,573	164	424	439	848	677	756	750	285	230	30,818	711	39,659	884
1 million or more	3,216	106	311	287	565	463	554	562	199	169	31,926	975	40,502	1,047
Under 1 million	1,356	58	113	152	283	213	202	188	86	61	28,107	1,582	37,659	1,649
Outside central cities	4,282	124	207	276	718	619	806	824	388	321	37,824	811	47,352	1,110
1 million or more	3,314	94	135	184	511	474	638	676	331	272	40,378	993	49,237	1,190
Under 1 million	967	30	72	92	207	145	168	148	57	49	30,613	1,749	40,893	2,712
Outside metropolitan areas	809	32	71	83	198	126	145	109	38	6	26,105	1,604	31,811	1,591
REGION														
Northeast	1,470	71	180	137	249	205	230	225	88	86	30,241	1,397	39,187	1,531
Midwest	697	20	33	49	114	103	120	139	63	56	37,845	2,423	47,955	2,362
South	3,529	109	260	314	636	490	643	618	264	196	33,591	1,408	43,305	1,347
West	3,967	121	229	299	766	624	713	700	296	218	33,838	1,074	41,836	873
TYPE OF HOUSEHOLD														
Family households	7,727	210	341	558	1,375	1,166	1,451	1,479	640	508	36,578	508	45,781	776
Married-couple families	5,246	72	142	307	847	766	1,032	1,124	522	433	41,116	806	50,840	1,015
Male householder, no wife present	736	12	19	46	124	120	146	167	56	46	39,015	1,905	46,709	2,247
Female householder, no husband present	1,746	126	180	205	403	280	272	188	61	29	23,671	1,039	30,191	1,077

TABLE 4.2

Household income by selected characteristics, 2000 [CONTINUED]

[Numbers in thousands. Based on a November 2001 weighting correction. Households as of March of the following year.]

	Total	Less than $5,000	$5,000 to $9,999	$10,000 to $14,999	$15,000 to $24,999	$25,000 to $34,999	$35,000 to $49,999	$50,000 to $74,999	$75,000 to $99,999	$100,000 and over	Median income Value (dollars)	Median income Standard Error (dollars)	Mean income Value (dollars)	Mean income Standard Error (dollars)
Nonfamily households	1,936	110	361	241	389	255	256	203	71	48	21,263	854	28,955	971
Male householder	1,024	51	130	100	219	163	155	124	50	32	25,488	1,102	32,666	1,369
Living alone	667	36	112	85	160	110	81	61	13	8	20,597	1,530	25,945	1,393
Female householder	911	60	231	141	170	92	101	80	21	16	16,074	1,019	24,783	1,341
Living alone	736	53	225	131	137	63	70	35	15	6	13,295	852	20,587	1,356
AGE OF HOUSEHOLDER														
Under 65 years	8,591	285	463	609	1,525	1,298	1,592	1,601	682	536	35,792	495	44,498	719
15 to 24 years	970	83	59	98	197	155	161	163	38	17	27,890	1,466	33,836	1,695
25 to 34 years	2,500	85	121	174	464	433	456	480	183	103	34,095	1,250	41,947	1,251
35 to 44 years	2,479	53	100	163	430	362	489	484	219	178	38,060	1,154	47,360	1,456
45 to 54 years	1,636	35	73	98	255	204	327	317	152	175	41,107	1,200	51,624	1,742
55 to 64 years	1,006	29	110	75	178	144	159	157	90	63	32,186	1,567	42,486	1,976
65 years and over	1,072	35	239	190	240	124	114	81	29	20	17,258	918	25,685	1,190
65 to 74 years	660	18	136	95	147	82	82	55	25	19	20,166	1,379	29,008	1,726
75 years and over	413	17	103	95	93	42	32	26	4	1	14,512	928	20,378	1,293
Mean age of householder	42.54	38.95	52.38	46.71	42.75	40.73	40.83	40.12	41.93	43.44	(X)	(X)	(X)	(X)
SIZE OF HOUSEHOLD														
One person	1,402	89	338	216	297	173	151	96	28	14	16,221	621	23,134	978
Two people	2,055	77	137	207	424	335	335	287	131	121	30,357	962	39,787	1,244
Three people	1,813	72	102	124	346	257	347	328	132	105	35,166	1,142	42,670	1,308
Four people	1,986	43	60	117	298	286	420	419	189	155	40,475	1,008	50,893	1,937
Five people	1,248	15	44	80	219	189	242	263	117	80	38,744	1,767	47,330	1,791
Six people	670	11	8	39	110	121	109	160	68	44	40,378	2,076	49,379	2,637
Seven people or more	487	13	13	15	71	60	102	129	48	37	45,756	2,139	51,231	2,686
Mean size of household	3.48	2.76	2.19	2.83	3.27	3.52	3.74	4.01	4.06	3.91	(X)	(X)	(X)	(X)
NUMBER OF EARNERS														
No earners	1,189	182	422	225	226	68	39	18	7	3	9,893	387	13,486	599
One earner	3,352	121	237	452	963	626	492	303	86	71	23,647	628	30,779	900
Two earners or more	5,121	18	42	121	576	728	1,176	1,361	618	482	48,422	886	56,742	974
Two earners	3,597	16	36	113	507	617	851	841	343	273	42,961	895	51,825	1,140
Three earners	1,036	2	6	8	63	96	261	325	151	124	55,238	1,754	64,216	2,266
Four earners or more	488	—	—	—	6	15	63	195	123	85	69,477	2,222	77,093	2,675
Mean number of earners	1.65	0.49	0.47	0.88	1.25	1.56	1.93	2.28	2.54	2.51	(X)	(X)	(X)	(X)
WORK EXPERIENCE OF HOUSEHOLDER														
Total	9,663	320	702	798	1,764	1,422	1,707	1,682	711	556	33,455	678	42,411	659
Worked	7,301	106	220	480	1,246	1,138	1,437	1,502	658	514	38,834	707	47,894	787
Worked at full-time jobs	6,487	54	152	381	1,049	1,025	1,324	1,392	629	481	40,617	631	49,548	843
50 weeks or more	5,357	15	58	249	831	840	1,144	1,224	562	432	42,765	748	52,277	968
27 to 49 weeks	697	9	36	72	121	125	122	126	44	41	33,566	2,179	41,499	1,913
26 weeks or less	433	30	57	60	97	61	57	41	23	8	21,959	1,687	28,753	1,770
Worked at part-time jobs	814	52	68	99	197	113	113	110	30	33	24,436	1,581	34,712	2,018
50 weeks or more	410	12	21	52	97	59	57	73	17	22	28,809	2,376	40,061	3,262
27 to 49 weeks	166	12	19	19	39	26	24	18	5	3	22,811	3,517	29,410	3,145
26 weeks or less	239	28	28	28	60	28	33	20	8	7	20,683	2,033	29,211	3,197
Did not work	2,362	214	482	318	519	284	270	181	52	43	17,437	642	25,461	982

TABLE 4.2

Household income by selected characteristics, 2000 [CONTINUED]

[Numbers in thousands. Based on a November 2001 weighting correction. Households as of March of the following year.]

	Total	Less than $5,000	$5,000 to $9,999	$10,000 to $14,999	$15,000 to $24,999	$25,000 to $34,999	$35,000 to $49,999	$50,000 to $74,999	$75,000 to $99,999	$100,000 and over	Median income Value (dollars)	Median income Standard Error (dollars)	Mean income Value (dollars)	Mean income Standard Error (dollars)
EDUCATIONAL ATTAINMENT														
Total	8,692	237	643	701	1,567	1,267	1,546	1,519	673	539	34,299	733	43,368	706
Less than 9th grade	2,321	90	326	294	534	338	340	259	109	30	23,105	826	30,076	862
9th to 12th grade (no diploma)	1,364	55	115	136	352	211	252	156	52	34	25,735	943	32,693	1,185
High school graduate (includes equivalency)	2,270	52	120	171	407	381	427	456	148	107	35,100	1,048	42,716	1,437
Some college, no degree	1,163	17	42	55	144	162	255	268	132	88	44,774	1,839	50,142	1,519
Associate degree	478	3	12	23	51	77	91	111	67	43	47,203	3,132	54,179	2,739
Bachelor's degree or more	1,096	20	28	21	79	98	181	269	164	236	60,365	1,506	74,250	3,080
Bachelor's degree	794	14	25	11	65	83	149	192	119	135	56,497	2,935	69,434	3,690
Master's degree	203	1	2	4	6	10	23	61	37	56	71,852	3,461	81,171	5,504
Professional degree	58	—	—	4	5	7	7	3	7	25	(B)	(B)	(B)	(B)
Doctorate degree	41	—	1	2	3	—	1	13	2	19	(B)	(B)	(B)	(B)
TENURE														
Owner occupied	4,485	69	183	229	600	571	851	1,028	507	446	44,735	959	54,349	1,178
Renter occupied	5,031	235	507	557	1,119	824	841	640	198	109	25,903	518	32,138	602
Occupier paid no cash rent	147	16	12	12	45	27	15	14	6	1	22,746	2,250	29,764	5,088
WHITE NON-HISPANIC														
ALL HOUSEHOLDS	79,375	1,776	4,228	5,115	9,823	9,771	11,968	15,600	9,033	12,061	45,910	263	61,240	397
TYPE OF RESIDENCE														
Inside metropolitan areas	61,592	1,293	2,811	3,579	7,008	7,035	9,076	12,342	7,531	10,916	49,986	320	65,848	478
Inside central cities	18,700	552	1,151	1,227	2,413	2,372	2,742	3,484	1,978	2,782	43,378	648	59,637	801
1 million or more	10,775	315	635	652	1,285	1,245	1,546	1,992	1,259	1,846	46,868	816	64,790	1,193
Under 1 million	7,925	237	516	575	1,128	1,126	1,196	1,492	719	936	39,567	870	52,630	957
Outside central cities	42,892	741	1,660	2,352	4,596	4,663	6,334	8,858	5,553	8,134	52,394	376	68,556	590
1 million or more	28,759	464	951	1,498	2,781	2,928	3,971	5,754	4,015	6,398	57,065	479	74,795	807
Under 1 million	14,133	277	709	855	1,815	1,735	2,363	3,105	1,538	1,736	44,944	628	55,859	685
Outside metropolitan areas	17,783	483	1,417	1,535	2,815	2,735	2,892	3,258	1,502	1,145	34,587	541	45,278	728
REGION														
Northeast	15,924	360	882	1,017	1,857	1,748	2,215	3,172	1,892	2,782	49,091	682	64,693	812
Midwest	20,809	439	987	1,269	2,639	2,562	3,151	4,391	2,517	2,854	46,934	504	59,191	690
South	26,837	643	1,661	1,887	3,497	3,560	4,141	5,073	2,684	3,691	42,004	407	57,917	687
West	15,805	335	698	941	1,830	1,901	2,461	2,965	1,940	2,734	48,118	698	66,098	1,099
TYPE OF HOUSEHOLD														
Family households	52,876	662	969	1,703	4,989	5,899	8,324	12,203	7,617	10,510	57,182	320	72,455	506
Married-couple families	43,624	414	469	1,063	3,416	4,440	6,576	10,485	6,915	9,847	62,109	299	77,922	583
Male householder, no wife present	2,571	39	103	110	335	321	491	622	244	306	45,694	1,307	59,648	2,073
Female householder, no husband present	6,681	210	396	529	1,239	1,137	1,257	1,097	459	356	33,163	658	41,688	728
Nonfamily households	26,499	1,114	3,260	3,412	4,834	3,872	3,644	3,397	1,416	1,552	26,331	257	38,861	572
Male householder	11,614	430	964	1,024	1,869	1,854	1,837	1,908	824	903	32,386	450	47,111	1,112
Living alone	8,860	402	909	961	1,611	1,491	1,372	1,208	472	436	28,019	616	39,873	1,076
Female householder	14,886	684	2,295	2,387	2,965	2,018	1,807	1,488	592	648	21,567	287	32,424	519
Living alone	12,982	655	2,267	2,321	2,795	1,793	1,475	1,000	330	345	19,062	302	27,115	378
AGE OF HOUSEHOLDER														
Under 65 years	61,008	1,350	2,063	2,326	5,629	6,853	9,624	13,814	8,328	11,022	53,829	344	68,936	485

TABLE 4.2

Household income by selected characteristics, 2000 [CONTINUED]

[Numbers in thousands. Based on a November 2001 weighting correction. Households as of March of the following year.]

	Total	Less than $5,000	$5,000 to $9,999	$10,000 to $14,999	$15,000 to $24,999	$25,000 to $34,999	$35,000 to $49,999	$50,000 to $74,999	$75,000 to $99,999	$100,000 and over	Median income Value (dollars)	Median income Standard Error (dollars)	Mean income Value (dollars)	Mean income Standard Error (dollars)
15 to 24 years	4,037	178	287	341	796	779	689	572	189	207	29,782	626	39,616	1,150
25 to 34 years	12,300	263	317	399	1,249	1,609	2,328	3,154	1,455	1,526	49,889	537	60,322	853
35 to 44 years	17,135	267	435	518	1,321	1,694	2,647	4,258	2,711	3,284	59,785	605	73,449	957
45 to 54 years	16,593	297	455	494	1,108	1,508	2,271	3,680	2,715	4,066	63,904	703	79,271	1,018
55 to 64 years	10,943	346	569	574	1,156	1,262	1,689	2,149	1,259	1,938	48,699	811	66,696	1,206
65 years and over	18,367	426	2,166	2,788	4,194	2,918	2,344	1,787	705	1,040	23,966	269	35,676	490
65 to 74 years	9,223	138	839	1,043	1,836	1,581	1,444	1,160	493	689	29,571	456	42,552	832
75 years and over	9,144	287	1,327	1,745	2,357	1,336	900	626	212	351	19,657	284	28,741	490
Mean age of householder	50.18	51.03	60.78	61.40	55.90	51.05	47.89	45.71	45.90	47.49	(X)	(X)	(X)	(X)
SIZE OF HOUSEHOLD														
One person	21,842	1,057	3,176	3,282	4,405	3,284	2,848	2,208	802	781	22,303	240	32,290	495
Two people	28,431	456	631	1,268	3,647	4,088	4,837	5,947	3,226	4,331	47,566	428	62,637	635
Three people	12,136	117	228	282	881	1,089	1,936	3,161	1,953	2,488	61,499	526	75,101	1,011
Four people	10,849	95	129	173	575	832	1,439	2,790	2,041	2,775	69,554	703	85,418	1,343
Five people	4,277	31	53	78	196	352	636	1,021	750	1,161	70,264	1,350	87,784	2,143
Six people	1,200	4	9	21	85	73	194	303	188	323	66,766	2,220	90,184	4,043
Seven people or more	640	16	2	11	34	51	79	171	74	202	69,153	2,232	82,769	4,158
Mean size of household	2.46	1.69	1.42	1.57	1.88	2.14	2.46	2.80	3.02	3.17	(X)	(X)	(X)	(X)
NUMBER OF EARNERS														
No earners	16,785	1,171	3,109	3,128	4,057	2,325	1,485	892	303	315	17,156	212	23,655	273
One earner	26,875	516	965	1,686	4,437	4,936	5,259	4,741	1,826	2,510	36,893	259	51,749	642
Two earners or more	35,716	89	155	300	1,330	2,510	5,224	9,968	6,904	9,237	70,287	339	86,044	665
Two earners	28,594	87	150	272	1,231	2,317	4,662	8,192	5,166	6,518	66,243	411	82,314	756
Three earners	5,312	2	5	28	94	167	468	1,446	1,270	1,832	82,918	905	97,801	1,619
Four earners or more	1,810	—	—	—	5	26	94	330	468	887	98,871	8,388	110,457	2,384
Mean number of earners	1.38	0.40	0.30	0.46	0.74	1.06	1.39	1.75	2.03	2.12	(X)	(X)	(X)	(X)
WORK EXPERIENCE OF HOUSEHOLDER														
Total	79,375	1,776	4,228	5,115	9,823	9,771	11,968	15,600	9,033	12,061	45,910	263	61,240	397
Worked	56,104	546	995	1,747	4,973	6,467	9,100	13,284	8,148	10,844	56,773	296	72,310	514
Worked at full-time jobs	48,262	271	577	1,145	3,918	5,446	7,896	11,915	7,383	9,712	59,198	431	74,469	562
50 weeks or more	41,648	142	241	712	2,918	4,555	6,777	10,667	6,748	8,888	61,614	277	77,566	627
27 to 49 weeks	4,471	37	126	266	604	579	814	884	528	633	46,182	1,157	59,407	1,227
26 weeks or less	2,144	91	210	167	397	313	305	364	107	190	31,016	1,177	45,709	1,953
Worked at part-time jobs	7,841	275	419	602	1,055	1,021	1,203	1,369	764	1,133	41,533	664	59,024	1,215
50 weeks or more	4,200	41	175	311	544	503	688	802	435	701	46,818	1,004	67,130	1,977
27 to 49 weeks	1,662	44	87	160	236	229	242	263	175	225	39,032	1,567	54,183	1,941
26 weeks or less	1,979	190	157	131	275	289	274	304	153	206	31,940	1,535	45,889	1,596
Did not work	23,272	1,230	3,233	3,367	4,851	3,304	2,868	2,316	886	1,217	22,579	255	34,550	447
EDUCATIONAL ATTAINMENT														
Total	75,338	1,598	3,941	4,774	9,028	8,991	11,279	15,028	8,844	11,854	47,089	270	62,398	412
Less than 9th grade	3,412	183	814	666	692	410	311	221	58	57	15,563	563	24,060	835
9th to 12th grade (no diploma)	5,638	192	788	812	1,114	871	764	705	221	170	24,239	491	34,226	1,131
High school graduate (includes equivalency)	23,635	579	1,342	1,794	3,622	3,417	3,989	4,860	2,315	1,717	38,330	404	47,091	400
Some college, no degree	14,130	263	512	793	1,734	1,952	2,381	3,094	1,703	1,698	45,998	539	58,364	840
Associate degree	6,419	91	178	264	609	781	1,095	1,488	978	935	52,475	873	63,121	1,165

TABLE 4.2

Household income by selected characteristics, 2000 [CONTINUED]

[Numbers in thousands. Based on a November 2001 weighting correction. Households as of March of the following year.]

	Total	Less than $5,000	$5,000 to $9,999	$10,000 to $14,999	$15,000 to $24,999	$25,000 to $34,999	$35,000 to $49,999	$50,000 to $74,999	$75,000 to $99,999	$100,000 and over	Median income Value (dollars)	Median income Standard Error (dollars)	Mean income Value (dollars)	Mean income Standard Error (dollars)
Bachelor's degree or more	22,104	291	307	446	1,255	1,561	2,739	4,660	3,569	7,276	73,566	774	94,239	1,056
Bachelor's degree	14,182	209	210	338	895	1,166	1,915	3,159	2,250	4,041	68,043	842	87,049	1,223
Master's degree	5,368	56	71	68	262	302	596	1,107	953	1,953	79,481	1,257	99,248	2,371
Professional degree	1,405	11	18	26	57	59	115	187	197	735	100,000	(X)	127,797	4,916
Doctorate degree	1,149	14	9	14	42	33	113	206	170	547	97,890	3,378	118,552	4,592
TENURE														
Owner occupied	58,902	958	2,123	3,107	6,300	6,561	8,781	12,394	7,776	10,902	52,441	310	68,521	499
Renter occupied	19,333	746	1,995	1,866	3,262	2,990	3,074	3,064	1,215	1,121	30,419	327	40,674	502
Occupier paid no cash rent	1,141	72	111	141	261	220	113	142	42	39	24,418	1,049	33,814	1,862

SOURCE: "Table 2. Selected Characteristics—Households by Total Money Income in 2000" in "Income 2000, Previously Published Tables from the *Money Income in the U.S. Reports*," U.S. Census Bureau, Washington, DC, February 1, 2002 [Online] http://www.census.gov/hhes/income/income00/inctab2.html [accessed July 22, 2002]

TABLE 4.3

Households by total money income, 1967–2000

(Income in 2000 CPI-U-RS adjusted dollars. Households as of March of the following year.)

	Number (1,000)	Total	Under $5,000	$5,000 to $9,999	$10,000 to $14,999	$15,000 to $24,999	$25,000 to $34,999	$35,000 to $49,999	$50,000 to $74,999	$75,000 to $99,999	$100,000 and over	Median income Value (dollars)	Median income Standard error (dollars)	Mean income Value (dollars)	Mean income Standard error (dollars)
2000	106,417	100.0	2.9	6.1	7.0	13.4	12.5	15.5	18.9	10.4	13.4	42,148	197	57,045	319
1999	104,705	100.0	2.8	6.1	7.1	13.8	12.4	15.8	18.5	10.5	13.2	42,187	198	56,684	297
1998	103,874	100.0	3.1	6.6	7.4	13.4	13.1	15.5	18.8	10.2	12.0	41,032	243	54,718	295
1997	102,528	100.0	3.2	7.0	7.6	14.2	12.7	16.0	18.5	9.7	11.1	39,594	183	53,169	297
1996	101,018	100.0	3.1	7.4	7.8	14.3	13.5	15.7	18.6	9.5	10.2	38,798	196	51,513	289
1995[1]	99,627	100.0	3.1	7.2	8.0	14.9	13.1	16.4	18.3	9.4	9.6	38,262	221	50,458	276
1994[2]	98,990	100.0	3.4	7.8	8.2	14.9	13.3	16.2	17.7	9.1	9.5	37,136	169	49,646	267
1993[3]	97,107	100.0	3.7	8.0	8.0	14.9	13.1	16.6	17.7	8.8	9.1	36,746	172	48,729	263
1992[4]	96,426	100.0	3.6	8.1	8.0	14.9	13.2	16.7	18.4	8.7	8.4	36,965	175	46,864	197
1991	95,676	100.0	3.3	8.1	7.6	14.7	13.7	16.8	18.4	9.0	8.4	37,314	179	46,970	193
1990	94,312	100.0	3.2	7.7	7.5	14.1	13.7	17.2	18.8	9.1	8.7	38,446	197	48,024	203
1989	93,347	100.0	3.0	7.6	7.4	14.1	13.1	17.1	19.2	9.2	9.3	38,979	214	49,246	214
1988	92,830	100.0	3.1	8.1	7.3	14.3	12.8	17.3	19.2	9.3	8.5	38,309	186	47,867	212
1987[5]	91,124	100.0	3.3	8.1	7.5	14.5	12.9	17.1	19.1	9.3	8.2	38,007	180	47,266	193
1986	89,479	100.0	3.6	8.2	7.3	14.8	13.3	17.2	18.7	9.1	7.8	37,546	194	46,387	189
1985[6]	88,458	100.0	3.5	8.4	7.7	15.1	13.7	17.7	18.3	8.7	6.8	36,246	196	44,607	176
1984	86,789	100.0	3.4	8.5	7.9	15.5	14.0	17.6	18.3	8.2	6.4	35,568	162	43,580	160
1983[7]	85,290	100.0	3.7	8.7	8.0	16.0	14.4	17.8	17.9	7.6	5.8	34,682	157	42,257	157
1982	83,918	100.0	3.6	8.9	8.3	15.7	14.5	18.2	17.9	7.4	5.5	34,667	157	41,779	155
1981	83,527	100.0	3.4	8.9	8.3	16.0	14.1	18.2	18.6	7.5	5.1	34,696	182	41,450	151
1980	82,368	100.0	3.1	8.9	8.2	15.5	14.0	18.9	18.7	7.5	5.2	35,239	182	41,910	153
1979[8]	80,776	100.0	3.0	8.7	7.6	15.2	13.8	18.5	19.7	7.8	5.6	36,399	173	43,238	164
1978	77,330	100.0	2.8	8.7	8.1	15.1	13.7	18.8	19.7	7.7	5.3	36,440	172	42,889	164
1977	76,030	100.0	3.0	9.1	8.5	15.8	14.3	19.1	18.9	6.7	4.4	34,242	139	40,620	124
1976[9]	74,142	100.0	3.0	9.3	8.5	16.0	14.8	19.4	18.6	6.4	4.0	34,050	142	40,051	123
1975[10]	72,867	100.0	3.2	9.5	8.7	16.0	15.4	19.4	18.2	6.0	3.7	33,489	123	39,105	122
1974[10][11]	71,163	100.0	3.1	9.1	7.9	15.8	15.3	20.0	18.4	6.5	4.0	34,409	121	40,239	126
1973	69,859	100.0	3.6	8.2	8.3	15.0	14.8	19.7	19.3	6.6	4.4	35,504	130	41,060	128
1972[12]	68,251	100.0	4.1	8.6	8.1	14.7	15.1	20.1	18.8	6.3	4.3	34,802	135	40,504	133
1971[13]	66,676	100.0	4.6	9.0	7.9	15.5	15.7	21.1	17.4	5.4	3.4	33,398	129	38,411	126
1970	64,778	100.0	4.8	8.7	7.6	15.2	16.3	21.0	17.6	5.4	3.4	33,746	127	38,641	131
1969	63,401	100.0	4.8	8.6	7.4	15.0	16.4	21.6	17.6	5.2	3.3	33,973	129	38,151	130
1968	62,214	100.0	5.1	8.6	7.8	15.4	17.8	21.2	16.8	4.5	2.7	32,723	128	37,021	152
1967[14]	60,813	100.0	5.9	9.1	7.9	16.1	17.4	21.8	14.9	4.1	2.8	31,397	117	35,115	136

[1]Full implementation of 1990 census-based sample design and metropolitan definitions, 7,000 household sample reduction, and revised race edits.
[2]Introduction of 1990 census-based sample design.
[3]Data collection method changed from paper and pencil to computer-assisted interviewing. In addition, the March 1994 income supplement was revised to allow for the coding of different income amounts on selected questionnaire items. Limits either increased or decreased in the following categories: earnings limits increased to $999,999; social security limits increased to $49,999; supplemental security income and public assistance limits increased to $24,999; veterans' benefits limits increased to $99,999; child support and alimony limits decreased to $49,999.
[4]Implementation of 1990 census population controls.
[5]Implementation of a new March CPS processing system.
[6]Recording of amounts for earnings from longest job increased to $299,999. Full implementation of 1980 census-based sample design.
[7]Implementation of Hispanic population weighting controls and introduction of 1980 census-based sample design.
[8]Implementation of 1980 census population controls. Questionnaire expanded to show 27 possible values from 51 possible sources of income.
[9]First year medians were derived using both Pareto and linear interpolation. Before this year all medians were derived using linear interpolation.
[10]These estimates were derived using Pareto interpolation and may differ from published data which were derived using linear interpolation.
[11]Implementation of a new March CPS processing system. Questionnaire expanded to ask 11 income questions.
[12]Full implementation of 1970 census-based sample design.
[13]Introduction of 1970 census-based sample design and population controls.
[14]Implementation of a new March CPS processing system.

SOURCE: Adapted from Carmen DeNavas-Walt, Robert W. Cleveland, and Mark I. Roemer, "Table A-1. Households by Total Money Income, Race, and Hispanic Origin of Householder: 1967 to 2000," in *Money Income in the United States: 2000,* Current Population Reports P60-213, U.S. Census Bureau, Washington, DC, September 2001

Ratio of Income to Poverty Levels

For purposes of analysis, the Census Bureau uses income-to-poverty ratios, which measure income in relation to the respective poverty threshold for each family size. Poor persons have a poverty ratio below 1.00. Persons above the poverty level are divided into two groups: the "near-poor" and the "non-poor." The "near-poor" have a poverty ratio between 1.00 and 1.24 (100 percent to 124 percent of the poverty level), and the "non-poor" have an income-to-poverty ratio of 1.25 (125 percent of the poverty level) and above.

In 2000, 11.3 percent of the total population had income-to-poverty ratios under 1.00; in other words, 31.1 million persons in the United States had incomes below the poverty threshold. Those under 18 years of age were

FIGURE 4.1

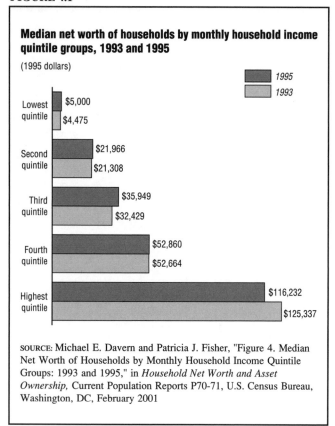

Median net worth of households by monthly household income quintile groups, 1993 and 1995

(1995 dollars)

■ 1995
□ 1993

Lowest quintile: $5,000 / $4,475
Second quintile: $21,966 / $21,308
Third quintile: $35,949 / $32,429
Fourth quintile: $52,860 / $52,664
Highest quintile: $116,232 / $125,337

SOURCE: Michael E. Davern and Patricia J. Fisher, "Figure 4. Median Net Worth of Households by Monthly Household Income Quintile Groups: 1993 and 1995," in *Household Net Worth and Asset Ownership,* Current Population Reports P70-71, U.S. Census Bureau, Washington, DC, February 2001

most likely to be poor (16.2 percent), followed by those ages 18 to 24 (14.4 percent). African Americans (22.1 percent) and Hispanics (21.2 percent) were almost three times as likely to have ratios below 1.00 as were non-Hispanic whites (7.5 percent). (See Table 3.4 in Chapter 3.) This represents an improvement over 1998, when 8.2 percent of non-Hispanic whites, 26.1 percent of African Americans, and 25.6 percent of Hispanics had ratios below 1.00.

Almost 17 percent of families with children under six years of age had income-to-poverty ratios below 1.00, driven by the large number of female-headed households, which typically have lower incomes. In addition, 21.6 percent of all single females had ratios below the poverty threshold. (See Table 3.4 in Chapter 3.)

Of the total population, 4.5 percent (12.3 million people) had an income classified as "near-poor," between 100 and 125 percent of the poverty threshold. (In Table 3.4 in Chapter 3, the right-hand column labeled "Under 1.25" includes all those with an income-to-poverty ratio of less than 1.25. Consequently, this figure includes both poor and near-poor. To calculate the figures on only the near-poor, figures in the middle column, "Under 1.00," must be subtracted from figures in the column "Under 1.25.") Eighteen percent of the 12.3 million "near-poor" were 65 years old or older.

NET WORTH OF HOUSEHOLDS

Income is one measure of a household's economic well-being; another measure is net worth, that is, the value of assets (what a person owns) minus any debts (what a person owes). In the publication *Household Net Worth and Asset Ownership, 1995* (Michael E. Davern and Patricia J. Fisher, Washington, D.C., 2001), the Census Bureau reported on the net worth of U.S. households. It reported that the 1995 median net worth of households was $40,200, up 1.5 percent from $39,590 in 1993 (in 1995 dollars). (See Figure 4.1.) Unless otherwise indicated, all figures include a household's equity in their house. The Census Bureau cautions that these figures might be somewhat low because the financial holdings of certain types of wealth tend to be underreported, and a large amount of wealth is concentrated in the hands of a very few people who are underrepresented in the survey.

As was the case with income, the highest quintile (the upper one-fifth) controlled the most wealth (50.1 percent) in 1995. While the median net worth of the lowest quintile was only $5,000, the median net worth of the highest quintile was $116,232. (See Figure 4.1.)

Race and Hispanic Origin

The Census Bureau found huge disparities in net worth among the various sectors of society. The overall median net worth of a white household ($49,030) was almost seven times that of an African American household ($7,073) or a Hispanic household ($7,255). However, overall net worth increased significantly for African American and Hispanic households between 1993 and 1995, in constant 1995 dollars. (See Table 4.4.) For white households, the increase was only 1.8 percent; for African Americans and Hispanics, the increases were 52 percent and 47.9 percent, respectively.

In 1995 the highest quintile among whites had a median worth of $123,781, while among African Americans, the median net worth of the highest one-fifth was only $40,866. Among Hispanics, the median net worth of the highest quintile was $80,416. In the lowest quintile, the median net worth of whites was $9,072, while for African Americans it was only $1,500, and $1,250 for Hispanics. (See Table 4.4.)

Age and Household Type

As householders age, they have greater opportunity to accumulate wealth. In 1995 net worth increased with age through age 69 and then dropped. (See Figure 4.2.) Households headed by married couples were worth considerably more in 1995 ($64,694) than were households headed by single men ($16,346) or women ($14,949). As expected, younger persons, many of whom are starting their working careers, tend to have lower net worth than older, more established persons. (See Table 4.5.)

TABLE 4.4

Median net worth and median net worth excluding home equity of households, by selected characteristics, 1993 and 1995

[Excludes group quarters]

Monthly household income quintile[1]	Total		White		Black		Hispanic origin[2]	
	1995	1993 (in 1995 dollars)	1995	1993 (in 1995 dollars)	1995	1993 (in 1995 dollars)	1995	1993 (in 1995 dollars)
All households (thousands)	99,088	96,468	84,224	82,190	11,719	11,248	8,161	7,403
Median net worth (dollars)	40,200	39,590	49,030	48,177	7,073	4,653	7,255	4,904
Excluding home equity	11,773	(NA)	14,398	(NA)	2,657	(NA)	2,900	(NA)
Net Worth by Income								
Lowest quintile								
Households (thousands)	19,838	19,327	15,085	14,662	4,077	4,066	2,416	2,272
Median net worth (dollars)	5,000	4,475	9,720	8,010	1,500	263	1,250	526
Excluding home equity	2,099	(NA)	3,000	(NA)	200	(NA)	500	(NA)
Second quintile								
Households (thousands)	19,812	19,306	16,742	16,162	2,617	2,663	1,979	1,760
Median net worth (dollars)	21,966	21,308	26,534	28,499	3,998	3,587	3,898	3,055
Excluding home equity	5,654	(NA)	7,359	(NA)	2,250	(NA)	1,700	(NA)
Third quintile								
Households (thousands)	19,811	19,279	17,066	16,591	2,164	2,126	1,564	1,437
Median net worth (dollars)	35,949	32,429	42,123	38,278	11,623	8,932	10,377	6,649
Excluding home equity	11,248	(NA)	12,837	(NA)	4,333	(NA)	4,181	(NA)
Fourth quintile								
Households (thousands)	19,812	19,304	17,489	17,218	1,684	1,454	1,416	1,115
Median net worth (dollars)	52,860	52,664	57,445	56,920	27,275	21,850	19,424	21,171
Excluding home equity	17,198	(NA)	19,225	(NA)	7,500	(NA)	6,823	(NA)
Highest quintile								
Households (thousands)	19,814	19,252	17,843	17,558	1,176	937	784	819
Median net worth (dollars)	116,232	125,337	123,781	129,923	40,866	47,422	80,416	58,903
Excluding home equity	42,523	(NA)	46,773	(NA)	14,672	(NA)	21,497	(NA)

(NA) Not available.

[1]Quintile upper limits for 1995 were: lowest quintile–$1,096; second quintile–$2,022; third quintile–$3,109; fourth quintile–$4,844. Upper limits for 1993 were: lowest quintile–$1,128; second quintile–$2,068; third quintile–$3,155; fourth quintile–$4,882.

[2]People of Hispanic origin may be of any race.

SOURCE: Michael E. Davern and Patricia J. Fisher, "Table G. Household Net Worth and Median Net Worth Excluding Home Equity of Households, by Monthly Household Income Quintile and Race and Hispanic Origin of Householder: 1993 and 1995," in *Household Net Worth and Asset Ownership,* Current Population Reports P70-71, U.S. Census Bureau, Washington, DC, February 2001

Type of Assets

In its 1993 and 1995 surveys, the Census Bureau asked respondents what type of financial assets they owned. The researchers found that in 1995, 69.1 percent of Americans had some type of interest-bearing account at a financial institution, while 7.7 percent owned other interest-bearing assets. Almost two-thirds (64.3 percent) had equity in their own homes, which represented the largest single asset held by most age groups. An overwhelming majority (89.2 percent) owned their own vehicles. About 1 in 5 (20.8 percent) held either stocks or mutual fund shares (which are usually invested in stocks), almost 1 in 4 (24.1 percent) had an IRA or Keogh account for retirement, and 1 in 10 (10.3 percent) held equity in his or her own business or profession. (See Table 4.6.)

Households with considerable net worth can generally offer their members greater opportunities. Householders with high net worth are better able to send their children to college, to travel, to help their children out as they get started in life, to buy the things they want, and to feel more secure. Considerable net worth can buy political influence and power, or at least present the opportunity to meet those who have that power. Net worth is a major factor determining a household's position and power in American society.

However, those with the fewest assets and net worth have the least to fall back on if they become ill or lose a job. They are the least able to help their children financially get started in life. In addition, they are the least likely to have political power. These are the Americans most likely to fall into poverty if misfortune strikes.

ENTERING AND LEAVING POVERTY

For most poor Americans, poverty is not a static condition. Some people near the poverty level improve their economic status within two years or less, while others at near-poverty levels become poor through economic catastrophes, such as illness or job loss. The Census Bureau collects annual poverty data in its *Current Population Surveys* (CPS). These surveys, however, do not reflect the dynamic nature of poverty for individual persons and families.

FIGURE 4.2

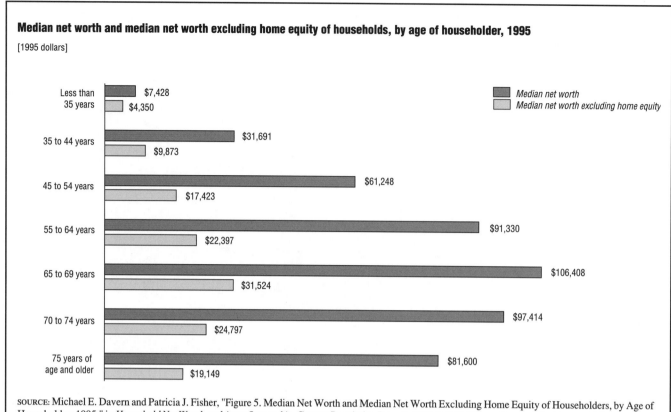

Median net worth and median net worth excluding home equity of households, by age of householder, 1995

[1995 dollars]

SOURCE: Michael E. Davern and Patricia J. Fisher, "Figure 5. Median Net Worth and Median Net Worth Excluding Home Equity of Householders, by Age of Householder: 1995," in *Household Net Worth and Asset Ownership,* Current Population Reports P70-71, U.S. Census Bureau, Washington, DC, February 2001

TABLE 4.5

Median net worth and median net worth excluding home equity of households, by type of household and age of householder, 1993 and 1995

[Excludes group quarters]

Type of household by age of householder	Number of households (thousands)	Median net worth (dollars)		Number of households (thousands)	Median net worth (in 1995 dollars)	
		Total	Excluding equity in own home		Total	Excluding equity in own home
		1995			**1993**	
Married-couple households	54,685	64,694	19,010	52,891	65,204	17,960
Less than 35 years	11,753	14,299	7,700	12,141	13,631	5,980
35 to 54 years	25,949	63,107	18,973	23,983	65,171	18,365
55 to 64 years	7,495	126,725	41,248	7,568	134,560	45,863
65 years and over	9,487	138,249	47,741	9,199	136,706	46,776
Male householders	16,044	16,346	7,375	15,397	14,219	5,432
Less than 35 years	5,402	5,425	4,311	5,285	4,529	3,044
35 to 54 years	6,336	22,150	7,899	6,157	19,408	6,484
55 to 64 years	1,539	39,045	9,849	1,437	47,050	11,486
65 years and over	2,767	67,697	15,374	2,518	63,978	13,616
Female householders	28,359	14,949	4,400	28,180	14,002	3,542
Less than 35 years	6,937	2,580	1,850	6,935	1,414	832
35 to 54 years	8,869	11,233	3,948	8,908	8,853	2,793
55 to 64 years	3,305	44,400	6,849	3,286	47,147	6,820
65 years and over	9,248	61,549	11,100	9,050	60,753	10,069

SOURCE: Michael E. Davern and Patricia J. Fisher, "Table I. Median Net Worth and Median Net Worth Excluding Home Equity of Householders, by Type of Household and Age of Householder: 1993 and 1995," in *Household Net Worth and Asset Ownership,* Current Population Reports P70-71, U.S. Census Bureau, Washington, DC, February 2001

TABLE 4.6

Asset ownership rates for households and median value of the holdings, by selected asset types, 1993 and 1995

[Excludes group quarters]

Monthly household income quintile[1]	Interest-earning assets at financial institutions	Other interest-earning assets	Stocks and mutual fund shares	Equity in own home	Equity in motor vehicles	Equity in own business or profession	IRA or Keogh accounts
Percent of Households Owning Assets							
1995							
Total	**69.1**	**7.7**	**20.8**	**64.3**	**89.2**	**10.3**	**24.1**
Lowest quintile	40.5	2.2	5.6	41.4	68.6	5.0	6.2
Second quintile	61.3	4.4	12.3	56.3	88.6	7.2	14.3
Third quintile	72.7	7.1	18.5	64.3	94.9	9.7	21.9
Fourth quintile	81.0	8.9	24.8	74.2	96.8	12.2	29.9
Highest quintile	90.2	15.9	42.6	85.1	97.3	17.5	48.3
1993							
Total	**71.1**	**8.6**	**20.9**	**64.3**	**85.7**	**10.8**	**23.1**
Lowest quintile	42.2	2.6	4.4	41.5	58.2	6.1	5.4
Second quintile	62.9	5.1	11.6	55.9	85.1	7.5	14.0
Third quintile	73.7	7.3	18.1	63.4	93.1	9.6	20.5
Fourth quintile	84.6	9.1	26.0	74.8	95.8	11.6	28.3
Highest quintile	92.2	19.1	44.3	86.0	96.4	19.4	47.1
Median Value of Holdings for Asset Owners							
1995 (dollars)							
Total	**2,537**	**15,000**	**9,000**	**50,000**	**6,675**	**8,000**	**15,000**
Lowest quintile	1,499	6,145	6,120	40,000	3,000	4,000	12,000
Second quintile	1,999	15,999	7,000	45,000	3,800	5,000	12,000
Third quintile	2,000	14,999	7,464	49,000	6,198	5,000	13,000
Fourth quintile	2,400	14,248	7,464	45,789	8,663	7,500	13,100
Highest quintile	5,000	16,349	11,000	65,061	12,975	15,000	17,800
1993 (in 1995 dollars)							
Total	**3,159**	**13,691**	**7,331**	**49,156**	**5,414**	**7,373**	**13,677**
Lowest quintile	1,679	10,532	3,476	41,015	1,745	996	10,533
Second quintile	2,106	13,692	5,178	43,156	3,526	2,086	11,586
Third quintile	2,104	13,165	4,898	45,274	4,871	5,056	10,006
Fourth quintile	2,893	10,532	6,214	44,080	6,837	10,006	12,429
Highest quintile	6,319	15,798	10,524	69,589	10,425	17,985	16,958

[1]Quintile upper limits for 1995 were: lowest quintile–$1,096; second quintile–$2,002; third quintile–$3,109; fourth quintile–$4,844. Upper limits for 1993 were: lowest quintile–$1,128; second quintile–$2,068; third quintile–$3,155; fourth quintile–$4,882.

SOURCE: Michael E. Davern and Patricia J. Fisher, "Table C. Asset Ownership Rates for Households and Median Value of the Holdings, by Monthly Household Income Quintile, for Selected Asset Types: 1993 and 1995," in *Household Net Worth and Asset Ownership,* Current Population Reports P70-71, U.S. Census Bureau, Washington, DC, February 2001

In its *Survey of Income and Program Participation* (SIPP), the Census Bureau gathered longitudinal information (measurements over time for specific individuals or families) in order to examine poverty over a 24-month period. This makes it possible to measure the movement of individuals and families into and out of poverty (entry and exit rates) and the duration of poverty spells (the number of months in poverty for those who were not poor during the first interview month, but who became poor at some point in the study). The study defined entry rates into poverty as the percentage of people who were not poor during 1993 but who were poor in 1994. Exit rates from poverty were defined as the percentage of people who were poor during 1993 but who were not poor in 1994.

Data from the 1993–95 SIPP survey are the most current data available and are now being used as a baseline to examine the impact of welfare reform. The 1996 welfare reform act (PRWORA) directed the Census Bureau to examine changes following the elimination of the Aid to Families with Dependent Children (AFDC) program and its replacement with TANF (Temporary Assistance for Needy Families). During a six-year period (1996 through 2001), the Census Bureau interviewed a sample of households that participated in the SIPP surveys from 1992 to 1994. Once the survey results are tabulated, this information will provide information on the effect of the new law upon the socioeconomic status of persons participating in public assistance programs.

In "Dynamics of Economic Wellbeing, Poverty 1993–94: Trap Door? Revolving Door? Or Both?" (*Current Population Reports*, July 1998), Mary Naifeh of the Census Bureau studied data from the 1993 SIPP panel to

FIGURE 4.3

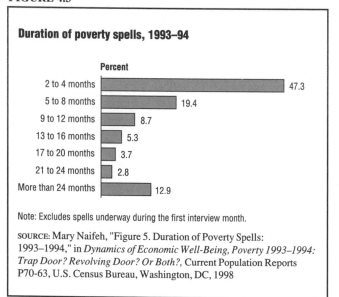

Duration of poverty spells, 1993–94

Percent

2 to 4 months	47.3
5 to 8 months	19.4
9 to 12 months	8.7
13 to 16 months	5.3
17 to 20 months	3.7
21 to 24 months	2.8
More than 24 months	12.9

Note: Excludes spells underway during the first interview month.

SOURCE: Mary Naifeh, "Figure 5. Duration of Poverty Spells: 1993–1994," in *Dynamics of Economic Well-Being, Poverty 1993–1994: Trap Door? Revolving Door? Or Both?,* Current Population Reports P70-63, U.S. Census Bureau, Washington, DC, 1998

FIGURE 4.4

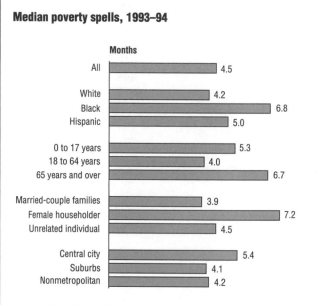

Median poverty spells, 1993–94

Months

All	4.5
White	4.2
Black	6.8
Hispanic	5.0
0 to 17 years	5.3
18 to 64 years	4.0
65 years and over	6.7
Married-couple families	3.9
Female householder	7.2
Unrelated individual	4.5
Central city	5.4
Suburbs	4.1
Nonmetropolitan	4.2

SOURCE: Mary Naifeh, "Figure 6. Median Poverty Spells: 1993–1994," in *Dynamics of Economic Well-Being, Poverty 1993–94: Trap Door? Revolving Door? Or Both?,* Current Population Reports P70-63, U.S. Census Bureau, Washington, DC, 1998

examine poverty in the period from October 1992 through December 1995. She focused on monthly measures of poverty, distinguishing between short- and long-term poverty. Some highlights of the survey include:

• The average annual monthly poverty rate in 1994 was 15.4 percent, representing about 10 million people, and not significantly different from the rate in 1993.

• More than one in five persons (21.4 percent) were poor at least two months in 1994.

• Some 5.3 percent of the population were chronically poor. That is, they were poor during all 24 months of 1993 and 1994.

• About 7.6 million persons who were poor in 1993 were not poor in 1994.

• Nonelderly adults were more likely to exit poverty than children and the elderly.

• Children had the highest entry rates into poverty and, along with retirement-age adults, had a low exit rate.

• Half of all poverty spells lasted 4.5 months or longer.

Spells of poverty reported from 1993 through 1994 lasted for varying lengths of time. Almost half (47.3 percent) lasted from 2 to 4 months, while 12.9 percent lasted more than 24 months. (See Figure 4.3.) African Americans (with a median poverty spell duration of 6.8 months) and Hispanics (with a median of 5 months) had longer poverty spells than whites (4.2 months). For the elderly, the median poverty spell lasted 6.7 months. The shortest poverty spells were for families headed by married couples (3.9 months). The longest spells were for female heads of households (7.2 months). (See Figure 4.4.)

More than 5 percent of the population were poor all 24 months of 1993 and 1994. African Americans (14.1 percent) and Hispanics (13.5 percent) were significantly more likely to be chronically poor (poor for a longer duration or more frequently recurring poverty) than whites (3.8 percent). Almost 18 percent of people in female-householder families were poor continuously for 24 months. (See Figure 4.5.)

Characteristics of Those Changing Their Poverty Status

Based on the SIPP interviews, 40 million people were poor in both 1993 and 1994. Between 1993 and 1994, the number of people who exited poverty (7.6 million) was similar to the number of people who entered poverty (6.9 million).

RACE AND AGE. Of the poor in 1993, whites (27.4 percent) were more likely to leave poverty in 1994 than either African Americans (17.7 percent) or Hispanics (23.6 percent). (See Figure 4.6.) Figure 4.7 shows the newly poor as a percent of the population that was not poor in 1993. Whites were less likely to enter poverty in 1994 than African Americans or Hispanics.

The elderly (often on fixed incomes) and children were less likely to exit poverty than were persons of other ages. Only 14.9 percent of the elderly and 20.1 percent of children under 18 years of age who were poor in 1993 were able to escape poverty in 1994. Adults 18 to 64 years of age were the most likely to escape—28.8 percent moved out of poverty. (See Figure 4.6.) However, only 2 percent of the

FIGURE 4.5

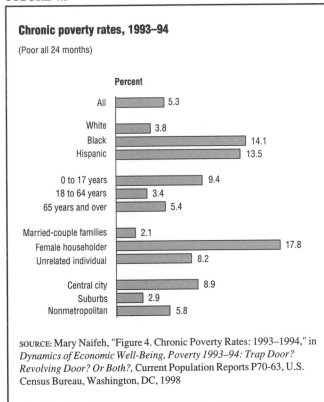

Chronic poverty rates, 1993–94

(Poor all 24 months)

SOURCE: Mary Naifeh, "Figure 4. Chronic Poverty Rates: 1993–1994," in *Dynamics of Economic Well-Being, Poverty 1993–94: Trap Door? Revolving Door? Or Both?,* Current Population Reports P70-63, U.S. Census Bureau, Washington, DC, 1998

FIGURE 4.6

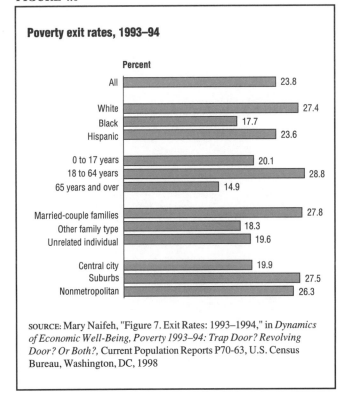

Poverty exit rates, 1993–94

SOURCE: Mary Naifeh, "Figure 7. Exit Rates: 1993–1994," in *Dynamics of Economic Well-Being, Poverty 1993–94: Trap Door? Revolving Door? Or Both?,* Current Population Reports P70-63, U.S. Census Bureau, Washington, DC, 1998

elderly entered poverty in 1994, compared to 4.4 percent of children under 18 years of age. (See Figure 4.7.)

FAMILY STATUS. Families headed by married couples were much more likely than other family types to leave poverty in 1994. Of the poor families headed by married couples in 1993, 27.8 percent were able to escape poverty during 1994. Only 18.3 percent of the poor families of other types recovered from poverty in 1994. (See Figure 4.6.) Families headed by married couples were also significantly less likely to enter poverty in 1994. (See Figure 4.7.) With at least two adults in the household, a family headed by a married couple is more likely to have at least one person working than a family headed by a single person.

FIGURE 4.7

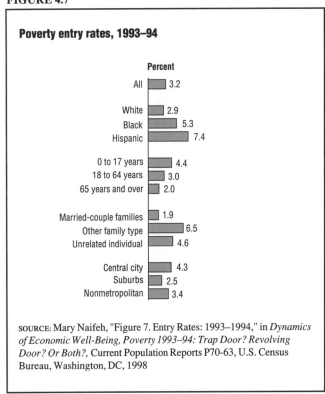

Poverty entry rates, 1993–94

SOURCE: Mary Naifeh, "Figure 7. Entry Rates: 1993–1994," in *Dynamics of Economic Well-Being, Poverty 1993–94: Trap Door? Revolving Door? Or Both?,* Current Population Reports P70-63, U.S. Census Bureau, Washington, DC, 1998

CHAPTER 5

FACTORS AFFECTING POVERTY AND WELFARE USE

Poverty is the largest single factor that drives people to apply for governmental assistance, commonly called "welfare." Many researchers agree that the major factors that create poverty are family size, family background, low educational achievement, unemployment (or under-employment, such as part-time workers who want to work full-time), low earnings, and the prevailing economic conditions in the labor market.

Children are the poorest group in America, having replaced the elderly in 1974. The major reason for the decline in elderly poverty rates was social insurance benefits, nearly all of which come from Social Security. In 2000, 16.2 percent of all children lived in families with incomes below the poverty level. (See Figure 3.2 in Chapter 3.) Changes in household and family composition, particularly the increase in the number of single-parent families, have contributed to high poverty rates, especially the high rate of child poverty. In 2000 almost half (45 percent) of children under the age of three who lived in female-headed families were poor, compared to 9 percent of children under three in families headed by married couples.

ASSISTANCE FROM THE GOVERNMENT

Women and children are most affected by poverty. The two largest cash assistance programs for families with children have been Temporary Assistance for Needy Families (TANF), which replaced Aid to Families with Dependent Children, or AFDC, under the 1996 welfare reform law and the Earned Income Tax Credit (EITC). States currently provide cash assistance from their TANF block grants to families that meet the work requirements (mandatory after two years on assistance) and who have not exceeded the five-year limit for assistance. The EITC is available to needy working households, and most of it goes to families with children.

Other cash and noncash programs targeted at helping women, children, and the elderly include Supplemental Security Income (SSI), the Low Income Home Energy Assistance Program (LIHEAP), Medicaid, the Food Stamp Program, the National School Lunch Program, the Child Care Food Program, the School Breakfast Program, the Summer Food Service Program, and Supplemental Food for Women, Infants, and Children (WIC).

Many poor families do not qualify for welfare benefits because of their income or resources. Most of these families are more likely to receive income from social insurance programs such as Social Security (benefits for children whose parents are dead, retired, or disabled) and unemployment compensation. Even though Social Security benefits are not means-tested, they help reduce the child poverty rate.

Poor Families More Likely to Need Government Assistance

In its 2001 report to Congress, *Indicators of Welfare Dependency,* the U.S. Department of Health and Human Services (HHS) examined dependence on welfare. The HHS found that, as one would expect, poor households relied far more heavily on government assistance to survive than did nonpoor households. In 1998 families with incomes below the poverty line received about half (48 percent) their income from wages or salaries, compared to 85 percent of nonpoor families. Poor families received one-third (32 percent) of their income from means-tested public assistance programs, including AFDC/TANF, SSI, and food stamps, compared to less than 1 percent of nonpoor families. (See Figure 5.1.) Means-tested benefits accounted for 37.7 percent of the income of poor families with children age five or under in 1998.

FAMILY STRUCTURE OF WELFARE RECIPIENTS

Single-Parent Families

An increasing number of children are being raised by one parent, usually the mother. The proportion of single-

FIGURE 5.1

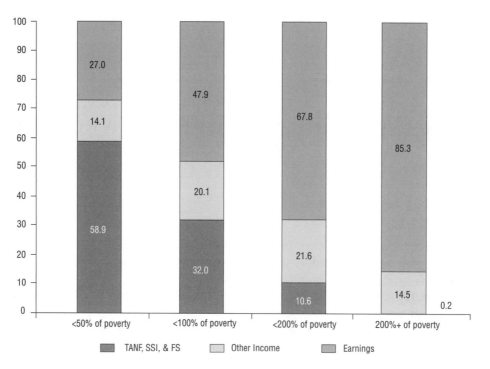

Percentage of total income from various sources, by poverty status, 1998

SOURCE: "Figure IND 1b. Percentage of Total Income from Various Sources, by Poverty Status: 1998," in *Indicators of Welfare Dependence, Annual Report to Congress, March 2001*, U.S. Department of Health and Human Services, Washington, DC, 2001

parent families grew rapidly between 1970 and 1990, while the proportion dropped for families headed by married couples. Since then the structure of American households and families has remained relatively stable. In 2000, 76.8 percent of all family households were families headed by married couples, down from 82.5 percent in 1980 and 87 percent in 1970. Meanwhile, the proportion of single-parent families headed by males rose from 2.4 percent in 1970 to 2.9 percent in 1980 and 5.6 percent in 2000. (See Table 5.1.)

The proportion of single-parent families headed by females grew from 11 percent in 1970 to 15 percent in 1980 and to 17.6 percent in 2000. (See Table 5.1.) Single-parent families, especially single-parent families headed by women, usually earn much less than families headed by married couples.

The increase in the number of single-parent families was most dramatic among African Americans and Hispanics and less so among whites. From 1970 to 2000, the proportion of white families headed by married couples declined from 89 percent to 81 percent. During the same period, the proportion of white single-parent families headed by males rose from 2.2 to 5.1 percent, and the proportion of white single-parent families headed by females grew from 9 to 13.9 percent. (See Table 5.1.)

Among Hispanics, the proportion of families headed by married couples dropped from 81 percent in 1970 to 67.9 percent in 2000, while the proportion of single-parent families headed by males rose from 4 to 8.7 percent, and the percentage of single-parent families headed by females increased from 15 to 23.4 percent. (See Table 5.1.)

The largest increase in the proportion of single-parent families occurred among African Americans. While the proportion of families headed by married couples fell from 68 percent in 1970 to less than half (47.8 percent) in 2000, the proportion of single-parent families headed by men grew from 4 to 8.1 percent, and the percentage headed by women increased from 28 percent to 44 percent of African American families. (See Table 5.1.)

Families with Children

Single parents make up an even larger proportion of families with children under 18 years of age. In 2000, 27 percent of families with minor children were single-parent families. Two-parent families made up 73 percent of all family groups with children, down from 87.1 percent in 1970 and 78.5 percent in 1980. Meanwhile, the proportion of families with children headed by men rose from 1.3 percent in 1970 and 2.1 percent in 1980 to 5.2 percent in 2000. Similarly, the proportion of families with

TABLE 5.1

Households by type and selected characteristics, March 2000

(In thousands, except average size)

Characteristic	All households	Family households Total	Married couple	Other families Male householder	Female householder	Nonfamily households Total	Male householder	Female householder
All households	104,705	72,025	55,311	4,028	12,687	32,680	14,641	18,039
Age of householder								
15 to 24 years old	5,860	3,353	1,450	560	1,342	2,507	1,286	1,221
25 to 34 years old	18,627	13,007	9,390	886	2,732	5,620	3,448	2,172
35 to 44 years old	23,955	18,706	14,104	1,102	3,499	5,250	3,261	1,989
45 to 54 years old	20,927	15,803	12,792	713	2,299	5,123	2,583	2,541
55 to 64 years old	13,592	9,569	8,138	351	1,080	4,023	1,533	2,490
65 years old and over	21,744	11,587	9,437	416	1,735	10,157	2,530	7,626
Race and ethnicity of householder								
White	87,671	60,251	48,790	3,081	8,380	27,420	12,204	15,215
Non-Hispanic	78,819	53,066	43,865	2,468	6,732	25,753	11,278	14,475
Black	12,849	8,664	4,144	706	3,814	4,185	1,876	2,309
Asian and Pacific Islander	3,337	2,506	1,996	179	331	831	432	399
Hispanic (of any race)	9,319	7,561	5,133	658	1,769	1,758	974	783
Presence of related children under 18								
No related children	67,350	34,670	28,919	1,826	3,924	32,680	14,641	18,039
With related children	37,355	37,355	26,392	2,202	8,762	(X)	(X)	(X)
One related child under 18	15,493	15,493	9,897	1,321	4,275	(X)	(X)	(X)
Two related children under 18	14,020	14,020	10,567	644	2,809	(X)	(X)	(X)
Three related children under 18	5,510	5,510	4,238	185	1,087	(X)	(X)	(X)
Four or more related children under 18	2,332	2,332	1,690	52	591	(X)	(X)	(X)
Presence of own children under 18								
No own children	70,100	37,420	30,062	2,242	5,116	32,680	14,641	18,039
With own children	34,605	34,605	25,248	1,786	7,571	(X)	(X)	(X)
With own children under 1	2,939	2,939	2,264	174	501	(X)	(X)	(X)
With own children under 3	8,786	8,786	6,784	441	1,561	(X)	(X)	(X)
With own children under 6	14,986	14,986	11,393	706	2,887	(X)	(X)	(X)
With own children under 12	25,885	25,885	19,082	1,235	5,568	(X)	(X)	(X)
Size of households								
1 person	26,724	(X)	(X)	(X)	(X)	26,724	11,181	15,543
2 people	34,666	29,834	22,899	1,730	5,206	4,832	2,607	2,225
3 people	17,152	16,405	11,213	1,106	4,086	746	570	177
4 people	15,309	15,064	12,455	682	1,927	245	179	66
5 people	6,981	6,894	5,723	307	864	87	70	17
6 people	2,445	2,413	1,916	130	366	32	26	6
7 or more	1,428	1,415	1,105	73	237	13	8	5
Average size	2.62	3.24	3.26	3.16	3.17	1.25	1.34	1.17

X Not applicable.
Note: Data are not shown separately for the American Indian and Alaska Native population because of the small sample size in the Current Population Survey in March 2000.

SOURCE: Jason Fields and Lynne M. Casper, "Table 1. Households by Type and Selected Characteristics: March 2000," in *America's Families and Living Arrangements,* Current Population Reports P20-537, U.S. Census Bureau, Washington, DC, June 2001

children headed by women rose from 11.5 percent in 1970 to 21.9 percent in 2000. (See Table 5.1.)

BY RACE. Table 5.2 shows the living arrangements of children by race for selected years from 1980 to 1998. African American children are far more likely to live with a single parent than are white or Hispanic children. In 1998 a majority of African American children (55 percent) lived in a single-parent family, 51 percent living with the mother only. About one-third (31 percent) of Hispanic children lived with one parent; 64 percent lived in two-parent families. Twenty-three percent of white children lived with one parent, while 74 percent lived with two parents.

In 1998 a higher percentage of African American children (9 percent) than whites (3 percent) and Hispanics (5 percent) lived with neither parent. In part, this is because African American children are more likely to live with grandparents without the presence of either parent. (See Table 5.2.)

DIVORCE

The divorce rate in the United States has risen markedly in every decade since the 1950s, although at a somewhat lower rate in the 1990s. In 1985 almost one-quarter of those living in the United States who had ever been married had also been divorced at one time or another. Divorce is a

TABLE 5.2

Children under 18 years old by presence of parents, 1980–98

[As of March (63,427 represents 63,427,000). Excludes persons under 18 years old who maintained households or family groups.]

Race, Hispanic origin, and year	Number (1,000)	Both parents	Percent living with—					Father only	Neither parent
			Mother only						
			Total	Divorced	Married, spouse absent	Never married	Widowed		
ALL RACES [1]									
1980	63,427	77	18	8	6	3	2	2	4
1985	62,475	74	21	9	5	6	2	3	3
1990	64,137	73	22	8	5	7	2	3	3
1995	70,254	69	23	9	6	8	1	4	4
1998	71,377	68	23	8	5	9	1	4	4
WHITE									
1980	52,242	83	14	7	4	1	2	2	2
1985	50,836	80	16	8	4	2	1	2	2
1990	51,390	79	16	8	4	3	1	3	2
1995	55,327	76	18	8	5	4	1	3	3
1998	56,124	74	18	8	4	5	1	5	3
BLACK									
1980	9,375	42	44	11	16	13	4	2	12
1985	9,479	40	51	11	12	25	3	3	7
1990	10,018	38	51	10	12	27	2	4	8
1995	11,301	33	52	11	11	29	2	4	11
1998	11,414	36	51	9	9	32	1	4	9
HISPANIC [2]									
1980	5,459	75	20	6	8	4	2	2	4
1985	6,057	68	27	7	11	7	2	2	3
1990	7,174	67	27	7	10	8	2	3	3
1995	9,843	63	28	8	9	10	1	4	4
1998	10,863	64	27	6	8	12	1	4	5

[1] Includes other races not shown separately.
[2] Hispanic persons may be of any race.

SOURCE: "No. 69. Children Under 18 Years Old by Presence of Parents: 1980 to 1998," in *Statistical Abstract of the United States: 2000,* U.S. Census Bureau, Washington, DC, 2000.

---

major factor in why women receive welfare, as divorced women are seldom as well off financially as they were when they were married. The fact that divorced women are more likely than men to receive custody of their children adds an additional financial burden. In 1997 some 85 percent of custodial parents were female. (See Table 5.3.)

According to U.S. Census Bureau data, by 2000 the number of people who had been divorced more than quadrupled from 1970, from 4.3 million to 19.9 million. This translated to 9.3 percent of the total U.S. adult population, compared to 3.2 percent in 1970. Further, there were more single women then men because men are more likely to marry after divorce. Figure 5.2 shows the percentages of married, never married, separated/divorced, and widowed men and women each decade from 1970 to 2000.

NEVER-MARRIED ADULTS

The number of adults age 18 or older who had never married rose from 24.9 percent in 1970 to 28.1 percent in 2000. The proportion of the never-married has increased as young adults delay the age at which they marry for the first time. (See Figure 5.2.)

Single-parent women are more likely to never have been married (43 percent) than single-parent men (34 percent). In 2000, 47.4 percent of African American mothers, 16 percent of Hispanic mothers, and 34 percent of non-Hispanic white mothers with children under age 18 had never been married. In addition to a growing trend away from marriage, these percentages could also be explained by marriages following the birth of the first child.

CHILD SUPPORT

In 1997, 22.9 million children under the age of 21 lived with a custodial parent. Most of these children lived with their mother. Of the 14 million custodial parents in 1997, about 11.9 million, or 85 percent, were women, according to the U.S. Census Bureau. (See Table 5.3.)

Child support is becoming an increasingly important source of income for women with the growing number of families headed by women, coupled with the time limits now in place for receiving cash assistance. About 59.5 percent of custodial mothers and 38.2 percent of custodial fathers were awarded child support in 1997. (See Table 5.3.) In that same year, more than 7.8 million custodial

TABLE 5.3

Child support payments agreed to or awarded custodial parents, 1997

(Numbers in thousands, spring 1998. Parents living with own children under 21 years of age whose other parent is not living in the home)

		Child support agreed to or awarded							Child support not awarded	
		Supposed to receive child support payments in 1997								
			Received payments in 1997				Received no payments in 1997			
Characteristic	Number	Number	Number	Number	Average child support	Average total money income	Number	Average total money income	Number	Average total money income
ALL CUSTODIAL PARENTS										
Total	13,987	7,876	7,006	4,720	$3,622	$24,741	2,286	$18,370	6,111	$19,925
Standard error	304	231	218	180	$108	$693	125	$709	204	$560
Custodial mothers	11,905	7,080	6,331	4,335	$3,655	$23,249	1,996	$16,659	4,825	$15,643
Standard error	281	219	207	172	$114	$622	117	$729	181	$425
Custodial fathers	2,082	796	674	385	$3,251	$41,529	289	$30,179	1,286	$35,986
Standard error	120	74	68	52	$304	$4,522	45	$2,058	94	$1,927
Poverty Status in 1997										
Family income below poverty level	4,038	2,101	1,794	978	$2,317	$7,222	816	$6,336	1,937	$5,673
Standard error	166	120	111	82	$152	$254	75	$281	116	$173
Visitation and Joint Custody Arrangements With Non-custodial Parents in 1997										
Visitation privileges only	7,630	4,736	4,301	3,014	$3,406	$23,085	1,287	$18,828	2,894	$19,077
Joint custody only[1]	77	40	35	11	(B)	(B)	23	$26,559	37	$38,259
Visitation and joint custody	2,680	1,795	1,567	1,303	$4,546	$30,094	264	$26,918	885	$37,697
Neither	3,601	1,305	1,103	392	$2,191	$20,249	711	$14,098	2,295	$13,846
CUSTODIAL MOTHERS										
Race and Hispanic Origin										
White	8,264	5,307	4,752	3,475	$3,886	$24,098	1,277	$17,512	2,957	$16,771
Non-Hispanic	6,673	4,559	4,109	3,076	$3,996	$25,106	1,033	$18,877	2,114	$18,897
Black	3,321	1,607	1,434	764	$2,600	$18,612	670	$14,716	1,714	$13,958
Hispanic (of any race)	1,710	798	688	433	$3,012	$17,023	256	$12,467	912	$11,560
Current Marital Status										
Married	2,607	1,703	1,559	1,174	$3,977	$21,087	385	$18,241	904	$15,592
Divorced	3,673	2,585	2,357	1,738	$4,326	$29,752	619	$23,005	1,087	$21,049
Separated	1,565	880	765	507	$3,547	$20,510	258	$14,828	685	$16,849
Widowed[2]	230	125	104	62	(B)	(B)	42	(B)	106	$21,346
Never married	3,831	1,788	1,547	855	$1,966	$13,769	692	$10,771	2,043	$12,088
Educational Attainment										
Less than high school diploma	2,385	1,132	976	536	$2,127	$10,131	440	$6,791	1,253	$8,167
High school graduate	4,399	2,608	2,336	1,513	$3,398	$19,413	823	$15,002	1,791	$13,805
Some college, no degree	2,624	1,626	1,476	1,041	$3,615	$21,520	435	$18,138	998	$18,159
Associate degree	1,043	728	653	515	$3,733	$25,607	138	$24,743	315	$19,109
Bachelors degree or more	1,454	987	891	730	$5,312	$41,656	161	$41,183	467	$35,035

B Represents base less than 75,000.
[1]Joint custody may be physical, legal, or both. Legal custody does not necessarily include visitation.
[2]Widowed parents have children from a previous marriage that ended in divorce or from a previous nonmarital relationship.

SOURCE: Timothy Grall, "Table B. Child Support Payments Agreed to or Awarded to Custodial Parents: 1997," in *Child Support for Custodial Mothers and Fathers 1997*, Current Population Reports P60-212, U.S. Census Bureau, Washington, DC, October 2000

parents were entitled to receive child support. The other 6.1 million custodial parents did not receive financial support from an ex-partner. Of those custodial parents receiving child support, about 7.2 million had legal agreements established by a court or other government institution. Another 600,000 had some sort of extralegal agreement. (See Figure 5.3.)

According to the U.S. Census Bureau, 67.4 percent of custodial parents who were due child support in 1997 actually received partial or full payment. While the overall proportion of custodial parents who received partial or full payments remained stable from 1993 to 1997, the pro-

portion receiving full payment increased from 34.1 percent in 1993 to 40.9 percent in 1997.

Those Living in Poverty

For the custodial mothers who do receive child support, often it is not enough to keep them and their children out of poverty. According to the U.S. Census Bureau, in 1997 about 29 percent (4 million) of custodial parents had family incomes considered below the poverty level, compared to about 16 percent of all parents. Thirty-two percent (3.8 million) of custodial mothers lived below the poverty threshold. Only 10.7 percent (222,000) of custodial fathers were below

FIGURE 5.2

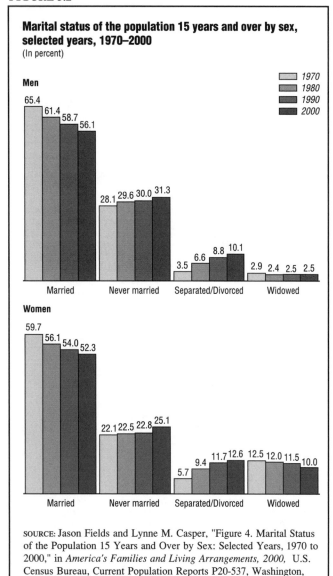

Marital status of the population 15 years and over by sex, selected years, 1970–2000

(In percent)

SOURCE: Jason Fields and Lynne M. Casper, "Figure 4. Marital Status of the Population 15 Years and Over by Sex: Selected Years, 1970 to 2000," in *America's Families and Living Arrangements, 2000*, U.S. Census Bureau, Current Population Reports P20-537, Washington, DC, 2001

FIGURE 5.3

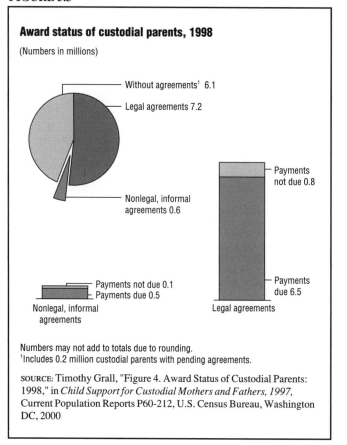

Award status of custodial parents, 1998

(Numbers in millions)

Numbers may not add to totals due to rounding.
[1]Includes 0.2 million custodial parents with pending agreements.

SOURCE: Timothy Grall, "Figure 4. Award Status of Custodial Parents: 1998," in *Child Support for Custodial Mothers and Fathers, 1997*, Current Population Reports P60-212, U.S. Census Bureau, Washington DC, 2000

the poverty threshold during the same period. Almost all (94.5 percent) custodial parents below the poverty line in 1997 were mothers. (See Figure 5.4 and Table 5.4.)

The U.S. Census Bureau reported that approximately 35.7 percent of custodial parents who were due child support, but did not receive it in 1997, were poor. In addition, a similar percentage (31.7 percent) of custodial parents who were not awarded child support at all were considered poor in 1997. Of parents awarded child support, 54.5 percent of poor custodial parents actually received payments in 1997 compared to 67.4 percent of all custodial parents. (See Table 5.4.)

Child Support Received

In 1997 custodial mothers received an average amount of $3,655 in child support for the year. The average amount for custodial fathers was $3,251. (See Table 5.4.)

According to the Census Bureau, the total individual incomes of custodial mothers who actually received child support were 56 percent of the amount received by custodial fathers who received child support ($23,249 versus $41,529). On average, these support payments constituted 15.7 percent of the women's income compared to 7.8 percent of the men's. (See Table 5.3.)

One of the reasons women tend to have lower incomes than men is that fewer women participate in the workforce permanently and full-time. Although about 78.6 percent of custodial mothers who received child support worked in 1997, only 46.9 percent of them worked full-time year-round (compared to 76.9 percent of custodial fathers). And when both custodial mothers and fathers did work full-time year-round, the average income of custodial mothers ($34,356) was considerably less than that of custodial fathers ($54,429) in 1997. The percentage of custodial mothers working increased from 40.9 percent in 1993 to 46.9 percent in 1997.

Socioeconomic Factors

Other socioeconomic factors that prevent custodial mothers from lifting themselves out of poverty were highlighted by the U.S. Census Bureau in 1997. (See Table 5.3.) They included:

TABLE 5.4

Child support—award and recipiency status of custodial parent, 1997

[In thousands except as noted (13,987 represents 13,987,000). Custodial parents 15 years and older with own children under 21 years of age present from absent parents as of spring 1998. Covers civilian noninstitutional population.]

Award and recipiency status	All custodial parents				Custodial parents below the poverty level			
	Total		Mothers	Fathers	Total		Mothers	Fathers
	Number	Percent distribution			Number	Percent distribution		
Total	**13,987**	**(X)**	**11,905**	**2,082**	**4,038**	**(X)**	**3,816**	**222**
With child support agreement or award	7,876	(X)	7,080	796	2,101	(X)	2,021	81
Supposed to receive payments in 1997	7,006	100.0	6,331	674	1,794	100.0	1,723	72
Actually received payments in 1997	4,720	67.4	4,335	385	978	54.5	947	31
Received full amount	2,863	40.9	2,650	213	436	24.3	415	21
Received partial payments	1,857	26.5	1,685	172	542	30.2	532	10
Did not receive payments in 1997	2,286	32.6	1,996	289	816	45.5	776	41
Child support not awarded	6,111	(X)	4,825	1,286	1,937	(X)	1,795	141
MEAN INCOME AND CHILD SUPPORT								
Received child support payments in 1997:								
Mean total money income (dol.)	24,741	(X)	23,249	41,529	7,222	(X)	7,306	(B)
Mean child support received (dol.)	3,622	(X)	3,655	3,251	2,317	(X)	2,290	(B)
Received the full amount due:								
Mean total money income (dol.)	27,533	(X)	25,899	47,815	6,977	(X)	7,226	(B)
Mean child support received (dol.)	4,719	(X)	4,780	3,955	3,646	(X)	3,663	(B)
Received partial payments:								
Mean total money income (dol.)	20,435	(X)	19,083	33,712	7,418	(X)	7,369	(B)
Mean child support received (dol.)	1,931	(X)	1,886	2,375	1,247	(X)	1,217	(B)
Received no payments in 1997:								
Mean total money income (dol.)	18,370	(X)	16,659	30,179	6,336	(X)	6,108	(B)
Without child support agreement or award:								
Mean total money income (dol.)	19,925	(X)	15,643	35,986	5,673	(X)	5,657	(B)

B Base too small to meet statistical standards for reliability.
X Not applicable.

SOURCE: "No. 547. Child Support—Award and Recipiency Status of Custodial Parent: 1997," in *Statistical Abstract of the United States: 2001*, U.S. Census Bureau, Washington, DC, 2001

- Of poor women due child support payments in 1997, 55 percent actually received payments. (See Table 5.4.) For nonpoor women, the receipt rate for due payments was 68.5 percent.

- Some 73.1 percent of white women received child support payments that were due to them in 1997, compared to 53.3 percent of African American women and 62.9 percent of Hispanic women. (See Table 5.3.)

- The percentage of never-married women who received payments in 1997 was much lower (53.3 percent) than that of ever-married women (72.7 percent).

- Women with at least a bachelor's degree were more likely to receive the child support due them (82 percent) than women with less education (66.3 percent).

Government Assistance in Obtaining Child Support

In 1975 Congress established the Child Support Enforcement program to ensure that children had financial support from both parents. Though improvements in paternity establishment and child support collections have followed, much more needs to be done. In 1997 only about 40.9 percent of custodial parents due child support received

FIGURE 5.4

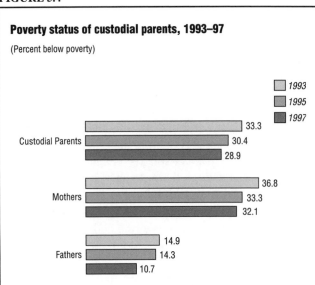

Poverty status of custodial parents, 1993–97

(Percent below poverty)

SOURCE: Timothy Grall, "Figure 2. Poverty Status of Custodial Parents: 1993–1997," in *Child Support for Custodial Mothers and Fathers 1997*, Current Population Reports P60-212, U.S. Census Bureau, Washington, DC, October 2000

TABLE 5.5

Insured unemployment as a percent of total unemployment, by month, 1967–99

Year	Jan.	Feb.	Mar.	Apr.	May	June	July	Aug.	Sept.	Oct.	Nov.	Dec.	Avg.
1967	52	52	54	54	50	30	39	41	33	33	35	47	43
1968	57	50	52	50	45	26	34	38	33	34	38	48	42
1969	54	54	52	48	43	27	35	36	31	33	40	51	41
1970	57	54	52	53	53	36	42	45	42	44	48	53	48
1971	58	58	61	59	56	42	45	48	44	46	47	55	52
1972	56	58	56	52	49	36	41	38	33	34	38	47	45
1973	51	46	46	44	43	31	36	37	34	38	38	48	41
1974	53	54	57	60	54	40	43	44	39	42	48	60	50
1975	66	73	77	81	79	72	77	79	73	74	76	80	75
1976	78	75	76	73	72	58	66	66	60	59	60	63	67
1977	67	66	66	66	59	45	52	49	47	48	49	57	56
1978	54	54	50	47	44	36	39	42	35	37	34	43	43
1979	48	48	47	47	42	33	39	38	36	38	40	49	42
1980	51	51	53	52	49	45	49	49	54	49	49	54	50
1981	54	50	49	46	40	35	37	37	36	34	37	41	41
1982	47	44	48	49	45	40	42	42	43	48	49	47	45
1983	50	52	50	53	52	40	39	36	34	33	39	41	44
1984	40	38	38	36	34	30	31	30	30	31	31	38	34
1985	40	41	41	39	32	28	30	30	28	27	32	37	34
1986	38	36	37	35	32	29	32	32	29	30	32	37	33
1987	37	37	38	35	31	28	30	29	28	26	29	34	32
1988	37	37	37	35	31	28	30	29	27	27	30	34	32
1989	35	35	40	37	30	29	33	33	29	31	29	38	33
1990	40	42	44	41	37	33	36	34	32	34	34	40	37
1991	47	46	48	49	41	37	39	37	35	34	38	51	42
1992	56	54	59	59	54	46	48	48	49	50	50	51	52
1993	50	48	51	52	48	43	47	48	47	44	46	49	48
1994	43	48	43	38	36	31	33	33	30	32	34	39	37
1995	39	41	40	37	35	32	35	34	32	34	31	40	36
1996	41	43	42	40	34	33	34	34	32	31	33	39	36
1997	39	39	38	38	33	30	34	33	30	32	35	37	35
1998	40	41	40	41	35	31	36	34	31	32	36	39	36
1999	44	43	44	41	38	33	36	35	32	33	35	41	38

SOURCE: "Table 4-2. Insured Employment as a Percent of Total Unemployment, By Month, Selected Years, 1967–1999," in *The Green Book,* U.S. House of Representatives, Committee on Ways and Means, Washington, DC, 2000

full payments. About one-fourth (26.5 percent) received partial payments, and one-third (32.6 percent) received none at all. (See Table 5.4.) Provisions in the Personal Responsibility and Work Opportunity Reconciliation Act of 1996 (PL 104-193, or PRWORA) strengthened and improved child support collection and enforcement activities.

Under PRWORA, states must have child support assignment (requirement that families receiving assistance must assign child support rights to the state) and good-faith cooperation requirements for TANF participants. The cooperation provision requires the custodial parent to provide the name and other identifying information about the absent parent. However, states have the flexibility to develop their own "good cause" exceptions to the cooperation requirements, such as a serious threat of domestic violence and/or sexual abuse. In addition, they may decide the penalty for noncooperation, although PRWORA mandates a minimum penalty of 25 percent of the monthly cash assistance.

The welfare-reform law (PRWORA) also required states to have child support automation systems in place by October 1, 2000. Each state must have in effect a computerized child support enforcement system to account for funds, to record data, to facilitate the collection and dis-

bursement of support payments, and to keep records that improve the state's ability to locate missing parents and/or their assets. Enforcement procedures include denying or revoking driver's licenses, withholding wages, and seizing income tax refunds or unemployment compensation benefits. Data must be kept confidential for several reasons, including the possibility of family violence.

Child Support Assurance

A family that receives assistance in the state's TANF program must assign any child support rights to the state in order to reimburse some of the cost of that assistance. If child support is then collected on the case, the state is required to give a predetermined portion to the federal government. As an alternative to this provision, a state may choose to use its maintenance-of-effort funds (the 80 percent of its historic welfare expenditure level a state is required to spend on welfare) to run a Child Support Assurance program (CSA). Any eligible family with a support order could then choose to participate in the CSA program rather than the TANF.

In a CSA program, children with child support orders are guaranteed to receive a minimum amount of support each month. The child support agency will collect the

TABLE 5.6

Unemployment insurance recipiency rates, 2001

State	Total	Male	Female	State	Total	Male	Female
United States	43.3%	45.9%	40.0%	Missouri	40.4%	39.6%	41.2%
Alabama	31.2%	32.1%	30.2%	Montana	41.9%	47.0%	35.1%
Alaska	58.1%	58.9%	56.9%	Nebraska	34.3%	37.0%	31.3%
Arizona	28.2%	32.9%	23.6%	Nevada	50.5%	56.7%	43.7%
Arkansas	51.5%	52.0%	51.0%	New Hampshire	24.4%	24.8%	23.9%
California	45.9%	47.5%	44.0%	New Jersey	61.0%	NA	NA
Colorado	33.7%	36.8%	30.6%	New Mexico	28.8%	30.8%	26.3%
Connecticut	73.9%	75.2%	72.3%	New York	48.4%	47.8%	49.0%
Delaware	51.4%	46.1%	58.4%	North Carolina	38.6%	38.6%	38.6%
DC	31.9%	31.3%	32.4%	North Dakota	41.2%	51.2%	25.0%
Florida	27.0%	27.6%	26.3%	Ohio	44.2%	50.8%	35.9%
Georgia	34.9%	33.8%	34.6%	Oklahoma	27.8%	26.3%	29.6%
Hawaii	38.6%	42.8%	33.8%	Oregon	51.2%	54.9%	46.1%
Idaho	46.5%	56.3%	34.3%	Pennsylvania	62.1%	66.4%	56.5%
Illinois	43.6%	49.0%	37.2%	Rhode Island	57.6%	57.1%	58.3%
Indiana	41.4%	44.8%	37.0%	South Carolina	43.5%	44.0%	43.0%
Iowa	51.1%	61.6%	39.6%	South Dakota	20.8%	24.4%	17.0%
Kansas	34.5%	35.2%	33.5%	Tennessee	48.0%	50.6%	45.4%
Kentucky	35.0%	41.5%	28.1%	Texas	29.8%	31.7%	27.8%
Louisiana	21.8%	20.3%	23.9%	Utah	32.0%	38.1%	25.6%
Maine	38.1%	38.6%	37.4%	Vermont	48.4%	63.4%	35.7%
Maryland	32.4%	31.8%	33.1%	Virginia	26.0%	26.9%	25.1%
Massachusetts	73.6%	70.3%	78.9%	Washington	47.6%	52.1%	41.6%
Michigan	49.3%	56.3%	40.4%	West Virginia	37.8%	42.3%	30.7%
Minnesota	44.7%	46.0%	42.1%	Wisconsin	54.8%	58.0%	50.2%
Mississippi	35.7%	36.3%	35.1%	Wyoming	28.6%	34.3%	22.5%

SOURCE: Maurice Emsellem, Jessica Goldberg, Rick McHugh, Wendell Primus, Rebecca Smith, and Jeffrey Wenger, "Table 1. Unemployment Insurance Recipiency Rates," in *Failing the Unemployed: A State by State Examination of Unemployment Insurance Systems,* Economic Policy Institute, Washington DC, Center on Budget and Policy Priorities, Washington, DC, and National Employment Law Project, New York, 2002

ordered support and, if necessary, supplement it up to the assured level. If the noncustodial parent does not pay the support, the CSA agency pays the family the guaranteed support and steps up its enforcement efforts for nonpayment. In return, the custodial parent would have to use the state's child support system, which keeps records of support collections and disbursements. Collecting back payments would allow the state to recover or partially recover the cost of the guaranteed payment. In addition, states would determine at what point assistance should be phased out as a family's income increases.

With a Child Support Assurance program, the state saves money. When the state is using federal money from the TANF program, it must turn over a portion (maximum 50 percent) of the child support it gets from the TANF recipient to the federal government. In a state-funded CSA program, the recipient keeps the child support payment, and the state pays the difference between the TANF assistance amount and the assured child support. The state saves money in this case because no money goes to the federal government. In addition, the CSA program recipient continues getting the assured support payment each month following employment, encouraging custodial parents to enter and stay in the paid labor force.

Government Enforcement

About 5.5 million custodial parents made 12.3 million contacts to a child support enforcement office (IV-D office), department of social services, or other government agency for assistance related to child support in 1998. The most common reasons for the contacts were to collect due child support (25.8 percent of the contacts), to establish a legal agreement (22.9 percent of the contacts), to receive Temporary Assistance for Needy Families or Medicaid (17 percent), or to locate the other parent (13.9 percent).

UNEMPLOYMENT COMPENSATION

In order to qualify for unemployment compensation benefits, an unemployed person usually must have worked recently for a covered employer for some period of time and for a certain amount of pay. In 2000 about 125 million individuals were covered by unemployment compensation—97 percent of all wage and salary workers and 89 percent of the civilian labor force. Most of those not covered were the self-employed, agricultural or domestic workers, certain alien farm workers, and railroad workers (who have their own unemployment program).

Although the unemployment compensation system covers 97 percent of all wage and salary workers, only 38 percent of unemployed workers received unemployment benefits in 1999. This compares with a peak of 75 percent of the unemployed receiving benefits in 1975 and a low of 32 percent in both 1987 and 1988. (See Table 5.5.)

TABLE 5.7

Unemployment compensation program data, fiscal years 1989–2000

Statistic	1989	1990	1991	1992	1993	1994	1995	1996	1997	1998	1999	2000 (estimated)[1]
Total civilian unemployment rate (percent)	5.3	5.4	6.5	7.3	7.0	6.3	5.6	5.5	5.1	4.6	4.3	4.2
Insured unemployment rate (percent)[2]	2.1	2.3	3.1	3.1	2.7	2.6	2.3	2.3	2.1	1.9	1.8	1.8
Coverage (millions)	104.3	106.1	105.1	104.9	106.6	109.7	112.9	115.4	118.2	121.6	124.2	125.1
Average weekly benefit amount:												
Current dollars	145	154	163	167	172	175	179	182	185	190	202	213
In 1999 dollars[3]	196	198	200	198	198	197	196	193	192	194	202	208
State unemployment compensation:												
Beneficiaries (millions)	7.0	8.1	10.2	9.6	7.8	8.2	7.9	8.1	7.5	7.3	7.1	7.2
Regular benefit exhaustions (millions)	1.9	2.2	3.2	3.9	3.3	3.1	2.7	2.7	2.6	2.3	2.3	2.3
Regular benefits paid (billions of dollars)	13.5	16.8	24.4	25.6	21.9	21.7	20.9	22.0	20.3	19.4	20.7	21.3
Extended benefits (State share: billions of dollars)	(6)	0.03	0.01	0.02	0.00	0.15	0.04	0.01	(6)	(6)	0.01	0.01
State tax collections (billions of dollars)	17.3	16.0	15.3	17.6	21.0	22.5	23.2	22.7	22.1	21.0	20.0	21.5
State trust fund impact (income-outlays: billions of dollars)[4]	+3.80	-0.88	-9.13	-8.03	-0.93	+0.66	+2.24	+0.75	+1.80	+1.6	-0.71	+0.19
Federal unemployment accounts:												
Federal tax collections (billions of dollars)[5]	4.45	5.36	5.33	5.41	4.23[7]	5.46	5.70	5.85	6.10	6.37	6.48	6.67
Outlays: federal EB share plus federal supplemental benefits (billions of dollars)	(6)	0.03	0.01	11.15	13.17	4.37	0.05	-0.01[8]	(6)	0.01	0.01	0.01
State administrative costs (billions of dollars):												
Unemployment Insurance Service	1.71	1.74	1.95	2.49	2.52	2.43	2.38	2.31	2.34	2.55	2.50	2.50
Employment Service	1.00	1.01	1.05	1.02	0.90	0.90	1.05	1.06	1.02	1.01	1.05	1.11
Total administrative costs	**2.71**	**2.75**	**3.00**	**3.51**	**3.42**	**3.33**	**3.43**	**3.36**	**3.36**	**3.56**	**3.55**	**3.61**

[1] Based on the President's fiscal year 2001 budget.
[2] The average number of workers claiming state unemployment compensation benefits as a percent of all workers covered.
[3] Adjusted using the Consumer Price Index for All Urban Consumers.
[4] Excludes interest earned.
[5] Net of reduced credits.
[6] Less than $5 million.
[7] Reflects a book adjustment of minus $967 million.
[8] Reflects reclaimed benefits in excess of benefits paid.

SOURCE: "Table 4-1. Unemployment Compensation Program Data, Fiscal Years 1989–2000," in *The Green Book*, U.S. House of Representatives, Committee on Ways and Means, Washington, DC, 2000

TABLE 5.8

Amount and duration of weekly benefits for total unemployment under the regular state programs, 1999–2000

State	1999 average weekly benefit	2000 weekly benefit amount[1]		1999 average duration (weeks)	2000 potential duration (weeks)	
		Minimum	Maximum		Minimum	Maximum
Alabama	$158	$45	$190	10	15	26
Alaska	194	44–68	248–320	15	16	26
Arizona	164	40	205	14	12	26
Arkansas	206	55	309	13	9	26
California	158	40	230	16	14	26
Colorado	252	25	337	12	13	26
Connecticut	233	15–30	382–457	15	26	26
Delaware	233	20	315	13	24	26
District of Columbia	239	50	309	20	20	26
Florida	214	32	275	14	26	26
Georgia	206	39	264	9	9	26
Hawaii	280	5	371	16	26	26
Idaho	201	51	273	12	10	26
Illinois	242	51	284–376	16	26	26
Indiana	214	50	252	11	8	26
Iowa	234	39–47	263–323	11	7	26
Kansas	247	76	306	13	10	26
Kentucky	214	39	316	12	15	26
Louisiana	161	10	258	15	26	26
Maine	198	41–60	254–381	13	26	26
Maryland	206	25–33	250	14	26	26
Massachusetts	288	27–40	431–646	17	10	30
Michigan	237	87	300	12	15	26
Minnesota	279	38	331–410	14	10	26
Mississippi	156	30	190	14	13	26
Missouri	180	45	220	13	11	26
Montana	180	63	254	14	8	26
Nebraska	183	36	206	12	20	26
Nevada	221	16	282	14	12	26
New Hampshire	221	32	301	10	26	26
New Jersey	285	0	429	17	15	26
New Mexico	184	48	254	16	19	26
New York	245	40	365	18	26	26
North Carolina	225	30	356	10	13	26
North Dakota	202	43	283	15	12	26
Ohio	228	77	279–375	13	20	26
Oklahoma	211	16	283	14	20	26
Oregon	230	84	360	15	4	26
Pennsylvania	258	35–40	408–416	16	16	26
Puerto Rico	104	7	133	19	26	26
Rhode Island	253	52–102	383–478	13	15	26
South Carolina	188	20	248	11	15	26
South Dakota	172	28	214	11	15	26
Tennessee	188	30	255	12	12	26
Texas	225	48	294	16	9	26
Utah	205	20	309	12	10	26
Vermont	208	40	287	13	26	26
Virginia	192	50	230	10	12	26
Virgin Islands	168	32	233	15	13	26
Washington	279	94	441	18	16	30
West Virginia	194	24	318	14	26	26
Wisconsin	228	44	297	12	12	26
Wyoming	200	19	261	13	12	26
U.S. average	**215**	**NA**	**NA**	**15**	**NA**	**NA**

[1] A range of amounts is shown for those States that provide dependents' allowances.
NA—Not applicable.

SOURCE: "Table 4-5. Amount and Duration of Weekly Benefits for Total Unemployment Under the Regular State Programs, 1999," in *The Green Book,* U.S. House of Representatives, Committee on Ways and Means, Washington, DC, 2000

Unemployment compensation varies widely by state. Table 5.6 shows the percentages of unemployed receiving benefits in each state in 2001. Recipiency rates were highest in Connecticut (73.9 percent) and Massachusetts (73.6 percent) and lowest in South Dakota (20.8 percent), Louisiana (21.8 percent), and New Hampshire (24.4 percent).

In 1999, 1.8 percent of the workforce covered by unemployment compensation received benefits, at a time when the total civilian unemployment rate was about 4.3 percent. The average weekly unemployment compensation benefit was $202. The amount of average weekly compensation remained relatively stable (in 1999 dollars) between 1989 and 1999. (See Table 5.7.)

While the maximum a state may offer is 39 weeks of coverage (except for special programs), all states provide up to 26 weeks of benefits, except Massachusetts and Washington, which offer 30 weeks. Benefits vary dramatically from state to state. The average weekly benefits in Hawaii ($280), Massachusetts ($288), Minnesota ($279), New Jersey ($285), and Rhode Island ($253) were significantly higher in 1999 than those offered by Puerto Rico ($104), Alabama ($158), California ($158), Mississippi ($156), and Louisiana ($161). (See Table 5.8.)

Unemployment Compensation Important in Avoiding Poverty

Two recent studies have examined the extent to which unemployment insurance serves as a safety net for low-income workers. The first, conducted by the General Accounting Office (GAO), *Unemployment Insurance: Role as Safety Net for Low-Wage Workers Is Limited* (Washington, D.C., 2000), examined recipiency rates by low-wage and higher-wage workers from 1992 to 1995. The GAO found that while low-wage workers are twice as likely as higher-wage workers to be unemployed, they are only half as likely to receive unemployment insurance benefits. They attribute this in part to the sectors in the economy in which low-wage workers tend to be employed, such as the service and retail sectors, which often do not provide unemployment insurance.

However, a more recent study conducted by Ann Rangarajan, Walter Corson, and Robert G. Wood of Mathematica Policy Research did find evidence that the unemployment insurance system was protecting low-wage workers following the enactment of welfare reform in 1996. In *Is the Unemployment Insurance System a Safety Net for Welfare Recipients Who Exit Welfare for Work?* (Washington, DC, 2001), they examined a group of former welfare recipients who exited welfare between July 1997 and June 1998. They found that between 50 and 60 percent of persons leaving welfare for work are eligible for unemployment insurance, compared to 20 to 35 percent found in earlier studies. Nonetheless, almost 40 percent of those who leave welfare for work are ineligible for benefits. Some of those who leave the welfare rolls are ineligible for benefits because they quit their jobs. This study was conducted during a strong economic period, and more research is needed to determine whether unemployment insurance provides a safety net to low-wage workers and those leaving welfare during periods of slower economic growth and recessions.

Minorities Hardest Hit by Unemployment

The unemployment rate of African American and Hispanic workers is higher than that of whites. In January 2002, the unemployment rate for white workers was 5.0 percent, compared to 9.8 percent for African Americans and 8.1 percent for Hispanics in the same age group. (See Table 5.9.)

THE FEDERAL MINIMUM WAGE— A RELATIVE DECLINE

The federal minimum wage dates back to the passage of the Fair Labor Standards Act (PL 75-718) in 1938, which established basic national standards for minimum wages, overtime pay, and the employment of child workers. (The minimum wage is a "cash wage" only and does not include any fringe benefits. Consequently, the total compensation for minimum-wage workers is even lower than the total compensation for higher-paid workers, who generally receive some kind of benefits in addition to wages. Most minimum-wage workers do not receive any benefits.) The provisions of the act have been extended to cover many other areas of employment since 1938.

The first minimum wage instituted in 1938 was $0.25 an hour. Over the years, it gradually increased, reaching $3.35 hour in 1981. The minimum wage was increased to $3.80 in 1990 and $4.25 in 1991. In July 1996, Congress passed legislation that raised the minimum wage to $5.15 in 1997 by means of two 45-cent increases. (See Table 5.10.) In 2001 the minimum wage was still $5.15, although as of January 2002 nine states (including California, Alaska, and Connecticut) had minimum wage rates higher than the federal rate, and three states (Kansas, New Mexico, and Ohio) had minimum wage rates lower than the federal rate.

The minimum wage remained unchanged from 1981 to 1990. When inflation is taken into account, the minimum wage actually lost about half its value over this period. The increases in 1996 and 1997 still left the real value of the minimum wage well below the 1978 value. (See Figure 5.5.) A person working 40 hours a week for 50 weeks a year at minimum wage ($5.15 per hour) would gross $206 per week, or $10,300 per year, well below the poverty level for a family of three ($14,150 in 2000). For adults, this means that "day laborers" (those without a permanent job) who look for a job every day and those employed in many service jobs for minimum wages are unlikely to earn enough to escape from poverty.

The number of people working at or below the minimum wage dropped sharply from 7.8 million in 1981 to 3.2 million in 1989. The decrease was caused mainly by the sharp decline in the purchasing power of the minimum wage. As the value of the minimum wage dropped, the number of those hired at that minimum level also fell. After the recession of 1990–91 and the slow recovery in

TABLE 5.9

Selected unemployment indicators, monthly data seasonally adjusted, 2000 through January 2002

[Unemployment rates]

Selected categories	Annual average		2001												2002
	2000	2001	Jan.	Feb.	Mar.	Apr.	May	June	July	Aug.	Sept.	Oct.	Nov.	Dec.	Jan.
Characteristic															
Total, 16 years and over	4.0	4.8	4.2	4.2	4.3	4.5	4.4	4.6	4.6	4.9	5.0	5.4	5.6	5.8	5.6
Both sexes, 16 to 19 years	13.1	14.7	13.7	13.5	13.8	14.2	13.6	14.4	14.8	15.8	14.9	15.4	15.7	16.2	16.1
Men, 20 years and over	3.3	4.2	3.6	3.5	3.8	3.9	3.9	4.1	4.0	4.4	4.3	4.8	5.2	5.2	5.2
Women, 20 years and over	3.6	4.1	3.5	3.6	3.6	3.8	3.8	3.9	4.0	4.2	4.4	4.8	4.9	52.0	4.8
White, total	3.5	4.2	3.6	3.7	3.7	3.9	3.9	4.0	4.1	4.3	4.3	4.7	5.0	5.1	5.0
Both sexes, 16 to 19 years	11.4	12.7	11.7	11.2	11.7	11.9	12.0	12.7	13.2	13.8	12.7	23.1	13.5	13.7	14.2
Men, 16 to 19 years	12.3	13.8	13.1	12.7	12.3	12.9	13.3	14.3	13.8	15.1	13.6	14.7	15.8	14.6	13.7
Women, 16 to 19 years	10.4	11.4	10.2	9.6	11.0	10.9	10.7	11.0	12.6	12.4	11.7	11.5	11.1	12.8	14.6
Men, 20 years and over	2.8	3.7	3.1	3.1	3.3	3.4	3.4	3.6	3.5	3.8	3.8	4.4	4.7	4.6	4.7
Women, 20 years and over	3.1	3.6	3.0	3.3	3.1	3.4	3.4	3.4	3.5	3.6	3.8	4.1	4.2	4.5	4.2
Black, total	7.6	8.7	8.2	7.5	8.4	8.2	8.0	8.4	8.1	9.0	8.8	9.6	9.9	10.2	9.8
Both sexes, 16 to 19 years	24.7	29.0	27.5	28.1	28.3	30.5	25.7	28.0	26.6	30.1	28.5	30.2	32.1	33.4	30.7
Men, 16 to 19 years	26.4	30.5	27.3	31.1	28.7	33.5	30/0	6.0	28.1	31.4	430.8	31.2	31.6	32.0	32.1
Women, 16 to 19 years	23.0	27.5	27.6	25.1	28.0	27.7	21.5	25.7	25.2	28.7	26.1	29.1	32.6	34.8	29.0
Men, 20 years and over	7.0	8.0	7.0	6.7	8.2	8.1	7.6	7.8	7.9	8.8	7.8	8.2	8.7	9.1	8.9
Women, 20 years and over	6.3	7.0	6.9	5.9	6.3	5.9	6.4	6.7	6.2	7.0	7.7	8.5	8.4	8.7	8.4
Hispanic origin, total	5.7	6.6	5.9	6.2	6.2	6.3	6.2	6.6	6.2	6.4	6.5	7.1	7.4	7.9	8.1
Married men, spouse present	2.0	2.7	2.3	2.3	2.4	2.5	2.6	2.6	2.7	2.8	2.8	3.1	3.3	3.4	3.5
Married women, spouse present	2.7	3.1	2.6	2.6	2.7	2.8	2.9	3.0	2.9	3.1	3.3	3.6	3.6	3.7	3.4
Women who maintain families	5.9	6.6	6.4	6.0	6.1	6.3	6.2	6.3	6.3	6.8	7.1	6.8	8.0	8.0	7.9
Full-time workers	3.9	4.7	4.0	4.0	4.1	4.3	4.3	4.5	4.5	4.8	5.0	5.4	5.6	5.8	5.7
Part-time workers	4.8	5.1	4.9	4.8	4.9	5.3	4.8	5.2	5.1	5.4	4.6	5.5	5.6	5.6	5.2
Industry															
Nonagricultural wage and salary workers	4.1	5.1	4.2	4.4	4.5	4.6	4.6	4.8	4.8	5.2	5.2	5.8	6.0	6.2	5.9
Mining	3.9	4.7	2.2	4.5	4.0	4.8	4.9	5.9	3.9	4.7	5.0	5.8	5.3	6.1	5.9
Construction	6.4	7.3	6.7	6.8	6.4	6.9	6.7	6.9	7.1	7.6	7.8	8.3	8.9	8.9	9.4
Manufacturing	3.6	5.2	4.1	4.5	4.8	4.6	4.8	5.0	5.2	5.7	5.6	6.0	6.4	6.8	6.6
Durable goods	3.4	5.3	4.0	4.1	4.7	4.4	4.8	5.0	5.0	5.8	5.8	6.5	6.9	7.2	7.0
Nondurable goods	4.0	5.1	4.4	4.9	4.9	4.9	4.8	4.9	5.5	5.4	5.4	5.3	5.5	6.1	5.9
Transportation and public utilities	3.1	4.1	2.9	3.0	3.2	4.0	3.6	4.1	3.4	3.6	3.9	6.0	6.1	6.1	6.2
Wholesale and retail trade	5.0	5.6	4.9	5.1	5.3	5.2	5.2	5.4	5.3	5.6	5.9	6.1	6.4	7.1	6.3
Finance, insurance, and real estate	2.3	2.8	2.3	2.4	2.5	2.6	2.4	2.6	3.1	2.7	2.8	2.8	3.6	3.0	2.2
Services	3.8	4.6	3.9	4.1	4.1	4.1	4.2	4.4	4.4	4.9	4.8	5.5	5.4	5.5	5.4
Government workers	2.1	2.2	2.2	1.6	2.1	2.2	2.0	2.1	2.1	2.1	2.2	2.3	2.4	2.4	2.3
Agricultural wage and salary workers	7.5	9.7	9.0	9.2	11.1	9.4	8.4	9.5	10.5	10.0	7.6	9.0	9.3	9.6	10.3
Educational attainment*															
Less than a high school diploma	6.4	7.3	6.7	7.4	6.8	6.7	6.7	6.9	6.8	7.3	7.7	7.8	8.1	8.8	8.1
High school graduates, no college	3.5	4.2	3.7	3.7	3.8	3.8	3.9	3.9	4.1	4.3	4.3	4.6	5.0	4.9	5.2
Some college, less than a bachelor's degree	2.7	3.3	2.9	2.7	2.7	2.9	3.0	3.1	3.1	3.3	3.5	3.9	4.2	4.3	4.2
College graduates	1.7	2.3	1.6	1.6	1.9	2.2	2.1	2.1	22.2	2.2	2.5	2.7	2.9	3.1	2.9

*Data refer to persons 25 years and over.

SOURCE: "6. Selected Unemployment Indicators, Monthly Data Seasonally Adjusted," in "Current Labor Force Statistics," *Monthly Labor Review*, U.S. Department of Labor, Bureau of Labor Statistics, Washington, DC, March 2002

1992, 4.2 million workers in 1993 earned the minimum wage or less. In 1996 nearly 10 million workers were directly affected by the minimum-wage increase. Often employers use the minimum wage as a standard for low-paying jobs, perhaps paying $1 or $2 above minimum wage for a particular job.

Who Works for Minimum Wage?

In *The Low-Wage Labor Market: Does the Minimum Wage Help or Hurt Low-Wage Workers?* (Urban Institute, Washington, DC), Mark D. Turner reports that most workers affected by minimum wage increases are adults age 20 and older (72.7 percent). The majority (62.3 percent) of minimum-wage workers in 1998 were women; some 82.6 percent of minimum-wage workers were employed in part-time jobs. Those who work for the minimum wage are more likely to be employed in the retail (46.8 percent) and service (34.2 percent) sectors. About 80.8 percent of minimum-wage workers are white, while 13.8 percent are African American. (See Table 5.11.) Turner asserts that raising the minimum wage does not substantially benefit persons living in poverty.

While workers must receive at least the minimum wage for most jobs, there are some exceptions in which a

TABLE 5.10

History of federal minimum wage rates under the fair labor standards act

Effective Date	1938 Act[1]	1961 Amendments[2]	1966 and subsequent amendments[3]	
			Nonfarm	Farm
Oct. 24, 1938	$0.25			
Oct. 24, 1939	$0.30			
Oct. 24, 1945	$0.40			
Jan. 25, 1950	$0.75			
Mar. 1, 1956	$1.00			
Sept. 3, 1961	$1.15	$1.00		
Sept. 3, 1963	$1.25			
Sept. 3, 1964		$1.15		
Sept. 3, 1965		$1.25		
Feb. 1, 1967	$1.40	$1.40	$1.00	$1.00
Feb. 1, 1968	$1.60	$1.60	$1.15	$1.15
Feb. 1, 1969			$1.30	$1.30
Feb. 1, 1970			$1.45	
Feb. 1, 1971			$1.60	
May 1, 1974	$2.00	$2.00	$1.90	$1.60
Jan. 1, 1975	$2.10	$2.10	$2.00	$1.80
Jan. 1, 1976	$2.30	$2.30	$2.20	$2.00
Jan. 1, 1977			$2.30	$2.20
Jan. 1, 1978	$2.65 for all covered, nonexempt workers			
Jan. 1, 1979	$2.90 for all covered, nonexempt workers			
Jan. 1, 1980	$3.10 for all covered, nonexempt workers			
Jan. 1, 1981	$3.35 for all covered, nonexempt workers			
Apr. 1, 1990[4]	$3.80 for all covered, nonexempt workers			
Apr. 1, 1991	$4.25 for all covered, nonexempt workers			
Oct. 1, 1996[5]	$4.75 for all covered, nonexempt workers			
Sept. 1, 1997	$5.15 for all covered, nonexempt workers			

[1] The 1938 Act was applicable generally to employees engaged in interstate commerce or in the production of goods for interstate commerce.

[2] The 1961 Amendments extended coverage primarily to employees in large retail and service enterprises as well as to local transit, construction, and gasoline service station employees.

[3] The 1966 Amendments extended coverage to state and local government employees of hospitals, nursing homes, and schools, and to laundries, dry cleaners, and large hotels, motels, restaurants, and farms. Subsequent amendments extended coverage to the remaining federal, state and local government employees who were not protected in 1966, to certain workers in retail and service trades previously exempted, and to certain domestic workers in private household employment.

[4] Grandfather Clause: Employees who do not meet the tests for individual coverage, and whose employers were covered by the FLSA, on March 31, 1990, and fail to meet the increased annual dollar volume (ADV) test for enterprise coverage, must continue to receive at least $3.35 an hour.

[5] A subminimum wage—$4.25 an hour—is established for employees under 20 years of age during their first 90 consecutive calendar days of employment with an employer.

SOURCE: "Federal Minimum Wage Rates Under the Fair Labor Standards Act," U.S. Department of Labor, Employment Standards Administration, Washington, DC [Online] http://www.dol.gov/esa/minwage/chart.htm [accessed August 5, 2002]

TABLE 5.11

Characteristics of minimum wage and other wage earners, 1998

Characteristics	Workers directly affected by proposed minimum wage ($5.15–$6.14)	Other low-wage workers ($6.15–$6.64)	Workers above minimum wage ($6.65+)	All workers
Average hourly wage	$5.64	$6.41	$12.49	$11.04
Employment (in millions)	11,166	3,344	52,447	66,958
Share of total	17%	5%	78%	100%
Demographics				
Men	37.7%	40.2%	53.5%	50.2%
Women	62.3%	59.8%	46.5%	49.8%
White	80.8%	82.2%	82.3%	82.0%
Men	30.9%	32.6%	45.0%	42.0%
Women	50.0%	49.6%	37.3%	40.0%
Black	13.8%	14.2%	13.2%	13.4%
Men	4.7%	5.2%	6.3%	6.0%
Women	9.1%	9.1%	6.9%	7.4%
Teenagers (16–19)	27.3%	20.6%	2.5%	7.5%
Young adults (20–24)	19.5%	21.6%	11.5%	13.3%
Adults (25+)	53.2%	57.9%	86.0%	79.1%
Parents	19.4%	24.6%	38.0%	34.3%
Work hours				
Full-time (35+)	17.3%	22.2%	44.8%	39.1%
Part-time				
20–34 hours	7.5%	7.6%	3.5%	4.4%
1–19 hours	75.1%	70.2%	51.7%	56.5%
Average weekly hours	9.2	11.2	19.6	17.5
Poverty status				
Below poverty	16.4%	11.4%	4.8%	7.1%
100–124% poverty	7.2%	4.8%	2.8%	3.6%
125–149% poverty	5.1%	4.8%	3.0%	3.5%
150% or more of poverty	71.3%	79.0%	89.4%	85.9%
Industry				
Manufacturing	9.3%	13.6%	22.8%	20.1%
Retail trade	46.8%	35.3%	13.3%	20.0%
Service	34.2%	37.8%	37.3%	36.8%
Occupation				
Managerial & professional	5.5%	6.9%	16.8%	14.4%
Technical, sales	35.3%	33.9%	32.2%	32.8%
Service	39.2%	33.0%	29.0%	30.9%
Operators & laborers	20.0%	26.2%	22.0%	21.8%

SOURCE: Mark D. Turner, "Table 1. Characteristics of Minimum Wage and Other Wage Earners, 1998," in *The Low-Wage Labor Market: Does the Minimum Wage Help or Hurt Low-Wage Workers?*, U.S. Department of Health and Human Services, Washington, DC, January 14, 2000 [Online] http://aspe.hhs.gov/hsp/lwlm99/turner.htm [accessed May 21, 2002]

person may be paid less than the minimum wage. Full-time students working on a part-time basis in the service and retail industries or at the student's academic institution, certain disabled persons, and workers who are "customarily and regularly" tipped may receive less than the minimum wage.

TRENDS IN TOTAL EARNINGS

In the 1980s and 1990s the median personal income of American men declined substantially. For all males, median earnings (half earned more and half earned less) reached $27,209 in 1973 (in adjusted 2000 dollars) and then began dropping, hitting a low of $23,975 in 1982, a year of deep recession. Male earnings then began a slow recovery, reaching $26,825 in 1989. Then, male earnings began to fall, dipping to $24,681 in 1992, lower than the median earnings during the recession of the early 1980s, and more than 10 percent below male earnings in 1973. In 2000 median male earnings reached $28,269, an increase of only 3.9 percent since 1973. This trend applied to white, African American, and Hispanic men. (See Table 5.12.)

Female earnings rose 71.4 percent from 1973 to 2000. It should be noted, however, that the median income of female workers in 2000 ($16,188) was still only 57 percent that of male workers ($28,269). (See Table 5.12.)

FIGURE 5.5

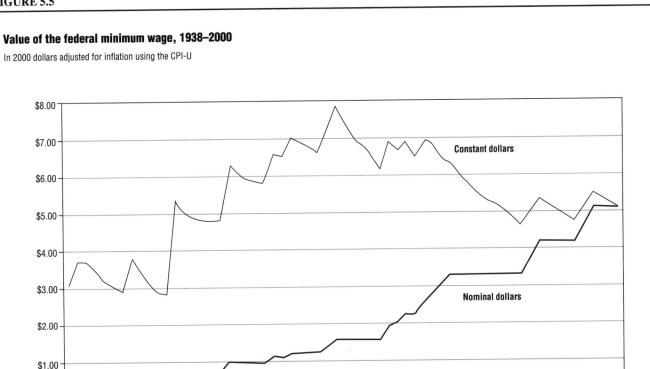

Value of the federal minimum wage, 1938–2000

In 2000 dollars adjusted for inflation using the CPI-U

Note: CPI-U = Consumer Price Index for all urban consumers.

SOURCE: "Value of the Federal Minimum Wage, 1938–2000," in *The Minimum Wage,* U.S. Department of Labor, Bureau of Labor Statistics, Washington, DC [Online] http://www.dol.gov/esa/minwage/chart2.htm [accessed May 31, 2002]

SOMETIMES HAVING A JOB DOES NOT MEAN GETTING OUT OF POVERTY

In *A Profile of the Working Poor, 1999* (Bureau of Labor Statistics, Washington, DC, 2001), Thomas Beers examined the status of the working poor. The term "working poor" refers to those who participated in the labor force for at least 27 weeks (either working or looking for work) and who lived in families with incomes below the official poverty level. He found that for 6.8 million workers in 1999 (5.1 percent of those in the labor force), their jobs were not enough to keep them out of poverty. (See Table 5.13.)

Beers reported that working women (5.9 percent) had a higher poverty rate than working men (4.4 percent). Nearly three-fourths of the working poor were white workers (71.1 percent), but African American and Hispanic workers continued to experience poverty rates at more than twice the rates of whites. African Americans (10.2 percent) and Hispanics (10.7 percent) with at least six months in the labor force had a far higher poverty rate than whites (4.3 percent). Younger workers were more likely to be in poverty than older workers. Much of the

reason for this is that many younger workers are still in school and work at part-time or entry-level jobs that often do not pay well. (See Table 5.13.)

In general, the lower the educational level, the higher the risk of poverty. Among workers in the labor force for at least half of 1999, those with less than a high school diploma had a much higher poverty rate (14.3 percent) than high school graduates (6.0 percent). Far lower poverty rates were reported for workers with an associate degree (2.9 percent) or a four-year college degree (1.3 percent). African American workers, regardless of education levels, had higher poverty rates than white workers. The highest poverty rate (33.7 percent) was for African American women workers with less one year of high school.

In 1999 working families headed by married couples without children were least likely to be poor (1.5 percent), while the presence of children under age 18 increased the married-couple poverty rate to 5.2 percent. Single women with families were most likely to be living in poverty (23.9 percent), although the working-poor population included a significant proportion of single men with children (10.7 percent). (See Table 5.14.)

TABLE 5.12

Persons by total money income, race, Hispanic origin, and sex, 1967–2000

[Income in 2000 CPI-U-RS 28/ adjusted dollars. People 15 years old and over beginning with March 1980, and people 14 years and over as of March of the following year for previous years.]

Race, Hispanic origin, sex, and year	Number (thous.)	Number with income (thous.)	With income — Percent distribution: Total	$1 to $2,499 or loss	$2,500 to $4,999	$5,000 to $9,999	$10,000 to $14,999	$15,000 to $24,999	$25,000 to $49,999	$50,000 to $74,999	$75,000 and over	Median income Value (dols)	Median income Standard error (dols)	Mean income Value (dols)	Mean income Standard error (dols)
ALL RACES - MALE															
2000	104,273	96,983	100.0	4.9	3.1	8.5	9.6	18.1	30.8	13.8	11.2	28,269	231	40,290	305
1999	103,114	96,023	100.0	5.1	3.4	8.9	9.4	18.1	31.0	13.3	10.8	28,191	136	39,640	277
1998	102,048	94,948	100.0	5.1	3.5	9.2	9.7	17.5	32.0	13.2	9.8	27,955	136	38,320	271
1997	101,123	94,168	100.0	5.3	3.4	9.7	10.8	18.1	31.4	12.2	9.3	26,976	132	37,229	280
1996	100,159	93,439	100.0	5.5	3.6	10.2	10.9	18.1	31.6	11.8	8.4	26,054	172	35,855	270
1995	98,593	92,066	100.0	5.7	4.0	9.4	11.2	19.4	30.1	12.1	8.1	25,333	164	35,318	260
1994	97,704	91,254	100.0	6.1	3.8	10.2	11.3	18.8	30.3	11.5	8.0	25,000	127	34,953	246
1993	96,768	90,194	100.0	6.5	4.2	10.4	10.8	19.4	30.0	11.4	7.4	24,821	125	34,039	242
1992	95,652	90,175	100.0	6.4	4.4	10.6	10.8	19.2	30.2	11.4	6.9	24,681	129	32,349	168
1991	93,760	88,653	100.0	5.9	4.3	10.5	10.8	18.9	31.0	11.7	7.0	25,353	130	32,660	166
1990	92,840	88,220	100.0	5.5	4.0	10.2	10.2	18.6	31.9	12.3	7.3	26,056	131	33,436	176
1989	91,955	87,454	100.0	5.5	4.2	9.9	10.0	18.1	31.7	13.0	7.6	26,825	165	34,718	190
1988	91,034	86,584	100.0	5.8	4.3	10.1	9.5	17.9	32.4	12.9	7.2	26,606	182	33,847	184
1987	90,256	85,713	100.0	6.2	4.4	9.8	10.3	18.1	30.9	13.2	7.0	25,939	178	33,248	166
1986	89,368	84,471	100.0	6.5	4.5	10.0	9.2	18.7	31.5	12.3	7.3	25,809	138	32,909	163
1985	88,478	83,631	100.0	6.8	4.7	10.4	9.6	19.2	30.9	11.9	6.6	25,032	139	31,694	153
1984	87,034	82,183	100.0	7.1	4.9	11.0	9.6	18.4	31.5	11.4	6.1	24,754	143	30,844	136
1983	86,014	80,795	100.0	7.7	5.1	10.9	9.9	19.0	31.3	10.6	5.6	24,193	153	30,002	134
1982	84,955	79,722	100.0	7.5	4.7	10.8	10.1	19.0	31.5	10.9	5.6	23,975	156	29,872	134
1981	83,958	79,688	100.0	7.0	4.8	10.9	10.2	18.2	32.7	11.3	5.1	24,508	166	30,041	133
1980	82,949	78,661	100.0	6.8	4.4	10.4	9.5	18.8	33.4	11.2	5.2	24,932	156	30,523	135
1979	81,947	78,129	100.0	6.3	4.6	10.6	9.4	17.9	33.6	12.1	5.7	26,046	132	31,645	144
1978	80,969	75,609	100.0	6.9	4.4	10.8	9.3	17.2	33.7	12.3	5.5	26,452	139	31,720	148
1977	79,863	74,015	100.0	7.0	4.6	10.7	9.6	17.2	34.2	11.5	5.2	25,540	128	30,435	131
1976	78,782	72,775	100.0	7.1	4.6	11.1	9.7	17.9	34.5	10.8	4.6	25,300	139	29,967	129
1975	77,560	71,234	100.0	7.0	4.6	10.4	9.9	17.6	35.2	10.4	4.3	25,125	137	29,598	131
1974	76,363	70,863	100.0	7.3	4.6	9.9	8.8	18.1	35.4	10.5	4.9	25,974	143	30,304	132
1973	75,040	69,387	100.0	7.2	4.8	9.7	8.6	16.6	36.8	12.0	5.4	27,209	148	31,374	138
1972	73,572	67,474	100.0	6.9	5.0	10.4	9.1	16.3	37.2	11.0	5.0	26,737	138	30,990	140
1971	72,469	66,486	100.0	7.6	5.1	10.2	9.2	17.0	37.4	9.4	4.1	25,537	133	29,196	133
1970	70,592	65,015	100.0	7.6	5.5	10.0	8.5	17.3	37.9	9.4	4.2	25,771	132	29,121	135
1969	69,027	64,105	100.0	7.6	5.7	10.0	8.7	16.9	38.4	8.9	4.1	26,036	130	29,166	138
1968	67,611	62,494	100.0	7.5	6.0	10.2	8.7	17.7	38.1	8.2	3.6	25,272	119	28,002	131
1967	66,519	61,452	100.0	7.8	6.4	10.5	8.8	18.7	37.4	7.0	3.3	24,408	114	26,610	127

TABLE 5.12

Persons by total money income, race, Hispanic origin, and sex, 1967–2000 [CONTINUED]

[Income in 2000 CPI-U-RS 28/ adjusted dollars. People 15 years old and over beginning with March 1980, and people 14 years and over as of March of the following year for previous years.]

Race, Hispanic origin, sex, and year	Number (thous.)	Number with income (thous.)	With income Percent distribution — Total	$1 to $2,499 or loss	$2,500 to $4,999	$5,000 to $9,999	$10,000 to $14,999	$15,000 to $24,999	$25,000 to $49,999	$50,000 to $74,999	$75,000 and over	Median income — Value (dols)	Median income — Standard error (dols)	Mean income — Value (dols)	Mean income — Standard error (dols)
ALL RACES – FEMALE															
2000	111,735	99,974	100.0	10.4	6.4	16.9	13.5	19.4	24.1	6.5	2.9	16,188	103	22,320	134
1999	110,660	99,613	100.0	10.6	7.0	17.3	13.7	19.8	23.0	5.8	2.9	15,825	101	22,027	136
1998	109,628	98,694	100.0	11.0	6.7	18.0	14.2	18.9	22.9	5.6	2.6	15,227	108	21,592	147
1997	108,168	97,447	100.0	10.6	7.2	19.0	14.4	19.7	21.5	5.2	2.4	14,662	116	20,876	136
1996	107,076	96,558	100.0	10.9	7.8	19.7	13.9	19.5	21.4	4.6	2.1	14,009	115	20,080	137
1995	106,031	96,007	100.0	12.0	7.9	19.3	14.5	19.6	20.3	4.6	1.8	13,620	84	19,386	124
1994	105,028	95,147	100.0	12.7	8.2	19.7	14.7	18.7	20.1	4.1	1.7	13,197	82	18,966	124
1993	104,032	94,417	100.0	13.0	8.8	20.0	13.9	19.0	19.8	4.0	1.5	12,993	83	18,538	124
1992	102,954	93,517	100.0	13.3	9.0	19.6	14.2	18.6	20.2	3.8	1.3	12,928	85	18,005	94
1991	101,483	92,569	100.0	13.1	8.9	20.1	14.1	19.1	19.7	3.6	1.4	12,975	86	17,896	92
1990	100,680	92,245	100.0	13.2	9.4	19.1	13.8	19.3	19.9	3.9	1.3	12,930	92	17,864	94
1989	99,838	91,399	100.0	13.6	9.4	19.1	13.7	19.3	19.9	3.8	1.2	12,978	93	17,835	93
1988	99,019	90,593	100.0	14.4	9.4	20.0	13.1	18.8	19.9	3.4	1.1	12,501	107	17,323	96
1987	98,225	89,661	100.0	14.9	9.7	19.5	14.1	18.9	18.8	3.1	1.0	12,097	96	16,827	88
1986	97,320	87,822	100.0	16.0	9.9	20.1	12.6	19.3	18.5	2.6	1.0	11,476	98	16,198	83
1985	96,354	86,531	100.0	16.5	10.4	20.2	13.1	19.2	17.4	2.4	.8	11,076	70	15,612	80
1984	95,282	85,555	100.0	17.1	10.1	20.6	13.4	19.0	16.9	2.1	.8	10,898	68	15,208	75
1983	94,269	83,781	100.0	17.8	10.6	20.7	13.3	19.3	15.8	1.9	.6	10,569	72	14,684	73
1982	93,145	82,505	100.0	18.4	10.2	21.3	13.9	18.8	15.1	1.7	.5	10,118	74	14,084	70
1981	92,228	82,139	100.0	18.5	10.7	21.7	14.1	18.9	14.4	1.5	.3	9,928	78	13,534	65
1980	91,133	80,826	100.0	19.0	11.0	21.5	13.6	19.1	14.0	1.3	.4	9,790	57	13,475	68
1979	89,914	79,921	100.0	19.9	11.2	20.9	13.2	19.3	13.8	1.3	.4	9,623	64	13,325	69
1978	88,617	71,864	100.0	17.2	12.1	22.0	13.9	19.1	13.9	1.3	.4	9,840	69	13,544	70
1977	87,399	65,407	100.0	14.5	12.9	22.9	14.9	19.5	13.8	1.1	.3	9,943	65	13,349	63
1976	86,153	63,170	100.0	15.3	13.2	23.2	14.8	19.4	12.7	1.0	.3	9,598	69	13,085	64
1975	84,982	60,807	100.0	15.4	13.2	23.4	15.3	18.9	12.7	.9	.2	9,667	73	12,808	60
1974	83,599	59,642	100.0	16.4	13.2	23.3	13.9	19.8	12.2	.9	.3	9,471	80	12,787	65
1973	82,244	58,029	100.0	16.6	14.3	21.4	14.8	18.9	12.7	1.0	.3	9,444	91	12,831	68
1972	80,896	54,487	100.0	16.9	14.5	21.1	14.5	18.4	13.3	1.0	.3	9,328	99	12,838	72
1971	79,565	52,603	100.0	17.6	15.5	20.8	14.5	18.7	11.8	.8	.3	8,908	49	12,330	70
1970	77,649	51,647	100.0	19.2	15.3	20.4	13.0	19.3	11.7	.8	.3	8,643	49	12,124	70
1969	76,277	50,224	100.0	19.6	16.0	19.4	13.9	19.7	10.5	.7	.3	8,634	50	11,927	69
1968	74,889	48,544	100.0	19.5	16.1	20.0	14.5	18.6	10.4	.7	.2	8,533	52	11,546	68
1967	73,584	46,843	100.0	21.5	16.9	19.1	14.2	18.3	8.8	.7	.4	7,916	53	10,914	84

SOURCE: "Table P-54. Total Money Income of People, by Race, Hispanic Origin, and Sex: 1967 to 2000," in *Historical Income Tables—People*, U.S. Department of Commerce, Economic Statistics Administration, Census Bureau, Washington, DC, April 2002 [Online] http://www.census.gov/hhes/income/histinc/p54.html [accessed May 23, 2002]

TABLE 5.13

Poverty status of persons in the labor force for 27 weeks or more, by age, sex, race, and Hispanic origin, 1999

(Numbers in thousands)

Age and sex	Total	White	Black	Hispanic origin	Below poverty level				Poverty rate[1]			
					Total	White	Black	Hispanic origin	Total	White	Black	Hispanic origin
Total, 16 years and older	133,651	111,714	15,698	13,971	6,796	4,830	1,596	1,496	5.1	4.3	10.2	10.7
16 to 19 years	5,207	4,405	596	622	527	365	127	93	10.1	8.3	21.4	15.0
20 to 24 years	12,412	10,240	1,675	1,866	1,312	894	367	253	10.6	8.7	21.9	13.6
25 to 34 years	30,695	24,839	4,096	4,178	1,835	1,290	433	486	6.0	5.2	10.6	11.6
35 to 44 years	36,945	30,612	4,564	3,917	1,726	1,246	387	417	4.7	4.1	8.5	10.7
45 to 54 years	29,965	25,468	3,158	2,255	851	631	165	167	2.8	2.5	5.2	7.4
55 to 64 years	14,066	12,240	1,271	938	419	313	89	64	3.0	2.6	7.0	6.8
65 years and older	4,361	3,909	338	195	127	91	27	15	2.9	2.3	8.0	7.7
Men, 16 years and older	71,790	61,163	7,260	8,267	3,165	2,526	447	898	4.4	4.1	6.2	10.9
16 to 19 years	2,700	2,312	264	383	234	183	29	60	8.7	7.9	10.9	15.6
20 to 24 years	6,488	5,487	741	1,152	575	438	115	156	8.9	8.0	15.5	13.5
25 to 34 years	16,728	13,865	1,899	2,558	852	707	93	315	5.1	5.1	4.9	12.3
35 to 44 years	19,949	16,877	2,153	2,254	833	674	119	243	4.2	4.0	5.5	10.8
45 to 54 years	15,764	13,594	1,455	1,253	402	311	52	91	2.5	2.3	3.5	7.3
55 to 64 years	7,595	6,704	582	546	200	159	30	28	2.6	2.4	5.2	5.1
65 years and older	2,566	2,325	166	122	69	53	10	6	2.7	2.3	5.8	4.9
Women, 16 years and older	61,861	50,551	8,438	5,704	3,631	2,303	1,149	598	5.9	4.6	13.6	10.5
16 to 19 years	2,507	2,093	332	239	293	181	99	34	11.7	8.7	29.7	14.1
20 to 24 years	5,924	4,753	934	714	737	456	252	98	12.4	9.6	27.0	13.7
25 to 34 years	13,967	10,975	2,197	1,620	983	582	340	172	7.0	5.3	15.5	10.6
35 to 44 years	16,996	13,735	2,411	1,663	893	571	269	174	5.3	4.2	11.1	10.5
45 to 54 years	14,201	11,874	1,703	1,002	450	320	114	76	3.2	2.7	6.7	7.6
55 to 64 years	6,472	5,537	689	393	219	154	58	36	3.4	2.8	8.5	9.2
65 years and older	1,795	1,584	172	73	57	38	17	9	3.2	2.4	10.1	[2]

[1] Number below the poverty level as a percent of the total in the labor force for 27 weeks or more.
[2] Data not shown where base is less than 75,000.
Note: Detail for race and Hispanic-origin groups will not sum to totals because data for the "other races" group are not presented and Hispanics are included in both the white and black population groups.

SOURCE: "Table 2. Persons in the Labor Force for 27 Weeks or More: Poverty Status by Age, Sex, Race, and Hispanic Origin, 1999," in *A Profile of the Working Poor, 1999*, U.S. Department of Labor, Bureau of Labor Statistics, Report 947, Washington, DC, February 2001

In a family headed by a married couple, a greater likelihood exists that two people are working than with a single-parent family. Two-income families are rarely poor. Only 1.4 percent of families headed by married couples with two or more wage earners were poor in 1999. Of the 3.8 million working-poor families, nearly half were families maintained by women. Working women who were the sole supporters of their families had the highest poverty rate, 25.4 percent. (See Table 5.14.)

Several factors affect the poverty status of working families: the size of the family, the number of workers in the family, the characteristics of the worker(s), and various labor market problems. The addition of a child puts a financial strain on the family and increases the chances that a parent might have to stay home to care for the child. While a child in a single-parent family may work, children are usually employed for lower pay and at part-time jobs. In addition, the more education a person has, the more his or her job is likely to pay. Single mothers are more likely to have less education than married women.

Finally, the labor market plays a major role in whether a working family lives in poverty. Beers named three major labor market problems contributing to poverty among workers in 1999—unemployment, low earnings, and involuntary part-time employment. Only 0.7 percent of workers who did not suffer from any of these problems were poor in 1999, while 20.2 percent of low-paid workers were in poverty. Unemployment (7.8 percent) and involuntary part-time work (2.1 percent) were also important reasons. However, it was the combination of two or more factors that had the most devastating effect on families. Unemployment coupled with low earnings accounted for 42.5 percent of those in poverty. (See Table 5.15.)

TABLE 5.14

Poverty status and presence of related children among primary families with at least one member in the labor force for 27 weeks or more, 1999

(Numbers in thousands)

Characteristic	Total families	At or above poverty level	Below poverty level	Poverty rate[1]
Total primary families	60,454	56,699	3,755	6.2
With related children under 18	34,542	31,337	3,205	9.3
Without children	25,912	25,362	550	2.1
With one member in the labor force	24,649	21,506	3,143	12.8
With two or more members in the labor force	35,805	35,193	612	1.7
With two members	29,970	29,421	550	1.8
With three or more members	5,835	5,772	62	1.1
Married-couple families:				
With related children under 18	25,658	24,314	1,343	5.2
Without children	21,158	20,845	313	1.5
With one member in the labor force	15,285	14,083	1,202	7.9
Husband	11,413	10,476	937	8.2
Wife	3,175	2,967	207	6.5
Relative	698	639	58	8.4
With two or more members in the labor force	31,530	31,076	454	1.4
With two members	26,518	26,112	406	1.5
With three or more members	5,012	4,964	48	1.0
Families maintained by women:				
With related children under 18	6,920	5,269	1,651	23.9
Without children	3,154	2,973	181	5.7
With one member in the labor force	7,189	5,498	1,691	23.5
Householder	5,870	4,380	1,490	25.4
Relative	1,319	1,118	201	15.2
With two or more members in the labor force	2,885	2,744	141	4.9
Families maintained by men:				
With related children under 18	1,965	1,754	211	10.7
Without children	1,600	1,543	56	3.5
With one member in the labor force	2,175	1,925	250	11.5
Householder	1,795	1,602	193	10.8
Relative	380	323	57	14.9
With two or more members in the labor force	1,390	1,372	18	1.3

[1] Number below the poverty level as a percent of the total in the labor force for 27 weeks or more.

SOURCE: "Table 6. Primary Families: Poverty Status, Presence of Related Children, and Work Experience of Family Members in the Labor Force for 27 Weeks or More, 1999," in *A Profile of the Working Poor, 1999,* U.S. Department of Labor, Bureau of Labor Statistics, Report 947, Washington, DC, February 2001

TABLE 5.15

Poverty status and labor market problems of full-time wage and salary workers in the labor force for 27 weeks or more, 1999

(Numbers in thousands)

Poverty status and labor market problems	Total	At or above poverty level	Below poverty level	Poverty rate[1]
Total, full-time wage and salary workers	104,968	101,369	3,599	3.4
No unemployment, involuntary part-time employment, or low earnings[2]	86,868	86,262	606	.7
Unemployment only	5,320	4,907	413	7.8
Involuntary part-time employment only	2,025	1,983	42	2.1
Low earnings only	7,444	5,939	1,505	20.2
Unemployment and involuntary part-time employment	883	800	83	9.4
Unemployment and low earnings	1,426	820	606	42.5
Involuntary part-time employment and low earnings	623	435	189	30.3
Unemployment, involuntary part-time employment, and low earnings	377	222	155	41.1

[1] Number below the poverty level as a percent of the total in the labor force for 27 weeks or more.
[2] The low earnings threshold in 1999 was $245.21 per week.

Note: Data refer to persons 16 years and older.

SOURCE: "Table 8. Persons in the Labor Force for 27 Weeks or More: Poverty Status and Labor Market Problems of Full-time Wage and Salary Workers, 1999," in *A Profile of the Working Poor, 1999,* U.S. Department of Labor, Bureau of Labor Statistics, Report 947, Washington, DC, February 2001

CHAPTER 6

WHO RECEIVES BENEFITS?

AN OVERVIEW OF WELFARE PROGRAM PARTICIPATION

With few exceptions, the demand for welfare assistance increased sharply in the 1990s. Nonetheless, one-third of the poor received no benefits in 2000. Several reasons explain why more than 33 percent of those living below the poverty line did not receive the assistance available to them. Some were ineligible because they had assets, such as a car or a savings account, which brought them above permitted limits. Others did not know they were eligible for benefits, while some knew they were eligible but chose not to accept benefits or felt the effort was not worth the amount of benefits they would receive.

How Many People Receive Benefits?

The U.S. Bureau of the Census reported that in 2000 about 64.9 million people, or 23.5 percent of the total U.S. population, lived in households that received some form of means-tested assistance—assistance based on earning below a certain amount. (See Table 6.1.) This number is considerably higher than the 53.2 million people, or 21 percent of the population, who received assistance in 1990.

In 2000, among the 31.1 million people living below the poverty level, 20.6 million, or 66.2 percent, were receiving some form of means-tested aid. (See Table 6.2.)

About 17 million persons, or 6.2 percent of the total population (down from 22.8 million, or 9 percent, in 1990), lived in households that received food stamps in 2000. Among the population living below the poverty level, 10.5 million people (33.8 percent of the poor) received food stamps. (See Tables 6.1 and 6.2.)

In 2000 Medicaid covered about 45.2 million people (up from 25.3 million in 1990), about 16.4 percent of the population. (See Table 6.1.)

What Type of Households Receive Assistance?

Certain types of households were more likely than others to receive means-tested assistance. Poor families with children under 18 years of age were most likely to receive government assistance. In 2000, 84.2 percent of all poor families with children and 88.6 percent of poor families headed by a single mother with children under six years of age received assistance. In unrelated subfamilies (two or more people living in the same household who are related to each other but are not related to the householder), 63.2 percent of poor children under the age of six received assistance. (See Table 6.2.)

Information on the age, gender, racial and ethnic background, and family status of welfare participants in 2000 is available from the Current Population Survey, a joint project of the U.S. Bureau of Labor Statistics and the U.S. Bureau of the Census.

Gender of Welfare Recipients

In 2000 there were slightly more female (24.7 percent) than male (22.3 percent) welfare recipients. About 34.8 million females received program assistance for at least a short time during 2000, compared to 30.1 million males. Among the poor, 11.8 million females (67 percent) received benefits during some part of the year, compared to 8.8 million males (65.3 percent). (See Table 6.2.)

One reason for the larger percentage of females receiving assistance is that women are more likely to live in a family without a spouse present. Another reason is that women, on average, earn only 70 percent of what men earn. Age may also play a role in the higher number of women in poverty; there are far more elderly women then men.

Racial and Ethnic Characteristics of Welfare Recipients

The U.S. Census Bureau reported that in 2000, 15.2 percent of white non-Hispanics lived in households receiving some form of means-tested assistance, 44 percent of

TABLE 6.1

Program participation status of households, 2000

(Numbers in thousands. Based on a November 2001 weighting correction.)

Characteristic	Total	In household that received means-tested assistance		In household that received means tested assistance excl.school lunch		In household that received means tested cash assistance		In household that received food stamps		In household in which one or more persons were covered by Medicaid		Live in public or subsidized housing	
		Number	Percent	Number	Percent	Number	Percent	Number	Percent	Number	Percent	Number	Percent
Both Sexes													
Total	275,924	64,939	23.5	52,299	19.0	17,871	6.5	17,028	6.2	45,161	16.4	10,682	3.9
Under 18 years	71,936	25,332	35.2	18,793	26.1	5,966	8.3	7,706	10.7	16,894	23.5	4,092	5.7
18 to 24 years	26,965	6,704	24.9	5,841	21.7	1,776	6.6	1,796	6.7	4,921	18.3	1,309	4.9
25 to 34 years	37,440	8,711	23.3	6,945	18.6	2,134	5.7	2,208	5.9	6,030	16.1	1,314	3.5
35 to 44 years	44,780	8,985	20.1	6,705	15.0	2,265	5.1	1,979	4.4	5,845	13.1	1,118	2.5
45 to 54 years	38,040	5,711	15.0	4,874	12.8	2,047	5.4	1,263	3.3	4,124	10.8	803	2.1
55 to 59 years	13,338	1,976	14.8	1,844	13.8	934	7.0	473	3.5	1,585	11.9	333	2.5
60 to 64 years	10,447	1,653	15.8	1,550	14.8	683	6.5	417	4.0	1,331	12.7	288	2.8
65 years and over	32,978	5,867	17.8	5,747	17.4	2,065	6.3	1,185	3.6	4,430	13.4	1,424	4.3
65 to 74 years	17,878	3,055	17.1	2,956	16.5	1,137	6.4	680	3.8	2,383	13.3	665	3.7
75 years and over	15,100	2,812	18.6	2,791	18.5	928	6.1	505	3.3	2,047	13.6	759	5.0
Male													
Total	134,943	30,107	22.3	24,006	17.8	7,967	5.9	7,332	5.4	20,781	15.4	4,355	3.2
Under 18 years	36,830	13,044	35.4	9,676	26.3	3,003	8.2	3,872	10.5	8,721	23.7	2,068	5.6
18 to 24 years	13,476	2,990	22.2	2,499	18.5	734	5.4	666	4.9	2,068	15.3	531	3.9
25 to 34 years	18,451	3,706	20.1	3,051	16.5	883	4.8	735	4.0	2,605	14.1	449	2.4
35 to 44 years	22,177	4,029	18.2	3,020	13.6	1,035	4.7	802	3.6	2,610	11.8	373	1.7
45 to 54 years	18,578	2,690	14.5	2,269	12.2	917	4.9	545	2.9	1,932	10.4	306	1.6
55 to 59 years	6,406	826	12.9	774	12.1	384	6.0	170	2.7	675	10.5	106	1.7
60 to 64 years	4,847	647	13.4	599	12.4	256	5.3	153	3.1	514	10.6	87	1.8
65 years and over	14,179	2,174	15.3	2,117	14.9	756	5.3	388	2.7	1,657	11.7	433	3.1
65 to 74 years	8,187	1,239	15.1	1,192	14.6	454	5.5	243	3.0	949	11.6	253	3.1
75 years and over	5,992	934	15.6	925	15.4	302	5.0	145	2.4	708	11.8	180	3.0
Female													
Total	140,981	34,832	24.7	28,293	20.1	9,903	7.0	9,696	6.9	24,380	17.3	6,327	4.5
Under 18 years	35,107	12,288	35.0	9,116	26.0	2,964	8.4	3,834	10.9	8,173	23.3	2,024	5.8
18 to 24 years	13,489	3,714	27.5	3,342	24.8	1,042	7.7	1,130	8.4	2,853	21.2	778	5.8
25 to 34 years	18,989	5,005	26.4	3,895	20.5	1,251	6.6	1,473	7.8	3,425	18.0	865	4.6
35 to 44 years	22,603	4,956	21.9	3,684	16.3	1,229	5.4	1,177	5.2	3,236	14.3	745	3.3
45 to 54 years	19,462	3,022	15.5	2,604	13.4	1,131	5.8	718	3.7	2,192	11.3	497	2.6
55 to 59 years	6,932	1,150	16.6	1,070	15.4	550	7.9	302	4.4	910	13.1	227	3.3
60 to 64 years	5,600	1,005	18.0	952	17.0	427	7.6	265	4.7	817	14.6	201	3.6
65 years and over	18,799	3,693	19.6	3,630	19.3	1,309	7.0	797	4.2	2,773	14.8	991	5.3
65 to 74 years	9,691	1,815	18.7	1,764	18.2	683	7.0	437	4.5	1,434	14.8	412	4.3
75 years and over	9,108	1,877	20.6	1,866	20.5	626	6.9	360	4.0	1,339	14.7	578	6.3
Household relationship													
Total	275,924	64,939	23.5	52,299	19.0	17,871	6.5	17,028	6.2	45,161	16.4	10,682	3.9
65 years and over	32,978	5,867	17.8	5,747	17.4	2,065	6.3	1,185	3.6	4,430	13.4	1,424	4.3
In families	229,482	56,421	24.6	44,164	19.2	14,855	6.5	14,540	6.3	39,057	17.0	8,079	3.5
Householder	72,388	15,146	20.9	12,205	16.9	4,180	5.8	3,921	5.4	10,629	14.7	2,442	3.4
Under 65 years	60,782	13,374	22.0	10,478	17.2	3,457	5.7	3,573	5.9	9,175	15.1	2,249	3.7
65 years and over	11,606	1,772	15.3	1,727	14.9	723	6.2	348	3.0	1,454	12.5	193	1.7
Related children													
Under 18 years	70,767	24,785	35.0	18,364	26.0	5,840	8.3	7,574	10.7	16,519	23.3	4,023	5.7
Under 6 years	23,243	8,263	35.5	6,867	29.5	2,085	9.0	2,829	12.2	6,274	27.0	1,492	6.4
6 to 17 years	47,524	16,523	34.8	11,497	24.2	3,755	7.9	4,745	10.0	10,245	21.6	2,531	5.3
Own children 18 years and over	21,298	5,180	24.3	4,394	20.6	1,868	8.8	1,068	5.0	3,875	18.2	568	2.7
In married-couple families	180,272	32,673	18.1	24,458	13.6	6,704	3.7	5,561	3.1	21,582	12.0	2,738	1.5
Husbands	55,611	7,873	14.2	6,168	11.1	1,746	3.1	1,319	2.4	5,324	9.6	755	1.4
Under 65 years	45,531	6,689	14.7	5,022	11.0	1,313	2.9	1,120	2.5	4,396	9.7	598	1.3
65 years and over	10,080	1,184	11.7	1,146	11.4	433	4.3	199	2.0	929	9.2	157	1.6
Wives	55,611	7,873	14.2	6,168	11.1	1,746	3.1	1,319	2.4	5,324	9.6	755	1.4
Under 65 years	47,954	7,021	14.6	5,336	11.1	1,450	3.0	1,179	2.5	4,663	9.7	634	1.3
65 years and over	7,657	852	11.1	832	10.9	295	3.9	140	1.8	661	8.6	120	1.6
Related children													
Under 18 years	51,926	13,166	25.4	9,049	17.4	2,011	3.9	2,447	4.7	8,131	15.7	1,069	2.1
Under 6 years	17,426	4,507	25.9	3,518	20.2	667	3.8	939	5.4	3,180	18.2	438	2.5
6 to 17 years	34,499	8,659	25.1	5,530	16.0	1,345	3.9	1,508	4.4	4,951	14.4	631	1.8
Own children 18 years and over	13,802	2,576	18.7	2,073	15.0	877	6.4	354	2.6	1,862	13.5	133	1.0

TABLE 6.1

Program participation status of households, 2000 [CONTINUED]

(Numbers in thousands. Based on a November 2001 weighting correction.)

Characteristic	Total	In household that received means-tested assistance		In household that received means tested assistance excl. school lunch		In household that received means tested cash assistance		In household that received food stamps		In household in which one or more persons were covered by Medicaid		Live in public or subsidized housing	
		Number	Percent	Number	Percent	Number	Percent	Number	Percent	Number	Percent	Number	Percent
In families with female house-holder, no spouse present	37,422	19,831	53.0	16,463	44.0	7,003	18.7	8,103	21.7	14,607	39.0	4,866	13.0
Householder	12,525	5,996	47.9	4,972	39.7	2,041	16.3	2,306	18.4	4,361	34.8	1,532	12.2
Under 65 years	10,798	5,453	50.5	4,438	41.1	1,785	16.5	2,173	20.1	3,877	35.9	1,486	13.8
65 years and over	1,727	543	31.5	533	30.9	257	14.9	134	7.7	484	28.0	46	2.7
Related children													
Under 18 years	15,382	10,098	65.6	8,152	53.0	3,491	22.7	4,707	30.6	7,316	47.6	2,756	17.9
Under 6 years	4,655	3,189	68.5	2,868	61.6	1,298	27.9	1,696	36.4	2,646	56.8	981	21.1
6 to 17 years	10,727	6,908	64.4	5,284	49.3	2,193	20.4	3,012	28.1	4,670	43.5	1,775	16.5
18 years and over	6,177	2,295	37.2	2,049	33.2	871	14.1	675	10.9	1,783	28.9	414	6.7
In families with male house-holder, no spouse present	11,788	3,918	33.2	3,243	27.5	1,147	9.7	876	7.4	2,868	24.3	475	4.0
Householder	4,252	1,276	30.0	1,065	25.1	393	9.2	295	6.9	943	22.2	155	3.7
Under 65 years	3,835	1,140	29.7	935	24.4	329	8.6	266	6.9	833	21.7	151	3.9
65 years and over	417	136	32.6	130	31.1	64	15.4	29	7.0	110	26.4	4	1.0
Related children													
Under 18 years	3,460	1,522	44.0	1,164	33.6	337	9.8	420	12.1	1,072	31.0	198	5.7
Under 6 years	1,162	566	48.7	481	41.4	120	10.3	194	16.7	448	38.6	73	6.3
6 to 17 years	2,298	955	41.6	682	29.7	217	9.5	225	9.86	24	27.2	125	5.5
18 years and over	1,319	309	23.4	271	20.5	120	9.1	39	2.9	230	17.5	21	1.6
In unrelated subfamilies	1,326	647	48.8	502	37.9	149	11.3	178	13.5	442	33.3	73	5.5
Under 18 years	760	389	51.2	291	38.3	90 1	1.8	103	13.6	255	33.6	46	6.0
Under 6 years	224	115	51.7	99	44.5	24	10.8	24	10.5	81 3	6.2	14	6.2
6 to 17 years	536	273	51.0	191	35.7	66	12.2	80	14.8	174	32.5	32	5.9
18 years and over	566	258	45.6	212	37.4	60	10.5	75	13.3	187	33.0	27	4.8
Unrelated individuals	45,117	7,871	17.4	7,633	16.9	2,866	6.4	2,309	5.1	5,662	12.6	2,530	5.6
Male	21,629	3,569	16.5	3,415	15.8	1,264	5.8	1,027	4.8	2,594	12.0 9	63	4.5
Under 65 years	18,747	2,924	15.6	2,773	14.8	1,082	5.8	896	4.8	2,164	11.5	708	3.8
Living alone	9,107	1,026	11.3	1,026	11.3	420	4.6	360	4.06	97	7.7	443	4.9
65 years and over	2,882	645	22.4	643	22.3	18	2 6.3	131	4.6	430	14.9	255	8.9
Living alone	2,464	536	21.8	536	21.8	142	5.8	101	4.1	347	14.1	247	10.0
Female	23,488	4,303	18.3	4,217	18.0	1,602	6.8	1,282	5.5	3,068	13.1	1,567	6.7
Under 65 years	15,711	2,597	16.5	2,513	16.0	1,121	7.1	880	5.6	1,967	12.5	771	4.9
Living alone	8,858	1,367	15.4	1,367	15.4	675	7.6	556	6.3	1,001	11.3	630	7.1
65 years and over	7,777	1,706	21.9	1,704	21.9	482	6.2	402	5.2	1,101	14.2	796	10.2
Living alone	7,449	1,619	21.7	1,619	21.7	443	5.9	373	5.0	1,028	13.8	794	10.7

Note: Hispanics may be of any race.

SOURCE:"Table 3. Program Participation Status of Household—Poverty Status of Persons in 2000, All Races, Below Poverty Level," in *CPS Annual Demographic Survery,* U.S. Census Bureau, March 2001 [Online] http://ferret.bls.census.gov/macro/032001/pov/new03_001.htm [accessed June 5, 2002]

African Americans, and 48.5 percent of persons of Hispanic origin (persons of Hispanic origin can be of any race). Among those with incomes below the poverty line, 53.1 percent of white non-Hispanics, 80.8 percent of African Americans, and 77.9 percent of Hispanics received benefits.

Age of Welfare Recipients

More than one-third (35.2 percent) of children under 18 years old received assistance at some time during 2000. Approximately one out of six elderly (17.8 percent) received assistance. (See Table 6.1.)

Family Relationships of Welfare Recipients

Only 18.1 percent of recipients who received benefits for some part of 2000 were living in families headed by married couples. By contrast, 53 percent of individuals in female-headed families with no spouse present received benefits. The highest rate of assistance was provided to families headed by women with children under the age of six (68.5 percent). (See Table 6.1.)

USE OVER A PERIOD A TIME

The *Survey of Income and Program Participation* (SIPP), conducted periodically by the U.S. Census Bureau, is a longitudinal (over a period of time) survey of the same households that measures changes in their economic activity. Among the many areas covered in the 1993–95 survey, the bureau studied the use of major means-tested programs: Aid to Families with Dependent Children (AFDC), General Assistance, Supplemental Security Income (SSI),

TABLE 6.2

Program participation status of households, all races below the poverty level, 2000

(Numbers in thousands. Based on a November 2001 weighting correction.)

Characteristic	Total	In household that received means-tested assistance		In household that received means tested assistance excl.school lunch		In household that received means tested cash assistance		In household that received food stamps		In household in which one or more persons were covered by Medicaid		Live in public or subsidized housing	
		Number	Percent	Number	Percent	Number	Percent	Number	Percent	Number	Percent	Number	Percent
Both Sexes													
Total	31,054	20,567	66.2	17,902	57.6	7,814	25.2	10,500	33.8	15,567	50.1	5,749	8.5
Under 18 years	11,553	9,611	83.2	8,096	70.1	3,490	30.2	5,313	46.0	7,304	63.2	2,664	23.1
18 to 24 years	3,890	2,042	52.5	1,877	48.3	680	17.5	1,015	26.1	1,577	40.5	625	16.1
25 to 34 years	3,892	2,529	65.0	2,194	56.4	940	24.2	1,309	33.6	1,933	49.7	652	16.8
35 to 44 years	3,678	2,461	66.9	2,033	55.3	856	23.3	1,119	30.4	1,768	48.1	567	15.4
45 to 54 years	2,441	1,422	58.3	1,282	52.5	651	26.7	684	28.0	1,080	44.3	394	16.2
55 to 59 years	1,175	613	52.2	582	49.5	344	29.2	261	22.2	486	41.3	186	15.8
60 to 64 years	1,066	504	47.3	475	44.6	256	24.0	251	23.5	382	35.9	172	16.1
65 years and over	3,359	1,385	41.2	1,363	40.6	597	17.8	549	16.3	1,036	30.8	489	14.6
65 to 74 years	1,592	755	47.4	738	46.3	334	21.0	346	21.7	571	35.9	272	17.1
75 years and over	1,767	630	35.6	625	35.4	263	14.9	202	11.5	465	26.3	217	12.3
Male													
Total	13,417	8,755	65	7,462	55.6	3,136	23.4	4,220	31.5	6,478	48.3	2,240	16.7
Under 18 years	5,836	4,850	83.1	4,027	69.0	1,697	29.1	2,582	44.2	3,654	62.6	1,309	22.4
18 to 24 years	1,568	709	45.2	628	40.1	200	12.8	316	20.1	496	31.6	201	12.8
25 to 34 years	1,421	806	56.7	689	48.5	270	19.0	328	23.1	598	42.1	169	11.9
35 to 44 years	1,520	927	61.0	763	50.2	335	22.0	377	24.8	649	42.7	175	11.5
45 to 54 years	1,122	631	56.2	565	50.4	258	23.0	289	25.7	480	42.8	129	11.5
55 to 59 years	477	240	50.2	226	47.3	130	27.2	92	19.2	183	38.3	58	12.1
60 to 64 years	411	175	42.6	160	39.0	76	18.5	82	20.0	122	29.7	56	13.7
65 years and over	1,063	417	39.2	403	37.9	171	16.1	154	14.5	297	27.9	143	13.5
65 to 74 years	575	264	45.9	253	44.0	111	19.4	105	18.2	186	32.4	97	17.0
75 years and over	488	154	31.5	150	30.8	59	12.1	49	10.1	110	22.6	46	9.4
Female													
Total	17,637	11,811	67.0	10,440	59.2	4,678	26.5	6,280	35.6	9,089	51.5	3,510	19.9
Under 18 years	5,717	4,761	83.3	4,069	71.2	1,793	31.4	2,731	47.8	3,650	63.9	1,355	23.7
18 to 24 years	2,323	1,333	57.4	1,249	53.8	481	20.7	699	30.1	1,081	46.6	424	18.2
25 to 34 years	2,472	1,722	69.7	1,505	60.9	670	27.1	981	39.7	1,335	54.0	484	19.6
35 to 44 years	2,158	1,534	71.1	1,270	58.8	521	24.2	742	34.4	1,119	51.9	392	18.2
45 to 54 years	1,319	791	60.0	717	54.4	393	29.8	395	30.0	600	45.5	266	20.2
55 to 59 years	698	373	53.5	357	51.1	214	30.6	169	24.2	303	43.4	128	18.3
60 to 64 years	655	330	50.3	315	48.0	180	27.5	169	25.8	260	39.7	115	17.6
65 years and over	2,296	967	42.1	959	41.8	426	18.6	394	17.2	740	32.2	346	15.1
65 to 74 years	1,017	491	48.3	485	47.7	222	21.9	241	23.7	384	37.8	175	17.2
75 years and over	1,279	476	37.2	474	37.1	204	16.0	153	12.0	355	27.8	171	13.4
Household relationship													
Total	31,054	20,567	66.2	17,902	57.6	7,814	25.2	10,500	33.8	15,567	50.1	5,749	18.5
65 years and over	3,359	1,385	41.2	1,363	40.6	597	17.8	549	16.3	1,036	30.8	489	14.6
In families	22,015	16,581	75.3	14,076	63.9	6,043	27.4	8,894	40.4	12,547	57.0	4,431	20.1
Householder	6,222	4,364	70.1	3,788	60.9	1,629	26.2	2,355	37.8	3,343	53.7	1,260	20.3
Under 65 years	5,595	4,103	73.3	3,538	63.2	1,494	26.7	2,250	40.2	3,136	56.0	1,220	21.8
65 years and over	627	261	41.5	250	39.9	134	21.4	105	16.8	207	33.0	40	6.4
Related children													
Under 18 years	11,018	9,273	84.2	7,827	71.0	3,411	31.0	5,214	47.3	7,075	64.2	2,615	23.7
Under 6 years	3,917	3,274	83.6	2,925	74.7	1,271	32.4	1,923	49.1	2,689	68.6	1,000	25.5
6 to 17 years	7,101	5,998	84.5	4,902	69.0	2,141	30.1	3,291	46.3	4,386	61.8	1,616	22.8
Own children 18 years and over	1,311	887	67.7	762	58.1	390	29.8	474	36.2	668	51.0	210	16.0
In married-couple families	10,138	6,599	65.1	5,211	51.4	1,692	16.7	2,850	28.1	4,573	45.1	1,040	10.3
Husbands	2,638	1,488	56.4	1,212	45.9	405	15.4	652	24.7	1,040	39.4	246	9.3
Under 65 years	2,179	1,345	61.7	1,076	49.4	336	15.4	588	27.0	939	43.1	214	9.8
65 years and over	459	143	31.2	136	29.6	69	5.1	64	14.0	102	22.2	32	7.0
Wives	2,638	1,488	56.4	1,212	45.9	405	15.4	652	24.7	1,040	39.4	246	9.3
Under 65 years	2,305	1,392	60.4	1,120	48.6	3.62	15.7	609	26.4	968	42.0	230	10.0
65 years and over	334	96	28.6	92	27.6	43	13.0	43	12.9	73	21.7	16	4.8

TABLE 6.2

Program participation status of households, all races below the poverty level, 2000

(Numbers in thousands. Based on a November 2001 weighting correction.)

Characteristic	Total	In household that received means-tested assistance		In household that received means tested assistance excl.school lunch		In household that received means tested cash assistance		In household that received food stamps		In household in which one or more persons were covered by Medicaid		Live in public or subsidized housing	
		Number	Percent	Number	Percent	Number	Percent	Number	Percent	Number	Percent	Number	Percent
Related children													
Under 18 years	4,219	3,246	76.9	2,498	59.2	769	18.2	1,415	33.5	2,232	52.9	493	11.7
Under 6 years	1,490	1,142	76.6	916	61.4	248	16.6	516	34.6	833	55.9	187	12.5
6 to 17 years	2,728	2,104	77.1	1,583	58.0	521	19.1	899	32.9	1,399	51.3	306	11.2
Own children 18 years and over	477	280	58.7	217	45.6	97	20.3	108	22.6	195	40.9	49	10.2
In families with female house-													
holder, no spouse present	10,425	8,957	85.9	8,026	77.0	4,049	38.8	5,649	54.2	7,239	69.4	3,176	30.5
Householder	3,096	2,547	82.3	2,302	74.4	1,120	36.2	1,580	51.0	2,062	66.6	944	30.5
Under 65 years	2,921	2,439	83.5	2,195	75.1	1,058	36.2	1,543	52.8	1,961	67.1	933	31.9
65 years and over	175	108	61.6	107	61.5	62	35.4	36	20.8	102	58.0	12	6.6
Related children													
Under 18 years.	6,116	5,489	89.8	4,904	80.2	2,487	40.7	3,578	58.5	4,465	73.0	1,994	32.6
Under 6 years	2,196	1,945	88.6	1,844	84.0	973	44.3	1,323	60.2	1,718	78.2	766	34.9
6 to 17 years	3,920	3,544	90.4	3,060	78.1	1,514	38.6	2,255	57.5	2,746	70.1	1,228	31.3
18 years and over	753	568	75.5	515	68.5	285	37.8	349	46.3	449	59.6	161	21.3
In families with male householder													
no spouse present	1,452	1,025	70.6	840	57.8	301	20.7	395	27.2	735	50.6	215	14.8
Householder	488	329	67.5	274	56.1	104	21.2	123	25.1	240	49.2	70	14.3
Under 65 years	448	300	67.0	248	55.3	94	20.9	110	24.6	218	48.7	66	14.7
65 years and over	40	29	(B)	26	(B)	10	(B)	13	(B)	22	(B)	4	(B)
Related children													
Under 18 years	684	538	78.6	425	62.1	156	22.8	221	32.3	379	55.4	129	18.9
Under 6 years	231	187	81.1	165	71.7	50	21.6	84	36.5	137	59.6	47	20.2
6 to 17 years	453	351	77.4	259	57.3	106	23.4	137	30.2	241	53.3	82	18.2
18 years and over	81	39	48.3	29	35.5	9	10.7	17	21.2	24	29.9	1	1.1
In unrelated subfamilies	510	383	75.1	300	58.8	93	18.2	127	25.0	258	50.6	48	9.4
Under 18 years	306	240	78.3	181	59.1	60	19.7	79	25.9	155	50.7	32	10.4
Under 6 years	113	72	63.2	59	52.3	16	14.4	12	10.8	51	44.6	5	4.3
6 to 17 years	193	168	87.2	122	63.2	44	22.9	67	34.7	105	54.3	27	14.0
18 years and over	204	143	70.4	119	58.3	32	15.9	48	23.7	103	50.4	16	7.8
Unrelated individuals	8,529	3,602	42.2	3,526	41.3	1,678	19.7	1,479	17.3	2,762	32.4	1,270	14.9
Male	3,459	1,400	40.5	1,364	39.4	640	18.5	558	16.1	1,052	30.4	464	13.4
Under 65 years	2,931	1,170	39.9	1,134	38.7	552	18.8	486	16.6	889	30.3	362	12.3
Living alone	1,155	550	47.6	550	47.6	268	23.2	267	23.1	399	34.5	246	21.3
65 years and over	528	230	43.5	230	43.5	88	16.7	72	13.6	164	31.0	102	19.3
Living alone	437	179	40.9	179	40.9	70	15.9	60	13.8	121	27.7	98	22.3
Female	5,071	2,202	43.4	2,162	42.6	1,039	20.5	922	18.2	1,709	33.7	807	15.9
Under 65 years	3,378	1,501	44.4	1,460	43.2	743	22.0	632	18.7	1,194	35.3	498	14.7
Living alone	1,575	848	53.8	848	53.8	498	31.6	434	27.6	671	42.6	421	26.7
65 years and over	1,692	702	41.5	702	41.5	296	17.5	290	17.1	516	30.5	309	18.2
Living alone	1,584	669	42.2	669	42.2	281	17.8	276	17.4	489	30.8	307	19.4

Note: Hispanics may be any race.

SOURCE: "Table 3. Program Participation Status of Household—Poverty Status of Persons in 2000," in *CPS Annual Demographic Survey,* U.S. Census Bureau, March 2001 [Online] http://ferret.bls.census.gov/macro/032001/pov/new03_002.htm [accessed June 5, 2002]

Medicaid, Food Stamps, and housing assistance. In "Dynamics of Economic Well-Being: Program Participation, 1993 to 1995: Who Gets Assistance?" (*Current Population Reports*, September 2001), the Census Bureau released information on the characteristics of recipients of means-tested programs and the length of time for which they received benefits during a 33-month period.

Education Levels of Welfare Recipients

The SIPP found a strong correlation between a low level of education and receipt of welfare benefits. Adults who did not graduate from high school were most likely to receive assistance for all 33 months from January 1993 though September 1995:

- Those who did not finish high school—18.9 percent;

- Those who were high school graduates—5.6 percent;

- Those with one or more years of college—2.1 percent.

According to the study, the median duration of welfare assistance for recipients without a high school diploma (7.1 months) was much longer than the median for

TABLE 6.3

Median duration of spells of program participation by program, 1993–95

[In months]

Characteristic	Any means-tested programs[1]		AFDC/GA		Supplemental Security Income[2]		Food stamps		Medicaid		Housing assistance	
	Median	Standard error	Median	Standard error	Median	Standard error	Median	Standard error	Median	Standard error	Median	Standard error
All recipients[3]	**5.0**	**0.4**	**7.3**	**0.4**	**(X)**	**(X)**	**5.8**	**0.4**	**4.9**	**0.6**	**7.8**	**0.6**
Race and Hispanic Origin												
White	4.8	0.4	5.9	0.7	(X)	(X)	5.3	0.4	4.8	0.6	7.3	0.5
Not of Hispanic origin[4]	4.8	0.4	5.4	0.8	(X)	(X)	5.3	0.5	5.2	0.6	7.1	0.5
Black	6.1	1.1	8	0.3	(X)	(X)	7.6	0.3	5.3	0.6	11.8	0.8
Hispanic origin[4]	4.9	1.3	7.6	0.8	(X)	(X)	5.5	1.3	3.9	0.1	12.6	2.0
Not of Hispanic origin	5.0	0.4	7.2	0.4	(X)	(X)	5.8	0.4	5.3	0.5	7.6	0.6
Age[5]												
Under 18 years	4.6	0.6	7.7	0.5	(X)	(X)	7.2	0.6	4.3	0.9	12.4	1.5
18 to 64 years	5.1	0.5	6.3	1.8	(X)	(X)	5.0	0.5	5.2	0.7	7.1	0.6
65 years and over	7.7	0.9	(B)	(B)	(X)	(X)	5.6	2.8	7.8	0.6	7.9	1.3
Sex												
Men	4.4	0.5	5.8	0.8	(X)	(X)	5.2	0.7	4.2	0.9	7.1	0.9
Women	5.6	0.6	7.8	0.5	(X)	(X)	6.4	1.1	5.4	0.7	9.4	2.8
Educational Attainment (people 18 years and over)												
Less than 4 years of high school	7.1	0.5	6.3	1.8	(X)	(X)	5.9	0.8	7.1	0.4	10.2	1.7
High school graduate, no college	4.9	0.7	6.7	4.3	(X)	(X)	4.8	0.5	5.4	0.7	6.0	2.3
1 or more years of college	4.0	0.1	4.6	1.9	(X)	(X)	4.1	1.0	4.0	0.2	5.5	3.1
Disability Status (people 15 to 64 years old)												
With a work disability	7.4	0.6	6.7	4.5	(X)	(X)	6.7	1.9	7.5	0.4	10.9	1.2
With no work disability	4.3	0.6	6.0	0.8	(X)	(X)	4.7	0.5	3.9	0.1	5.8	1.6
Residence												
Metropolitan	5.3	0.5	7.6	0.4	(X)	(X)	6.6	1.0	5.4	0.7	9.8	5.1
Central city	5.7	0.8	7.7	0.4	(X)	(X)	7.3	0.4	6.0	1.0	11.3	1.2
Noncentral city	4.9	0.7	7.2	0.6	(X)	(X)	5.6	0.5	4.8	1.0	6.9	6.4
Nonmetropolitan	4.5	0.6	4.9	0.6	(X)	(X)	4.7	0.6	4.2	0.8	6.3	7.4
Region												
Northeast	4.0	0.1	7.7	0.5	(X)	(X)	6.2	1.5	4.9	3.5	8.9	3.0
Midwest	4.4	0.7	7.1	0.8	(X)	(X)	5.2	0.8	5.9	1	7.5	0.7
South	5.1	0.7	6.0	2.2	(X)	(X)	6.3	1.1	4.0	0.1	5.3	1.5
West	6.2	1.6	7.7	0.7	(X)	(X)	5.6	0.8	6.9	1.7	13.2	1.5
Family Status												
In families	4.9	0.4	7.4	0.4	(X)	(X)	5.8	0.4	4.6	0.6	8	0.7
In married-couple families	4.0	0.1	5.9	1.0	(X)	(X)	4.8	0.4	4.0	0.1	5.0	1.7
In families with a female householder, no spouse present	7.2	0.4	7.9	0.5	(X)	(X)	7.6	0.6	5.5	0.8	13.1	0.7
Unrelated individuals	5.7	2.2	3.8	0.4	(X)	(X)	5.8	4.0	7.8	0.5	7.4	0.9
Employment and Labor Force Status (people 18 years and over)												
Employed full-time	3.8	0.1	3.8	0.2	(X)	(X)	3.7	0.2	3.7	0.1	3.9	0.1
Employed part-time	6.2	1.9	6.7	1.6	(X)	(X)	4.6	0.7	6.6	2.3	8.0	2.1
Unemployed	6.1	1.8	7.7	1.0	(X)	(X)	6.7	2.4	4.8	2.9	7.9	2.3
Not in labor force	7.5	0.4	7.4	0.7	(X)	(X)	7.0	0.6	7.4	0.3	11.2	1.0

high school graduates (4.9 months) and people with some college experience (4 months). (See Table 6.3.)

Employment Status of Welfare Recipients

More than one-quarter (25.7 percent) of the unemployed and more than one-fifth (21 percent) of those individuals not in the labor force received welfare assistance in an average month in 1995. However, only 3.7 percent of full-time employees and 9.3 percent of part-time workers received these benefits. In addition to receiving means-tested benefits, unemployed workers may also be eligible for unemployment compensation. (See Table 6.4.) In an average month in 1995, 18.5 percent of the unemployed were receiving unemployment compensation benefits.

Duration of Program Spells

The length of time people received assistance, referred to as a spell, differed by program. The average number of months for receiving means-tested assistance during the 33-month period from January 1993 to

TABLE 6.3

Median duration of spells of program participation by program, 1993–95 [CONTINUED]

[In months]

Characteristic	Any means-tested programs[1]		AFDC/GA		Supplemental Security Income[2]		Food stamps		Medicaid		Housing assistance	
	Median	Standard error	Median	Standard error	Median	Standard error	Median	Standard error	Median	Standard error	Median	Standard error
Family Income-to-Poverty Ratio												
Under 1.00	7.4	0.4	7.8	0.5	(X)	(X)	7.5	0.4	7.2	0.3	13.5	0.9
1.00 and over	3.9	0.1	5.5	0.9	(X)	(X)	4.1	0.5	3.9	0.1	4.0	0.1

X Not applicable.
[1]Major means-tested programs include Aid to Families with Dependent Children (AFDC), General Assistance, Supplemental Security Income (SSI), food stamps, medicaid, and housing assistance.
[2]Median duration cannot be computed when more than half of the spells are continuing in the last month of data collection. (This situation is especially likely to occur for elderly recipients whose incomes from other sources are unlikely to rise over time.)
[3]Median duration for each program is derived only for those who begin participating in each program at some point in the survey, while those who are already in the program before the start of the survey (i.e., the left-censored cases) are excluded from the analysis.
[4]Persons of Hispanic origin may be of any race.
[5]Age, educational attainment, and other variables are measured at the time the spells begin.

SOURCE: Jan Tin and Charita Castro, "Table A7. Median Duration of Spells of Program Participation and Standard Errors by Program: 1993-95," in *Dynamics of Economic Well-Being: Program Participation, 1993 to 1995: Who Gets Assistance?*, Current Population Reports P70-77, U.S. Census Bureau, Washington, DC, September 2001

September 1995 was five months. The spell length for housing assistance (7.8 months) and AFDC/general assistance (7.3 months) was longer than that for food stamps (5.8 months) and Medicaid (4.9 months). (See Figure 6.1.) People in families maintained by a female householder had longer spells (7.2 months) than married-couple families (4 months). (See Table 6.3.)

SURVEY OF PROGRAM DYNAMICS FOR EVALUATING WELFARE REFORM

Data from the 1993–95 SIPP survey are being used as a baseline to examine the impact of welfare reform. The 1996 welfare reform act (PRWORA) directed the U.S. Census Bureau to examine changes following the elimination of the AFDC program and its replacement with TANF. During a six-year period (1996 through 2001) the Census Bureau interviewed a sample of households that participated in the SIPP surveys from 1992 to 1994. Once tabulation is complete, these surveys will provide information on the effect of the new law upon the demographic and socioeconomic characteristics of persons participating in public assistance programs. Changes in the composition and characteristics of AFDC/TANF recipients over time are examined in Chapter 10.

OVERLAPPING SERVICES

Not surprisingly, poor individuals who receive one form of social welfare assistance are likely to qualify for and receive others. For example, during 1997 and 1998, 32.2 percent of those receiving TANF also received housing assistance, 60.3 percent received free or reduced-price

FIGURE 6.1

Median spell length (in months) by program, January 1993–September 1995

SOURCE: Jan Tin and Charita Castro, "Figure 25. Median Spell Length (in months) by Program: January 1993–September 1995," in *Dynamics of Economic Well-Being: Program Participation, 1993 to 1995, Who Gets Assistance?*, Current Population Reports P70-77, U.S. Census Bureau, Washington, DC, September 2001

school meals, 81 percent received food stamps, and almost all (97.3 percent) were on Medicaid. Similarly, among SSI recipients, 43.7 percent received food stamps, 18.4 percent received free or reduced-price school meals, 23.4 percent lived in public or subsidized rental housing, and 95 percent were on Medicaid. About 16.9 percent of those receiving Social Security and 17.2 percent of people receiving Medicare were also on Medicaid. (See Table 6.5.)

At the same time, among households receiving food stamps, 35.1 percent received TANF, 30.1 percent

TABLE 6.4

Average monthly program participation rates for any means-tested programs by selected characteristics, 1993–95

| | Program participation rates (in percent) | | | | | |
| | Any major means-tested programs[1] | | | | | |
Characteristics	1993	Standard error	1994	Standard error	1995	Standard error
Total number of recipients[2]	39,162	670	39,514	669	38,995	682
As percent of the population	15.2	0.3	15.2	0.3	14.9	0.3
Race and Hispanic Origin[3]						
White	11.7	0.3	11.8	0.3	11.6	0.3
Not of Hispanic origin	9.4	0.3	9.4	0.3	9.2	0.6
Black	36.6	0.9	36.0	0.9	35.0	0.4
Hispanic origin	32.3	1.1	31.7	1.1	30.6	1.1
Not of Hispanic origin		0.0	13.2	0.3	12.6	0.3
Age						
Under 18 years	26.2	0.6	26.5	0.6	26.1	0.6
18 to 64 years	11.0	0.3	10.8	0.3	10.6	0.3
65 years and over	12.0	0.7	11.7	0.7	11.6	0.7
Sex						
Men	13.0	0.4	13.0	0.4	12.5	0.4
Women	17.2	0.4	17.3	0.4	17.1	0.4
Educational Attainment (people 18 years and over)						
Less than 4 years of high school	25.8	0.9	25.6	0.9	24.8	0.9
High school graduate, no college	10.5	0.4	10.5	0.4	10.3	0.4
1 or more years of college	4.6	0.3	4.5	0.3	4.5	0.3
Disability Status (people 15 to 64 years old)						
With a work disability	25.0	1.0	25.5	1.0	25.3	1.0
With no work disability	8.7	0.3	8.5	0.3	8.3	0.3
Residence						
Metropolitan	14.7	0.3	14.7	0.3	14.5	0.3
Central city	23.0	0.6	22.4	0.6	22.0	0.6
Noncentral city	9.3	0.3	9.5	0.3	9.2	0.3
Nonmetropolitan	17.0	0.6	16.6	0.6	16.1	0.6
Region						
Northeast.	14.8	0.6	14.6	0.6	14.5	0.6
Midwest	12.5	0.5	12.6	0.5	12.2	0.5
South	16.5	0.5	16.4	0.5	16.0	0.5
West	16.7	0.6	16.8	0.6	16.5	0.6
Family Status						
In families	15.6	0.3	15.6	0.3	15.3	0.3
In married-couple families	9.1	0.3	8.9	0.3	8.6	0.3
In families with a female householder, no spouse present	44.3	1.0	44.3	0.9	44.2	1.0
Unrelated individuals	12.8	0.7	12.4	0.7	12.3	0.4
Employment and Labor Force Status (people 18 years and over)						
Employed full-time	4.0	0.2	3.8	0.2	3.7	0.2
Employed part-time	8.6	0.7	9.2	0.7	9.3	0.8
Unemployed	26.6	1.9	26.9	2.2	25.7	2.3
Not in labor force	21.3	0.6	21.3	0.6	21.0	0.6
Marital Status (people 18 years and over)						
Married	6.6	0.3	6.2	0.3	5.9	0.3
Separated, divorced, or widowed	19.6	0.8	19.6	0.8	19.1	0.8
Never married	15.6	0.7	15.6	0.7	15.6	0.7
Family Income-to-Poverty Ratio						
Under 1.00	60.5	0.9	60.3	0.9	60.2	1.0
1.00 and over	6.7	0.2	7.0	0.2	6.9	0.2

[1]Major means-tested programs include Aid to Families with Dependent Children (AFDC), General Assistance, Supplemental Security Income, food stamps, medicaid, and housing assistance.
[2]In thousands.
[3]People of Hispanic origin may be of any race.

SOURCE: Jan Tin and Charita Castro, "Table A-1. Average Monthly Program Participation Rates for Any Means-Tested Programs by Selected Characteristics: 1993–95," in *Dynamics of Economic Well-Being: Program Participation, 1993 to 1995: Who Gets Assistance?*, Current Population Reports P70–77, U.S. Census Bureau, Washington DC, September 2001

TABLE 6.5

Percent of recipients in programs within the jurisdiction of the Committee on Ways and Means receiving assistance from other major federal assistance programs, 1997–98

| Other assistance program | Ways and Means assistance program | | | | |
	TANF	SSI	Social Security	Unemploy-ment compen-sation	Medi-care
Food stamps	81.0	43.7	7.3	7.0	7.3
WIC	30.6	5.5	1.3	7.9	0.9
Medicaid	97.3	95.0	16.9	16.9	17.2
Free or reduced-price school meals	60.3	18.4	4.0	18.0	2.9
Public or subsidized rental housing	32.2	23.4	5.7	4.0	5.8
VA compensation or pensions	1.1	2.8	4.9	1.2	4.9
Number of households receiving benefits (in thousands)	3,008	4,772	28,833	1,546	26,525

Note: Table shows number of households for December 1997–March 1998. Table reads that 81.0 percent of TANF households also receive food stamps. SSI recipients living in California receive a higher SSI payment in lieu of food stamps, and thus are not included in the food stamp percentages.

SOURCE: "Table 15–1. Percent of Recipients in Programs Within the Jurisdiction of the Committee on Ways and Means Receiving Assistance from Other Major Federal Programs, 1997–98," in *The Green Book*, U.S. House of Representatives, Committee on Ways and Means, Washington, DC, 2000

TABLE 6.6

Percent of recipients in other major federal assistance programs receiving assistance under programs within the jurisdiction of the Committee on Ways and Means, 1997–98

| Ways and Means assistance program | Other assistance program | | | | | |
	Food stamps	WIC	Free or reduced-price school meals	Public or sub-sidized rental housing	Medicaid	VA com-pensa-tion or pensions
TANF	35.1	25.6	21.5	21.6	22.5	1.4
SSI	30.1	7.4	10.4	24.9	34.8	5.7
Social Security	30.5	10.2	13.6	36.3	37.4	59.3
Unemployment compensation	1.6	3.4	3.3	1.4	2.0	0.8
Medicare	27.9	6.3	9.0	34.3	35.2	55.2
Number of house-holds receiving benefits (in thousands)	6,932	3,585	8,444	4,487	13,014	2,369

Note: Table shows households for December 1997–March 1998. Table reads that 35.1 percent of food stamp recipient households receive TANF. SSI recipients living in California receive a higher SSI payment in lieu of food stamps, and thus are not included in the food stamp percentages.

SOURCE: "Table 15–2. Percent of Recipients in Other Major Federal Assistance Programs Receiving Assistance Under Programs Within the Jurisdiction of the Committee on Ways and Means, 1997–98," in *The Green Book,* U. S. House of Representatives, Committee on Ways and Means, Washington, DC, 2000

TABLE 6.7

Percent of households receiving AFDC/TANF or SSI and also receiving assistance from other programs for selected time periods, 1984–98

| Assistance program | Year | | | | | | | |
	1984	1987	1990	1992	1993	1994	1995	1997–98
AFDC/TANF:								
Food stamps	81.4	81.7	82.7	86.2	88.9	88.3	87.2	81.0
WIC	15.3	18.6	18.7	21.5	18.5	21.4	24.7	30.6
Free or reduced-price school meals	49.2	55.6	52.7	55.5	56.9	57.5	63.1	60.3
Public or subsidized rental housing	23.0	19.4	34.7	29.5	33.1	30.3	31.1	32.2
Medicaid	93.2	95.5	97.6	96.2	97.6	96.4	97.2	97.3
VA compensation or pensions	2.8	1.9	1.3	1.9	1.1	1.1	0.8	1.1
Number of households receiving benefits (in thousands)	3,585	3,527	3,434	4,057	4,831	4,906	4,652	3,008
SSI:								
Food stamps	46.5	39.7	41.3	46.2	48.0	50.1	50.0	43.7
WIC	2.5	2.5	3.0	4.3	3.7	5.4	5.6	5.5
Free or reduced-price school meals	12.7	11.9	15.3	18.2	21.3	23.8	25.2	18.4
Public or subsidized rental housing	21.6	20.0	21.4	23.8	23.9	24.9	24.1	23.4
Medicaid	100.0	99.6	99.7	99.8	99.5	100.0	100.0	95.0
VA compensation or pensions	4.7	7.7	5.7	4.0	4.5	3.9	3.6	2.8
Number of households receiving benefits (in thousands)	3,008	3,341	3,037	3,957	3,861	4,223	4,580	4,772

Note: Data on households interviewed between December 1997 and March 1998. SSI recipients living in California receive a higher SSI payment in lieu of food stamps, and thus are not included in the food stamp percentages; in 1997, the TANF Program replaced the Aid to Families with Dependent Children (AFDC) Program.

SOURCE: "Table 15–3. Percent of households Receiving AFDC/TANF or SSI and Also Receiving Assistance from Other Programs for Selected Time Periods," in *The Green Book,* U.S. House of Representatives, Committee on Ways and Means, Washington DC, 2000

received SSI, 30.5 percent received Social Security, and 27.9 percent were on Medicare. (The figures do not add up to 100 percent because some people received more than one benefit.) About 25.6 percent of those receiving WIC (Special Supplemental Nutrition Program for Women, Infants, and Children) also received TANF benefits. (See Table 6.6.)

Between 1984 and 1998 the percentage of AFDC/TANF and SSI households who received other benefits fluctuated. But basically the coverage for most benefits, except VA (veterans) compensation or pensions, increased between 1984 and 1995. However, following the passage of PRWORA in 1996, welfare requirements became more stringent. The percentage of households receiving both AFDC/TANF and food stamps declined (from 87.2 percent in 1995 to 81 percent in 1997–98). The percentage receiving both SSI and food stamps also declined over this period, from 50 percent to 43.7 percent. (See Table 6.7.)

CHAPTER 7

COMPARING THE NEW (TANF) WITH THE OLD (AFDC)

The Personal Responsibility and Work Opportunity Reconciliation Act (PL 104-193), the welfare-reform law enacted in 1996, ended the Aid to Families with Dependent Children (AFDC) program and replaced it with the Temporary Assistance for Needy Families (TANF) program. AFDC was an entitlement program that guaranteed benefits to all recipients whose income and resources were below state-determined eligibility levels. However, state-determined tests of financial need for cash assistance were subject to federal guidelines and limits. Under TANF, a federal block-grant program, states have the authority to determine eligibility requirements and benefit levels. Unlike AFDC, TANF is not an entitlement program. Because of this, there is no requirement that states aid, or apply uniform rules to, all families determined financially needy. (See Chapter 2 for the specific provisions of TANF.)

For several years prior to the passage of the controversial welfare-reform law, critics challenged many aspects of the existing program. On the one hand, many thought that a new welfare-to-work system would merely push welfare recipients deeper into poverty after former recipients tended to gain employment in low-wage service-sector jobs. On the other hand, many felt that the old entitlement system did not reward hard work and that it discouraged the formation and stability of two-parent families. Others charged that the program actually harmed recipients by creating "welfare dependency." Welfare dependency refers to individuals' spending a good part of their potential working lives on welfare and passing welfare dependency from one generation to another. Tied to the issue of welfare dependency was a growing belief that the living patterns of many of the poor supposedly contributed to their condition.

GALLUP PUBLIC OPINION POLLS

A 1994 Gallup poll found that about two-thirds (68 percent) of respondents believed that most welfare recipients were taking advantage of the system rather than truly needing help. As a result, 44 percent wanted to reduce welfare payments, and another 10 percent wanted to cut off payments altogether.

When asked what government could do to "help welfare recipients get off welfare and become self-sufficient," respondents most often favored job training (94 percent) and child care (90 percent). Other actions favored by the respondents included financing welfare reform with funds taken from existing welfare benefits (78 percent), cutting off all benefits to welfare recipients after two years (67 percent), paying transportation costs to a job or job-training class (66 percent), and providing government-paid jobs when there is a lack of private sector jobs (60 percent). (See Table 7.1.)

In November 1996, following the passage of the welfare-reform law, Americans were asked their opinion of the

TABLE 7.1

Public opinion on things government could do to get people off welfare, 1994

Next, I am going to read a list of some things government could do as part of a plan to help welfare recipients get off welfare and become self-sufficient. Please tell me whether you would favor or oppose each one. First . . . help provide child care so a parent on welfare can work or look for work; provide job training to teach welfare recipients new skills; pay the costs of commuting to a job or job training classes; provide a government-paid job to welfare recipients when there are not enough private sector jobs available; cut off all benefits to people who had not found a job or become self-sufficient after two years; finance welfare reform by reducing or eliminating some existing welfare benefits. (RANDOM ORDER)

	Favor	Oppose	No opinion
Job training	94%	5%	1%
Provide child care	90	9	1
Finance from within	78	18	4
Cut off after 2 years	67	30	3
Pay commuting costs	66	32	2
Provide job if needed	60	37	3
	100%	100%	100%

SOURCE: *The Gallup Poll Monthly*, May 1994

new law and its probable success or failure in improving the welfare system. The majority (54 percent) of the respondents felt it would be a success, while 31 percent thought it would be a failure, and 15 percent had no opinion.

A BRIEF BACKGROUND OF AFDC

Because the U.S. welfare system was based on the Aid to Families with Dependent Children (AFDC) program for about 60 years, it is important to understand that program before comparing TANF to it. Following this brief background, the rest of the chapter will compare the old system with the new.

Part of the Social Security Act

The Great Depression of the 1930s brought enormous suffering to many Americans. The administration of President Franklin Delano Roosevelt (1933–45) introduced a large amount of social legislation designed to ease some of that misery. The Social Security Act (August 14, 1935) was the most significant piece of legislation passed during that time. Title IV of the act was a cash grant program that would enable states to aid needy children who lacked one or both parents. Renamed Aid to Families with Dependent Children (AFDC) in the 1950s, the program became active in all 50 states, the District of Columbia, Guam, Puerto Rico, and the Virgin Islands in the 1960s.

Helping Widows

The primary goal of Title IV of the Social Security program was to provide economic support for children whose parent (usually the father) had died, had left, or had become disabled. The AFDC program was modeled after the many state Mother's Pension funds, which had provided assistance to single mothers, mainly widows.

The AFDC program was not controversial when it was first enacted. At that time, many women did not work and widows were generally considered unemployable and morally deserving of aid. After all, it was not their fault that their husbands had died. Furthermore, during a time when there were few jobs, legislators, having a bias toward providing jobs to male breadwinners first, considered it wiser to pay a widow a small pension than to have her take a "man's" job. Finally, most legislators believed that a mother belonged in the home, raising her children and that AFDC support helped to maintain that situation. Since that time, widows and their children have been increasingly covered under the survivor's insurance provided by the Social Security Act. By 1961 widows made up barely 7 percent of the AFDC caseload.

Although congressional representatives were thinking mostly of widows, benefits were granted to poor mothers who were alone for reasons other than the deaths of their spouses. They did not expect that a significant percentage of those eligible for AFDC would be single mothers other than widows. Furthermore, no one at the time could have foreseen the huge increase in the number of female-headed households that would later lead to the large growth of the AFDC program. Finally, many legislators thought paying AFDC to mothers was a better alternative than having to pay to care for the children in orphanages, where many poor mothers had been forced to put their children when they could not afford to take care of them.

Growing AFDC Caseloads Lead to Reevaluation

In 1962, 3.5 million Americans were receiving AFDC. Just five years later, in 1967, the number had grown to 5 million. Eligibility rules had been expanded. Poor, rural African Americans who had often been denied benefits were moving to the cities, which added to urban poverty. Community-action groups and advocates for the needy were helping the poor get benefits for which they were eligible. Divorces were increasing, and more babies were being born outside marriage. All these factors contributed to the increase in AFDC recipients, as well as a growing concern about caseloads, their cost, and the characteristics of the recipients.

CHANGING ATTITUDES TOWARD WOMEN. The AFDC rolls and programs grew as divorced, separated, and never-married women sought help. While these women were still generally considered unemployable and best suited to staying at home with their children, many Americans considered that the behavior that led to such women receiving AFDC should disqualify them. They believed that a mother's single status was immoral and threatening to the ideal of the traditional family of a father, mother, and children. This led legislators and many others to look upon welfare as a moral issue. Since the 1970s, the stigma once attached to divorce and separation has nearly disappeared, and those concerned about the moral issues have focused primarily on the never-married mother.

Several other factors contributed to the changing attitudes toward women on welfare. In the 1960s the number of African American women on the AFDC rolls began to increase. Discriminatory practices had often prevented their receiving the assistance to which they were legally entitled. However, as these barriers slowly fell, the number of African American women receiving support began to grow. The eventual overrepresentation of African American women receiving AFDC payments tended to reinforce existing racial stereotypes and to lessen support for the AFDC program.

Finally, as the number of women entering the workforce grew, it seemed increasingly difficult to justify poor women receiving AFDC payments that allowed them to stay at home with their children. The "traditional" value that the mother belonged at home with her children was beginning to erode as a greater number of women began entering the workforce. Many people reasoned that welfare recipients should not be at home when many millions of nonpoor women were out in the labor force, either supporting themselves or increasing the family income. This attitude contributed greatly to the idea sometimes known as "workfare," in which the welfare recipient is expected to do some kind of work for his or her assistance, an old idea that has reappeared throughout American history.

AFDC-UP

As of October 1, 1990, states that operated AFDC were required to offer AFDC to children in two-parent families who were needy because one or both of their parents were unemployed. This program was called AFDC-UP (unemployed parent). Eligibility for AFDC-UP was limited to families in which the principal wage earner was unemployed but had a history of working. States that did not have an unemployed parent program as of September 26, 1988, could limit benefits under the AFDC-UP program to as few as 6 months in any 13-month period. AFDC-UP was intended to eliminate one of the major criticisms of the AFDC program. Previously, recipients were eligible for AFDC in many cases only when there was no father in the house. This contributed to many poor fathers' leaving home as a survival strategy in order to permit their families to get welfare support. Many observers believed this weakened the structure of numerous poor families.

After years of criticism and suggested modifications, the controversial 1996 Personal Responsibility and Work Opportunity Reconciliation Act (PL 104-193) replaced the AFDC program with the TANF block-grant program. The rest of this chapter discusses the differences between the two programs.

FEDERAL SPENDING ON AFDC AND TANF

Under the prior law, the federal government reimbursed states for a portion of AFDC, the related expenditures for Emergency Assistance (EA), and Job Opportunity and Basic Skills (JOBS). Federal funds paid from 50 to 80 percent of the state AFDC benefit costs, depending on per capita income. In addition, the federal government paid 50 percent of the administrative costs for the programs. Figure 7.1 shows the federal and state shares of the $28.2 billion spent on these programs in 1996. Federal funds accounted for 53.2 percent ($15 billion), while state funds made up the remaining 46.8 percent ($13.2 billion).

States were required to end the AFDC program and begin TANF by July 1, 1997, but many began the new system earlier. The federal block grant for TANF ($16.5 billion per year from 1997 through 2002) is based on each state's peak level of federal expenditures for AFDC and related programs; for most, this was the 1994 level. Federal condi-

FIGURE 7.1

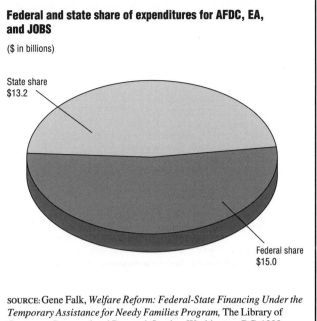

Federal and state share of expenditures for AFDC, EA, and JOBS

($ in billions)

State share
$13.2

Federal share
$15.0

SOURCE: Gene Falk, *Welfare Reform: Federal-State Financing Under the Temporary Assistance for Needy Families Program,* The Library of Congress, Congressional Research Service, Washington, DC, 1998

tions apply to the federally funded TANF, such as work participation requirements, five-year time limits, child support assignment and distribution, and aid to only those unwed minor parents living in an adult-supervised setting.

Though TANF is called a block-grant program, it combines seven different grants, each having federal funding caps (limited maximums):

- State family assistance grant—the $16.5 billion grant based on historic state welfare expenditures.

- Bonuses to reward decreases in illegitimacy—$20 million grant to each of the five states with the largest reduction in out-of-wedlock birth rates combined with a decline in abortion rates.

- Supplemental grants for population increases in certain states—formula grants to states with above-average population growth and below-average federal spending per poor person in AFDC and related programs.

- Bonuses to reward high-performance states—bonus funds for states meeting the goals of the TANF program.

- Welfare-to-work formula grants—matching grants to states to fund welfare-to-work initiatives targeting long-term welfare recipients, with an 85 percent pass-through of funds to localities (Job Training Partnership Act Service Delivery areas).

- Welfare-to-work competitive grants—grants competitively awarded to private industry councils and cities or counties with welfare-to-work projects.

TABLE 7.2

Summary of total TANF expenditures funding for 50 states and the District of Columbia, 1997–2002

($ in millions)

Grant	Fiscal Year						Total: FY1997 to FY2002
	1997	1998	1999	2000	2001	2002	
State family assistance grant (403(a)(1))	$16,489	$16,489	$16,489	$16,489	$16,489	$16,489	$98,932
Bonus to reward decrease in illegitimacy (403(a)(2))	–	–	100	100	100	100	400
Supplemental grant for population increases in certain states (403(a)(3))		79	161	244	315	–	800
Bonus to reward high performance states (403(a)(4))	–	–	200	300	200	200	900
Welfare-to-Work formula grants (403(a)(5)(A))	–	1,069	996	–	–	–	2,135
Welfare-to-Work competitive grants (403(a)(5)(B))	–	368	343	–	–	–	712
Contingency fund (403(b))							1,960
Total TANF	**16,489**	**18,005**	**18,289**	**17,133**	**17,104**	**16,789**	**105,768**

Note: Detail may not sum to totals due to rounding.

SOURCE: Gene Falk, "Table 2. Summary of Total TANF Funding for 50 States and the District of Columbia," in *Welfare Reform: Federal-State Financing Under the Temporary Assistance for Needy Families Program,* The Library of Congress, Congressional Research Service, Washington, DC, 1998

• Contingency—fund-matching grants to states that experience high unemployment rates or increased food stamp caseloads.

Almost all of the TANF program funds the state family assistance grant. This grant is capped at $16.5 billion for fiscal years 1997 through 2002 and was $1.5 billion more than the federal share of the AFDC and related programs in 1996. (See Table 7.2.)

Figure 7.2 compares the federal share of expenditures under the prior system with its share of total TANF funding. The lighter bars show federal expenditures under AFDC, EA, and JOBS, while the darker bars show the total TANF grants available through fiscal year 2002. The figure at the bottom represents the expenditures in constant dollars, showing an actual decrease of funds when adjusted for inflation. Using constant 1996 dollars, the estimated federal share of TANF funding in 2002 was $14.7 billion, a lower amount than the AFDC expenditures for each year from 1991 to 1996.

The funds for the state family assistance grant are distributed to each state according to its historic welfare spending under the prior law. Table 7.3 shows the amount granted to each state and its percentage of the total grant. California (22.6 percent) and New York (14.8 percent) together receive over one-third of the total grant, while 26 states each receive less than 1 percent of the funding. Native American tribes are permitted to administer their own tribal assistance programs with funds deducted from their state's family assistance grant.

STATE SPENDING ON AFDC AND TANF

State expenditures accounted for 46 percent of total expenditures for AFDC, EA, and JOBS in 1996. The welfare-reform law requires states to maintain at least 75 per-

cent of their "historic state expenditures" (the state share of 1994 AFDC, EA, and JOBS expenditures). This cost-sharing requirement (in order to receive the full family assistance grant) is called the maintenance-of-effort (MOE) level. If a state fails to meet the federal work requirements, its MOE level becomes 80 percent. Failure to meet the MOE level results in a dollar-for-dollar reduction of the state's family assistance grant. Table 7.4 provides historic state expenditures for each state as well as the 75 percent and 80 percent MOE thresholds.

ELIGIBILITY AND BENEFIT PAYMENTS

Aid to Families with Dependent Children

Under the Aid to Families with Dependent Children program, states determined the eligibility of needy families with children. But it had to be done within federal guidelines. If the state determined that a family was financially needy, the family was guaranteed AFDC benefits.

The individual states defined "need" as what a person must have to exist: food, shelter, clothing, household supplies, utilities, and personal care items. States set their own benefits levels, established (within federal limitations) income and resource limits, and administered the program or supervised its administration. Eligible recipients received benefits no matter what the status of the economy, even in recessions and fiscal downturn. Eligibility for AFDC ended at a child's 18th birthday or, at state option, at a child's 19th birthday if the child was a full-time student in a secondary or technical school and was expected to complete the program before she or he reached age 19.

To receive AFDC payments, a family had to pass two tests. First, the family's gross income could not be greater than 185 percent of the need standard set by the state. For

FIGURE 7.2

Federal share of expenditures for AFDC, EA, and JOBS compared with total TANF funding, 1990–2002

Billions
AFDC, EA, and JOBS FY 1990–96; TANF FY 1992–2002

$12.0, $13.2, $14.6, $14.8, $15.7, $16.3, $15.0, $16.5, $18.0, $18.3, $17.1, $17.1, $16.8

1990 1992 1994 1996 1998 2000 2002

Billions of constant FY 1996 dollars
AFDC, EA, and JOBS FY 1990–96; TANF FY 1992–2002

$14.1, $15.0, $16.1, $15.9, $16.5, $16.7, $15.0, $16.1, $17.3, $17.2, $15.8, $15.4, $14.7

1990 1992 1994 1996 1998 2000 2002

Constant dollars for FY1998–FY2002 were computed using forecast inflation.

SOURCE: Gene Falk, *Welfare Reform: Federal-State Financing Under the Temporary Assistance for Needy Families Program,* The Library of Congress, Congressional Research Service, Washington, DC, 1998

TABLE 7.3

State family assistance grants, by state

($ in thousands)

State	State family assistance grant	% of total for 50 states and D.C.
Alabama	93,315	0.6%
Alaska	63,609	0.4%
Arizona	222,420	1.3%
Arkansas	56,733	0.3%
California	3,733,818	22.6%
Colorado	136,057	0.8%
Connecticut	266,788	1.6%
Delaware	32,291	0.2%
District of Columbia	92,610	0.6%
Florida	562,340	3.4%
Georgia	330,742	2.0%
Hawaii	98,905	0.6%
Idaho	31,938	0.2%
Illinois	585,057	3.5%
Indiana	206,799	1.3%
Iowa	131,525	0.8%
Kansas	101,931	0.6%
Kentucky	181,288	1.1%
Louisiana	163,972	1.0%
Maine	78,121	0.5%
Maryland	229,098	1.4%
Massachusetts	459,371	2.8%
Michigan	775,353	4.7%
Minnesota	267,985	1.6%
Mississippi	86,768	0.5%
Missouri	217,052	1.3%
Montana	45,534	0.3%
Nebraska	58,029	0.4%
Nevada	43,977	0.3%
New Hampshire	38,521	0.2%
New Jersey	404,035	2.5%
New Mexico	126,103	0.8%
New York	2,442,931	14.8%
North Carolina	302,240	1.8%
North Dakota	26,400	0.2%
Ohio	727,968	4.4%
Oklahoma	148,014	0.9%
Oregon	167,925	1.0%
Pennsylvania	719,499	4.4%
Rhode Island	95,022	0.6%
South Carolina	99,968	0.6%
South Dakota	21,894	0.1%
Tennessee	191,524	1.2%
Texas	486,257	2.9%
Utah	76,829	0.5%
Vermont	47,353	0.3%
Virginia	158,285	1.0%
Washington	404,332	2.5%
West Virginia	110,176	0.7%
Wisconsin	318,188	1.9%
Wyoming	21,781	0.1%
TOTAL	**16,488,667**	**100.0%**

SOURCE: Gene Falk, *Welfare Reform: Federal-State Financing Under the Temporary Assistance for Needy Families Program,* The Library of Congress, Congressional Research Service, Washington, DC, 1998

example, in Colorado, where the state had established a 1996 need standard of $421 per month for a three-person family, the family could earn no more than $779 per month to be eligible for AFDC. Second, the family's net income (income after taxes and certain other deductions) had to be below the state's payment standard (the amount the state pays), which in most states was below the need standard. (See Table 7.5.)

Need standards, based on 100 percent of "need," varied widely from state to state. For example, in 1996 the states of New Hampshire ($2,034), Washington ($1,252), Hawaii ($1,140), and Vermont ($1,148) believed the monthly cost of maintaining a basic life for a family of

three in their respective states was much higher than did the states of Indiana ($320), Delaware ($338), Nebraska ($364), New Mexico ($389), Mississippi ($368), and the territories of the Virgin Islands ($300) and Puerto Rico ($360). The U.S. average need standard for a three-person family in 1996 was $675 a month, while the median (half were higher, half were lower) need standard among the 50 states and the District of Columbia was $645. (See Table 7.5.)

TABLE 7.4

TANF maintenance of effort thresholds

($ in thousands)

State	100% of historic state expenditures	75% of historic state expenditures	80% of historic state expenditures
Alabama	52,285	39,214	41,828
Alaska	65,257	48,942	52,205
Arizona	126,704	95,028	101,363
Arkansas	27,785	20,839	22,228
California	3,635,855	2,726,892	2,908,684
Colorado	110,495	82,871	88,396
Connecticut	244,561	183,421	195,649
Delaware	29,028	21,771	23,222
District of Columbia	93,932	70,449	75,146
Florida	494,559	370,919	395,647
Georgia	231,158	173,369	184,926
Hawaii	97,309	72,981	77,847
Idaho	18,238	13,679	14,591
Illinois	573,451	430,088	458,761
Indiana	151,367	113,526	121,094
Iowa	82,618	61,963	66,094
Kansas	82,333	61,750	65,866
Kentucky	89,891	67,418	71,913
Louisiana	73,887	55,415	59,109
Maine	50,032	37,524	40,026
Maryland	235,954	176,965	188,763
Massachusetts	478,597	358,948	382,877
Michigan	624,691	468,518	499,753
Minnesota	239,660	179,745	191,728
Mississippi	28,966	21,724	23,173
Missouri	160,161	120,121	128,129
Montana	20,955	15,716	16,764
Nebraska	38,173	28,629	30,538
Nevada	33,985	25,489	27,188
New Hampshire	42,820	32,115	34,256
New Jersey	400,213	300,160	320,171
New Mexico	49,795	37,346	39,836
New York	2,291,438	1,718,578	1,833,150
North Carolina	205,568	154,176	164,454
North Dakota	12,092	9,069	9,674
Ohio	521,108	390,831	416,887
Oklahoma	81,667	61,250	65,334
Oregon	123,006	92,255	98,405
Pennsylvania	542,834	407,126	434,267
Rhode Island	80,489	60,367	64,392
South Carolina	47,902	35,927	38,322
South Dakota	11,699	8,774	9,359
Tennessee	110,413	82,810	88,331
Texas	319,301	235,726	251,441
Utah	33,721	25,291	26,977
Vermont	34,067	25,550	27,253
Virginia	170,898	128,173	136,718
Washington	362,748	272,061	290,198
West Virginia	43,058	32,294	34,446
Wisconsin	22,638	169,229	180,511
Wyoming	14,220	10,665	11,376
U.S. Totals	**13,911,583**	**10,433,687**	**11,129,266**

SOURCE: Gene Falk, *Welfare Reform: Federal-State Financing Under the Temporary Assistance for Needy Families Program,* The Library of Congress, Congressional Research Service, Washington, DC, 1998

In addition, Table 7.5 shows typical 1996 maximum AFDC payments for three-member families. As in the need standards, states varied widely in typical monthly payments. In all cases, the typical annual AFDC payments were well below the 1996 federal poverty guidelines for a family of three ($12,516, or $1,043 per month). The typical 1996 AFDC payments for a family of three in Alaska ($923), Hawaii ($712), New York, Suffolk County ($703), Connecticut ($636), Vermont ($650), and California

($607) were much higher than in Mississippi ($120), Alabama ($164), Tennessee ($185), Texas ($188), and Louisiana ($190). The U.S. average payment for a family of three was $399, and the median payment was $389.

Most AFDC families were eligible for and received food stamps, an important supplement to the cash assistance paid under AFDC. Table 7.5 shows the combined benefit amounts and their percentage of 1996 poverty guidelines (based on the guideline for a family of three in the 48 contiguous states). Mississippi had the lowest combined benefits ($433), which amounted to 40 percent of the poverty rate ($1,082 a month). Hawaii had the highest at $1,183, or 95 percent of Hawaii's poverty rate of $1,244 per month.

In 1996, in almost four-fifths (78 percent) of the states and territories, typical payment amounts were well below the state-established need standards. Only one-fifth (22 percent) of the states/territories had typical payment amounts equal to their need standard for a three-person family. In 1980 payments were more likely to equal need standards; 32 states and territories (60.4 percent) had payments equal to need standards. Measured in constant (1996) dollars, the average need standard declined by 30 percent from 1970 to 1996, while the maximum benefit declined by 51 percent.

Similarly, typical monthly AFDC payments dropped sharply in real value (buying power). The typical monthly payment per four-person family changed from $178 in 1970 to $377 in 1995. However, in constant 1995 dollars, the typical benefit fell from $704 in 1970 to $377 in 1995, a 46 percent drop. Because the average family size became smaller over this period, average benefits per person dropped less sharply (25.8 percent). (See Table 7.6.)

Temporary Assistance for Needy Families (TANF)

Under the Temporary Assistance for Needy Families program, states decide how much to aid a needy family. No federal guidelines exist for determining eligibility and no requirement mandates that states aid all needy families. Though TANF does not require states to have a need standard or a gross income limit, as did AFDC, many states have based their TANF programs in part on their earlier practices.

The maximum benefit is the amount paid to a family with no countable income. (Federal law specifies what income counts toward figuring benefits and what income, such as child support, is to be disregarded by the state.) The maximum benefit is only to be paid to those families that comply with TANF's work requirements or other program requirements established by the state, such as parental and personal responsibility rules.

Though most states vary benefits according to family size, some eliminate or restrict benefit increases due to

TABLE 7.5

Gross income limit, need standard, and maximum monthly potential benefits, AFDC and food stamps, one-parent family of three persons, January 1996

State	Gross income limit (185 percent of need standard)	100 percent of "need"	Maximum AFDC grant[2]	Food stamp benefit[3]	Combined benefits	Combined benefits as a percent of 1996 poverty guidelines[4]	AFDC benefits as a percent of 1996 poverty guidelines[4]
Alabama	$1,245	$ 673	$164	$313	$ 477	44	15
Alaska	1,902	1,028	923	321	1,244	92	68
Arizona	1,783	964	347	313	660	61	32
Arkansas	1,304	705	204	313	517	48	19
California	1,351	730	607	245	852	79	56
Colorado	779	421	421	301	722	67	39
Connecticut	1,613	872	636	236	872	81	59
Delaware	625	338	338	313	651	60	31
District of Columbia	1,317	712	420	301	721	67	39
Florida	1,943	1,050	303	313	616	57	28
Georgia	784	424	280	313	593	55	26
Guam	611	330	330	461	791	73	31
Hawaii	2,109	1,140	712	471	1,183	95	57
Idaho	1,833	991	317	313	630	58	29
Illinois	1,782	963	5377	313	690	64	35
Indiana	592	320	288	313	601	56	27
Iowa	1,571	849	426	299	725	67	39
Kansas	794	429	5429	313	742	69	30
Kentucky	973	526	262	313	575	53	24
Louisiana	1,217	658	190	313	503	47	18
Maine	1,023	553	418	301	719	66	39
Maryland	956	517	5373	313	686	63	34
Massachusetts	1,045	565	565	257	822	76	52
Michigan:							
(Washtenaw Co.)	1,086	587	489	280	769	71	45
(Wayne Co.)	1,019	551	459	289	748	69	42
Minnesota	984	532	532	267	799	74	49
Mississippi	681	368	120	313	433	40	11
Missouri	1,565	846	292	313	605	56	27
Montana	1,001	541	425	299	724	67	39
Nebraska	673	364	364	313	677	63	34
Nevada	1,293	699	348	313	661	61	32
New Hampshire	3,763	2,034	550	262	812	75	51
New Jersey	1,822	985	5424	307	731	68	39
New Mexico	720	389	389	310	699	65	36
New York:							
(New York City)	1,067	577	5577	270	847	78	53
(Suffolk Co.)	1,301	703	5703	232	935	86	65
North Carolina	1,006	544	272	313	585	54	25
North Dakota	797	431	431	298	729	67	40
Ohio	1,709	924	5341	313	654	60	32
Oklahoma	1,193	645	307	313	620	57	28
Oregon	851	460	5460	313	773	71	43
Pennsylvania	1,136	614	421	301	722	67	39
Puerto Rico	666	360	180	NA	180	NA	17
Rhode Island	1,025	554	5554	299	853	79	51
South Carolina	969	524	200	313	513	47	18
South Dakota	938	507	430	298	728	67	40
Tennessee	1,079	583	185	313	498	46	17
Texas	1,389	751	188	313	501	46	17
Utah	1,051	568	426	299	725	67	39
Vermont	2,124	1,148	650	232	882	82	60
Virgin Islands	555	300	246	402	642	59	22
Virginia	727	393	354	313	667	62	33
Washington	2,316	1,252	5546	289	835	77	50
West Virginia	1,833	991	253	313	566	52	23
Wisconsin	1,197	647	517	272	789	73	48
Wyoming	1,247	674	360	313	673	62	33
Median AFDC State	720	645	389	310	699	65	36

[1] In most states these benefit amounts apply also to two-parent families of three (where the second parent is incapacitated or unemployed). Some, however, increase benefits for such families.

[2] In states with area differentials, figure shown is for area with highest benefit.

the birth of a new child to a recipient already receiving benefits. Instead benefits depend on family size at the time of enrollment in 16 states. Idaho pays a flat monthly grant that is the same regardless of family size. Wisconsin pays benefits based on work activity of the recipient and not on family size. Five states provide an increase in benefits to TANF families following the birth of an additional child.

TABLE 7.5

Gross income limit, need standard, and maximum monthly potential benefits, AFDC and food stamps, one-parent family of three persons, January 1996 [CONTINUED]

[3]Food stamp benefits are based on maximum AFDC benefits shown and assume deductions of $381 monthly ($134 standard household deduction plus $247 maximum allowable deduction for excess shelter cost) in the 48 contiguous states and the District of Columbia. In the remaining four jurisdictions these maximum allowable food stamp deductions are assumed: Alaska, $658, Hawaii, $542, Guam, $569; and Virgin Islands, $300. If only the standard deduction were assumed, food stamp benefits would drop by about $74 monthly in most of the 48 contiguous states and the District of Columbia. Maximum food stamp benefits from October 1995 through September 1996 are $313 for a family of three except in these four jurisdictions, where they are as follows: (urban) Alaska, $401; Hawaii, $522; Guam, $461; and Virgin Islands, $402.

[4]This column is based on the 1996 poverty guideline for a family of three persons in the 48 contiguous states, $12,980, converted to a monthly rate of $1,082. For Alaska, the guideline is $16,220; for Hawaii, $14,930.

[5]In these states part of the AFDC cash payment has been designated as energy aid and is disregarded by the state in calculating food stamp benefits. Illinois disregards $18. Kansas disregards $57. Maryland disregards $43. New Jersey disregards $25. New York disregards $53. Ohio disregards $14. Oregon disregards $118. Rhode Island disregards $127.85. Washington disregards $86.

NA—Not available

Note: Puerto Rico does not have a food stamp program; instead a cash nutritional assistance payment is given to recipients.

SOURCE: Congressional Research Service telephone survey of the states

---

TABLE 7.6

Historic trends in average payment per recipient and per family and maximum and median benefits for a family of four, selected years 1970–95

AFDC payments	Year									
	1970	1975	1980	1985	1987	1989	1991	1992	1993	1995
Average monthly benefit per family	$178	$210	$274	$331	$359	$381	$388	$389	$373	$377
In 1995 dollars[2]	704	601	518	470	484	471	434	423	394	377
Average monthly benefit per person	46	63	94	113	123	131	135	136	131	135
In 1995 dollars[2]	182	180	178	160	166	162	151	148	138	135
Median State benefit in July for a family unit of four with no income[1]	221	264	350	399	420	432	435	435	435	435
In 1995 dollars[2]	874	756	662	566	566	534	487	473	459	435

[1]Among 50 states and the District of Columbia.
[2]The constant dollar numbers were calculated using the CPI-U.

Note: AFDC benefit amounts have not been reduced by child support enforcement collections.

SOURCE: U.S. Department of Health and Human Services, Family Support Administration, and the Congressional Research Service

---

In a comparison of AFDC and TANF maximum benefits for a family of three, the majority of states did not change their maximum benefits between July 1994 and January 2000. When inflation is taken into account, the value of benefits in most states has actually declined. Guam, Kentucky, Mississippi, Montana, New Mexico, West Virginia, and Wisconsin increased benefits, while benefit payments actually decreased in Connecticut, the District of Columbia, Idaho, and Oklahoma. (See Table 7.7.)

Most families receiving TANF benefits are also eligible for food stamps. A single benefit determination is made for both cash and food assistance. Though the eligibility and benefit amounts for TANF are determined by the states, food stamp eligibility and benefit amounts are determined by federal law and are consistent in all states.

Food stamp benefits, administered by the U.S. Department of Agriculture, are not counted in determining the TANF cash benefit. However, TANF benefits are considered part of a family's countable income in determining food stamp benefits, which are reduced 30 cents for each dollar of countable income. Therefore, food stamp benefits are higher in states with lower TANF

benefits and vice versa. In 2000, combined monthly benefits for a family of three were lowest in Puerto Rico ($379), Alabama ($490), Mississippi ($494), Tennessee ($504), and Texas ($515). Alaska ($1,101) and Hawaii ($1,061) had the highest combined benefit for a family of three. (Poverty guidelines are higher in these two states because of higher costs of living.) Other states/territories with generous benefits included California ($813 in region 1), Connecticut ($820), Guam ($942), New York ($867 in Suffolk County), Vermont ($870), and Wisconsin ($846 for those in community service). (See Table 7.8.)

HOW MANY GET AFDC AND TANF BENEFITS?

The number of AFDC recipients increased sharply in the early 1970s and then generally leveled off somewhat until 1979. During the economic downturn of 1979–81, the number of cases increased 10 percent. In 1982, following the passage of the Omnibus Budget Reconciliation Act (OBRA), the number of family participants dropped by 8 percent. (See Table 7.9.) The OBRA legislation included provisions that restricted AFDC eligibility.

TABLE 7.7

Maximum combined AFDC/TANF benefits for a family of three (parent with two children), July 1994–January 2000

State	July 1994	July 1996	July 1998	January 2000	Percent real change from July 1994– January 2000
Alabama	$164	$164	$164	$164	−10.7
Alaska	923	923	923	923	−10.7
Arizona	347	347	347	347	−10.7
Arkansas	204	204	204	204	−10.7
California	607	596	565	626	−7.9
Colorado	356	356	356	357	−10.5
Connecticut	680	636	636	636	−16.5
Delaware	338	338	338	338	−10.7
District of Columbia	420	415	379	379	−19.5
Florida	303	303	303	303	−10.7
Georgia	280	280	280	280	−10.7
Guam	330	673	673	673	82.0
Hawaii:					
Work exempt	712	712	712	712	−10.7
Nonexempt	712	712	570	570	−28.5
Idaho	317	317	276	293	−17.5
Illinois	377	377	377	377	−10.7
Indiana	288	288	288	288	−10.7
Iowa	426	426	426	426	−10.7
Kansas	429	429	429	429	−10.7
Kentucky	228	262	262	262	2.6
Louisiana	190	190	190	190	−10.7
Maine	418	418	439	461	−1.6
Maryland	373	373	388	417	−0.2
Massachusetts:					
Work exempt	579	579	579	579	−10.7
Nonexempt	579	565	565	565	−12.9
Michigan:					
Washtenaw County	489	489	489	489	−10.7
Wayne County	459	459	459	459	−10.7
Minnesota	532	532	532	532	−10.7
Mississippi	120	120	120	170	26.5
Missouri	292	292	292	292	−10.7
Montana	416	438	461	469	0.6
Nebraska	364	364	364	364	−10.7
Nevada	348	348	348	348	−10.7
New Hampshire	550	550	550	575	−6.7
New Jersey	424	424	424	424	−10.7
New Mexico	381	389	489	439	2.8
New York:					
New York City	577	577	577	577	−10.7
Suffolk County	703	703	703	703	−10.7
North Carolina	272	272	272	272	−10.7
North Dakota	431	431	440	457	−5.4
Ohio	341	341	362	373	−2.4
Oklahoma	324	307	292	292	−19.6
Oregon	460	460	460	460	−10.7
Pennsylvannia	421	421	421	421	−10.7
Puerto Rico	180	180	180	180	−10.7
Rhode Island	554	554	554	554	−10.7
South Carolina	200	200	201	204	−9.1
South Dakota	430	430	430	430	−10.7
Tennessee	185	185	185	185	−10.7
Texas	188	188	188	201	−4.6
Utah	414	416	451	451	−2.8
Vermont	650	633	656	708	−2.8
Virgin Islands	240	240	240	240	−10.7
Virginia	354	354	354	354	−10.7
Washington	546	546	546	546	−10.7
West Virginia	253	253	253	328	15.7

Participation increased again in 1983 as the United States suffered its worst recession since World War II. It remained fairly steady until increases began again in 1990. By 1994 the number of recipients had swelled to 14.2 million, a 24 percent increase in only four years. In 1996, the last year for AFDC, the number of recipients

TABLE 7.7

Maximum combined AFDC/TANF benefits for a family of three (parent with two children), July 1994–January 2000 [CONTINUED]

State	July 1994	July 1996	July 1998	January 2000	Percent real change from July 1994– January 2000
Wisconsin:					
Community service	517	517	673	673	16.2
W2 transition	517	517	628	628	8.4
Wyoming	360	360	340	340	−15.7
Median State	381	415	421	421	−10.5

Note: The Consumer Price Index for All Urban Consumers inflation adjustment factor for converting July 1994 dollars to January 2000 dollars is 1.1203.

SOURCE: "Table 7–7. Maximum Combined AFDC/TANF Benefits for a Family of Three (Parent with Two Children), July 1994–January 2000" in *The Green Book*, U.S. House of Representatives, Committee on Ways and Means, Washington, DC, 2000

had dropped to 12.6 million from the record high in 1994. The number of AFDC families also increased between 1990 and 1994, from nearly 4 million to more than 5 million (again, a record high). In 1996 AFDC families numbered close to 4.6 million. (See Table 7.9.)

Although both the number of recipients and the number of cases (families) increased most years until 1994, the number of recipients per case declined significantly after the late 1960s. The number of recipients per case is figured by dividing the number of recipients by the number of families (cases). In 1969 the average AFDC family size was four recipients. By 1973 the number had dropped to 3.5. By 1980 the average number of recipients per family was 2.9, and in 1996 the average number per family was 2.8, the same as in 1994. (See Table 7.9.) Family size declined further in 2000, to 2.6 persons per TANF family.

California continued to have the largest TANF caseload, with a monthly average of 501,000 in 2001. New York was second with a monthly average of 258,000 families. Together California and New York account for one-third of total TANF families and one-half of total TANF cash payments.

Following the enactment of the welfare-reform law, caseloads for families dropped by an average of 53.3 percent from 1996 to 2001. (See Table 7.10.) In 26 states, caseloads fell by 50 percent or more.

CHARACTERISTICS OF AFDC/TANF RECIPIENTS

Children make up the majority of AFDC/TANF recipients. The proportion of children receiving benefits remained relatively steady from 1980 to 1999. In 1980, 69.1 percent of AFDC recipients were children. Of the 7.2 million Americans who received TANF support in 1999, about 5.1 million (71 percent) were children. Meanwhile, the percentage of all children on AFDC/TANF fell from 11.5 percent in 1980 to 7.2 percent in 1999. (See Table 7.9.)

TABLE 7.8

Maximum combined TANF and food stamp benefit for families of one to six persons, January 1, 2000

State	Family size					
	1	2	3	4	5	6
Alabama	$238	$370	$490	$602	$703	$823
Alaska	558	904	1,101	1,285	1,456	1,652
Arizona	310	466	618	758	888	1,039
Arkansas	208	387	518	639	746	878
California:						
Region 1	384	627	813	988	1,140	1,314
Region 2	373	610	792	963	1,111	1,282
Colorado	316	471	625	768	905	1,060
Connecticut	448	633	820	984	1,130	1,301
Delaware	307	463	611	751	878	1,028
District of Columbia	334	482	640	790	919	1,086
Florida	293	442	587	721	844	988
Georgia	275	438	571	697	810	934
Guam	498	717	942	1,131	1,303	1,510
Hawaii:						
Work exempt	531	800	1,061	1,305	1,533	1,794
Nonexempt	473	721	962	1,185	1,392	1,632
Idaho	372	479	580	671	751	852
Illinois	315	468	639	756	885	1,028
Indiana	264	434	576	708	829	971
Iowa	295	526	673	812	929	1,074
Kansas	354	520	675	814	936	1,080
Kentucky	297	431	558	695	814	949
Louisiana	199	370	508	630	740	868
Maine	320	515	697	872	1,034	1,217
Maryland	296	503	667	818	954	1,095
Massachusetts:						
Work exempt	441	614	780	933	1,078	1,245
Nonexempt	435	606	770	921	1,064	1,229
Michigan:						
Washtenaw County	380	554	717	881	1,028	1,222
Wayne County	360	533	696	860	1,007	1,201
Minnesota	358	629	789	934	1,061	1,207
Mississippi	237	376	494	602	698	816
Missouri	262	438	579	705	817	948
Montana	361	536	703	861	1,007	1,175
Nebraska	322	479	630	770	900	1,051
Nevada	327	476	618	751	872	1,014
New Hampshire	474	628	777	912	1,034	1,192
New Jersey	280	499	672	807	932	1,078
New Mexico	363	526	682	829	964	1,121
New York:						
New York City	413	601	779	947	1,106	1,266
Suffolk County	479	677	867	1,043	1,210	1,373
North Carolina	293	439	565	674	773	891
North Dakota	356	528	695	850	995	1,161
Ohio	323	487	636	788	923	1,067
Oklahoma	293	431	579	718	841	985
Oregon	384	550	697	861	1,008	1,175
Pennsylvania	317	505	669	826	971	1,128
Puerto Rico[1]	206	296	379	453	522	601
Rhode Island	396	588	763	910	1,046	1,203
South Carolina	248	387	518	637	746	876
South Dakota	380	540	676	800	915	1,051
Tennessee	222	373	504	624	731	860
Texas	211	396	515	634	733	862
Utah	349	527	690	835	966	1,111
Vermont	519	697	870	1,020	1,162	1,305
Virginia	321	480	623	753	887	1,021
Virgin Islands	308	511	703	878	1,038	1,230
Washington	411	582	757	915	1,064	1,235
West Virginia	324	467	604	737	850	988

TABLE 7.8

Maximum combined TANF and food stamp benefit for families of one to six persons, January 1, 2000 [CONTINUED]

State	Family size					
	1	2	3	4	5	6
Wisconsin:						
Community service	(²)	745	846	937	1,017	1,118
W2 transition	(²)	713	814	905	985	1,086
Wyoming	303	498	613	704	798	899

Note: Food stamp calculations assume that the family does not receive an excess shelter deduction. In very low benefit states, combined benefits shown reflect the maximum food stamp allotment for the family size, but in some states the excess shelter deduction would increase food stamps (by up to $83 monthly—more in Alaska and Hawaii). Calculations assume a single-parent family with no earned income and use normal rounding rules.
[1] Puerto Rico does not have a standard Food Stamp Program, but it operates a program of nutritional cash assistance under a block grant. The table shows TANF benefits plus amounts from the Nutritional Cash Assistance Program.
[2] Wisconsin has no one-person families in its regular W–2 (TANF) Program. Pregnant women without children are ineligible and "child-only" recipients have been moved into special programs.

SOURCE: "Table 7–9. Maximum Combined TANF and Food Stamp Benefit for Families of One to Six Persons, January 1, 2000," in *The Green Book*, U.S. House of Representatives, Committee on Ways and Means, Washington, DC, 2000

number of children, with an average number of two children per family in 2000.

Most children receiving TANF benefits were children of the head of household in TANF families; 8 percent were grandchildren of the head of the household. In cases where only the child received TANF benefits, 63 percent lived with their parents and 23 percent with grandparents.

In 2000 African American families were 38.6 percent of the TANF cases; white families, 31.2 percent; Hispanics, 25 percent; Asians, 2.2 percent; and Native Americans, 1.6 percent. This represents a decline in the percentage of white recipients, from 38.1 percent in 1990, and an increase in the percentage of Hispanics, from 16.6 percent. The percentage of African American recipients declined slightly over this period. (See Table 7.11.)

The proportion of African American children remained relatively stable from 1990 to 2000 as well. During the same period, the number of Hispanic children significantly increased, from 17.7 percent in 1990 to 26.8 percent in 2000. (See Table 7.11.)

The majority of adults receiving TANF benefits in 2000 had a high school education or less. Almost half (46.3 percent) had not graduated from high school; 47.5 percent had graduated from high school; and only 3.4 percent had education beyond high school. (See Table 7.12.)

The percentage of TANF adults who were employed increased dramatically between 1990 and 2000, from 7 percent in 1990 to 26.4 percent in 2000.

AFDC recipients were likely to participate in one or more other programs. TANF recipients are also eligible

While one of the major criticisms of the AFDC program was the belief that welfare mothers had many children in order to get additional benefits, the average AFDC family had only 1.9 children. Between 1980 and 2000 the average AFDC/TANF family changed very little in the

for other types of assistance. Of the almost 4.6 million families on AFDC in 1996, 89.3 percent received food stamps. In 2000, 79.9 percent of TANF families received food stamps. Almost all families (98.8 percent) received Medicaid. TANF families received an average of $348.93 in cash assistance per month in 2000. Family income from all other sources averaged $579.83 per month. (See Table 7.12). (For a more complete discussion of participation of TANF recipients in multiple programs, see Chapter 6.)

Although the largest expenditure for most families is for shelter, only 17.7 percent of TANF families received subsidized housing assistance in 2000. Some 6.5 percent lived in public housing and 11.2 percent received rent subsidies. The availability of public housing and rent subsidies varies significantly by state/territory, with Illinois, Iowa, Utah, the Virgin Islands, Virginia, and Washington providing no housing assistance, and the District of Columbia, Massachusetts, North Dakota, Puerto Rico, and South Dakota providing assistance to more than 30 percent of their TANF families (See Table 7.13.) See Chapter 8 for more information on federal housing.

LENGTH OF TIME ON WELFARE

A number of studies have investigated the length of time AFDC recipients received assistance. While most recipients left the program after a fairly short period, many returned later, potentially cycling in and out of welfare a number of times. Therefore, researchers measured not just the length of a given spell but also the total time of all spells in an individual's lifetime.

An analysis of AFDC recipients by the U.S. Department of Health and Human Services revealed that almost half of AFDC recipients beginning any given spell received assistance for two or fewer years; 19 percent had welfare spells longer than seven years. For persons beginning their first AFDC spell, 36.5 percent spent less than two years on AFDC in their lifetimes, and 29 percent spent eight or more years.

TABLE 7.9

Historical trends in AFDC/TANF enrollments, fiscal years 1970–99

	Average monthly number (in thousands)			Total child population (under age 18)[1]	Percent all children on AFDC/TANF
Fiscal year	Families	Recipients	Children		
1970	1,909	7,415	5,494	69,759	7.9
1971	2,532	9,556	6,963	69,806	9.9
1972	2,918	10,632	7,698	69,417	11.1
1973	3,124	11,038	7,965	68,762	11.6
1974	3,170	10,845	7,824	67,984	11.5
1975	3,357	11,094	7,952	67,164	11.8
1976	3,575	11,386	8,054	66,250	12.2
1977	3,593	11,130	7,846	65,461	12.0
1978	3,539	10,672	7,492	64,773	11.6
1979	3,496	10,318	7,197	64,106	11.2
1980	3,642	10,597	7,320	63,754	11.5
1981	3,871	11,160	7,615	63,213	12.0
1982	3,569	10,431	6,975	62,813	11.1
1983	3,651	10,659	7,051	62,566	11.3
1984	3,725	10,866	7,153	62,482	11.4
1985	3,692	10,813	7,165	62,623	11.4
1986	3,748	10,997	7,300	62,865	11.6
1987	3,784	11,065	7,381	63,056	11.7
1988	3,748	10,920	7,325	63,246	11.6
1989	3,771	10,934	7,370	63,457	11.6
1990	3,974	11,460	7,755	63,942	12.1
1991	4,374	12,592	8,513	65,069	13.1
1992	4,768	13,625	9,226	66,075	14.0
1993	4,981	14,143	9,560	66,963	14.3
1994	5,046	14,226	9,611	67,804	14.2
1995	4,879	13,659	9,280	68,438	13.6
1996	4,552	12,644	8,671	69,023	12.6
1997	3,947	10,954	7,781	69,528	10.5
1998	3,179	8,770	6,330	70,229	8.9
1999	2,648	7,203	[2]5,114	70,548[1]	7.2

[1] Census Bureau estimates of the resident child population (under age 18) as of July 1 each year. Figures for 1998 and 1999 are "middle series" projections.
[2] Rough estimate, based on ratio of children to total recipients in 1998.

SOURCE: "Table 7–4. Historical Trends in AFDC/TANF Enrollments, Fiscal Years 1970–1999," in *The Green Book*, U.S. House of Representatives, Committee on Ways and Means, Washington, DC, 2000

TABLE 7.10

Change in number of Aid to Families with Dependent Children (AFDC)/Temporary Assistance for Needy Families (TANF) families, fiscal years 1996–2001

	FY96	FY97	FY98	FY99	FY00	FY01	Net change FY1996–2001	
Average monthly families	4,543,397	3,936,610	3,199,700	2,673,610	2,268,653	2,123,306	-2,420,091	-53.3

	Percent change from prior years				
	To: FY97	FY98	FY99	FY00	FY01
From: FY96	-13.4	-29.6	-41.2	-50.1	-53.3
FY97		-18.7	-32.1	-42.2	-46.1
FY98			-16.4	-29.1	-33.6
FY99				-15.1	-20.6
FY00					-6.4

source: "Table 2:3. Change in Number of AFDC/TANF Families—Fiscal Years 1996-2001," in *2001 TANF Annual Report to Congress*, U.S. Department of Health and Human Services, Administration for Children and Families, Washington, DC, 2002

TABLE 7.11

Trends in Aid to Families with Dependent Children (AFDC)/Temporary Assistance for Needy Families (TANF) recipient characteristics, fiscal years 1990, 1992, 1994, 1996, 1998, and 2000

	FY 1990	FY 1992	FY 1994	FY 1996	FY 1998	FY 2000
Families						
Total	3,976,000	4,769,000	5,046,000	4,553,000	3,176,000	2,269,000
Child-only cases	459,000	707,000	869,000	978,000	743,000	782,000
Percent	11.6	14.8	17.2	21.5	23.4	34.5
Race (percent of all families)						
White	38.1	38.9	37.4	35.9	32.7	31.2
Black	39.7	37.2	36.4	36.9	39.0	38.6
Hispanic	16.6	17.8	19.9	20.8	22.2	25.0*
Asian	2.8	2.8	2.9	3.0	3.4	2.2
American Native	1.3	1.4	1.3	1.4	1.5	1.6
Other	-	-	-	-	0.6	0.6
Unknown	1.5	2.0	2.1	2.0	0.7	0.8
Adults						
Age distribution (percent of all adults)						
Under 20	7.7	7.1	5.9	5.8	6.1	7.1
20–29	46.3	45.9	44.1	42.3	41.4	42.5
30–39	32.5	33.3	34.8	35.2	33.8	32.1
Over 39	13.4	13.6	15.2	16.5	18.6	18.3
Average age	29.7	29.9	30.5	30.8	31.4	31.3
Employment rate	7.0	6.6	8.3	11.3	22.8	26.4
Children						
Age of youngest (percent of all families)						
Unborn	2.4	2.0	1.8	1.5	N/A	0.6
0–1	9.0	10.3	10.8	10.4	11.0	13.3
1–2	29.9	29.7	28.1	24.3	22.0	19.9
3–5	21.1	21.2	21.6	23.5	23.1	20.6
6–11	23.0	23.1	22.7	24.4	26.6	27.8
12–15	9.4	9.3	9.8	10.6	10.7	11.7
16 and older	3.4	3.5	3.5	3.8	4.7	5.1
Unknown	1.9	0.8	1.7	1.5	1.8	1.0
Race (percent of all children)						
White	33.1	33.9	33.0	31.6	28.3	26.8
Black	41.4	38.5	37.9	38.4	40.2	40.1
Hispanic	17.7	18.7	21.2	22.4	23.4	26.8*
Asian	3.9	3.9	3.6	3.8	4.2	2.8
American Native	1.3	1.6	1.4	1.4	1.5	1.6
Other	-	-	-	-	0.7	0.6
Unknown	2.7	3.4	2.9	2.4	1.8	1.3

*Can be of any race.

Note: N/A = Not available. Columns may not add to 100 percent due to rounding.

SOURCE: "Exhibit II. Trend of AFDC/TANF Recipient Characteristics FY 1990–FY 2000," in *2001 TANF Annual Report to Congress*, U.S. Department of Health and Human Services, Administration for Children and Families, Washington, DC, 2002

In "Targeting Would-Be Long-Term Recipients of AFDC," prepared for the U.S. Department of Health and Human Services, David T. Ellwood found that marital status was the single most powerful predictor of long-term welfare receipt. Single women receiving welfare averaged nine years on AFDC and represented 40 percent of those receiving welfare benefits at any one time. Thirty-nine percent were predicted to receive AFDC for 10 years or more.

Under TANF, most states have imposed a lifetime limit of five years for the receipt of benefits for adults, although states are allowed to provide benefits for longer to hardship cases or victims of domestic violence. Some states have set limits lower than 60 months. Families in which there is no adult head of household are exempt from time limits. New studies of the duration of time on welfare will need to be conducted of adult TANF recipients.

TEEN MOTHERS AND WELFARE

The new welfare-reform law contains provisions to encourage two-parent families and reduce out-of-wedlock births. Several provisions deal specifically with the reduction of births among teen mothers. According to Rebecca Maynard, in *Kids Having Kids: A Robin Hood Foundation Special Report on the Costs of Adolescent Childbearing* (The Robin Hood Foundation, New York, 1996), 70 percent of teen mothers received welfare and approximately 40 percent stayed on AFDC for five years or more. Teen mothers tend to have less education and fewer job skills. The Family Planning Councils of America estimates that approximately 80 percent of children whose unmarried mother did not graduate from high school live in poverty.

The birth rate for unmarried teens is high, although it declined throughout the 1990s. (See Figure 7.3.) Between

FIGURE 7.3

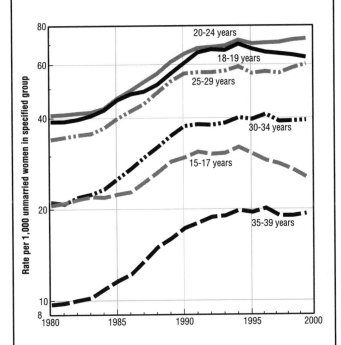

Birth rates for unmarried women, by age of mother, United States, 1980–2000

Note: Rates are plotted on a log scale.

SOURCE: Joyce A. Martin, et al., "Figure 3. Birth rates for unmarried women, by age of mother: United States, 1980–2000," in *Births: Final Data for 2000, National Vital Statistics Reports,* Centers for Disease Control and Prevention, National Center for Health Statistics, vol. 50, no. 5, February 12, 2002

1991 and 2000 the birth rate for 15-19 year olds fell 21.9 percent (from 62.1 per 1,000 to 48.5).

The approximately 470,000 births to teens in 2000 is a concern to society because teen mothers tend to have less education and less ability to support and care for their children. In addition, according to Maynard, in *Kids Having Kids,* babies born to teen mothers are:

- More likely to be born prematurely and to be of low birth weight.

- At risk for health problems, lower cognitive skills, and behavioral problems.

- Less likely to grow up in homes with their fathers, possibly causing emotional as well as financial problems.

- At greater risk to be abused.

By some estimates, teen parents under age 17 cost the United States close to $7 billion per year. These negative consequences motivated Congress to include provisions in the welfare-reform legislation to encourage the reduction of the incidence of births to unmarried women, with emphasis on teenagers.

TABLE 7.12

Temporary Assistance for Needy Families (TANF) recipient characteristics, October 1999–September 2000

	Total active families	Newly-approved families	Child-only families	Closed-case families
Families				
Monthly average	2,269,000	147,000	782,000	169,500
Child-only cases	782,000	31,500	-	42,900
Percent	34.5	21.4	-	25.3
Number of family members (percent of all families)				
1.0	20.3	17.1	-	22.8
2.0	34.0	38.5	-	34.5
3.0	23.2	24.1	-	22.7
4 or more	22.4	20.3	-	20.0
Average	2.6	2.6	-	2.5
Number of recipient children (percent of all families)				
1.0	44.2	47.4	53.7	47.8
2.0	28.4	27.2	26.9	25.7
3.0	15.3	12.9	12.0	12.2
4 or more	10.1	7.6	7.1	6.7
Unknown	2.0	4.9	0.3	7.6
Average	2.0	1.8	1.8	1.8
Type of assistance received (percent of all families)				
Medical	98.8	98.5	98.0	95.8
Food stamps	79.9	79.6	62.6	70.4
Subsidized housing	17.7	14.3	12.8	12.4
Ethnicity/race (percent of all families)				
White	31.2	36.7	29.5	37.5
Black	38.6	38.9	37.8	36.0
Hispanic*	25.0	19.9	27.7	21.3
Asian	2.2	0.8	1.8	1.7
American Native	1.6	2.0	1.3	1.8
Other	0.6	0.6	0.6	0.9
Unknown	0.8	0.9	1.2	0.8
TANF cash assistance (percent of all families)				
Percent	98.0	96.4	96.9	-
Monthly amount	$348.93	$276.66	$308.81	-
Non-TANF income (percent of all families)				
Percent	22.7	22.1	-	40.4
Monthly amount	$579.83	$477.91	-	$829.55
Adults				
Age distribution (percent of all adults)				
Under 20	7.1	11.1	-	11.0
20–29	42.5	47.6	-	43.5
30–39	32.1	29.1	-	30.5
Over 39	18.3	12.2	-	15.0
Average age	31.3	32.5	-	30.1
Marital status (percent of all adults)				
Married	12.4	13.8	-	13.7
Separated	13.1	14.9	-	13.0
Single	65.3	61.9	-	63.7
Widowed	0.7	0.4	-	0.6
Divorced	8.5	9.0	-	9.0
Education level (percent of all adults)				
1–6 years	3.8	2.5	-	2.4
7–9 years	12.5	11.6	-	9.1
10–11 years	30.0	28.4	-	29.6
12 years	47.5	48.7	-	48.7
More than 12	3.4	4.2	-	3.8
No formal	2.6	2.8	-	3.1
Unknown	0.4	1.8	-	3.3
Employment rate	26.4	19.7	-	37.9
Non-TANF income (percent of all adults)				
Percent	28.4	23.1	-	45.3
Monthly amount	$620.16	$503.81	-	$827.01

*May be of any race.
- Not applicable.
Columns may not add to 100 percent due to rounding.

SOURCE: Adapted from "Exhibit I. TANF Recipient Characteristics, October 1999–September 2000" in *2001 TANF Annual Report to Congress*, U.S. Department of Health and Human Services, Administration for Children and Families, Washington, DC, 2002

TABLE 7.13

Percent distribution of active Temporary Assistance for Needy Families (TANF) families receiving various types of assistance, October 1999–September 2000

State	Total families	Medical assistance	Food stamps		Subsidized housing		Subsidized child care	
			Percent	Monthly average	Public housing	Rent subsidy	Federal	State/local
U.S. total	2,269,131	98.8	79.9	224.01	6.5	11.2	6.2	1.8
Alabama	19,068	95.0	75.0	253.23	13.4	7.1	0.1	0.0
Alaska	7,317	97.7	71.9	303.46	3.1	7.3	12.9	0.0
Arizona	33,722	89.6	74.9	288.05	2.3	0.0	9.6	0.0
Arkansas	11,336	94.8	80.6	272.13	5.7	15.7	2.2	7.6
California	501,019	100.0	84.2	193.87	2.7	13.9	4.2	0.3
Colorado	11,154	93.2	70.3	240.85	18.6	10.2	15.9	0.0
Connecticut	28,095	100.0	79.4	194.90	2.0	31.0	0.0	0.0
Delaware	5,814	100.0	69.4	202.04	11.6	0.0	17.8	9.9
Dist . of Col.	17,563	99.4	82.5	244.86	24.6	6.7	6.2	3.3
Florida	67,355	100.0	73.7	237.24	9.6	8.3	7.2	0.0
Georgia	53,267	98.7	73.0	222.81	11.7	5.3	0.3	0.0
Guam*	2,721	—	—	—	—	—	—	—
Hawaii	14,705	100.0	85.6	377.18	2.0	6.6	12.6	0.3
Idaho	1,275	97.8	46.3	204.43	0.0	3.1	10.7	0.0
Illinois	88,493	99.7	79.5	269.45	0.0	0.0	0.3	14.7
Indiana	35,714	100.0	87.7	250.58	6.6	8.5	14.4	0.0
Iowa	19,952	67.1	72.7	208.20	0.0	0.0	9.2	0.0
Kansas	12,576	100.0	79.1	231.51	5.4	13.0	12.6	0.0
Kentucky	38,542	97.4	77.4	199.21	0.6	15.8	5.0	0.0
Louisiana	27,820	100.0	90.0	246.91	5.2	4.8	7.3	0.0
Maine	10,864	100.0	89.2	197.71	3.1	4.9	0.0	0.0
Maryland	27,523	100.0	75.1	269.54	9.4	14.7	0.5	0.0
Massachusetts	43,895	100.0	79.1	163.68	11.9	34.2	5.5	3.0
Michigan	74,211	97.7	82.0	217.39	0.6	8.6	15.2	0.0
Minnesota	39,293	99.2	99.7	251.80	0.0	26.7	11.1	0.0
Mississippi	14,970	100.0	82.1	184.98	1.3	6.1	2.5	0.0
Missouri	46,710	100.0	65.3	240.62	10.0	13.3	13.3	0.0
Montana	4,555	100.0	84.2	243.40	2.0	23.8	10.2	0.0
Nebraska	9,444	100.0	77.0	225.03	3.0	0.0	1.7	0.0
Nevada	6,274	99.6	52.3	241.12	3.1	15.8	6.5	0.2
New Hampshire	5,838	100.0	75.6	206.39	4.9	0.0	13.4	0.0
New Jersey	51,614	96.1	76.4	238.05	7.0	12.9	11.8	0.0
New Mexico	23,651	99.9	92.7	238.21	26.0	0.1	3.2	0.0
New York	257,790	100.0	88.4	221.47	13.8	11.8	1.8	0.0
North Carolina	48,157	100.0	22.3	206.87	13.7	9.4	5.0	4.3
North Dakota	2,890	99.9	81.6	240.90	7.4	47.2	20.5	0.0
Ohio	97,825	99.8	73.2	209.24	0.7	13.1	7.6	0.0
Oklahoma	15,112	100.0	64.5	270.10	0.0	26.6	27.2	0.0
Oregon	16,918	100.0	75.7	236.31	9.6	13.4	12.4	0.0
Pennsylvania	88,765	100.0	79.6	256.52	5.5	6.7	4.7	0.0
Puerto Rico	31,812	94.2	97.6	217.43	26.6	17.5	2.9	19.6
Rhode Island	16,320	100.0	91.9	209.76	9.5	18.6	2.6	12.6
South Carolina	16,059	100.0	75.5	226.73	11.6	13.2	8.7	0.0
South Dakota	2,802	100.0	68.4	229.26	34.7	0.0	5.1	0.0
Tennessee	53,788	100.0	90.4	209.60	1.1	1.5	0.0	20.2
Texas	131,162	100.0	86.8	259.79	11.3	15.5	8.0	0.4
Utah	8,409	100.0	79.8	250.82	0.0	0.0	17.8	0.0
Vermont	6,048	100.0	87.7	218.47	0.0	25.4	19.1	0.0
Virgin Islands	934	100.0	88.9	474.62	0.0	0.0	21.1	0.0
Virginia	31,834	100.0	67.5	233.37	0.0	0.0	12.2	0.0
Washington	57,008	99.9	80.9	219.29	0.0	0.0	16.7	0.0
West Virginia	11,830	99.7	91.0	245.05	11.6	11.7	3.6	0.6
Wisconsin	16,719	68.6	53.8	184.81	1.1	2.2	15.4	0.0
Wyoming	599	98.7	67.1	243.00	0.0	8.7	0.0	0.0

*Data not reported or reported in error.

SOURCE: "Table 10:12. Temporary Assistance for Needy Families—Active Cases Percent Distribution of TANF Families Receiving Assistance October–September 2000," in *2001 TANF Annual Report to Congress*, U.S. Department of Health and Human Services, Administration for Children and Families, Washington, DC, 2002

To receive TANF benefits, states were required to submit plans detailing their efforts to reduce out-of-wedlock births, especially among teenagers. In order to be eligible for TANF benefits, unmarried minor parents are required to remain in high school or its equivalent as well as to live in an adult-supervised setting. One provision in the law allows for the creation of second-chance homes for teen parents and their children, a type of home that already existed in some states. These homes require that all residents either enroll in school or participate in a job-training program. They also provide parenting and life skills classes as well as counseling and support services.

A performance bonus separate from the TANF block grant rewards states for reductions in births outside of marriage combined with a decline in the abortion rate. Grant money is also available for states to implement abstinence-only education programs. In addition, the welfare-reform law directs the Department of Health and Human Services to provide a strategy to prevent unmarried teen pregnancies and to ensure that 25 percent of the communities in the United States implement a teen pregnancy prevention program. These measures supplement already-existing federal and state efforts. Five states were awarded bonuses of $100 million in 1999 and 2000 and three states were awarded a total of $75 million in 2001 for successfully reducing the percentage of out-of-wedlock births.

CHAPTER 8
FEDERALLY ADMINISTERED MEANS-TESTED PROGRAMS

"Means-tested" programs provide benefits to those whose income and financial resources meet certain requirements. More than 80 benefit programs provide cash and/or non-cash aid to individuals who meet certain low-income qualifications. Cash assistance programs include Temporary Assistance for Needy Families (TANF), the Earned Income Tax Credit (EITC), and Supplemental Security Income (SSI).

SUPPLEMENTAL SECURITY INCOME

Supplemental Security Income (SSI) is a means-tested income assistance program authorized by Title XVI of the Social Security Act. The SSI program replaced the combined federal-state programs of Old Age Assistance, Aid to the Blind, and Aid to the Permanently and Totally Disabled in 50 states and the District of Columbia. However, these programs still exist in the U.S. territories of Guam, Puerto Rico, and the Virgin Islands. Since the first payments in 1974, SSI has provided monthly cash payments to needy aged, blind, and disabled individuals who meet the eligibility requirements. States may supplement the basic federal SSI payment.

Eligibility Requirements for SSI Recipients

There are a number of requirements that must be met in order to get financial benefits from Supplemental Security Income. First, a person must meet the program criteria for age, blindness, or disability. The aged, or elderly, are persons 65 years and older. To be considered legally blind, a person must have vision of 20/200 or less in the better eye with the use of corrective lenses, have tunnel vision of 20 degrees or less (can only see a small area straight ahead), or have met state qualifications for the earlier Aid to the Blind program.

A person is disabled if he or she cannot earn money at a job because of a physical or mental illness or injury that may cause his or her death, or if the condition lasts for 12 months or longer. Those who met earlier state Aid to the Permanently Disabled requirements may also qualify for assistance.

Children under age 18 (or 22 if a full-time student) and unmarried may qualify for SSI if they have a medically determinable physical or mental impairment that substantially reduces their ability to function independently as well as effectively engage in "age-appropriate" activities. This impairment must be expected to last for a continuous period of more than 12 months or to result in death.

The Personal Responsibility and Work Opportunity Act of 1996 (PL 104-193) abolished Aid to Families with Dependent Children (AFDC), but it did not eliminate SSI. However, the welfare reform law prohibited all non-citizens from receiving SSI, with the exception of veterans and those who have worked for 10 years and paid Social Security. It also made it harder for disabled children under 18 to get SSI. To be eligible, a disabled child must have "marked and severe functional limitations."

Because SSI is a means-tested benefit, a person's income and property must be counted before he or she can receive benefits. Table 8.1 shows the maximum income that an individual and couple can have, with some income exclusions, and still be eligible for SSI benefits in 2000. For example, the monetary limits placed on individuals and couples receiving Social Security benefits are $532 and $789 per month respectively. In addition, in 2000 a person could have no more than $2,000 worth of property, and a couple could have no more than $3,000 worth of property (mainly in savings accounts or stocks and bonds). Not included in countable resources are the person's home, as well as household goods and personal effects worth less than $2,000. A car is not counted if a member of the household uses it to go to and from work or to medical treatments or if it has been adapted, especially for a disabled person. Someone applying for SSI may have life insurance with a cash value of $1,500 or less and/or a burial policy up to the same value.

TABLE 8.1

Maximum income for eligibility for federal SSI benefits, 2000

	Receiving only Social Security		Receiving only wage income	
	Monthly	Annually	Monthly	Annually
Individual	$532	$6,384	$1,109	$13,308
Couple	789	9,468	1,623	19,476

SOURCE: "Table 3–2. Maximum Income for Eligibility for Federal SSI Benefits, 2000," in *The Green Book,* U.S. House of Representatives, Committee on Ways and Means, Washington, DC, 2000

FIGURE 8.1

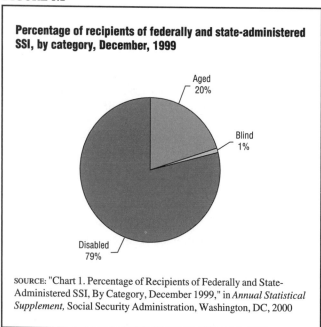

Percentage of recipients of federally and state-administered SSI, by category, December, 1999

Aged 20%
Blind 1%
Disabled 79%

SOURCE: "Chart 1. Percentage of Recipients of Federally and State-Administered SSI, By Category, December 1999," in *Annual Statistical Supplement,* Social Security Administration, Washington, DC, 2000

Recipients of SSI Benefits

More than 6.6 million persons received SSI payments in 1999, basically unchanged from the number of recipients in 1998. Of these, about 79 percent (5.2 million) were disabled, 20 percent (1.4 million) were elderly, and 1 percent (81,000) were blind. (See Figure 8.1.) Between 1975 and 1998 the number of elderly recipients declined significantly while the number of disabled nearly tripled. Table 8.2 shows the annual amount of payments by source of payment and category from 1974–99. In 2000 the leading causes of disability among adults and children were mental disorders (34 percent) and mental retardation (24.5 percent).

About 58.7 percent of SSI recipients in 1998 were women, and 41.3 percent were men. Almost two-thirds (60.3 percent) of those receiving SSI benefits were white, about one fourth (29.3 percent) were African American, and 9 percent were "other" races or ethnic groups. (See Table 8.3.)

Cost of the SSI Program

According to the Social Security Administration, as of 2002 an individual SSI recipient could receive up to

TABLE 8.2

Total amount of payments, by source of payment and category, 1974–99

[In thousands]

Calendar year	Total[1]	Federal SSI[1]	State supplementation Federally administered	State supplementation State administered[1]
All persons				
1974	$5,245,719	$3,833,161	$1,263,652	$148,906
1975	5,878,224	4,313,538	1,402,534	162,152
1980	7,940,734	5,866,354	1,848,286	226,094
1985	11,060,476	8,777,341	1,972,597	310,538
1990	16,598,680	12,893,805	3,239,154	465,721
1991	18,524,229	14,764,795	3,230,844	528,590
1992	22,232,503	18,246,934	3,435,476	550,093
1993	24,556,867	20,721,613	3,269,540	565,714
1994	25,876,571	22,175,233	3,115,854	585,483
1995	27,627,658	23,919,430	3,117,850	590,378
1996	28,791,924	25,264,878	2,987,596	539,450
1997	29,052,089	25,457,387	2,913,181	681,521
1998	30,216,345	26,404,793	3,003,415	808,137
1999	30,959,475	26,805,156	3,300,976	853,343
Aged				
1974	$2,503,407	$1,782,742	$631,292	$89,373
1975	2,604,792	1,842,980	673,535	88,277
1980	2,734,270	1,860,194	756,829	117,247
1985	3,034,596	2,202,557	694,114	137,925
1990	3,736,104	2,521,382	1,038,006	176,716
1991	3,890,412	2,691,681	998,652	200,079
1992	4,139,612	2,901,063	1,023,030	215,519
1993	4,250,092	3,097,616	933,852	218,624
1994	4,366,528	3,265,711	876,053	224,764
1995	4,467,146	3,374,772	864,450	227,924
1996	4,507,202	3,449,407	833,091	224,705
1997	4,531,973	3,479,948	823,581	228,444
1998	4,424,877	3,327,856	838,375	258,646
1999	4,724,748	3,514,689	921,332	271,003
Blind				
1974	$130,195	$91,308	$34,483	$4,404
1975	130,936	92,427	34,813	3,696
1980	190,075	131,506	54,321	4,248
1985	264,162	195,183	64,657	4,322
1990	334,120	238,415	90,534	5,171
1991	346,828	254,140	86,437	6,251
1992	370,769	275,606	87,783	7,380
1993	374,998	287,754	79,479	7,765
1994	372,461	292,102	72,596	7,763
1995	375,512	298,238	69,203	8,071
1996	371,869	298,897	65,894	7,077
1997	374,857	302,656	65,189	7,012
1998	366,452	291,050	67,137	8,265
1999	391,181	308,556	73,028	8,557
Disabled				
1974	$2,601,936	$1,959,112	$597,876	$44,948
1975	3,142,476	2,378,131	694,186	70,159
1980	5,013,948	3,874,655	1,037,137	102,156
1985	7,754,588	6,379,601	1,213,826	161,161
1990	12,520,568	10,134,007	2,110,615	275,946
1991	14,268,192	11,818,974	2,145,755	303,463
1992	17,710,514	15,070,265	2,324,664	315,585
1993	19,925,929	17,336,243	2,256,209	333,477
1994	21,131,001	18,617,421	2,167,205	346,375
1995	22,778,547	20,246,415	2,184,197	347,935
1996	23,905,578	21,516,579	2,088,610	300,389
1997	24,006,254	21,685,421	2,024,410	296,423
1998	25,304,721	22,785,879	2,097,903	420,939
1999	25,722,400	22,598,270	2,306,616	452,640

[1] Includes data not distributed by category.

SOURCE: "Table 7.A4.Total amount of payments, by source of payment and category, 1974–99," in *Social Security Bulletin, Annual Statistical Supplement 2000,* Social Security Administration, Office of Research, Evaluation, and Statistics, Baltimore, MD, 2000

TABLE 8.3

Number and percentage distribution of persons receiving federally administered payments, by selected characteristics, November 1998

[Based on 1-percent sample]

Sex and age	Total	White	Black	Other	Unknown
All recipients	6,589,000	60.3	29.3	9.0	1.4
Under 18	897,500	52.3	41.5	4.7	1.5
18–64	3,639,800	63.1	29.4	6.5	1.0
65 or older	2,051,700	58.8	23.9	15.4	2.0
Male	2,720,900	59.9	29.7	8.9	1.5
Under 18	570,700	52.0	41.7	4.9	1.4
18–64	1,589,100	63.2	29.1	6.6	1.2
65 or older	561,100	58.8	19.1	19.7	2.4
Female	3,868,100	60.5	29.1	9.1	1.4
Under 18	326,800	52.9	41.2	4.3	1.6
18–64	2,050,700	63.0	29.7	6.4	1.0
65 or older	1,490,600	58.7	25.7	13.8	1.9

[1] Codes for parents have been assigned to some recipients under age 42 with missing race codes.

SOURCE: "Table 7.E1. Number and percentage distribution of persons receiving federally administered payments, by race[1], sex, and age, November 1998," in *Social Security Bulletin, Annual Statistical Supplement 2000*, Social Security Administration, Office of Research, Evaluation, and Statistics, Baltimore, MD, 2000

$545 per month in benefits from the federal government. If both people in a couple were eligible, the pair could receive up to $817. Most states supplement the amount provided by the Federal government.

The cost of the program rose from $11 billion in 1985 to $16.6 billion in 1990 and to $31 billion in 1999. Expenditures for the disabled, which rose from 7.8 million in 1985 to 15.7 million in 1999, accounted for most of the increase. Table 8.4 provides a breakdown of the number of persons receiving payments by source of payment and category from 1974–99.

NON-CASH MEANS-TESTED BENEFITS

Non-cash benefits are those given in a form other than cash, such as vouchers, coupons, or commodities of some kind. The remainder of this chapter discusses some of the major non-cash means-tested programs, including food stamps; the National School Lunch and School Breakfast Programs; the Women, Infants, and Children (WIC) program; Medicaid; Head Start; home energy assistance; and housing assistance.

Under the Personal Responsibility and Work Opportunity Reconciliation Act (PL 104-193), the welfare-reform law enacted in August 1996, many of these programs are being funded as block grants (lump sums of money) from the federal government to the states. (For more information about this welfare law, see Chapter 2.)

FOOD STAMPS

The Food Stamp Program, administered by the U.S. Department of Agriculture, is America's largest food assistance program. Food stamps are designed to help low-income families purchase a nutritionally adequate, low-cost diet. Generally, food stamps may only be used to buy food to be prepared at home. They may not be used for alcohol, tobacco, or hot foods intended to be consumed immediately, such as restaurant or delicatessen food.

Title VIII of the 1996 Personal Responsibility and Work Opportunity Reconciliation Act continues to fund the Food Stamp Program, but the maximum benefits have been reduced. The welfare-reform law lowered the program's expenditures by more than $23 billion from 1997 to 2002. In addition to reduced benefits for many families, it created time limits for benefits to able-bodied adults without dependents and eliminated benefits to most legal immigrants.

In June 1997 the Supplemental Appropriations Act (PL 105-18) gave states the authority to purchase federal food stamps with which to provide state-funded food assistance to those who had been eliminated from the program under the new welfare-reform law. The Agricultural Research, Extension, and Education Reform Act of 1998 (PL 105-185) restored food stamp benefits to 250,000 of the 900,000 immigrants who had earlier lost eligibility.

Participation in the Food Stamp Program

The "typical" American household spends 30 percent of its monthly income on food purchases. The program calculates 30 percent of the family's earnings and then issues enough food stamps to make up the difference between that amount and the amount needed to buy an adequate diet. These monthly allotments of coupons are then redeemed for food at retail food stores. Some food stamp programs provide benefits electronically through an electronic benefit transfer (EBT), a debit card similar to a bank card. In an effort to reduce fraud and to save money, the 1996 welfare-reform law requires all states to convert to EBT issuance by fiscal year 2002.

TABLE 8.4

Number of persons receiving payments, by source of payment and category, 1974–99

Month and year	Total	Federally administered	Federal SSI	Total	State supplementation			
					Federally administered		State administered	
					Total	Only	Total	Only
All persons								
January 1974	3,248,949	3,215,632	2,955,959	1,838,602	1,480,309	259,673	358,293	33,317
December:								
1975	4,359,625	4,314,275	3,893,419	1,987,409	1,684,018	420,856	303,391	45,350
1980	4,194,100	4,142,017	3,682,411	1,934,239	1,684,765	459,606	249,474	52,083
1985	4,200,177	4,138,021	3,799,092	1,915,503	1,660,847	338,929	254,656	62,156
1990	4,888,180	4,817,127	4,412,131	2,343,803	2,058,273	404,996	285,530	71,053
1991	5,199,539	5,118,470	4,729,639	2,512,220	2,204,329	388,831	307,891	81,069
1992	5,646,877	5,566,189	5,202,249	2,684,371	2,371,564	363,940	312,807	80,688
1993	6,064,502	5,984,330	5,635,995	2,849,887	2,536,349	348,335	313,538	80,172
1994	6,377,111	6,295,786	5,965,130	2,950,470	2,628,431	330,658	322,039	81,325
1995	6,575,753	6,514,134	6,194,493	2,817,408	2,517,805	319,641	299,603	61,619
1996	6,676,729	6,613,718	6,325,531	2,731,681	2,421,470	288,187	310,211	63,011
1997	6,564,613	6,494,985	6,211,867	3,029,449	2,372,479	283,118	656,970	69,628
1998	6,649,465	6,566,069	6,289,070	3,072,392	2,411,707	276,999	660,685	83,396
1999	6,641,256	6,556,634	6,274,707	3,116,309	2,441,482	281,927	674,827	84,622
Aged								
January 1974	1,889,898	1,865,109	1,690,496	1,022,244	770,318	174,613	251,926	24,789
December:								
1975	2,333,685	2,307,105	2,024,765	1,028,596	843,917	282,340	184,679	26,580
1980	1,838,381	1,807,776	1,533,366	837,318	702,763	274,410	134,555	30,605
1985	1,529,674	1,504,469	1,322,292	698,634	583,913	182,177	114,721	25,205
1990	1,484,160	1,454,041	1,256,623	765,420	649,530	197,418	115,890	30,119
1991	1,497,817	1,464,684	1,278,674	785,366	665,406	186,010	119,960	33,133
1992	1,504,586	1,471,022	1,304,469	792,289	674,463	166,553	117,826	33,564
1993	1,507,463	1,474,852	1,323,577	801,226	685,779	151,275	115,447	32,611
1994	1,499,367	1,465,905	1,326,459	801,257	685,712	139,446	115,545	33,462
1995	1,479,415	1,446,122	1,314,720	777,841	663,390	131,402	114,451	33,293
1996	1,446,321	1,412,632	1,296,462	752,760	638,173	116,170	114,587	33,689
1997	1,395,845	1,362,350	1,251,374	750,168	619,516	110,976	130,652	33,495
1998	1,369,206	1,331,782	1,225,578	756,209	617,984	106,204	138,225	37,424
1999	1,346,771	1,308,062	1,203,056	759,681	620,261	105,006	139,420	38,709
Blind								
January 1974	73,850	72,390	55,680	45,828	37,326	16,710	8,502	1,460
December:								
1975	75,315	74,489	68,375	36,309	31,376	6,114	4,933	826
1980	79,139	78,401	68,945	39,863	36,214	9,456	3,649	738
1985	82,622	82,220	73,817	41,323	38,291	8,403	3,032	402
1990	84,109	83,686	74,781	43,376	40,334	8,905	3,042	423
1991	85,227	84,549	76,143	44,918	41,323	8,406	3,595	678
1992	86,070	85,400	77,634	45,234	41,682	7,766	3,552	670
1993	86,169	85,456	78,018	45,373	41,771	7,438	3,602	713
1994	85,609	84,911	78,033	44,779	41,253	6,878	3,526	698
1995	84,273	83,545	77,064	42,272	38,695	6,481	3,577	728
1996	82,815	82,137	76,180	40,173	36,759	5,957	3,414	678
1997	81,449	80,778	74,926	40,593	36,050	5,852	4,543	671
1998	81,029	80,243	74,623	40,828	36,193	5,620	4,635	786
1999	80,097	79,291	73,579	40,765	36,118	5,712	4,647	806
Disabled								
January 1974	1,285,201	1,278,122	1,209,783	769,501	672,575	68,350	96,926	7,068
December:								
1975	1,950,625	1,932,681	1,800,279	922,229	808,725	132,402	113,504	17,944
1980	2,276,130	2,255,840	2,080,100	1,050,155	945,788	175,740	104,367	20,290
1985	2,586,741	2,551,332	2,402,983	1,167,326	1,038,643	148,349	128,683	35,409
1990	3,319,911	3,279,400	3,080,727	1,535,007	1,368,409	198,673	166,598	40,511
1991	3,615,438	3,569,237	3,374,822	1,680,590	1,497,600	194,415	182,990	46,201
1992	4,055,105	4,009,767	3,820,146	1,845,464	1,655,419	189,621	190,045	45,338
1993	4,469,711	4,424,022	4,234,400	2,001,855	1,808,799	189,622	193,056	45,689
1994	4,790,658	4,744,970	4,560,638	2,102,711	1,901,466	184,332	201,245	45,688
1995	5,010,326	4,984,467	4,802,709	1,995,262	1,815,720	181,758	179,542	25,859
1996	5,145,850	5,118,949	4,952,889	1,933,493	1,746,538	166,060	186,955	26,901
1997	5,078,995	5,051,857	4,885,567	1,998,187	1,716,913	166,290	281,274	27,138
1998	5,190,815	5,154,044	4,988,869	2,067,530	1,757,530	165,175	310,000	36,771
1999	5,205,997	5,169,281	4,998,072	2,107,982	1,785,103	171,209	322,879	36,716

SOURCE: "Table 7.A3. Number of persons receiving payments, by source of payment and category, 1974–99," in *Social Security Bulletin, Annual Statistical Supplement 2000*, Social Security Administration, Office of Research, Evaluation, and Statistics, Baltimore, MD, 2000

The cash value of these benefits is based on the size of the household and how much the family earns. Households without an elderly or disabled member generally must have a monthly total (gross) cash income at or below 130 percent of the poverty level and may not have liquid assets (cash, savings, or other assets that can be easily sold) of more than $2,000. (If the household has an elderly member, the asset limit is $3,000.) The net monthly income limit (gross income minus any approved deductions for child care, some housing costs, and other expenses) must be 100 percent or less of the poverty level, $1,471 per month for a family of four in 2001. (See Table 8.5.)

With some exceptions, food stamps are automatically available to SSI (Supplemental Security Income) and TANF (Temporary Assistance to Needy Families) recipients. Food stamp benefits are higher in states with lower TANF benefits because those benefits are considered a part of a family's countable income. To receive food stamps, certain household members must register for work, accept suitable job offers, or fulfill work or training requirements (such as looking or training for a job).

While the federal government sets guidelines and provides funding, the Food Stamp Program is actually carried out by the states. They certify eligibility as well as calculate and issue benefit allotments. Most often, the welfare agency and staff that administer the TANF and Medicaid programs also run the food stamp program. The regular food stamp program operates in all 50 states, the District of Columbia, Guam, and the Virgin Islands. (Puerto Rico is covered under a separate nutrition-assistance program.)

With the exception of some small differences in Alaska, Hawaii, and the territories, the program is run the same way throughout the United States. While the states pay 50 percent of the administrative costs, the federal government pays 100 percent of food stamp benefits and the other 50 percent of the operating costs. In 1997 the federal government paid $21.5 billion in food stamp benefits, or an average monthly benefit of $71.27 per recipient. By 2001 the federal government paid only 17.8 billion in food stamp benefits, a decline of 17.2 percent. But because the number of recipients was down, the average monthly benefit per recipient actually rose to $74.77. (See Table 8.6.)

How Many Receive Food Stamps?

Food stamp participation increased significantly in the early and mid-1970s, remained relatively stable at between 18 and 22 million recipients per year throughout the 1980s, and then rose again in the 1990s. Participation generally peaks in periods of high unemployment, inflation, and recession. In 1994, 27.5 million persons (about 10 percent of the population) participated in the food stamp program, a 36.9 percent increase from the number of recipients in 1990. In 2001 the Food Stamp Program served an average of 17.3 million people each month, down 24.2 percent from 1997. (See Table 8.6.)

TABLE 8.5

Income chart for eligibility to receive food stamps, October 2001–September 2002

People in household	Gross monthly income limits	Net monthly income limits
1	$931.00	$716.00
2	$1,258.00	$968.00
3	$1,585.00	$1,220.00
4	$1,913.00	$1,471.00
5	$2,240.00	$1,723.00
6	$2,567.00	$1,975.00
7	$2,894.00	$2,226.00
8	$3,221.00	$2,478.00
Each additional person...	+$328.00	+$252.00

SOURCE: "Income Chart", U.S. Department of Agriculture, Food and Nutrition Service, Washington, DC [Online] http://www.fns.usda.gov/fsp/MENU?APPS/ELIGIBILITY/income/INCOMECHART.HTM [accessed May 1, 2002]

The food stamp program is the nation's largest source of food assistance, helping about 6 percent of all Americans. Approximately 55 percent of those who were eligible participated in 1998. Half are children, and more than 15 percent are elderly or disabled.

Table 6.2 (in Chapter 6) shows the numbers and percentages of poor households that received food stamps in 2000. One-third (33.8 percent) of all poor households received food stamps, with almost half (46 percent) of the recipients being under age 18. Recipiency rates were highest in households headed by women with children under 6—60.2 percent.

The percentage of poor white households receiving food stamps stood at 28.2 percent in 2000, compared to 49.9 of poor African American households and 33.7 percent of poor Hispanics.

Participation in the food stamp program has fallen markedly since the enactment of the PRWORA welfare reform in 1996. One reason for the decline is that many able-bodied adults age 18-50 who do not have children are no longer eligible for benefits. In addition, studies indicate that former TANF recipients who make the transition from welfare to work tend to give up their food stamp benefits even though they may still qualify on the basis of low income. The U.S. Department of Health and Human Services reported that the proportion of households eligible for food stamps that actually participated in the program fell from 63 percent in 1996 to 54 percent in 1998, a decrease of 9 percent.

Increase in Average Monthly Benefits

Average monthly benefits per person have risen from $34.47 in 1980 to $74.77 in 2001, not accounting for inflation. Table 8.7 shows the maximum monthly food stamp allotments for October 2001 to September 2002 for

TABLE 8.6

Food stamp program participation and costs, as of April 25, 2002

Fiscal year	Average participation	Average benefit per person[1]	Total benefits	All other costs[2]	Total costs
	Thousands	Dollars		Millions of dollars	
1969	2,878	6.63	228.8	21.7	250.5
1970	4,340	10.55	549.7	27.2	576.9
1971	9,368	13.55	1,522.7	53.2	1,575.9
1972	11,109	13.48	1,797.3	69.4	1,866.7
1973	12,166	14.60	2,131.4	76.0	2,207.4
1974	12,862	17.61	2,718.3	119.2	2,837.5
1975	17,064	21.40	4,385.5	233.2	4,618.7
1976	18,549	23.93	5,326.5	359.0	5,685.5
1977	17,077	24.71	5,067.0	394.0	5,461.0
1978	16,001	26.77	5,139.2	380.5	5,519.7
1979	17,653	30.59	6,480.2	459.6	6,939.8
1980	21,082	34.47	8,720.9	485.6	9,206.5
1981	22,430	39.49	10,629.9	595.4	11,225.2
1982[3]	21,717	39.17	10,208.3	628.4	10,836.7
1983	21,625	42.98	11,152.3	694.8	11,847.1
1984	20,854	42.74	10,696.1	882.6	11,578.8
1985	19,899	44.99	10,743.6	959.6	11,703.2
1986	19,429	45.49	10,605.2	1,033.2	11,638.4
1987	19,113	45.78	10,500.3	1,103.9	11,604.2
1988	18,645	49.83	11,149.1	1,167.7	12,316.8
1989	18,806	51.85	11,700.5	1,231.8	12,932.3
1990	20,067	58.92	14,186.7	1,304.4	15,491.1
1991	22,624	63.86	17,338.7	1,430.4	18,769.1
1992	25,406	68.57	20,905.7	1,556.6	22,462.3
1993	26,982	67.96	22,006.0	1,647.0	23,653.0
1994	27,468	69.01	22,748.6	1,744.1	24,492.7
1995	26,619	71.26	22,764.1	1,855.5	24,619.6
1996	25,542	73.21	22,441.5	1,885.5	24,327.0
1997	22,858	71.27	19,550.2	1,936.7	21,486.9
1998	19,788	71.12	16,889.1	2,003.5	18,892.6
1999	18,183	72.21	15,755.4	1,942.9	17,698.3
2000	17,158	72.78	14,984.8	2,073.3	17,058.1
2001 (P)	17,316	74.77	15,536.1	2,253.9	17,790.0

Fiscal Year 2001 data are preliminary; all data are subject to revision.

[1] Represents average monthly benefits per person.

[2] Includes the federal share of state administrative expenses and employment and training programs. Also includes other Federal costs (e.g., printing and processing of stamps; anti-fraud funding; program evaluation).

[3] Puerto Rico initiated Food Stamp operations during Fiscal Year 1975 and participated through June of Fiscal Year 1982. A separate Nutrition Assistance Grant was begun in July 1982.

SOURCE: "Food Stamp Program Participation and Costs (Data as of April 25, 2002)," U.S. Department of Agriculture, Food and Nutrition Service, Washington, DC [Online] http://www.fns.usda.gov/pd/fssummar.htm [accessed May 10, 2002]

TABLE 8.7

Maximum food stamp allotments, October 2001–September 2002

Household size	48 states and D.C.
1	$135
2	$248
3	$356
4	$452
5	$537
6	$644
7	$712
8	$814
Each additional person	$102

SOURCE: "Maximum Food Stamp Allotments," in *Food Stamp Program Monthly Allotments and Deductions,* U.S. Department of Agriculture, Food and Nutrition Service, Washington, DC, [Online] http://www.fns.usda.gov/fsp/MENU/ADMIN/CERTIFICATION/SUPPORT/MonthlyAllotmentsandDeductions1.htm [accessed May 23, 2002]

households of varying sizes within the continental United States. In 2000 the average monthly benefit for a 4-person household was $426; by 2002 it was $452.

In the early 1980s, Congress passed many laws designed to hold down the cost of the food stamp program by tightening administrative controls and setting tougher eligibility standards. The Omnibus Budget Reconciliation Act of 1981 (PL 97-35), the Agriculture and Food Act of 1981 (PL 97-98), and the Omnibus Budget Reconciliation Act of 1982 (PL 97-253) each contained provisions that held down costs. These measures included delaying inflation adjustments, establishing eligibility at 130 percent of poverty levels, ending eligibility for college students and strikers, and reducing benefits.

In 1985 the Food Security Act (PL 99-198) reversed the earlier trend, making food stamp rules easier and raising some benefits. However, the law required states to introduce employment and training programs for food stamp recipients. Several other pieces of legislation gave the homeless access to food stamps and increased benefits and accessibility for those receiving student aid, energy assistance, and income from employment programs for the elderly and charitable organizations. The Hunger Prevention Act of 1988 (PL 100-435) increased food stamp benefits and made it easier for people to get food stamps, as did the Mickey Leland Childhood Hunger Relief Act (PL 103-66).

Characteristics of Food Stamp Recipients

In 2000 most (89 percent) food stamp households earned less than the poverty guideline ($17,050 for a family of four). In fact, one third earned less than half of the 2000 poverty level. A report prepared for the Food and Nutrition Service of the U.S. Department of Agriculture, *Characteristics of Food Stamp Households: Fiscal Year 2000*, (Karen Cunningham and Jenny Genser, Alexandria, VA, 2001), presented detailed information on food stamp participants and households for 2000:

- Over half (51.3 percent) of participants were children.

- 21 percent were households with at least one elderly member.

- More than half of food stamp households also received either TANF (25.8 percent) or SSI benefits (31.7 percent).

- 43 percent of food stamp households with children had earned income.

- Almost all participants (95.3 percent) were U.S. citizens.

- 40 percent of food stamp participants were white, 35.8 percent African American and 18.5 percent Hispanic.

NATIONAL SCHOOL LUNCH AND SCHOOL BREAKFAST PROGRAMS

The National School Lunch Program (NSLP) and the School Breakfast Program (SBP) provide federal cash and commodity support to participating public and private schools and to nonprofit residential institutions that serve meals to children. Both programs have a three-level reimbursement system. Children from households with incomes at or below 130 percent of the poverty line receive free meals. Children from households with incomes between 130 percent and 185 percent of the poverty level receive meals at a reduced price (no more than 40 cents). Table 8.8 shows the income eligibility guidelines, based on the poverty line, effective from July 1, 2002, to June 30, 2003. The levels are higher for Alaska and Hawaii than in the 48 contiguous states, Washington, D.C., Guam and other U.S. territories. Children in TANF families are automatically eligible to receive free breakfasts and lunches. Almost 90 percent of federal funding for the NSLP is used to subsidize free and reduced-price lunches for low-income children.

Meals for children from households that do not qualify for free or reduced-price meals are also subsidized. There was a reimbursement of about 34 cents for each full-price school lunch during the 1999–2000 school year. Local school food authorities set their own prices for full-price meals. In 1999–2000 the reimbursement for each free school lunch was $2.13.

School Lunch Program

The National School Lunch Program (NSLP), created in 1946 under the National School Lunch Act (60 Stat 230), supplies subsidized lunches to children in almost all schools and in 6,000 residential and child-care institutions. In fiscal year 1999, about 91,000 elementary and secondary schools (99 percent of all public schools) participated in the program, and more than half (57.6 percent) of their students received free or reduced-price lunches. In 2000 the percentage of students receiving subsidized lunches declined slightly to 57.1 percent. In all, more than 27 million students were receiving subsidized lunches during the school year. (See Table 8.9.) The cost of the school lunch program in 1999 was $6.25 billion.

In the school year 1996–97, the U.S. Department of Agriculture changed certain policies so that school meals would meet the recommendations of the Dietary Guidelines for America, the federal standards for what constitutes a healthy diet. Federal spending for the NSLP in 2000 totaled $5.49 billion. (See Table 8.10 for 1980–2000 statistics.)

School Breakfast Program

The School Breakfast Program (SBP), created under the Child Nutrition Act of 1966 (PL 89-642), serves far fewer students than does the NSLP. The SBP also differs from the NSLP in that most schools offering the program are in low-income areas, and the children who participate in the program are mainly from low- and moderate-income families. In 1999 the program had an average daily participation of nearly 7.4 million students, 85.4 percent of whom received free or reduced-price (up to 30 cents) breakfasts. In 2000 about 7.6 million students participated, with 84.2 percent receiving subsidized breakfasts. The cost of this program in April 2000 was $1.4 billion. (See Table 8.10 for program costs; see Table 8.11 for statistics related to the number of participants and meals served from 1969 to 2001.)

WOMEN, INFANTS, AND CHILDREN (WIC)

The Special Supplemental Food Program for Women, Infants, and Children (WIC) provides food

TABLE 8.8

Income eligibility guidelines to receive free or reduced priced meals, effective from July 1, 2002–June 30, 2003

Household size	Federal poverty guidelines			Reduced price meals – 185%			Free meals – 130%		
	Annual	Month	Week	Annual	Month	Week	Annual	Month	Week
48 contiguous United States, District of Columbia, Guam and Territories									
1	8,860	739	171	16,391	1,366	316	11,518	960	222
2	11,940	995	230	22,089	1,841	425	15,522	1,294	299
3	15,020	1,252	289	27,787	2,316	535	19,526	1,628	376
4	18,100	1,509	349	33,485	2,791	644	23,530	1,961	453
5	21,180	1,765	408	39,183	3,266	754	27,534	2,295	530
6	24,260	2,022	467	44,881	3,741	864	31,538	2,629	607
7	27,340	2,279	526	50,579	4,215	973	35,542	2,962	684
8	30,420	2,535	585	56,277	4,690	1,083	39,546	3,296	761
For each additional family member add	+3,080	+257	+60	+5,698	+475	+110	+4,004	+334	+77
Alaska									
1	11,080	924	214	20,498	1,709	395	14,404	1,201	277
2	14,930	1,245	288	27,621	2,302	532	19,409	1,618	374
3	18,780	1,565	362	34,743	2,896	669	24,414	2,035	470
4	22,630	1,886	436	41,866	3,489	806	29,419	2,452	566
5	26,480	2,207	510	48,988	4,083	943	34,424	2,869	662
6	30,330	2,528	584	56,111	4,676	1,080	39,429	3,286	759
7	34,180	2,849	658	63,233	5,270	1,217	44,434	3,703	855
8	38,030	3,170	732	70,356	5,863	1,353	49,439	4,120	951
For each additional family member add	+3,850	+321	+75	+7,123	+594	+137	+5,005	+418	+97
Hawaii									
1	10,200	850	197	18,870	1,573	363	13,260	1,105	255
2	13,740	1,145	265	25,419	2,119	489	17,862	1,489	344
3	17,280	1,440	333	31,968	2,664	615	22,464	1,872	432
4	20,820	1,735	401	38,517	3,210	741	27,066	2,256	521
5	24,360	2,030	469	45,066	3,756	867	31,668	2,639	609
6	27,900	2,325	537	51,615	4,302	993	36,270	3,023	698
7	31,440	2,620	605	58,164	4,847	1,119	40,872	3,406	786
8	34,980	2,915	673	64,713	5,393	1,245	45,474	3,790	875
For each additional family member add	+3,540	+295	+69	+6,549	+546	+126	+4,602	+384	+89

SOURCE: "Income Eligibility Guidelines," U.S. Department of Agriculture, Food and Nutrition Service, published in *Federal Register*, vol. 67, no. 39, February 27, 2002

assistance as well as nutrition counseling and health services to low-income pregnant women, to women who have just given birth and their babies, and to low-income children up to 5 years old. Participants in the program must have incomes at or below 185 percent of poverty (all but five states use this cutoff level) and must be nutritionally at risk.

Under the Child Nutrition Act of 1966, nutritional risk includes abnormal nutritional conditions, medical conditions related to nutrition, health-impairing dietary deficiencies, or conditions that might predispose a person to these conditions. Pregnant women may receive benefits throughout their pregnancies and for up to six months after childbirth (up to one year for nursing mothers).

Those receiving WIC benefits get supplemental food each month in the form of actual food items or, more commonly, vouchers (coupons) for the purchase of specific items at the store. Permitted foods contain high amounts of protein, iron, calcium, vitamin A, and vitamin C. Items that may be purchased include milk, cheese, eggs, infant formula, cereals, and fruit or veg-

etable juices. Mothers participating in WIC are encouraged to breastfeed their infants if possible, but state WIC agencies will provide formula for mothers who choose to use it.

The U.S. Department of Agriculture estimated that the national average monthly cost of a WIC food package in 2001 was $34.31 per participant, including food and administrative costs. In fiscal year 2001 federal costs for the WIC program totaled $4.15 billion, and the program served approximately 7.3 million women, infants, and children. (See Table 8.12.) WIC works in conjunction with the Farmers' Market Nutrition Program, established in 1992, to provide WIC recipients with increased access, in the form of vouchers, to fresh fruits and vegetables.

WIC is not an entitlement program. That is, the number of participants is limited by the amount of funds available rather than by eligibility. In 1999 the federal government estimated that WIC reached about 97 percent of eligible women, infants, and children. Of the 7.3 million participants, 3.7 million were children, 1.9 million

TABLE 8.9

National School Lunch Program participation and lunches served, as of April 25, 2002

Fiscal year	Average participation				Total lunches served	Percent free/ RP of total
	Free	Reduced price	Full price	Total		
	Millions					%
1969	2.9	[1]	16.5	19.4	3,368.2	15.1
1970	4.6	[1]	17.8	22.4	3,565.1	20.7
1971	5.8	0.5	17.8	24.1	3,848.3	26.1
1972	7.3	0.5	16.6	24.4	3,972.1	32.4
1973	8.1	0.5	16.1	24.7	4,008.8	35.0
1974	8.6	0.5	15.5	24.6	3,981.6	37.1
1975	9.4	0.6	14.9	24.9	4,063.0	40.3
1976	10.2	0.8	14.6	25.6	4,147.9	43.1
1977	10.5	1.3	14.5	26.2	4,250.0	44.8
1978	10.3	1.5	14.9	26.7	4,294.1	44.4
1979	10.0	1.7	15.3	27.0	4,357.4	43.6
1980	10.0	1.9	14.7	26.6	4,387.0	45.1
1981	10.6	1.9	13.3	25.8	4,210.6	48.6
1982	9.8	1.6	11.5	22.9	3,755.0	50.2
1983	10.3	1.5	11.2	23.0	3,803.3	51.7
1984	10.3	1.5	11.5	23.4	3,826.2	51.0
1985	9.9	1.6	12.1	23.6	3,890.1	49.1
1986	10.0	1.6	12.2	23.7	3,942.5	49.1
1987	10.0	1.6	12.4	23.9	3,939.9	48.6
1988	9.8	1.6	12.8	24.2	4,032.9	47.4
1989	9.8	1.6	12.9	24.3	4,004.9	47.2
1990	9.9	1.7	12.6	24.1	4,009.1	48.3
1991	10.3	1.8	12.1	24.2	4,050.9	50.4
1992	11.2	1.7	11.7	24.6	4,101.9	53.0
1993	11.8	1.7	11.3	24.9	4,137.7	54.8
1994	12.2	1.8	11.3	25.3	4,201.8	55.9
1995	12.5	1.9	11.3	25.7	4,253.4	56.4
1996	12.7	2.0	11.3	25.9	4,313.2	56.9
1997	13.0	2.1	11.3	26.3	4,409.0	57.6
1998	13.1	2.2	11.3	26.6	4,424.9	57.8
1999	13.0	2.4	11.6	26.9	4,513.2	57.6
2000	13.0	2.5	11.8	27.2	4,574.9	57.1
2001 (P)	12.9	2.6	12.0	27.5	4,583.8	56.9

FY 2001 data are preliminary; all data are subject to revision. Participation data are 9 month averages (summer months are excluded).
[1] Included with free meals.

SOURCE: "National School Lunch Program: Participation and Lunches Served," U.S. Department of Agriculture, Food and Nutrition Service, Washington, DC, 2002 [Online] http://www.fns.usda.gov/pd/slsummar.htm [accessed May 1, 2002]

were infants, and 1.7 million were women. See Table 8.12 for overall statistics from 1974 to 2001.

A study conducted in 1998 for the Food and Nutrition Service of the U.S. Department of Agriculture *National Survey of WIC Participants, 2001 Final Report* (Nancy Cole and Julie Kresge, Alexandria, VA, 2001), found that almost two-thirds of WIC recipients reside in families whose income is below the poverty guidelines. Nonetheless, three-fourths of WIC families receive income from wages.

Most of the women participating in WIC were breast-feeding (60.8 percent), while 40.1 percent were pregnant and 39 percent had given birth. Almost half (45.2 percent) were never married, 44.1 percent were married, and the remaining 10.7 percent were widowed, separated, or divorced. The study found significant changes in caseloads and the racial composition of participants between 1988 and 1998. Caseloads in the western states grew from

13 percent to 24 percent of total WIC participants, primarily due to growth in the Hispanic population in the West. Hispanic participants increased from 21 percent of the caseload in 1988 to 32 percent in 1998.

MEDICAID

Medicaid, authorized under Title XIX of the Social Security Act, is a federal-state program that provides medical assistance for low-income people who are aged, blind, disabled, or members of families with dependent children and for certain other pregnant women and children. Within federal guidelines, each state designs and administers its own program. For this reason, there may be considerable differences from state to state as to who is covered, what type of coverage is provided, and how much is paid for medical services. States receive federal matching payments based on their Medicaid expenditures and the state's per capita income. The federal match ranges from 50 to 80 percent of Medicaid expenditures.

TABLE 8.10

Federal food programs, 1980–2000

[21.1 represents 21,100,000. Program data include Puerto Rico, Virgin Islands, Guam, American Samoa, Northern Marianas, and the former Trust Territory when a federal food program was operated in these areas. Participation data are average monthly figures except as noted. Participants are not reported for the commodity distribution programs. Cost data are direct federal benefits to recipients; they exclude federal administrative payments and applicable state and local contributions. Federal costs for commodities and cash-in-lieu of commodities are shown separately from direct cash benefits for those programs receiving both]

Program	Unit	1980	1985	1990	1995	1997	1998	1999	2000
Food stamp:									
Participants	Million	21.1	19.9	20.1	26.6	22.9	19.8	18.2	17.2
Federal cost	Mil. dol.	8,721	10,744	14,187	22,765	19,550	16,889	15,755	14,985
Monthly average coupon value per recipient	Dollars	34.47	44.99	58.92	71.26	71.27	71.12	72.20	72.75
Nutrition assistance program for Puerto Rico: [1]									
Federal cost	Mil. dol.	(X)	825	937	1,131	1,174	1,204	1,236	1,268
National school lunch program (NSLP):									
Free lunches served	Million	1,671	1,657	1,662	2,090	2,194	2,198	2,207	2,204
Reduced-price lunches served	Million	308	255	273	309	347	362	392	409
Children participating [2]	Million	26.6	23.6	24.1	25.7	26.3	26.6	26.9	27.2
Federal cost	Mil. dol.	2,279	2,578	3,214	4,466	4,934	5,102	5,314	5,489
School breakfast (SB):									
Children participating [2]	Million	3.6	3.4	4.1	6.3	6.9	7.1	7.4	7.5
Federal cost	Mil. dol	288	379	596	1,049	1,214	1,272	1,345	1,393
Special supplemental food program (WIC): [3]									
Participants	Million	1.9	3.1	4.5	6.9	7.4	7.4	7.3	7.2
Federal cost	Mil. dol.	584	1,193	1,637	2,517	2,815	2,808	2,853	2,847
Child and adult care (CC): [4]									
Participants [5]	Million	0.7	1.0	1.5	2.4	2.5	2.6	2.7	2.7
Federal cost.	Mil. dol.	207	390	720	1,296	1,393	1,372	1,438	1,495
Summer feeding (SF): [6]									
Children participating [7]	Million	1.9	1.5	1.7	2.1	2.2	2.2	2.2	2.1
Federal cost	Mil. dol.	104	103	145	212	217	234	238	233
Federal cost of commodities donated to— [8]									
Child nutrition (NSLP, CC, SF, and SB)	Mil. dol.	930	840	646	733	661	774	754	697

X Not applicable.

[1] Puerto Rico was included in the food stamp program until June 30, 1982.

[2] Average monthly participation (excluding summer months of June through August). Includes children in public and private elementary and secondary schools and in residential child care institutes.

[3] WIC serves pregnant and postpartum women, infants, and children up to age five.

[4] Program provides year-round subsidies to feed preschool children in child care centers and family day care homes. Certain care centers serving disabled or elderly adults also receive meal subsidies.

[5] Average quarterly daily attendance at participating institutions.

[6] Program provides free meals to children in poor areas during summer months.

[7] Peak month (July) average daily attendance at participating institutions.

[8] Includes the federal cost of commodity entitlements, cash-in-lieu of commodities, and bonus foods.

SOURCE: "Federal Food Programs: 1980–2000," in *Statistical Abstract of the U.S., 2001*, in U.S. Census Bureau, Washington, DC, 2001

Table 8.13 shows the number of recipients, the amount of payments, and the average payment per recipient for each state/territory.

Who Gets Medicaid?

Although Medicaid eligibility had been linked to receipt of, or eligibility to receive, benefits under Aid to Families with Dependent Children (AFDC) or Supplemental Security Income (SSI), legislation gradually extended coverage in the 1980s and 1990s. Beginning in 1986, benefits were extended to low-income children and pregnant women not on welfare. States must cover children less than 6 years of age and pregnant women with family incomes below 133 percent of the federal poverty level. Pregnant women are only covered for medical services related to their pregnancies, while children receive full Medicaid coverage. The states may cover infants under one year old and pregnant women with incomes more than 133 percent, but not more than 185 percent, of the poverty level. As of January 1, 1991, Medicaid also began to cover aged and disabled persons receiving Medicare whose income was below 100 percent of the poverty level.

Medicaid coverage is not guaranteed for recipients of Temporary Assistance for Needy Families (TANF) as it was for recipients of AFDC. However, the welfare-reform law of 1996 requires states to continue benefits to those who would have been eligible under the AFDC requirements each state had in place on July 16, 1996. As with pre-reform law, Medicaid coverage must be continued for one year for those families that have increased their earnings to the point where they are no longer eligible for cash

TABLE 8.11

School Breakfast Program participation and meals served, as of April 25, 2002

Fiscal year	Total participation[1]				Meals served	Free/RP of total meals
	Free	Red. price	Paid	Total		
	Millions					Percent
1969	—	—	—	0.22	39.7	71.0
1970	—	—	—	0.45	71.8	71.5
1971	0.60	[2]	0.20	0.80	125.5	76.3
1972	0.81	[2]	0.23	1.04	169.3	78.5
1973	0.99	[2]	0.20	1.19	194.1	83.4
1974	1.14	[2]	0.24	1.37	226.7	82.8
1975	1.45	0.04	0.33	1.82	294.7	82.1
1976	1.76	0.06	0.37	2.20	353.6	84.2
1977	2.02	0.11	0.36	2.49	434.3	85.7
1978	2.23	0.16	0.42	2.80	478.8	85.3
1979	2.56	0.21	0.54	3.32	565.6	84.1
1980	2.79	0.25	0.56	3.60	619.9	85.2
1981	3.05	0.25	0.51	3.81	644.2	86.9
1982	2.80	0.16	0.36	3.32	567.4	89.3
1983	2.87	0.15	0.34	3.36	580.7	90.3
1984	2.91	0.15	0.37	3.43	589.2	89.7
1985	2.88	0.16	0.40	3.44	594.9	88.6
1986	2.93	0.16	0.41	3.50	610.6	88.7
1987	3.01	0.17	0.43	3.61	621.5	88.4
1988	3.03	0.18	0.47	3.68	642.5	87.5
1989	3.11	0.20	0.51	3.81	658.4	86.8
1990	3.30	0.22	0.55	4.07	707.5	86.7
1991	3.61	0.25	0.57	4.44	772.1	87.3
1992	4.05	0.26	0.60	4.92	852.6	88.0
1993	4.41	0.28	0.66	5.36	923.6	87.9
1994	4.76	0.32	0.75	5.83	1,001.6	87.4
1995	5.10	0.37	0.85	6.32	1,078.9	86.8
1996	5.27	0.41	0.91	6.58	1,125.7	86.5
1997	5.52	0.45	0.95	6.92	1,191.2	86.5
1998	5.64	0.50	1.01	7.14	1,221.0	86.1
1999	5.71	0.56	1.10	7.37	1,267.6	85.4
2000	5.73	0.61	1.21	7.55	1,303.4	84.2
2001	5.80	0.66	1.32	7.78	1,333.3	83.3

Fiscal year 2001 data are preliminary; all data are subject to revision.
[1] Nine month average: October–May plus September.
[2] Included with free participation.

SOURCE: "School Breakfast Program Participation and Meals Served," U.S. Department of Agriculture, Food and Nutrition Service, Washington, DC, 2002 [Online] http://www.fns.usda.gov/pd/sbsummar.htm [accessed May 1, 2002]

aid and for four months to those who lose eligibility because of child or spousal support.

States may deny Medicaid benefits to adults who lose TANF benefits because they refuse to work. However, the law exempts poor pregnant women and children from this provision, requiring their continued Medicaid eligibility. In addition, the welfare law requires state plans to ensure Medicaid for children receiving foster care or adoption assistance.

The process to determine eligibility can take months. The Balanced Budget Act of 1997 (PL 105-33) gave states the option to grant interim coverage to children who appear to be eligible for Medicaid, based on age and family income. This "presumptive eligibility" option allows children and pregnant women to receive care immediately while waiting for Medicaid approval.

Many states, in an effort to reach the large number of uninsured children (by Census Bureau estimates, over

one-third of Medicaid-eligible children), are simplifying the Medicaid application process. According to the Center on Budget and Policy Priorities, as of February 1998, 38 states had dropped the assets test for Medicaid, 30 had developed shorter application forms, and 25 were allowing mail-in applications.

In addition, the 1996 welfare law gives states the option to use Medicaid to provide health care coverage to low-income working parents. About half (49 percent) of the working poor were uninsured in 1996; by 1999 the number remained relatively unchanged. (See Figure 8.2.) Although the income of these households is below the federal poverty line, working poor parents have been ineligible for publicly funded health insurance. In addition, low-wage jobs often do not offer affordable employer-sponsored coverage. The number of uninsured working poor parents is likely to grow as welfare recipients move into the work force, as required under the welfare-reform law, unless states expand Medicaid to cover this group.

TABLE 8.12

WIC program participation and costs, 1974–2001

Data as of April 25, 2002

Fiscal Year	Total participation	Program costs			Average monthly benefit per person
		Food	NSA	Total[1]	
	Thousands	Millions of dollars			Dollars
1974	88	8.2	2.2	10.4	15.68
1975	344	76.7	12.6	89.3	18.58
1976	520	122.3	20.3	142.6	19.60
1977	848	211.7	44.2	255.9	20.80
1978	1,181	311.5	68.1	379.6	21.99
1979	1,483	428.6	96.8	525.4	24.09
1980	1,914	584.1	140.5	727.7	25.43
1981	2,119	708.0	160.6	871.6	27.84
1982	2,189	757.6	190.5	948.8	28.83
1983	2,537	901.8	221.3	1,126.0	29.62
1984	3,045	1,117.3	268.8	1,388.1	30.58
1985	3,138	1,193.2	294.4	1,489.3	31.69
1986	3,312	1,264.4	316.4	1,582.9	31.82
1987	3,429	1,344.7	333.1	1,679.6	32.68
1988	3,593	1,434.8	360.6	1,797.5	33.28
1989	4,118	1,489.5	416.5	1,910.9	30.14
1990	4,517	1,636.9	478.7	2,122.2	30.20
1991	4,893	1,752.0	544.0	2,301.1	29.84
1992	5,403	1,958.6	632.7	2,596.7	30.21
1993	5,921	2,115.1	705.6	2,825.5	29.77
1994	6,477	2,325.2	834.4	3,169.5	29.92
1995	6,894	2,516.6	904.9	3,441.4	30.41
1996	7,186	2,689.9	985.1	3,695.3	31.20
1997	7,407	2,815.3	1,008.2	3,844.1	31.67
1998	7,367	2,807.8	1,061.4	3,889.9	31.76
1999	7,311	2,852.8	1,064.1	3,939.7	32.52
2000	7,192	2,852.2	1,102.6	3,971.1	33.05
2001 (P)	7,306	3,007.8	1,114.3	4,153.0	34.31

NSA = Nutrition Services and Administrative costs. Nutrition Services includes nutrition education, preventative and coordination services (such as health care), and promotion of breastfeeding and immunization.
FY 2001 data are preliminary; all data are subject to revision.
[1]In addition to food and NSA costs, total expenditures includes funds for program evaluation, Farmers' Market Nutrition Program (FY 1989 onward), special projects and infrastructure.

SOURCE: "Table 8.17. WIC Program Participation and Costs," in U.S. Department of Agriculture, Food and Nutrition Service, 2002 [Online] http://www.fns.usda.gov/pdf/wisummary.htm [accessed May 15, 2002]

Medicaid may also cover "medically needy" persons, those with income levels higher than the regular Medicaid levels. Each state may establish a higher income or resource level for the "medically needy" than the standards the states set for those who qualify for other social welfare benefits. They may also limit the categories of the "medically needy" who will receive Medicaid. As of January 2000, 39 states provided Medicaid to "medically needy" recipients.

MEDICAID RECIPIENTS. In 1998 approximately 40.6 million people were enrolled in Medicaid. Most were dependent children under 21 years of age (46.7 percent) and adults in families with dependent children (19.5 percent). The remainder of Medicaid recipients were permanently and totally disabled (16.3 percent), elderly (9.8 percent), or blind. The number receiving Medicaid coverage stayed around 22 million from 1975 through 1986, when it began to rise, reaching more than 36 million in 1995 and 1996. By 1998 the number had increased signif-

TABLE 8.13

Number of Medicaid recipients, amount of payments, and average amount per recipient, by state, fiscal year 1998

State	Recipients	Amount (in millions)	Average
Total	40,649,482	$142,318	$3,501
Alabama	527,078	1,902	3,609
Alaska	74,508	330	4,434
Arizona	507,668	1,644	3,238
Arkansas	424,727	1,376	3,239
California	7,082,175	14,237	2,010
Colorado	344,916	1,439	4,173
Connecticut	381,208	2,421	6,350
Delaware	101,436	420	4,138
District of Columbia	166,146	731	4,402
Florida	1,904,591	5,687	2,986
Georgia	1,221,978	3,012	2,466
Hawaii	184,614	507	2,749
Idaho	123,176	425	3,446
Illinois	1,363,856	6,173	4,526
Indiana	607,293	2,564	4,222
Iowa	314,936	1,289	4,092
Kansas	241,933	916	3,788
Kentucky	644,482	2,425	3,763
Louisiana	720,615	2,384	3,308
Maine	170,456	747	4,383
Maryland	561,085	2,489	4,437
Massachusetts	908,238	4,609	5,075
Michigan	1,362,890	4,345	3,188
Minnesota	538,413	2,924	5,432
Mississippi	485,767	1,442	2,969
Missouri	734,015	2,570	3,501
Montana	100,760	361	3,585
Nebraska	211,188	753	3,566
Nevada	128,144	462	3,606
New Hampshire	93,970	606	6,449
New Jersey	813,251	4,219	5,188
New Mexico	329,418	862	2,617
New York	3,073,241	24,299	7,907
North Carolina	1,167,988	4,014	3,437
North Dakota	62,280	341	5,476
Ohio	1,290,776	6,121	4,742
Oklahoma	342,475	1,178	3,439
Oregon	511,171	1,378	2,695
Pennsylvania	1,523,120	6,080	3,992
Rhode Island	153,130	919	6,004
South Carolina	594,962	2,019	3,393
South Dakota	89,537	356	3,974
Tennessee	1,843,661	3,167	1,718
Texas	2,324,810	7,140	3,071
Utah	215,801	619	2,867
Vermont	123,992	351	2,834
Virginia	653,236	2,118	3,243
Washington	1,413,208	2,044	1,447
West Virginia	342,668	1,243	3,628
Wisconsin	518,595	2,206	4,255
Wyoming	46,121	192	4,163
Outlying areas:			
Puerto Rico	964,015	250	259
Virgin Islands	19,764	10	511

SOURCE: "Table 8.H1. Number of Recipients, Amount of Payments, and Average Amount per Recipient, by State, Fiscal Year 1998," in *Annual Statistical Supplement, 2000* Social Security Administration, Washington, DC, 2000

icantly to 40.6 million, representing a 12.5 percent change since 1996. (See Table 8.14.)

Poor households were most likely to be covered by Medicaid. Some 39.8 percent of poor persons were covered in 2000. (See Table 8.15.) States are required to provide Medicaid coverage for pregnant women and children under age 6. One of every five children in the United States is covered under Medicaid. It is the single largest source of health insurance coverage for all children from families earning below 200 percent of the poverty line. African American and Hispanic children were far more likely to have Medicaid coverage than were white or Asian and Pacific Islander children. In 2000, 35.4 percent of African American children and 32.5 percent of Hispanic children were covered by Medicaid, compared to 13.3 percent of non-Hispanic white and 19.2 percent of Asian and Pacific Islander children. (See Table 8.16.)

Medicaid provides health care services, such as long-term care, for many elderly people not covered by Medicare. Medicaid pays for about half of all nursing home expenditures, which accounts for a large percentage of Medicaid expenditures. This proportion of spending on the elderly is expected to increase as more people live longer. The Census Bureau projects a 22 percent increase in the 85-and-over population between 1996 and 2002, from 3.7 million to 4.5 million.

Growth in Medicaid Costs

The rapid growth in spending for Medicaid has contributed to the concern over the rising cost of health care. Not accounting for inflation, spending skyrocketed from $6.3 billion in 1972 to $37.5 billion in 1985 and $142.3 billion in 1998. Of the $142.3 billion spent on Medicaid payments in 1998, most went for the disabled (42.4 percent) and the elderly (28.5 percent). In addition, considerable amounts were spent on dependent children under age 21 (16.0 percent) and adults in families with dependent children (10.4 percent). On average, the Medicaid program spent $10,242 on every elderly recipient, $1,203 on each dependent child under 21, and $9,095 on each disabled person in the program. (See Table 8.14.)

Transitional Medical Assistance

Families who leave welfare for work are at risk of losing the health care benefits that they received under Medicaid. Families with children who had previously been covered by Medicaid but are no longer eligible because of earnings from employment are eligible for Transitional Medical Assistance (TMA) for an additional 12 months through 2002.

STATE CHILD HEALTH INSURANCE PROGRAM

The Balanced Budget Act of 1997 (PL 105-33) set aside $24 billion over five years to fund the State Children's Health Insurance Program (SCHIP) in an effort to reach children who are uninsured. This was the nation's largest children's health care investment since the creation of Medicaid in 1965. SCHIP requires states to use the funding to cover uninsured children whose families earn

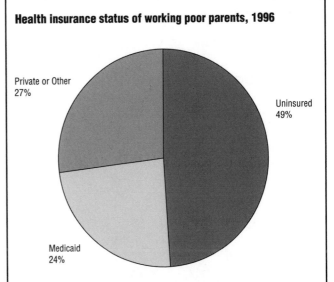

FIGURE 8.2

Health insurance status of working poor parents, 1996

Private or Other 27%

Uninsured 49%

Medicaid 24%

Based on adults in households with children who earn at least $5,150 a year (an amount equivalent to half-time, full-year work at the minimum wage), but whose income still falls below the poverty line.

SOURCE: Jocelyn Guyer and Cindy Mann, "Nearly Half of All Working Poor Parents Are Uninsured," in *Taking the Next Steps: States Can Now Expand Health Coverage to Low-Income Working Parents Through Medicaid,* Center on Budget and Policy Priorities, Washington, DC, July 1998

too much for Medicaid but too little to afford private coverage. States may use this money to expand their Medicaid programs, design new child health insurance programs, or create a combination of both.

States must enroll all children who meet Medicaid eligibility rules in the Medicaid program rather than in the new SCHIP plan. They are not allowed to use SCHIP to replace existing health coverage. In addition, states must decide on what kind of cost-sharing, if any, to require of low-income families without keeping them from access to the program. The only federal requirement is that cost-sharing cannot exceed 5 percent of family income.

HEAD START

Head Start began operating in 1965 under the general authority of the Economic Opportunity Act of 1964 (PL 88-452). Head Start is designed to help low-income children from birth to age 5 improve their social competence, learning skills, health, and nutrition so that they can begin school on a more level footing with more advantaged children.

Education is the service most directly provided by Head Start to enrolled children. Head Start services include language development; medical (including immunizations), dental, and mental health services; and nutritional and social services. Head Start often facilitates access to other social services, such as Medicaid, for

TABLE 8.14

Number of Medicaid recipients, total vendor payments, and average amounts, by type of eligibility category, fiscal years 1972–98

Fiscal year	Total	Aged 65 or older	Blind	Permanent and total disability	Dependent children under age 21	Adults in families with dependent children	Other
				Number (in thousands)			
1972	17,606	3,318	108	1,625	7,841	3,137	1,576
1975	22,007	3,615	109	2,355	9,598	4,529	1,800
1980	21,605	3,440	92	2,819	9,333	4,877	1,499
1985	21,814	3,061	80	2,937	9,757	5,518	1,214
1986	22,515	3,140	82	3,100	10,029	5,647	1,362
1987	23,109	3,224	85	3,296	10,168	5,599	1,418
1988	22,907	3,159	86	3,401	10,037	5,503	1,343
1989	23,511	3,132	95	3,496	10,318	5,717	1,175
1990	25,255	3,202	83	3,635	11,220	6,010	1,105
1991	28,280	3,359	85	3,983	13,415	6,778	658
1992	30,926	3,742	84	4,378	15,104	6,954	664
1993	33,432	3,863	84	4,932	16,285	7,505	763
1994	35,053	4,035	87	5,372	17,194	7,586	779
1995	36,282	4,119	92	5,767	17,164	7,604	1,537
1996	36,118	4,285	95	6,126	16,739	7,127	1,746
1997	34,872	3,955	…	6,129	15,791	6,803	2,195
1998	40,649	3,964	…	6,638	18,964	7,908	3,176
				Amount (in millions)			
1972	$6,300	$1,925	$45	$1,354	$1,139	$962	$875
1975	12,242	4,358	93	3,052	2,186	2,062	492
1980	23,311	8,739	124	7,497	3,123	3,231	596
1985	37,508	14,096	249	13,203	4,414	4,746	798
1986	41,005	15,097	277	14,635	5,135	4,880	980
1987	45,050	16,037	309	16,507	5,508	5,592	1,078
1988	48,710	17,135	344	18,250	5,848	5,883	1,198
1989	54,500	18,558	409	20,476	6,892	6,897	1,268
1990	64,859	21,508	434	23,969	9,100	8,590	1,257
1991	77,048	25,453	475	27,798	11,690	10,439	1,193
1992	90,814	29,078	530	33,326	14,491	12,185	1,204
1993	101,709	31,554	589	38,065	16,504	13,605	1,391
1994	108,270	33,618	644	41,654	17,302	13,585	1,467
1995	120,141	36,527	848	48,570	17,976	13,511	2,708
1996	121,685	36,947	869	51,196	17,544	12,275	2,853
1997	124,430	37,721	…	54,130	17,544	12,307	2,727
1998	142,318	40,602	…	60,375	22,806	14,833	3,702
				Average amount			
1972	$358	$580	$417	$833	$145	$307	$555
1975	556	1,205	850	1,296	228	455	273
1980	1,079	2,540	1,358	2,659	335	663	398
1985	1,719	4,605	3,104	4,496	452	860	658
1986	1,821	4,808	3,401	4,721	512	864	719
1987	1,949	4,975	3,644	5,008	542	999	761
1988	2,126	5,425	4,005	5,366	583	1,069	891
1989	2,318	5,926	4,317	5,858	668	1,206	1,079
1990	2,568	6,717	5,212	6,595	811	1,429	1,138
1991	2,725	7,577	5,572	6,979	871	1,540	1,813
1992	2,936	7,770	6,298	7,612	959	1,752	1,813
1993	3,042	8,168	7,036	7,717	1,013	1,813	1,824
1994	3,089	8,331	7,412	7,755	1,006	1,791	1,884
1995	3,311	8,868	9,256	8,422	1,047	1,777	1,762
1996	3,369	8,622	9,143	8,357	1,048	1,722	1,635
1997	3,568	9,538	…	8,832	1,111	1,809	3,597
1998	3,501	10,242	…	9,095	1,203	1,876	1,166

Notes: Fiscal year 1977 began in October 1976 and was the first year of the new federal fiscal cycle. Before 1977, the fiscal year began in July. Beginning in fiscal year 1980, recipients' categories do not add to unduplicated total because of the small number of recipients that are in more than one category during the year.

SOURCE: "Table 8.E2. Unduplicated Number of Recipients, Total Vendor Payments, and Average Amounts, by Type of Eligibility Category, Fiscal Years 1972–98," in *Social Security Bulletin: Annual Statistical Supplement, 2000,* Social Security Administration, Baltimore, MD, 2000

siblings and families, as well as for enrolled children. The program tries to involve parents in their children's education, either through volunteer participation or through employment of parents as Head Start staff.

Head Start's guidelines require that at least 90 percent of the children enrolled come from families with incomes at or below the poverty income level. At least 10 percent of the enrollment slots must be available for disabled children.

In 2000, 858,000 young children were served in Head Start programs at a total federal cost of nearly $5.3 billion. Money for the program is expected to increase so that an estimated 1 million children will be served by 2002. (See

TABLE 8.15

Type of health insurance and coverage status, 1999 and 2000

(Numbers in thousands) (Based on a November 2001 weighting correction)

	2000		1999		Change 1999 to 2000	
	Number	Percent	Number	Percent	Number	Percent
ALL PEOPLE						
Total	276,540	100.0	274,087	100.0	2,453	0.0
Total covered	237,857	86.0	234,807	85.7	*3,050	*0.3
Private	200,249	72.4	197,523	72.1	*2,727	*0.3
Employment-based	177,286	64.1	174,093	63.5	*3,193	*0.6
Government	66,935	24.2	66,582	24.3	353	-0.1
Medicare	37,028	13.4	36,109	13.2	*918	*0.2
Medicaid	28,613	10.3	28,221	10.3	392	0.1
Military	8,334	3.0	8,564	3.1	-229	*-0.1
Not covered	38,683	14.0	39,280	14.3	*-596	*-0.3
POOR PEOPLE						
Total	31,054	100.0	32,258	100.0	*-841	0.0
Total covered	21,870	70.4	22,233	68.9	-363	*1.5
Private	8,622	27.8	8,607	26.7	14	1.1
Employment-based	5,849	18.8	5,713	17.7	136	1.1
Government	15,563	50.1	15,917	49.3	-354	0.8
Medicare	4,566	14.7	4,255	13.2	311	*1.5
Medicaid	12,349	39.8	12,992	40.3	*-643	-0.5
Military	576	1.9	504	1.6	73	0.3
Not covered	9,184	29.6	10,025	31.1	*-841	*-1.5

*Statistically significant at the 90-percent confidence level.
Note: The estimates by type of coverage are not mutually exclusive; people can be covered by more than one type of health insurance during the year.
All numbers are derived from unrounded numbers. Some numbers and percentages may therefore appear to be slightly higher or lower than those computed with rounded figures from other columns.

SOURCE: "Table 1, Type of Health Insurance and Coverage Status, All People: 1999 and 2000," and "Table 2, Type of Health Insurance and Coverage Status, Poor People: 1999 and 2000," in *Health Insurance Coverage 2000*, U.S. Census Bureau, Washington, DC [Online] http://www.census.gov/hhes/hlthins/hlthin00/dtable1.html and http://www.census.gov/hhes/hlthins/hlthin00/dtable2.html [accessed May 6, 2002]

TABLE 8.16

Children covered by Medicaid by age, race and ethnicity, 1999 and 2000

Numbers in thousands. Based on a November 2001 weighting correction.

	2000			1999			Change 1999 to 2000	
		Covered			Covered		Covered	
	Total	Number	Percent	Total	Number	Percent	Number	Percent
ALL CHILDREN								
Under 18 years	72,553	14,739	20.3	72,325	14,572	20.1	167	0.2
Age								
Under 6 years	23,667	5,733	24.2	23,580	5,701	24.2	32	0.0
6 to 11 years	24,819	5,111	20.6	24,761	5,045	20.4	66	0.2
12 to 17 years	24,067	3,895	16.2	23,984	3,825	15.9	70	0.3
Race and Ethnicity								
White	56,817	9,671	17.0	56,666	9,432	16.6	239	0.4
Non-Hispanic	45,433	6,035	13.3	45,542	6,062	13.3	-27	0.0
Black	11,574	4,103	35.4	11,493	4,195	36.5	-92	-1.1
Asian\Pacific Island	3,129	602	19.2	3,066	520	17.0	*82	*2.2
Hispanic[1]	12,029	3,909	32.5	11,695	3,603	30.8	*306	*1.7

[1]Hispanics may be of any race. Statistically significant at the 90-percent confidence level.
Note: All numbers are derived from unrounded numbers. Some numbers and percentages may therefore appear to be slightly higher or lower than those computed with rounded figures from other columns.

SOURCE: "Table 10. Children Covered by Medicaid by Age, Race and Ethnicity: 1999 and 2000," in *Health Insurance Coverage 2000* U.S. Census Bureau, Washington, DC [Online] http://www.census.gov/hhes/hlthins/hlthin00/dtable10.html [accessed May 6, 2002]

FIGURE 8.3

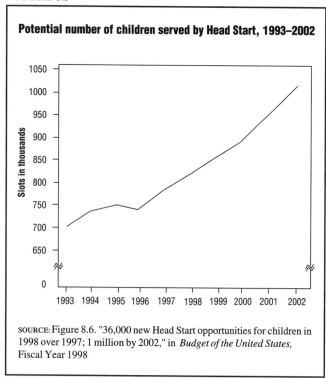

Potential number of children served by Head Start, 1993–2002

SOURCE: Figure 8.6. "36,000 new Head Start opportunities for children in 1998 over 1997; 1 million by 2002," in *Budget of the United States, Fiscal Year 1998*

Figure 8.3.) In 2000 African American children made up 35 percent of the enrollment; white children, 30 percent; Hispanic children, 29 percent; Native Americans, 3 percent; Asians, 2 percent; and Hawaiian/Pacific Islanders, 1 percent. Most of the children participating in the program were 4-year-olds (56 percent) and 3-year-olds (33 percent). (See Table 8.17.) A significant proportion (12.7 percent) were disabled children.

During the 2000–2001 operating year, 77 percent of Head Start families had incomes of less than $15,000 per year.

HELP IN PAYING THE HEATING BILL

What is now the Low-Income Home Energy Assistance Program (LIHEAP) began as Title III of the Crude Oil Windfall Profit Tax Act of 1980 (PL 96-223). The act provided funding for the states to create programs for three types of energy assistance:

- Helping poor households pay their heating and cooling bills.

- Using low-cost insulation to make homes more energy efficient.

- Providing financial aid to households during energy-related emergencies (unusually long cold or hot spells).

In 1981 Title XXVI of the Omnibus Budget Reconciliation Act (OBRA; PL 97-35) gave form and substance to the program. Funding peaked at an estimated $2.1 billion in 1985 and declined throughout the 1990s. In 2001 the U.S. Department of Health and Human Services increased funding by 27 percent over 2000, appropriating $1.41 billion in LIHEAP block grants.

Home heating assistance benefits, by far the major service of LIHEAP, served 4 million households in 2001. Average benefits varied dramatically, ranging from larger grants in colder states with higher costs of heating, such as Alaska ($2,450 per year), Montana ($1,454), and New Jersey ($1,400), to much lower grants in generally warmer states, such as Alabama ($200 per year), Florida ($150), and South Carolina ($150). Benefits apply to both heating and cooling in some states such as Texas.

States make payments directly to eligible households or to home energy suppliers to be used for eligible households. The highest level of assistance is given to households with the lowest income and highest energy costs in relation to income, taking into account family size and whether infants, children, or elderly are a part of the household.

FEDERAL HOUSING ASSISTANCE

The primary purpose of federal housing assistance is to improve housing quality and to reduce housing costs for low-income Americans. However, affordability rather than housing quality has become the predominant problem facing low-income renters and homeowners. The number of substandard housing units continues to decline. Affordability problems occur nationwide, affecting poor households in every region and in urban, suburban, and rural areas of the country alike. They are spread among all racial and ethnic groups and affect both working and non-working poor renters. In 1999 two-thirds of poor working families with children spent more than 30 percent of their income on shelter, the percentage the government considers affordable.

Financial Commitments for Housing Assistance

Housing assistance for low-income households comes through a number of programs and can be very confusing. Authorizations for housing assistance, especially for building low-cost public housing, may be committed for a dozen or two dozen years in the future. As a result, a financial authorization made in 1977 may well have affected spending by the U.S. Department of Housing and Urban Development (HUD) in 1996 and continue to affect spending into the twenty-first century. Spending patterns changed dramatically in the 1980s and 1990s. HUD has increasingly turned to using housing vouchers to help low-income families pay the rent in existing housing and has turned away from building low-income housing, which requires larger financial commitments over a longer time. Figure 8.4 shows the types of housing assistance provided by the federal government in 1999.

Vouchers give recipients more flexibility as to where they may live and are particularly helpful to those making

TABLE 8.17

Head Start—summary of children served, costs, and staffing, 1980–2000

[376 represents 376,000]

Year	Enrollment (1,000)	Appro- priation (mil. dol.)	Age and race	Enrollment, 2000 (percent)	Item	Number
1980	376	735	Under 3 years old	6	Average cost per child:	
1985	452	1,075	3 years old	33	1995	$4,534
1990	541	1,552	4 years old	56	1999	$5,403
1991	583	1,952	5 years old and over	5	2000	$5,951
1992	621	2,202				
1993	714	2,776			Paid staff (1,000):	
1994	740	3,326	White	30	1995	147
1995	751	3,534	Black	35	1999	172
1996	752	3,569	Hispanic	29	2000	180
1997	794	3,981	American Indian	3	Volunteers (1,000):	
1998	822	4,347	Asian	2	1995	1,235
1999	826	4,658	Hawaiian/		1999	1,327
2000	858	5,267	Pacific Islander	1	2000	1,252

SOURCE: "No. 553. Head Start—Summary: 1980 to 2000," in *Statistical Abstract of the United States: 2001* U.S. Census Bureau, Washington, DC, 2001

FIGURE 8.4

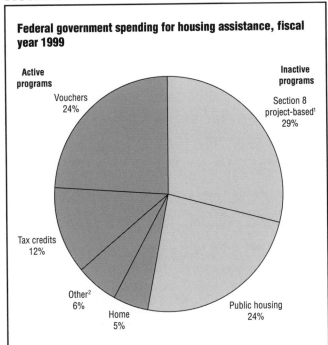

Federal government spending for housing assistance, fiscal year 1999

[1]Includes expenditures for New Construction/Substantial Rehabilitation, Loan Management Set-Aside, Property Disposition, Section 236, Rental Assistance Payment, and Rent Supplement.
[2]Includes expenditures for HOPE VI, Section 202, Section 811, Section 515, and Section 521.

SOURCE: "Enclosure I. Federal Government Spent about $29 Billion for Housing Assistance in FY 1999," in *Costs and Characteristics of Federal Housing Assistance*, GAO-01-901R, U.S. General Accounting Office, Washington, DC, 2001

FIGURE 8.5

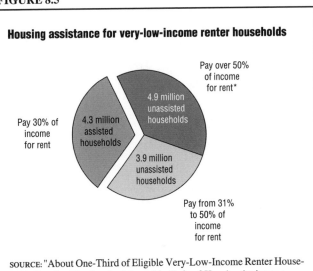

Housing assistance for very-low-income renter households

SOURCE: "About One-Third of Eligible Very-Low-Income Renter House-holds Receive Housing Assistance," in *Federal Housing Assistance Programs: Costs and Housing Characteristics*, General Accounting Office, Washington, DC, 2001

ments. The number of people receiving help depends on the amount of money authorized by Congress. Therefore, not all households or families that qualify receive assistance. Approximately one-third (32.8 percent) of the low-income families that qualify actually receive assistance. In 1999 some 4.3 million families received federal housing assistance even though about 13.1 million households qualified for it. (See Figure 8.5.)

In the 1980s and 1990s the number of new commitments to assist low-income families has dropped dramatically. Between 1977 and 1981 the federal government committed to increase rental assistance by an average of about 260,000 new households per year. From 1982 through 1999 the new assistance commitments fell to an

the transition from welfare to work. Families can use vouchers to move closer to areas with more job opportunities or better transportation to work.

Housing assistance is not an entitlement to which a person has a legal right if he or she meets certain require-

TABLE 8.18

Outlays for housing assistance administered by HUD, by broad program categories, 1977–2000

[In millions of current and 2000 dollars]

Fiscal Year	Direct housing assistance (in current dollars)			Homeless programs[3] (in current dollars)	Other housing block grants[4] (in current dollars)	Total outlays	
	Section 8 and other assisted housing[1]	Public housing[2]	Subtotal assisted housing			Current dollars	2000 dollars
1977	$1,331	$1,564	$2,895	0	0	$5,790	$15,791
1978	1,824	1,779	3,603	0	0	7,206	18,460
1979	2,374	1,815	4,189	0	0	8,378	19,709
1980	3,146	2,218	5,364	0	0	10,728	22,709
1981	4,254	2,478	6,732	0	0	13,464	25,901
1982	5,293	2,553	7,846	0	0	15,692	28,208
1983	6,102	3,318	9,420	0	0	18,840	32,428
1984	7,068	3,932	11,000	0	0	22,000	36,331
1985	7,771	17,261	25,032	0	$15	50,079	79,760
1986	8,320	3,859	12,179	0	142	24,500	38,075
1987	8,993	3,517	12,510	$2	165	25,187	38,046
1988	9,985	3,699	13,684	37	180	27,585	40,020
1989	10,689	3,774	14,463	72	275	29,273	40,553
1990	11,357	4,331	15,688	85	276	31,737	41,875
1991	12,107	4,786	16,893	125	168	34,079	42,802
1992	13,052	5,182	18,234	150	35	36,653	44,694
1993	14,032	6,447	20,479	180	276	41,414	49,002
1994	15,289	6,857	22,146	225	862	45,379	52,321
1995[5]	16,448	7,505	23,953	359	1,259	49,524	55,542
1996[5]	17,496	7,668	25,164	616	1,273	52,217	56,979
1997	17,131	7,809	24,940	718	1,263	51,861	55,104
1998[5]	16,975	8,028	25,003	916	1,316	52,238	54,617
1999[5]	17,171	7,805	24,976	1,032	1,367	52,351	53,710
2000 est.[5]	17,443	8,094	25,537	1,174	1,456	53,704	53,704

[1] Includes the following programs: section 8 Low-Income Housing Assistance, section 202/811 Housing for the Elderly and the Disabled, section 236 Rental Housing Assistance, Rent Supplement, section 235 Homeownership Assistance.

[2] Includes the following programs: Public Housing Capital, Public Housing Operating Subsidies, Public Housing Drug Elimination Grants, Revitalization of Severely Distressed Public Housing, Low-Rent Public Housing Loan Fund, Indian Housing Block Grants.

[3] Includes the following programs: Housing Opportunities for Persons with AIDS (HOPWA), Homeless Assistance Grants, Supplemental Assistance for Facilities to Assist the Homeless, Emergency Shelter Grants, Supportive Housing, Shelter Plus Care Program, section 8 Moderate Rehabilitation for Single Room Occupancy Dwellings Program, Innovative Homeless Initiatives Demonstration Program.

[4] Includes the following programs: HOME Investment Partnerships Program, Nehemiah Housing Opportunity Grant Program, Rental Housing Development Grants (HoDAG), Rental Rehabilitation Block Grant Program.

[5] In order to reflect trends more accurately, figures have been adjusted to account for advance spending in certain years. In 1995, $1.2 billion of spending occurred that should have occurred in 1996. In 1998, $680 million of spending occurred that should have occurred in 1999. The Congressional Budget Office also expects that $680 million of spending will occur in 2000 that should occur in 2001.

Note: The bulge in outlays for public housing in 1985 is caused by a change in the method of financing public housing, which generated close to $14 billion in one-time expenditures. That amount paid off—all at once—the capital cost of public housing construction and modernization activities undertaken between 1974 and 1985, which otherwise would have been paid off over periods of up to 40 years. Because of that expenditure, however, outlays for public housing since that time have been lower than they would have been otherwise.

SOURCE: "Table 15-32. Outlays for Housing Assistance Administered by HUD, by Broad Program Categories, 1977–2000," in *The Green Book*, U.S. House of Representatives, Committee on Ways and Means, Washington, DC, 2000

average of 55,000 per year. The limited level of housing assistance means most poor renters desiring housing assistance are placed on waiting lists and sometimes wait several years before receiving aid. In some areas, waiting lists are so long that they have been closed, and new families are not allowed to apply.

Availability of Low-Cost Housing

The Center on Budget and Policy Priorities, a non-profit advocacy organization for low-income people, reported in *Housing Strategies to Strengthen Welfare Policy and Support Working Families* (Barbara Sard and Margy Waller, Washington, DC, 2002), that the supply of low-cost housing has declined from 85 units per 100 poor families in 1987 to 75 units in 1999. The number of hous-

ing units that are both affordable and available for rent is even less: 39 units for each 100 renters.

The U.S. Conference of Mayors conducts an annual survey of hunger and homelessness in U.S. cities. Its 17th annual survey, conducted in 2001 in 27 cities, found an 86 percent increase in requests for housing from low income families and individuals. Only 38 percent of those eligible were currently receiving housing assistance. The wait for public housing in the cities surveyed averaged 16 months and the wait for housing vouchers was 22 months.

Observers attribute the decline in low-cost housing to a number of factors, including the conversion of rental units to condominiums, rapidly increasing costs of maintaining apartments, and urban-renewal programs that have destroyed low-cost housing. The decline in federal spending for public housing, both in funding the construction of new facilities and in refurbishing older, substandard units, has also contributed to the drop in low-cost housing.

Expenditures on Housing

Most federal housing aid goes to "very-low-income renters" through rental-assistance programs that either provide low-cost public housing or pay rent subsidies so that the low-income families may live in existing private apartments. Under the latter program, the low-income tenant pays 30 percent of his or her household income for rent, and the government pays the rest. The federal government also assists some lower moderate-income households in becoming homeowners by making long-term commitments to reduce their interest rates significantly.

In 1995 about 82 percent of all poor-renter households and 78 percent of working-poor renters with children spent at least 30 percent of their income on rent and utilities, the level set by HUD as "affordable housing." By 1999 the percentage of working poor paying more than 30 percent of their income for housing had increased to 88 percent. Around 4.9 million of these households (three of every five) spent more than 50 percent of their income on housing. HUD considers these families as "worst-case" and gives them priority for housing assistance.

Federal Funding for Housing

Budget authorizations for these programs dropped dramatically between the late 1970s and the late 1980s, but have risen since then. The budget authority for all housing assistance programs in 2000 was $25.9 billion, and the estimate for 2001 was $28.5 billion.

While the authorizations were declining, the actual yearly outlays, many fueled by earlier commitments, were increasing from $15.8 billion (in 2000 dollars) in 1977 to an estimated $53.7 billion in 2000, an increase of 240 percent. (See Table 8.18.)

Average annual federal outlays per unit for all programs have generally risen, from about $2,980 in 1977 (in 1997 dollars) to an estimated $5,490 in 1997. (See Table

TABLE 8.19

Per unit outlays for housing aid administered by HUD, 1977–97

[In current and 1997 dollars]

| Fiscal year | Per unit outlays | |
	Current dollars	1997 dollars
1977	$1,160	$2,980
1978	1,310	3,160
1979	1,430	3,160
1980	1,750	3,480
1981	2,100	3,810
1982	2,310	3,900
1983	2,600	4,220
1984	2,900	4,500
1985	6,420	9,620
1986	3,040	4,440
1987	3,040	4,320
1988	3,270	4,460
1989	3,390	4,420
1990	3,610	4,480
1991	3,830	4,530
1992	4,060	4,670
1993	4,450	4,960
1994	4,720	5,120
1995	5,080	5,360
1996	5,350	5,490
1997 (estimate)	5,490	5,490

Note: The peak in outlays per unit in 1985 of $6,420 is attributable to the bulge in 1985 expenditures associated with the change in the method for financing public housing. Without this change, outlays per unit would have amounted to around $2,860.

SOURCE: "Table 15-33. Per Unit Outlays for Housing Aid Administered by HUD, 1977–97," in *The Green Book,* U.S. House of Representatives, Committee on Ways and Means, Washington, DC, 2000

8.19.) Several factors have contributed to this growth. Rents in subsidized housing have probably risen faster than the income of assisted households, causing the subsidies to rise faster than inflation. In addition, housing aid is being targeted toward a poorer segment of the population, requiring larger subsidies per assisted household.

Increase in the Number of People Served

In 2000, 4.7 million renter households received subsidies, representing 13.6 percent of all renter households. Half of these households had incomes below the federal poverty line. More than one-third (35.6 percent) of those receiving subsidies were African American, 46.2 percent were non-Hispanic whites, and 13.8 percent were of Hispanic origin.

CHAPTER 9

WELFARE-TO-WORK PROGRAMS

WORK, A MAJOR ISSUE OF WELFARE REFORM

The focus of the welfare debate has changed dramatically since the 1980s. During the early 1980s President Ronald Reagan attacked waste, fraud, and abuse in the welfare system, the conventional attack upon public welfare at the time. Since the late 1980s, however, the issue of welfare reform has focused on work programs as a means of getting people off welfare and keeping them off. Both among Republicans and Democrats, a consensus developed that jobs, either in the private sector, subsidized by the government, or both, were the basic answer to the welfare problem. By the summer of 1996 a number of welfare reform proposals had been offered for consideration in Congress. Virtually all proposals contained a basic requirement that welfare recipients get jobs, either on their own or with the help of local welfare agencies. At the same time, because of the recognition that effective job training can be very expensive, job-training funds in many proposed welfare bills were dropped or severely limited.

These and similar proposals, which have been around for at least a generation, are generally referred to as "workfare" programs. Both liberals and conservatives agree that those able to work for their income should do so. A job allows individuals the independence and sense of accomplishment brought by providing for oneself and a family. Furthermore, finding people jobs reduces the financial burden on state, local, and federal governments.

The passage of the Personal Responsibility and Work Opportunity Reconciliation Act (PL 104-193) in August 1996 laid the foundation for a work-based welfare system. The welfare law replaced Aid to Families with Dependent Children (AFDC) and the JOBS (Job Opportunities and Basic Skills) training program with Temporary Assistance for Needy Families (TANF) and created financial incentives for welfare-to-work programs. States must require TANF recipients to work after two years on assistance or face reductions in funding. In addition, with few excep-

tions, they may not use federal funds to assist families for longer than five years. Funding for the various state work programs is included in federal block grants to states. Within the general guidelines of the act, each state designs its own program to promote job preparation and work.

HISTORY OF WORKFARE

In 1935, in the middle of the Great Depression, U.S. President Franklin Delano Roosevelt introduced the nation's first federal welfare program. At that time, 88 percent of welfare families received assistance because the father of the family had died. Since the nation had a surplus of workers and a shortage of work, keeping widows at home allowed mothers to care for their children and also kept these women from competing with men in the job market. Public work programs for men, such as the Civilian Conservation Corps (CCC) and the Works Progress Administration (WPA), were also created to combat unemployment.

Community Work and Training Program

The 1962 Public Welfare Amendments (PL 87-543) authorized the first federal workfare program—the Community Work and Training Program (CWTP). This program allowed the states to choose whether or not they wanted to enroll adult AFDC recipients in workfare programs. The CWTP provided standards for health and safety, minimum wages paid as welfare benefits, training, work expenses, and child care. Those enrolled had to work in meaningful public-service jobs that did not displace other workers. Between October 1962 and June 1968 CWTP workers received $195 million. When the program ended in June 1968, it had involved 13 states and as many as 27,000 participants.

Economic Opportunity Act

The next major initiative, Title V of the Economic Opportunity Act (EOA) of 1964 (PL 88-452), allowed

TABLE 9.1

Job training programs[1] for the disadvantaged: new enrollees, federal appropriations and outlays, fiscal years 1975–98

Fiscal year	New enrollees/ total participants[2]	Appropriations (millions)	Outlays (millions)	Budget authority in constant 1990 dollars	Outlays in constant 1990 dollars
1975	1,126,000	$1,580	$1,304	$3,755	$3,099
1976	1,250,000	1,580	1,697	3,515	3,775
1977	1,119,000	2,880	1,756	5,964	3,636
1978	965,000	1,880	2,378	3,658	4,627
1979	1,253,000	2,703	2,547	4,829	4,550
1980	1,208,000	3,205	3,236	5,154	5,203
1981	1,011,000	3,077	3,395	4,493	4,958
1982	NA	1,594	2,277	2,175	3,107
1983	NA	2,181	2,291	2,846	2,990
1984	716,200	1,886	1,333	2,361	1,669
1985	803,900	1,886	1,710	2,279	2,066
1986	1,003,900	1,783	1,911	2,101	2,252
1987	960,700	1,840	1,880	2,108	2,154
1988	873,600	1,810	1,902	1,991	2,092
1989	823,200	1,788	1,868	1,877	1,961
1990	630,000	1,745	1,803	1,745	1,803
1991	603,900	1,779	1,746	1,694	1,676
1992	602,300	1,774	1,767	1,637	1,632
1993	641,700	1,692	1,747	1,530	1,580
Adult	371,700	1,015	1,048	918	948
Youth	270,000	677	699	612	632
1994	635,300	1,597	1,693	1,415	1,500
Adult	370,400	988	1,016	875	900
Youth	264,900	609	677	540	600
1995	536,200	1,124	1,534	971	1,325
Adult	353,500	997	934	861	807
Youth	[3] 182,700	127	600	110	518
1996	480,600	977	1,023	825	865
Adult	338,600	850	866	718	732
Youth	142,000	127	157	107	133
1997	483,100	1,022	949	845	784
Adult	367,300	895	799	740	660
Youth	115,800	127	150	105	124
1998	452,400	1,085	1,162	886	949
Adult	333,600	955	900	780	735
Youth	118,800	130	262	106	214

[1] Figures shown in years 1975–83 are for training activities under the Comprehensive Employment and Training Act (CETA); public service employment under CETA is not included. Figures shown in years 1984–92 are for activities under title II–A of the Job Training Partnership Act (JTPA). For 1993–96 figures are for titles II–A (adult) and II–C(youth) of the JTPA, as amended in 1992.

[2] Figures for 1975–94 are new enrollees. Total participants are shown from 1995 forward.

[3] Reduced budget authority in fiscal year 1995 was insufficient to serve those already enrolled and to enroll a comparable number of new participants. In fiscal year 1996, transfers from II–B (summer youth) enabled more participants to be enrolled. This transfer authority continues to be used by States to serve more year-round youth.

NA—Not available.

SOURCE: "Table 15-39. Job Training Programs for the Disadvantaged: New Enrollees, Federal Appropriations and Outlays, Fiscal Years 1975–98," in *The Green Book*, U.S. House of Representatives, Committee on Ways and Means, Washington, DC, 2000

states to develop "work experience demonstration projects" using EOA funds instead of welfare funds intended for AFDC mothers, unemployed fathers, and other needy adults. If participants in the work-experience program were also AFDC recipients enrolled in the CWTP, Title V funds supplemented welfare benefits. The demonstration projects spent $300 million, with participation peaking at 72,000 persons in 1967. Title V expired in June 1969.

The available information on the EOA and the CWTP is not adequate to evaluate the programs' actual impact on the lives and futures of the participants. The sparse data available showed that 36 to 46 percent of the participants found employment after job training or after leaving a work-experience project. However, the researchers do not know what would have happened without the programs' intervention or how long these individuals remained employed.

Work Incentive Program

The Work Incentive (WIN) program was enacted through the 1967 Social Security Amendments (PL 90-248) to make AFDC recipients less dependent on welfare. The 1967 amendments were in response to a 24 percent increase in the number of female-headed families eligible for AFDC and were intended to provide training for these women.

The WIN program required registration of "appropriate AFDC recipients," with each state defining who was "appropriate." The program included regular counseling as well as referral and assistance in obtaining basic education and job skills. The recipients in classroom and on-the-job training might receive a small incentive payment. The program was supposed to develop an "employability" plan for each recipient. But by 1971 it became apparent that most participants in the program were not finding jobs.

The Social Security Act was amended in 1971, 1980, 1982, and 1984 to improve the WIN program. The WIN program was phased out by the Job Opportunities and Basic Skills Training Program (JOBS). All states enrolled in WIN had to introduce the JOBS program by October 1990.

Comprehensive Employment and Training Act of 1973

The Comprehensive Employment and Training Act (CETA) of 1973 (PL 93-203) consolidated several federal employment and training programs, not all of which focused solely on low-income job seekers. Targeted at economically disadvantaged people, including those on welfare, the CETA training programs lasted about 10 years. In 1979 about 90 percent of the 1.2 million participants in the major CETA programs were economically disadvantaged—71 percent were in poor families, and 18 percent were AFDC recipients.

Food Stamp Workfare

The Food Stamp Act of 1977 (PL 95-400) authorized seven urban and seven rural workfare demonstration projects that operated between 1979 and 1980. The 1981 amendments to the Food Stamp Act (PL 97-98) expanded the program and granted authority to all states and localities to establish workfare programs for food-stamp recipients. The work programs were similar to the previously discussed workfare programs. Noncompliance (not participating in the work program) resulted in the loss of eligibility for food stamps.

After the first year, a U.S. General Accounting Office (GAO) study could not determine the overall costs and benefits. A later GAO study found that during the 1981 expansion phase, those in the workfare demonstration projects reduced their receipt of food stamps at a greater rate than those not on workfare.

Job Training Partnership Act

In 1982 the Job Training Partnership Act (JTPA) (PL 97-300) replaced CETA. Title II-A of this act provided block grants to the states for training and related services for economically disadvantaged people, especially those receiving cash assistance and food stamps. State and local governments administered these programs within federal guidelines. The aid was intended to increase the participants' future employment possibilities and earnings and to reduce their dependence on welfare. Services provided by this program included job training, help in finding work, counseling, and other assistance designed to prepare the participant for a job.

In a typical year during the 1970s, more than 1 million new people were enrolled in the job-training program. By 1984 the number had dropped to 716,200 as budgets were cut in half. Budgets (in 1990 dollars) continued to drop after 1986. As a result, so did the number of new enrollees, which declined from 1 million in 1986 to 635,300 in 1994. While Table 9.1 does not provide figures on new enrollees for 1998, it shows that only 452,400 persons participated in the program during its final year of operation.

The number of terminees (people who had completed the program) also dropped sharply between 1990 and 1997, from 307,935 in 1990 to 175,647 in 1994 and 147,717 in 1997. Only 45 percent of those who enrolled in the program in 1997 completed it. In 1997, 68 percent of those participating in these programs were female and 32 percent were male. Almost half (45 percent) were non-Hispanic whites, about one third (34 percent) were non-Hispanic African Americans, 17 percent were Hispanics, and 5 percent were from other races.

In 1997 the majority (57 percent) of terminees were between 30 and 54 years of age, while 41 percent were between 22 and 29 years of age. Only 2 percent were 55 years and older. In the same year 57 percent of those who completed the program were high school graduates, and 21 percent had an education beyond high school.

Critics of the JTPA programs claimed that the most employable individuals from the eligible population were selected to participate in the program. They believed that this had been fostered by the heavy use of performance-based contracts, in which the amount paid to a private trainer of JTPA participants was based on the number of participants placed in jobs. Therefore, contractors tended to screen out eligible applicants who might be difficult to place. The strongest evidence of this selection process was in the educational attainment of those in the program, over half of whom were high school graduates. However, it is also possible that those people with higher educational levels were more likely to apply for the program.

The JTPA program was repealed by Congress in 1998 and replaced in 2000 by the Workforce Investment Act, discussed later in this chapter.

SUMMER EMPLOYMENT. Title II-B of JTPA authorized a summer employment and training program for economically disadvantaged youngsters ages 16 to 21. Under this program, 100 percent of the participants had to be economically disadvantaged. Services included a full range of remedial education, classroom and on-the-job training, and some work experience for which the young people were paid a minimum wage.

As with the training program discussed earlier, outlays and participation dropped after 1985. Funding decreased from $776 billion in 1985 to $698 billion (in

TABLE 9.2

Summer youth employment and training program, federal appropriations, outlays, and participants, fiscal years 1984–98[1]

[In millions of dollars]

| | Appropria-tions[2] | Outlays | | Participants[3] |
		Current dollars	Constant 1990 dollars	
1984	$824	$584	$731	672,000
1985	724	776	938	767,600
1986	636	746	879	785,000
1987	750	723	828	634,400
1988	718	707	778	722,900
1989	709	697	732	607,900
1990	700	699	699	585,100
1991	683	698	663	555,200
1992	[3]995	958	912	782,100
1993	[4]1,025	915	827	647,400
1994	[5]888	834	739	574,400
1995	[6]185	883	763	495,300
1996	[7]625	1,030	870	410,700
1997	[8]871	913	754	492,900
1998	[9]871	787	643	495,100

[1] Appropriations and outlays are for fiscal years; participants are for calendar years.
[2] Because JTPA is an advance-funded program, appropriations for the Summer Youth Employment and Training Program in a particular fiscal year are generally spent the following summer. For example, fiscal year 1991 appropriations were spent during the summer of calendar year 1992. The pattern has varied somewhat in recent years. These variations are noted.
[3] Fiscal year 1992 funding includes a $500 million supplemental appropriation for summer 1992 and $495 million for summer 1993.
[4] Fiscal year 1993 funding includes $354 million for summer 1993 and $671 million for summer 1994.
[5] Fiscal year 1994 funding includes $206 million for summer 1994 and $682 million for summer 1995.
[6] Public Law 104–19 rescinded $682 million in fiscal year 1995 funds which were to be available for the summer of 1996. The remaining $185 million was for the summer of 1995.
[7] Fiscal year 1996 funds are for the summer of 1996.
[8] Fiscal year 1997 funds are for the summer of 1997.
[9] Fiscal year 1998 funds are for the summer of 1998.

SOURCE: "Table 15–40. "Summer Youth Employment Program: Federal Appropriations, Outlays, and Participants, Fiscal Years 1984–98," in *The Green Book*, U.S. House of Representatives, Committee on Ways and Means, Washington DC, 2000

current dollars) in 1991, while participation dropped from 767,600 in 1985 to 555,200 in 1991, rose to 782,100 in 1992, and dropped again to 410,700 in 1996. Approximately $787 million was spent in the summer of 1998 to serve an estimated 495,100 young people. (See Table 9.2.)

The summer employment and training program was repealed by the Workforce Investment Act of 1998. Summer employment programs for young persons are continuing as part of other programs for low-income youth.

Job Opportunities and Basic Skills Training Program

The Job Opportunities and Basic Skills Training Program (JOBS) was another program intended to help welfare families obtain education, training, and employment so that they could become self-sufficient. JOBS, administered by the U.S. Department of Health and Human Services (HHS), was also designed to provide these individuals with supportive services, such as child care. Each state was responsible for determining the structure of its JOBS program. This responsibility helped direct the training toward unique needs and job opportunities within each state. The Family Support Act of 1988 (PL 100-485) required states to replace any existing WIN programs with JOBS programs.

The target groups for the JOBS program were persons who had received AFDC for at least 36 months over the previous 60 months, parents under 24 years of age who did not have a high school diploma or a GED and who were not in school when they applied for AFDC, parents under 24 years of age with little or no work experience in the previous year, and members of families in which the youngest child was 16 years or older. In a majority of cases, the parent was female. Unlike previous laws, the act required participation in JOBS by parents of children as young as three years old and permitted states to include participation of mothers with children as young as one year old. As described by the HHS, the JOBS program:

- Emphasized education, particularly literacy and remedial education. Basic education, in this context, was defined as literacy and remedial education, English as a second language, and a high school diploma or the equivalent.

- Provided training and work experience for jobs that existed. Emphasis was on short-term, goal-oriented training. JOBS was designed to use and coordinate with other job-training programs that were already in existence. It encouraged community participation in programs such as community-based business and volunteer organizations. Work-training programs were targeted at areas that needed specific types of skills to match job opportunities.

- Gave states flexibility in program design. The federal government created the broad standards. But the states designed the programs to best suit their needs.

- Allowed women to choose relatives, independent contractors, or day care centers, within state fiscal constraints, as child-care providers. States used vouchers, direct payments, or other types of financing to compensate child-care workers.

Every state JOBS program was required to include plans to provide education to those without a high school education, offer job-skills training, and teach the person how to get and hold a job. With few exceptions, the program had to provide some form of schooling designed to get a high school or equivalent diploma if the person was a parent under 20 years old with no high school education. Similarly, the state had to provide educational programs unless the person had a specific employment goal that did not require a high school diploma if the person was over 20 years of age and without a high school or equivalent diploma.

JOBS required the state to supply child care to mothers who needed it. The state also had to provide transportation and other services if the parent needed them. If the family lost AFDC eligibility because the parent had found a job, the family could get a year of transitional child care and Medicaid. This transition period was intended to help the family adjust to its new situation and be able to somehow replace the child care and health services offered under the JOBS program. Basically, the JOBS program created a new government compact with welfare recipients. It promised to give them more training, supply transportation, furnish day care for their children, and provide Medicaid to protect their health, while the welfare recipient was required to get either an education or a job.

Funding for the JOBS program significantly increased potential federal financing. The federal matching rate was 90 percent, up to a state's WIN allocation for 1987. Funds for JOBS programs beyond that amount were matched at the Medicaid rate or 60 percent, whichever was greater. The total federal financing matched was set at a cap of $800 million in 1990 to rise to a cap of $1.3 billion in 1995. There were no limits on child-care funding, which was matched at the Medicaid rate, which ranges from 50 to 80 percent, depending on the state. Generally, federal authorizations permitted about 10 percent of welfare recipients to participate in JOBS programs at any one time. In a typical month in 1994, 579,213 people were participating in JOBS programs.

The JOBS program was replaced by Temporary Assistance for Needy Families (TANF) under the Personal Responsibility and Work Opportunity Reconciliation Act of 1996.

Job Corps

The Job Corps program was first authorized in 1964 by the Economic Opportunity Act. After 1982, it was authorized by Title IV-B of JTPA. The program serves economically disadvantaged youth ages 16 to 24 who show both the need for and the ability to benefit from an intensive and wide range of social services provided in a residential setting. In 2001 there were 118 Job Corps centers in the United States offering basic education, vocational skills training, work experience, counseling, health care, and other job-related services. About 88 percent of the trainees live at the centers while they are enrolled in the program.

In the 1997–98 program year, about 60 percent of the enrollees were male; 50 percent of new students were African American; 28 percent, white; and 16 percent, Hispanic. Seventy-eight percent were high school dropouts, and 63 percent had never worked full time. Thirty-three percent of Job Corps enrollees in 1997 came from families on public assistance.

In 2000 the average enrollee stayed in the program for 7.1 months. Those who graduated from the program were

TABLE 9.3

Job Corps, federal appropriations, outlays, and new enrollees, fiscal years 1982–98

[In millions of dollars]

| | Appropriations[2] | Outlays | | New enrollees |
		Current dollars	Constant 1990 dollars	
1982	$590	$595	$812	53,581
1983	618	563	735	60,465
1984	599	581	727	57,386
1985	617	593	716	63,020
1986	612	594	701	64,964
1987	656	631	723	65,150
1988	716	688	757	68,068
1989	742	689	724	62,550
1990	803	740	740	61,453
1991	867	769	769	62,205
1992	919	834	789	61,762
1993	966	936	846	62,749
1994	1,040	981	869	58,460
1995	1,089	1,011	873	68,540
1996	1,094	994	840	67,774
1997	1,154	1,165	963	65,705
1998	1,246	1,197	977	67,425

[1] Appropriations and outlays are for fiscal years; enrollees are for program years.

SOURCE: "Table 15–41. Job Corps: Federal Appropriations, Outlays, and New Enrollees, Fiscal Years 1982–98," in *The Green Book*, U.S. House of Representatives, Committee on Ways and Means, Washington DC, 2000

enrolled longer, an average of 10.6 months. Almost all (91 percent) program graduates (those either receiving their high school diploma/GED or completing a vocational trade course) got a job after leaving, continued their education, or entered the military. The hourly wage received by graduates was $7.97 per hour, up 6.4 percent from 1999.

Unlike most work programs, funding for the Job Corps was not cut as dramatically as that for other programs had been, and participation remained relatively stable. Following a decline between 1982 and 1986, outlays increased gradually each year to $977 million (in constant 1990 dollars) in 1998. The number of new enrollees per year averaged around 63,350 from 1983 to 1998, when it hit 67,400. (See Table 9.3.)

A four-year longitudinal study was conducted for the U.S. Department of Labor by Mathematica Policy Research. Called *Does Job Corps Work? Summary of the National Job Corps Study* (J. Burghardt, P. Schochet, S. McConnell, T. Johnson, R. M. Gritz, S. Glazerman, J. Homrighausen, and R. Jackson, Princeton, N.J., 2001), the study found that compared to a control group of youth who did not participate in the Job Corps, the Job Corps participants:

• Showed positive gains in education and training. (See Figure 9.1.)

• Were employed in higher-paying jobs.

• Were less dependent upon public assistance.

The Job Corps has been administered under the Workforce Investment Act since July 2000, following the repeal of the JTPA.

FIGURE 9.1

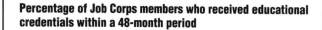

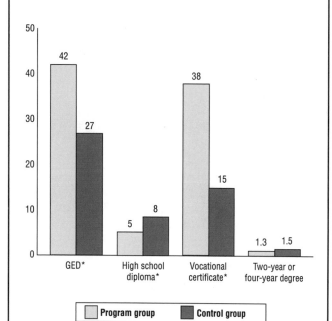

Percentage of Job Corps members who received educational credentials within a 48-month period

*Difference is statistically significant.

Note: Sampled eligible Job Corps applicants who applied between November 1994 and December 1995 were assigned randomly to either a program group or a control group. Program group members could enroll in Job Corps. Control group members could not, but they could enroll in all other programs available to them in their communities.

SOURCE: John Burghardt, et al., "Figure 4: Percentage Who Received Credential During the 48-Month Period," in *Does Job Corps Work? Summary of the National Job Corps Study,* Mathematica Policy Research, Inc., Princeton, NJ, June 2001

Workforce Investment Act

The Workforce Investment Act (WIA, Public Law 105-220) was passed by Congress in 1998 and replaced the JTPA. The WIA differs from the JTPA in several ways:

- Under the WIA, "one-stop" centers have been created to improve service delivery to adults. These centers provide training, assistance with job searches, and comprehensive assessment.

- The minimum income eligibility standards of the JTPA were eliminated under the WIA. All unemployed adults over age 22 who have had difficulty locating a job through traditional channels are eligible for the program.

- Participants in the WIA may choose their training courses and providers.

WORK REQUIREMENTS FOR TANF RECIPIENTS

The purpose of the TANF provisions differs significantly from that of the JOBS program. The stated purpose

TABLE 9.4

Work activity requirements for single parents at least 20 years old and for non-parental caretakers who receive TANF

Work activities	Average Weekly Hours Required		
	FY1997–FY1998	FY1999	FY2000 and later
1. Unsubsidized job 2. Subsidized private job 3. Subsidized public job 4. Work experience	20 hours, all in first 9 activities	25 hours*	30 hours*
5. On-the-job training 6. Job search and job readiness (6 weeks usual maximum) 7. Community service 8. Vocational educational training (12 months maximum)** 9. Caring for child of community service participant		— at least 20 hours in first 9 activities:	— at least 20 hours in first 9 activities:
10. Job skills training directly related to work 11. Education directly related to work (high school drop-out) 12. Satisfactory attendance at high school or equivalent (high school drop-out)		— 5 hours countable in last 3 activities	— 10 hours countable in last 3 activities

*20 hours for a single parent or caretaker relative caring for a child under 6.
**No more than 30% of TANF recipients who are treated as "engaged in work" may consist of persons who are engaged in activity number 8, vocational educational training. After FY2000, no more that 30% pf persons counted as workers may consist of persons engaged in activities number 8, 11a, and 12a.

SOURCE: Vee Burke, "Table 1. Work Activity Requirements for Single Parents at Least 20 Years Old and for Non-Parental Caretakers Who Receive TANF," in *New Welfare Law: Role of Education and Training,* The Library of Congress, Congressional Research Service, Washington, DC, 1998

of JOBS was to ensure that needy families with children "obtain the education, training and employment that will help them avoid long-term welfare dependence." The purpose of the TANF is to "end the dependence of needy parents on government benefits by promoting job preparation, work, and marriage." The 1996 welfare law imposed work conditions but did not specifically fund work programs. However, the 1997 Balanced Budget Act established a $3 billion welfare-to-work grant program for 1998–99. The president's fiscal-year 1998 budget proposed funding of $4.1 billion over five years to create or subsidize jobs.

TANF recipients are expected to participate in work activities while receiving benefits. After 24 months of assistance, states must require recipients to work at least part-time in order to continue to receive cash benefits. States are permitted to exempt certain groups from the work-activity requirements, including parents of very young children (up to one year) and disabled adults. The TANF law defines the "work activities" that count when determining a state's work participation rate. Table 9.4 lists the work-activity requirements for single parents who are at least 20 years old and nonparental caretakers.

To be counted as a work participant, a TANF recipient was required to work at least 20 hours a week in 1997 and

TABLE 9.5

Qualifying education activites for parent who is under age 20 and household head or married

(without high school diploma)

Work activity	FY1997–FY1998	FY1999	FY2000 and thereafter
11 a. Education directly related to work*	20 hours weekly	20 hours weekly	20 hours weekly
12a. High school attendance (or equivalent)*	"satisfactory attendance"	"satisfactory attendance"	"satisfactory attendance"

*No more than 30% of TANF recipients who are treated as "engaged in work" may consist of persons who are engaged in activity number 8, vocational educational training. After FY2000, no more than 30% of persons counted as workers may consist of persons engaged in activities number 8, 11a and 12a.

SOURCE: Vee Burke, Table 2. Qualifying Educational Activities for Parent Who Is Under Age 20 and Household Head or Married," in *New Welfare Law: Role of Education and Training*, The Library of Congress, Congressional Research Service, Washington, DC, 1997

1998. This requirement rose to 25 hours in 1999 and 30 in 2000, unless the recipient has a child under six. In the first two years, the 20 required hours must be spent in one or more of these nine high-priority activities:

- An unsubsidized job (no government help),
- A subsidized private job,
- A subsidized public job,
- Work experience,
- On-the-job training,
- Job search and job readiness (a usual maximum of six weeks),
- Community service,
- Vocational educational training (a 12-month maximum),
- Providing child care for a community service participant.

Three activities listed—work-related job skills training, work-related education, and satisfactory attendance at high school or its equivalent—become countable only if the parent or caretaker spends 20 hours in the other nine activities. Therefore, after 1998, when recipients must work 5 or 10 hours more, they may spend the hours beyond 20 in activities 10 to 12 and receive credit for them as a work participant. (In able-bodied two-parent families, one parent must work, or the two parents can share, 35 hours a week, with 30 hours in one or more of the first nine activities.) (See Table 9.4.)

Table 9.5 shows the additional provisions that apply to young parents who are under age 20 and are either household heads or married and who lack a high school diploma. They will be considered "engaged in work" if they either maintain satisfactory attendance in high school (no hours specified) or participate in education directly related to work (20 hours a week).

Education and Training

Reflecting a "work-first" philosophy, the 1996 welfare law limits the number of TANF recipients who may get work credit through participation in education and training. No more than 30 percent of TANF families who are counted as engaged in work may consist of persons who are participating in vocational educational training. Vocational educational training is the only creditable work activity not explicitly confined to high school dropouts.

In contrast, the prior law funded, and states were required to offer, education and training. Participants in the JOBS program were allowed to count postsecondary education as a JOBS activity. In 1995 higher education activities accounted for nearly 23 percent of the monthly average of JOBS participants. Because very few education and training programs count as work activities, many groups have urged that the definition of vocational educational training be more broadly defined to include training and education for persons beyond high school. For the estimated one-third of welfare recipients with a low literacy level, the National Governors' Association in 1997 urged "greater flexibility to count basic education activities toward the work requirement." However, the proponents of putting work first believe that education and training are more valuable and meaningful after a recipient is employed. They contend that participation in JOBS education and training programs often became the end in itself rather than the intended transition to a job.

FINDING AND CREATING JOBS FOR TANF RECIPIENTS

Job availability is one of the most difficult challenges facing states in moving recipients to work from welfare. This challenge includes both the location of job opportunities and the suitability of jobs for the skill levels and past work experience of most welfare recipients. If suitable jobs cannot be found, states must create work-activity placements. The challenge of appropriate job opportunities was made easier by the economic prosperity of the 1990s. However, issues could arise as the economy contracts in a recession, causing a scarcity of jobs.

Welfare agencies have had to change their focus and train staff to function more as job developers and counselors than as caseworkers. They make an initial assessment of recipients' skills as required by the TANF law. They may then develop personal responsibility plans for recipients, identifying what is needed (training, job-placement services, support services) to move them into the workforce.

States have developed a variety of approaches to finding and creating job opportunities. Though most rely on existing unemployment offices, many states have tried other options to help recipients find work:

- Collaboration with the business community to develop strategies that provide recipients with the skills and training employers want.

- Use of several types of subsidies for employers who hire welfare recipients directly (subsidizing wages, providing tax credits to employers, subsidizing workers' compensation and unemployment compensation taxes).

- Targeting state jobs for welfare recipients.

- Financial encouragement for entrepreneurship and self-employment.

- Creation of community service positions, often within city departments, such as parks and libraries. (Recipients usually participate in this "workfare" as a condition of continuing to receive benefits rather than for wages.)

These ideas are not yet fully tested, so their potential to meet the goals of welfare reform is unknown. The different approaches provide an opportunity to learn which programs succeed and which fall short. Careful state evaluation of their programs is crucial.

An In-Depth Evaluation of "Work First" Programs in Five States

A study by the Urban Institute, *Building an Employment Focused Welfare System: Work First and Other Work-Oriented Strategies in Five States* (Washington, D.C., 1998), was one of the first in-depth comparative analyses of how states are succeeding in moving to work-oriented welfare systems. The study of five selected states showed that strategies to promote employment, supported by a strong economy, have been effective in moving significant numbers of welfare recipients into jobs. The report was based on site visits in early 1997 to Indiana, Massachusetts, Oregon, Virginia, and Wisconsin, states that have experienced large caseload declines. These five states had begun reorganizing their welfare systems to emphasize a "work first" approach before Congress passed the 1996 welfare reform law.

Typical practices in all five states included (1) making the job search the first and major activity, (2) restricting participation in education and training, (3) imposing stricter participation and work requirements, (4) enforcing heavy penalties for noncompliance, and (5) setting time limits on

assistance. Nonetheless, despite the similarities, each state had its own unique plan for welfare reform. For instance, Virginia gave recipients the greatest opportunity to combine assistance with employment but also imposed harsh penalties for noncompliance. Both Virginia and Massachusetts required work sooner than the other states and depended heavily on community-service programs to engage recipients in some form of work. Of the states studied, Oregon had developed the most successful program for creating subsidized job opportunities for welfare recipients.

However, the researchers warn that a "work first" approach by itself cannot help all welfare recipients. It works best for individuals who are already fairly employable. It is less effective in helping those with significant barriers to employment or in helping recipients stay employed. Tracking a sample of recipients over a one-year period, the study found that, by the end of the year, 31 to 44 percent of the participants were still receiving cash assistance or were back on welfare, whether they had a job or not. Pamela Holcomb, the Urban Institute senior research associate who directed the study, said, "It's a strategy that gets a lot of people off the rolls quickly, but that's not the same as keeping them off welfare or moving families out of poverty."

More recently, states have turned their attention to the needs of those with barriers to employment, including health problems, low educational and skill levels, difficulties speaking English, substance abuse, mental health problems, and victimization by domestic violence. These are people who require intensive supportive services in order to obtain employment and for whom a "work first" approach is not appropriate.

As part of its Assessing the New Federalism project, the Urban Institute initiated case studies at 17 sites in 13 states in 1996 and 1997 to examine the impact of welfare reform. Follow-up case studies conducted in 2000 found that 9 out of the 17 sites had begun to use an enhanced mixed model to assist those with barriers to employment, compared to only one county in 1997. This approach generally includes an in-depth assessment of barriers to employment and specialized services for hard-to-employ individuals.

SUPPORT SERVICES NECESSARY FOR MOVING RECIPIENTS TO WORK

Child Care

The offer of affordable child care is one critical element in encouraging low-income mothers to seek and keep jobs. A recent U.S. General Accounting Office report noted that "any effort to move more low-income mothers from welfare to work will need to take into account the importance of child care subsidies to the likelihood of success." A study in Minneapolis discovered that about one-fourth of the former welfare recipients on the waiting list for child care went back on welfare when the child care services never materialized. According to the 1998 *Kids Count,* an annual report produced by the Annie E. Casey Foundation, child care expenses consume about one-fourth of the earnings of low-income families earning less than $1,200 a month.

The 1996 welfare reform law created a block grant to states for child care. The amount of the block grant was equivalent to what states received under AFDC. However, states that maintain the amount that they spent for child care under AFDC are eligible for additional matching funds. The block grant and the supplemental matching funds are referred to as the Child Care Development Fund (CCDF). In addition, states were given the option of transferring some of their TANF funds to the CCDF or spending them directly on child care services. As a result, the amount allocated for child care through the CCDF and TANF ($7.1 million in 2000) has more than tripled since 1997, when $2.1 million was allocated to the states.

Because states may use TANF funds for child care, they have more flexibility than before to design child care programs, not only for welfare recipients but also for working-poor families who may need child care support to continue working and stay off welfare. States determine who is eligible for child care support, how much those parents will pay (often using a sliding fee scale), and the amount a state will reimburse providers of subsidized care.

In 2000 states provided child care subsidies to 1.9 million low-income children, up from 1 million children in 1996. Approximately 70 percent of the children are cared for in child care centers or licensed family child care homes. The remaining 30 percent of children are cared for in more informal settings, including arrangements with friends and relatives. Despite the dramatic increase in the provision of child care to low-income families, many eligible families are still not receiving assistance.

Transportation, Access to Jobs

Transportation is another critical factor facing welfare recipients moving into a job. Recipients without a car must depend on public transportation. Yet two of three new jobs are in suburban areas, often outside the range of public transportation. Even when jobs are accessible to public transportation, many day-care centers and schools are not. Some jobs require weekend or night shift work, when public transportation schedules are limited. Even for those recipients with cars, the expense of gas and repairs can deplete earnings.

To promote employment, the vehicle asset limits under TANF are broader than under AFDC. While each state has the flexibility to determine its own vehicle asset level, all states have chosen to increase the limit for the value of the primary automobile in the family beyond that set under AFDC. In addition, 28 states disregard the value of at least one vehicle in the family. The remaining states exclude from $3,959 to $12,000 of the car's value.

According to the U.S. Department of Transportation, states use a variety of approaches to provide transportation for TANF recipients moving into the workforce:

- Reimbursing work-related transportation expenses (automobile expenses or public transportation).

- Providing financial assistance in the form of loans or grants in order to purchase or lease an automobile.

- Filling transit service gaps, such as new routes or extended hours.

- Providing transit alternatives, such as vanpools or shuttle services.

- Offering entrepreneurial opportunities for recipients to become transportation providers.

- Transferring TANF funds to the Social Services Block Grant in order to develop the transportation infrastructure for the working poor in rural areas and inner cities.

CHAPTER 10

WELFARE REFORM—THE FIRST SIX YEARS

Six years after the passage of the Personal Responsibility and Work Opportunity Reconciliation Act (PL 104-193), most observers view welfare-reform efforts with guarded optimism. In April 2002 the U.S. Department of Health and Human Services (HHS) issued its Fourth Annual TANF Report to Congress, which states that "the strategies of requiring work and responsibility and rewarding families who have gone to work are paying off. Since the welfare reform effort began there has been a dramatic increase in work participation (including employment, community service, and work experience) among welfare recipients, as well as an unprecedented reduction in the caseload because recipients have left welfare for work."

Even many welfare recipients appear willing to give welfare reform a try. In *What Welfare Recipients and the Fathers of Their Children Are Saying about Welfare Reform* (Linda Burton et al., Johns Hopkins University, Baltimore, MD, 1998), a report about 15 focus group discussions in Baltimore, Boston, and Chicago, the general tone of the focus group interviews was one of cautious optimism. In Boston, an African-American male focus group participant called welfare reform a definite step forward. By giving recipients the necessary assistance to enter the workforce, it not only encourages them to get training and find work, but it also helps build character and self-esteem.

As proposals to reauthorize TANF are being debated, the National Governors' Association (NGA) recommended continuing the primary focus on work and allowing states more flexibility in defining work activities. States are finding that a combination of activities, including training, education, and treatment of substance abuse produces the greatest success, particularly for the harder to serve clients.

CHARACTERISTICS OF THOSE WHO LEAVE WELFARE AND THOSE WHO REMAIN ON THE ROLLS

Welfare caseloads (the average monthly number of recipients) declined by 56.3 percent between 1996 and 2001, from 12.6 million to 5.5 million. Figure 10.1 provides a look at AFDC/TANF recipient changes from 1996 to 2001. The total number of families also declined by half, from 4.5 million in 1996 to 2.3 million in 2000.

The percentage of African Americans on the welfare rolls remained relatively stable between 1990 (39.7 percent) and 2000 (38.6 percent) and the percentage of whites declined (from 38 percent in 1990 to 31.2 percent in 2000). However, the percentage of Hispanic families increased significantly, from 16.6 percent in 1990 to 25 percent in 2000. (See Table 7.11 in Chapter 7.) The growing numbers of Hispanics on the welfare rolls can be partially explained by the fact that they represent an ever-increasing share of the total population in the United States. While the white population increased by 5.3 percent between 1990 and 2000 and African Americans increased by 21 percent, the Hispanic population skyrocketed by 58 percent. However, minority population groups are also over-represented among the more disadvantaged and are thus less likely to leave the welfare rolls.

The proportion of families with a teen mother has decreased. In 1994, 288,879 mothers who were 19 years old and under received assistance; in 1997 the number had fallen to 201,182. In 2000, 138,000 teen mothers received benefits, 14 percent of all teen recipients. The birthrate for women 15-19 years old fell to a record low of 48.5 per 1,000 women, down 22 percent from the high of 62.1 in 1991. However, the proportion of child-only cases has increased. The percentage of cases with no adult receiving assistance increased from 17.2 percent in 1994 to 34.5 percent in 2000. (See Table 7.11 in Chapter 7.) Child-only families are those in which the caretaker is not eligible for benefits, in most cases due to a lack of need or a lack of U.S. citizenship. Child-only cases are exempt from the work requirements and time limits imposed on other TANF families.

FIGURE 10.1

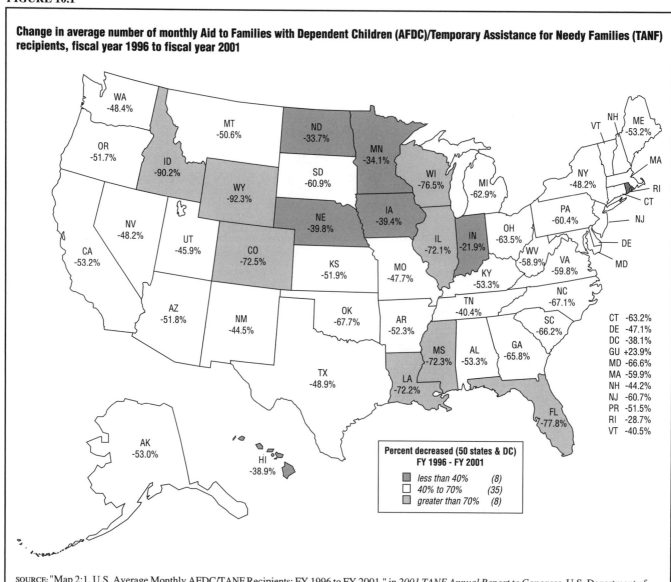

Change in average number of monthly Aid to Families with Dependent Children (AFDC)/Temporary Assistance for Needy Families (TANF) recipients, fiscal year 1996 to fiscal year 2001

SOURCE: "Map 2:1. U.S. Average Monthly AFDC/TANF Recipients: FY 1996 to FY 2001," in *2001 TANF Annual Report to Congress*, U.S. Department of Health and Human Services, Administration for Children and Families, Washington, DC, 2002

Although many recipients leave welfare for work, some have trouble keeping a job. Lack of understanding about workplace behavior, problems with child care or transportation, and the instability of the low-skilled labor market are all factors contributing to job loss. States must find ways to keep recipients employed, helping them build a work history so that they can move into higher-skilled, better-paying jobs. In its 1999 National Survey of American Families (NSAF), the Urban Institute found that 22 percent of those who left welfare between 1997 and 1999 were back on welfare when re-interviewed in 1999. The Department of Health and Human Services reviewed a number of surveys of people who left welfare that were conducted in various states. HHS found that a median of 27 percent of those who had exited the welfare rolls within the past year had returned at the time of the survey. While those who return to the welfare rolls are limited to a lifetime receipt of 60 months of TANF benefits, those who lose their TANF benefits are in most cases still eligible for other forms of assistance, including food stamps and Medicaid.

WORK PARTICIPATION

Sixty percent of TANF recipients are required to participate in work activities. The other 40 percent are exempt:

- Some 7 percent are single custodial parents with a child under 12 months.

- About 11 percent have been sanctioned (usually due to non-participation in work or a research project or as part of an approved waiver).

- Approximately 10 percent are exempt for good cause, such as disability or poor health.

TABLE 10.1

Average monthly percentage of adults in Temporary Assistance for Needy Families (TANF) with hours of participation in various work activities, fiscal year 2000

State	Total adults	Adults with hours of participation*	Unsubsidized employment	Subsidized private employment	Subsidized public employment	Work experience	On-the-job training	Job search	Community service	Vocational education	Job skills training	Education related to employment	Satisfactory school attendance	Providing child care	Additional waiver activities	Other
United States	1,588,651	631,132	60.6%	0.6%	0.7%	9.8%	0.3%	12.5%	6.5%	8.7%	2.7%	2.7%	4.0%	0.1%	4.9%	4.3%
Alabama	9,308	3,396	64.6%	1.2%	4.9%	4.9%	0.1%	17.3%	0.8%	10.6%	0.1%	0.0%	6.1%	0.0%	0.0%	2.9%
Alaska	8,739	3,483	63.3%	0.2%	0.1%	2.4%	0.2%	19.1%	8.8%	18.3%	0.0%	0.0%	1.8%	0.0%	0.0%	13.9%
Arizona	20,871	8,573	76.9%	0.0%	0.0%	16.2%	0.2%	21.6%	0.9%	7.9%	0.9%	0.3%	3.7%	0.0%	0.0%	0.0%
Arkansas	7,272	2,129	37.2%	3.1%	1.4%	6.0%	2.0%	13.3%	0.2%	29.2%	3.2%	2.5%	5.5%	0.0%	0.0%	3.4%
California	304,705	103,961	72.7%	0.4%	0.9%	1.6%	1.0%	14.1%	0.7%	9.4%	1.5%	2.9%	2.2%	0.1%	0.4%	0.9%
Colorado	7,050	3,176	51.0%	0.1%	3.9%	10.4%	0.3%	9.9%	11.3%	20.4%	0.0%	0.0%	11.6%	0.0%	0.0%	0.0%
Connecticut	19,485	8,299	80.2%	0.0%	0.0%	0.3%	0.6%	23.6%	0.1%	5.5%	0.0%	5.7%	1.5%	0.0%	0.0%	0.0%
Delaware	4,448	1,292	88.7%	0.0%	0.0%	8.6%	0.8%	8.5%	0.0%	0.1%	0.9%	0.0%	0.0%	0.0%	17.5%	0.0%
Dist. of Col.	12,623	4,356	86.1%	0.5%	0.3%	8.3%	0.0%	5.0%	0.0%	1.8%	0.9%	0.7%	0.0%	0.0%	0.0%	4.5%
Florida	32,164	12,647	67.9%	0.2%	0.5%	9.7%	0.0%	5.0%	6.5%	12.1%	0.7%	1.4%	8.0%	0.2%	0.0%	0.0%
Georgia	32,019	6,446	41.3%	0.3%	0.2%	9.2%	0.8%	4.6%	8.0%	24.6%	1.1%	0.3%	7.5%	0.1%	0.0%	13.6%
Guam	58	-	-	-	-	-	-	-	-	-	-	-	-	-	-	-
Hawaii	13,429	6,205	82.5%	0.0%	0.0%	16.4%	0.5%	14.0%	0.1%	7.4%	0.5%	0.5%	1.0%	0.0%	0.0%	0.0%
Idaho	424	365	32.5%	0.3%	0.0%	7.1%	0.0%	36.4%	3.6%	27.4%	0.0%	0.0%	2.5%	0.0%	0.0%	44.1%
Illinois	66,143	35,478	71.8%	0.0%	0.0%	8.4%	0.0%	0.9%	2.1%	12.3%	2.0%	4.6%	1.2%	0.0%	0.0%	6.4%
Indiana	27,378	14,824	88.1%	0.6%	0.0%	0.5%	0.1%	3.3%	0.0%	1.6%	0.5%	3.4%	0.4%	0.0%	14.1%	0.0%
Iowa	17,148	10,430	88.7%	0.6%	0.0%	0.7%	0.0%	1.8%	0.3%	9.4%	0.0%	0.0%	4.4%	0.0%	0.0%	8.6%
Kansas	8,812	6,191	51.2%	0.0%	0.0%	11.0%	0.1%	0.0%	0.3%	1.6%	1.2%	0.6%	7.4%	0.0%	55.2%	0.0%
Kentucky	24,447	7,450	53.5%	0.5%	0.0%	6.6%	0.3%	2.6%	14.7%	21.3	1.9%	2.4%	0.0%	0.0%	0.0%	3.5%
Louisiana	17,255	5,824	66.6%	0.1%	0.4%	15.2%	0.2%	5.3%	0.0%	19.1%	0.0%	0.6%	3.8%	0.0%	0.0%	0.0%
Maine	9,044	5,270	70.8%	0.0%	0.0%	5.5%	0.2%	17.1%	9.0%	3.8%	7.3%	0.1%	4.3%	0.4%	0.0%	5.0%
Maryland	16,160	3,351	31.6%	2.4%	1.9%	7.3%	0.8%	27.1%	2.2%	21.0%	1.9%	2.8%	10.7%	0.0%	0.0%	0.0%
Massachusetts	29,025	7,909	63.6%	2.6%	0.6%	0.0%	0.0%	6.4%	3.9%	5.3%	10.3%	2.7%	8.0%	0.0%	0.0%	0.0%
Michigan	54,679	24,684	88.2%	0.8%	0.0%	0.3%	0.2%	11.6%	0.2%	1.6%	0.4%	0.3%	2.3%	0.0%	0.0%	0.0%
Minnesota	34,677	18,000	68.6%	0.0%	0.0%	0.0%	0.0%	24.3%	0.4%	5.3%	0.2%	3.5%	10.0%	0.0%	7.1%	0.0%
Mississippi	6,946	2,094	67.0%	0.0%	0.0%	11.7%	0.0%	13.3%	12.0%	3.0%	0.0%	1.9%	2.5%	0.0%	0.0%	0.0%
Missouri	35,447	15,644	45.9%	0.1%	0.0%	4.5%	0.2%	17.3%	0.0%	5.4%	7.5%	7.1%	2.2%	0.0%	17.0%	8.0%
Montana	5,548	4,009	14.2%	0.0%	0.0%	69.2%	0.0%	16.1%	0.9%	5.5%	0.0%	0.0%	1.0%	0.0%	73.5%	0.0%
Nebraska	6,568	2,616	46.6%	0.0%	0.0%	2.0%	0.5%	24.7%	0.2%	7.5%	7.8%	0.0%	14.4%	0.0%	10.2%	5.9%
Nevada	3,882	2,003	50.4%	0.0%	0.0%	0.6%	0.0%	42.6%	2.6%	9.8%	0.4%	0.0%	1.8%	0.0%	0.0%	16.9%
New Hampshire	4,398	2,022	51.4%	0.0%	0.0%	2.7%	0.1%	35.1%	0.0%	3.5%	11.2%	0.0%	12.7%	0.0%	22.1%	0.0%
New Jersey	33,058	15,299	43.5%	0.0%	0.0%	39.3%	0.1%	15.6%	0.2%	22.9%	4.4%	12.4%	1.4%	0.1%	0.0%	0.0%
New Mexico	22,337	8,771	76.8%	0.3%	1.3%	2.1%	0.2%	0.9%	10.0%	8.1%	5.4%	5.0%	0.4%	1.1%	0.0%	0.3%
New York	232,540	76,842	59.2%	1.0%	0.2%	19.0%	0.0%	3.5%	13.8%	4.9%	0.2%	0.9%	0.7%	0.0%	0.0%	0.0%
North Carolina	23,211	6,474	58.3%	1.5%	0.6%	4.9%	0.2%	11.6%	0.0%	24.8%	0.5%	6.0%	4.4%	0.0%	0.0%	0.0%
North Dakota	2,891	863	52.0%	0.1%	0.0%	23.9%	0.1%	19.8%	1.9%	12.5%	1.5%	5.8%	1.7%	0.0%	0.0%	0.0%
Ohio	65,129	45,067	45.0%	0.1%	0.1%	31.3%	0.1%	7.7%	0.0%	19.0%	1.0%	0.2%	7.8%	0.0%	0.0%	19.0%
Oklahoma	7,880	4,257	36.8%	0.2%	0.0%	4.4%	0.1%	35.8%	0.0%	10.5%	12.4%	4.6%	3.1%	0.0%	0.0%	0.0%
Oregon	11,865	7,924	17.0%	4.7%	1.0%	5.6%	0.2%	32.8%	1.8%	0.0%	8.1%	7.1%	3.3%	0.0%	93.2%	8.5%
Pennsylvania	63,879	18,514	85.9%	0.0%	0.0%	6.8%	0.0%	7.9%	0.3%	0.9%	3.8%	2.8%	0.0%	0.0%	0.0%	0.1%

TABLE 10.1

Average monthly percentage of adults in Temporary Assistance for Needy Families (TANF) with hours of participation in various work activities, fiscal year 2000 [CONTINUED]

State	Total adults	Adults with hours of participation*	Unsubsidized employment	Subsidized private employment	Subsidized public employment	Work experience	On-the-job training	Job search	Community service	Vocational education	Job skills training	Education related to employment	Satisfactory school attendance	Providing child care	Additional waiver activities	Other
Puerto Rico	28,022	6,810	16.3%	5.9%	5.1%	3.4%	2.8%	38.5%	12.1%	14.3%	5.7%	1.7%	0.5%	0.2%	0.7%	2.1%
Rhode Island	14,076	5,734	72.6%	0.7%	0.0%	3.7%	0.1%	5.8%	0.0%	12.2%	0.0%	6.7%	1.8%	0.0%	0.0%	5.5%
South Carolina	8,244	3,183	58.4%	0.2%	0.0%	2.8%	0.5%	7.1%	0.1%	7.4%	3.1%	0.1%	7.6%	0.0%	27.8%	0.3%
South Dakota	1,275	790	25.4%	0.0%	0.1%	0.0%	2.9%	7.8%	63.4%	5.7%	1.6%	8.9%	1.8%	0.0%	0.0%	0.0%
Tennessee	44,033	20,443	42.3%	0.0%	0.2%	1.2%	0.0%	28.5%	1.5%	10.0%	8.8%	0.0%	21.5%	0.0%	23.5%	3.6%
Texas	90,275	13,327	43.0%	0.8%	0.4%	3.1%	0.0%	42.1%	0.4%	5.7%	0.6%	8.6%	2.3%	0.0%	30.4%	0.0%
Utah	6,265	4,892	29.6%	0.0%	0.0%	1.8%	0.3%	19.8%	0.0%	4.0%	13.6%	2.7%	1.6%	0.0%	0.0%	67.5%
Vermont	5,797	2,776	52.4%	0.0%	1.4%	3.7%	0.3%	26.0%	0.0%	16.1%	1.9%	0.0%	9.4%	0.0%	0.0%	22.4%
Virgin Islands	935	106	19.8%	0.0%	0.0%	9.4%	16.0%	15.1%	9.4%	6.6%	7.5%	1.9%	24.5%	5.7%	0.0%	0.0%
Virginia	19,415	6,676	77.4%	0.5%	0.0%	3.5%	1.5%	31.3%	0.0%	0.3%	2.9%	1.0%	0.2%	0.0%	0.0%	0.0%
Washington	48,307	42,476	40.3%	1.3%	4.9%	4.5%	0.2%	10.6%	48.0%	1.1%	6.5%	1.6%	5.4%	0.0%	0.0%	10.3%
West Virginia	10,157	2,504	25.2%	0.2%	0.3%	31.0%	0.7%	13.2%	23.8%	7.9%	0.0%	7.9%	0.8%	0.0%	0.0%	0.0%
Wisconsin	5,710	5,078	8.6%	0.1%	0.0%	63.5%	0.0%	14.3%	11.6%	4.7%	29.2%	20.4%	19.2%	0.0%	0.0%	0.0%
Wyoming	228	108	32.4%	0.9%	0.0%	50.0%	2.8%	33.3%	0.0%	11.1%	0.0%	0.0%	4.6%	0.0%	0.0%	3.7%

*Adults participating in more than one activity are included once in this total.

SOURCE: "Table 3:4:b. Average Monthly Number of Adults with Hours of Participation by Work Activity Fiscal Year 2000," in *2001 TANF Annual Report to Congress*, U.S. Department of Health and Human Services, Administration for Children and Families, Washington, DC, 2002

TABLE 10.2

Employment status of single and married mothers, 1988–2000

	1988	1989	1990	1991	1992	1993	1994	1995	1996	1997	1998	1999	2000
Married mothers													
with children under 6													
employed	53.2	54.8	55.8	55.2	55.2	55.7	57.8	59.7	59.9	60.8	60.6	59.5	60.7
unemployed	3.5	2.4	2.8	4.0	4.2	3.7	3.6	3.3	2.4	2.8	2.9	2.3	2.1
not in labor force	43.1	42.7	41.2	40.6	40.4	40.5	38.4	36.9	37.6	36.3	36.3	38.0	37.1
with children under 18													
employed	60.9	62.3	62.7	62.1	62.9	63.3	64.7	66.4	66.8	67.6	67.1	67.1	67.7
unemployed	3.1	2.5	2.8	3.5	3.9	3.2	3.5	3.0	2.4	2.5	2.7	2.1	2.1
not in labor force	35.8	35.1	34.4	34.3	33.1	33.4	31.7	30.5	30.7	29.7	30.1	30.7	30.0
Married mothers under 200% of poverty													
with children under 6													
employed	34.71	38.29	38.36	35.8	35.3	36.0	38.5	39.1	39.0	39.7	41.2	39.3	42.3
unemployed	6.02	4.27	4.24	6.1	6.8	6.8	5.9	4.6	4.2	4.4	5.2	3.9	3.9
not in labor force	59	57.4	57.23	58.03	57.9	57.9	55.4	56.3	56.7	55.8	53.5	56.6	53.7
with children under 18													
employed	40.4	42.7	42.6	40.5	41.0	41.8	43.7	44.2	44.4	44.6	44.5	43.4	46.2
unemployed	5.6	4.6	4.6	5.5	6.4	5.7	5.6	5.1	4.3	4.6	5.4	3.9	4.1
not in labor force	53.8	52.6	52.7	54.0	52.6	52.3	50.5	50.7	51.3	50.8	50.0	52.6	49.6
Single mothers													
with children under 6													
employed	42.9	44.5	47.8	46.0	44.0	45.8	46.4	50.1	52.6	57.6	58.8	61.9	64.5
unemployed	9.2	9.5	7.9	8.7	8.7	8.4	9.7	8.0	8.4	9.8	9.2	8.2	6.9
not in labor force	47.8	46.0	44.3	45.2	47.3	45.8	43.7	41.9	39.1	32.6	32.0	29.8	28.5
with children under 18													
employed	57.0	57.2	58.9	57.4	56.2	56.8	57.1	59.7	62.1	64.2	66.4	68.4	70.2
unemployed	7.3	7.3	7.2	7.4	8.0	7.3	8.1	6.9	6.7	8.2	7.2	6.4	5.6
not in labor force	35.6	35.5	33.9	35.1	35.8	35.9	34.7	33.4	31.2	27.6	36.4	25.4	24.1
Single mothers under 200% of poverty													
with children under 6													
employed	34.73	36.4	38.34	37.2	34.8	39.1	39.4	42.6	44.4	50.4	51.1	54.6	58.5
unemployed	10.4	10.45	9.53	10	9.8	9.1	10.6	8.7	9.6	11.8	11.0	9.5	8.0
not unemployed	46.7	53.15	52.11	52.75	55.5	51.8	50.0	48.8	46.0	37.8	37.8	35.9	33.5
with children under 18													
employed	44.0	45.4	46.3	45.7	44.1	46.0	46.1	48.2	51.1	54.4	56.6	59.0	60.8
unemployed	9.3	8.9	9.5	9.0	9.7	8.7	10.0	8.3	8.6	10.3	9.3	7.9	7.4
not in labor force	46.7	45.7	44.3	45.3	46.2	45.2	43.8	43.5	40.4	35.4	34.1	33.1	31.8

SOURCE: "Table 4:1. Employment Status of Single and Married Mother, 1988–2000," in *2001 TANF Annual Report to Congress*, U.S. Department of Health and Human Services, Administration for Children and Families, Washington, DC, 2002

- Around 8 percent are teen parents participating in educational activities.

- The remaining 4 percent of exemptions include victims of domestic violence, pregnant women, and persons who lack transportation or live in remote areas.

In 2000 the work participation rates declined somewhat, down from 38.3 percent in 1999 to 33 percent. This still represents a dramatic increase over the rate of 7 percent in the early 1990s. Some of the recent decline may be due to an increase in the number of hours of work participation required, which increased from 25 hours in 1999 to 30 hours in 2000 and some may be due to a weakening of the economy with fewer employment opportunities. Of those participating in work activities in 2000, 60.6 percent were participating in unsubsidized employment, 9.8 percent in work experience programs, 12.5 percent in job searches, 11.4 percent in job skills or vocational training, and nearly 7 percent in some type of educational activity. (See Table 10.1.)

EMPLOYMENT AND EARNINGS

Because caseload reductions mean lower expenditures, states have additional resources to offer further services to help welfare recipients overcome the barriers to finding work and supporting their families and to help them avoid a return to welfare. Several state employment-focused strategies, combined with the use of education and training to help recipients become employable and to find better jobs, have been effective in moving substantial numbers of welfare recipients into jobs. These strategies, supported by a strong economy, have resulted in initial welfare-reform successes. Employment rates for current and former welfare recipients have tripled since TANF was enacted. In 1996, only 11 percent of recipients were working; by 1999 some 33 percent of adult recipients had a job.

Earnings have increased for many welfare families. The average earnings per welfare recipient family increased from $466 per month in 1996 to $688 per month in 2000, an overall increase of 47.6 percent.

Reports also show sharp increases in employment for low-income (under 200 percent of poverty levels) single mothers. In 1992, 34.8 percent of these single mothers with children under 6 were employed, compared to more than 58.5 percent in 2000, an increase of 68.1 percent. In addition, employment rates increased somewhat among low-income married mothers with children under 6, from 35.3 percent in 1992 to 42.3 percent in 2000, an increase of 19.8 percent. (See Table 10.2.)

Earnings for female-headed households have increased, particularly for low-income women. For those in the lowest income quintile (the bottom 20 percent), earnings increased from $315 in 1996 to $1,646 in 2000.

Stronger Incentives to Work

States are finding ways to make work more attractive than welfare. In most states both policies and spending choices have focused on work and support for working families. Financial incentives include earnings disregards, Individual Development Accounts, the Earned Income Tax Credit, and increased asset levels.

EARNINGS DISREGARDS. In order to help families make the transition from welfare to work, all states disregard a certain portion of earnings in determining benefits. States disregard either a certain percentage of earnings or a specific dollar amount. For example, Idaho disregards 60 percent of earnings; Wyoming disregards $200 per month per adult. Ten states ignore from 20 to 67 percent of earnings.

INDIVIDUAL DEVELOPMENT ACCOUNTS. Thirty-one states permit those eligible for TANF to establish Individual Development Accounts (IDAs). Earnings deposited into these savings accounts are not counted toward program eligibility or benefit levels. These funds may be used for educational purposes, the purchase of a first home, or business capitalization.

EARNED INCOME TAX CREDIT. The Earned Income Tax Credit (EITC), which is discussed in Chapter 3, provides tax relief for low-income families. The U.S. Census Bureau has estimated that the additional income provided by the EITC in 1999 lifted 4.7 million people above the poverty level, more than any other government program.

INCREASED ASSET LEVELS. Eligibility for AFDC permitted individuals to have only $1,000 in assets. Most states have increased the amount of allowable assets, ranging from $1,500 to $8,000, and higher for disabled persons. Most states have also increased the allowable vehicle asset level.

Hiring Welfare Recipients

In a national survey of 500 employers, the Urban Institute found that nearly 75 percent of employers who have hired a welfare recipient are pleased with that employee's performance. Ninety-four percent of companies who have hired a welfare recipient report that they would hire another recipient in the future. More than 80 percent who have not hired someone from welfare say they are likely to do so in the next year, if they have entry-level job openings. Sixty percent of employers sought "reliability" and "a positive attitude" more than specific skills.

Harry Holzer and Michael Stoll, in *Meeting the Demand: Hiring Patterns of Welfare Recipients in Four Metropolitan Areas* (Brookings Institution, Washington, DC, 2001), reported on a survey of 750 employers in four metropolitan areas (Los Angeles, Chicago, Cleveland, and Milwaukee) in 1998 and 1999. Between 30 to 40 percent of employers reported having hired welfare recipients in the prior two years. While most employers expressed a willingness to hire welfare recipients, in actual practice many of the available jobs were in locations that were not accessible to welfare recipients. Minorities and those with low educational attainment faced particular difficulties in finding employment.

The federal government committed to hiring at least 10,000 welfare recipients between 1997 and 2000. By mid-1999, federal agencies had already exceeded the goal, employing 14,000 former welfare recipients. By 2001, more than 50,000 ex-welfare recipients had been hired by the federal government under the welfare-to-work initiative, although many of these were temporary positions.

Job Retention and Advancement

If welfare recipients are to make their way out of poverty, they must develop better employment histories, as well as increase the quality of their jobs over time through higher wages, improved benefit packages, and greater job security.

To promote career advancement and increased earnings for clients with significant barriers, the state of Virginia is developing innovative employment and training partnerships with business and industry.

Detroit's Focus: HOPE program provides workforce development for well-paying jobs, including training as machinists, engineers, and information technology specialists. Programs are open to high school graduates or those with GEDs, and help with tuition is available.

Pennsylvania provides specialized services to current and former TANF families with employment barriers to help them begin employment or continue to work. It uses TANF funds for job retention, advancement, and rapid re-employment services and a place-based employment collaboration with public housing authorities.

Employing the Hard-to-Serve

As caseloads decrease, a growing proportion of those who remain on the rolls have significant barriers to employment. Based on data from the National Survey of American Families, the Urban Institute identified six barriers to employment:

- Poor physical or mental health
- Less than a high school education
- A child less than one year of age
- A child on SSI
- Low proficiency in English
- Lack of work experience.

States are beginning to focus more attention on "hard-to-serve" families. For instance, many states have chosen

the Family Violence Option to ensure that victims of domestic violence get both protection and services. Most states exempt mothers of infants from work requirements.

New initiatives have been developed by the states to assist those with particular difficulties in obtaining employment:

- Project Early Intervention in Texas provides intensive case management to low-income families as well as employment assistance, substance abuse treatment, assessment for learning disabilities, adult education classes/GED preparation, and related services.

- A pilot project sponsored by the state of Missouri identifies welfare recipients with substance abuse and mental health problems and links them to the appropriate treatment services.

The U.S. Department of Labor administers the Welfare-to-Work grant program created to improve opportunities for those with employment barriers. In Boston, a program has been established to provide pre-employment skills training followed by internships and hiring. Philadelphia is using its grant to provide pre-employment services, paid work experience with close supervision, and ongoing counseling and support.

WELFARE SAVINGS

Dramatic reductions in welfare caseloads in recent years have substantially decreased the amount spent on cash welfare assistance. In addition, TANF block grant funding is based on the historically high caseload levels reached in the mid-1990s. As a result, most states now have money to fund supportive services, such as child care and transportation programs, to help needy families with children, and to strengthen their welfare reforms. Figure 10.2 shows how the allocation of TANF funds changed between 1996 and 2000.

Surplus funds can be used to increase job training and to provide child care and transportation, not just for recipients but also for some of those who have left the welfare rolls. States can also leave block grant money with the federal government to create a reserve fund for when the economy faces a recession. As of September 2000, HHS reported only $3.2 billion in unspent TANF funds, 5 percent of the $64 billion allocated by the federal government between 1997 and 2000.

Flexibility with TANF

Because of the flexibility inherent to TANF, states are permitted to decide how to appropriate the money they receive as long as they address at least one of the four TANF objectives:

1. Provide assistance to needy families so children may be cared for in their own homes or in the homes of relatives.

FIGURE 10.2

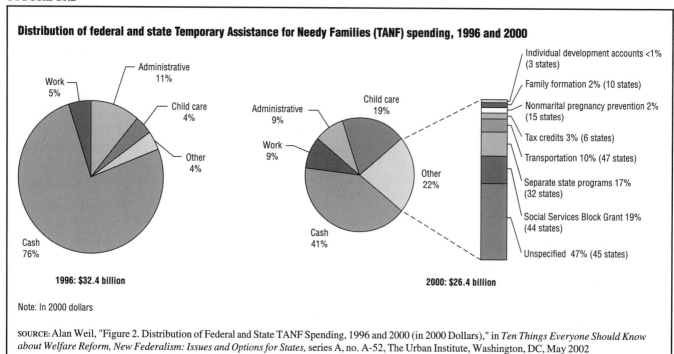

Distribution of federal and state Temporary Assistance for Needy Families (TANF) spending, 1996 and 2000

Note: In 2000 dollars

SOURCE: Alan Weil, "Figure 2. Distribution of Federal and State TANF Spending, 1996 and 2000 (in 2000 Dollars)," in *Ten Things Everyone Should Know about Welfare Reform, New Federalism: Issues and Options for States,* series A, no. A-52, The Urban Institute, Washington, DC, May 2002

2. End the dependence of needy parents on government benefits by promoting job preparation, work, and marriage.

3. Reduce the incidence of out-of-wedlock pregnancies.

4. Encourage two-parent families.

Federal officials are encouraging states to interpret these requirements broadly, allowing spending for any services that "reasonably" accomplish their intended purpose. A few restrictions limit the programs that states can develop. But the basic principle is that states can use these resources to fund services that strengthen low-income families and help their children.

SUPPORT SERVICES

Because of the additional services offered, overall state spending on welfare efforts has actually increased. According to the National Governors' Association (NGA), states are spending significantly more on child care and other support services to help people find and keep jobs. Providing child care is a significant aid in getting low-income families into the workforce. The number of children receiving subsidized child care doubled between 1996 and 2000.

However, some families leaving welfare for work have turned to unlicensed, informal types of child care. This type of care is often lower quality than regulated care. In addition, many eligible families are not receiving child care, in some cases because of complex application processes.

In order to help those leaving welfare get to their jobs, asset levels for automobile ownership have been increased in most states. In addition, several states are using TANF funds to develop strategies to provide transportation assistance to low-income persons. Delaware provides information about public transportation, off-hour transportation services, transitional transportation in areas not served by public transit, van pools and vehicle ownership programs in rural areas, and reverse commuting routes to suburban industrial sites. The State of Kentucky has established the Human Service Transportation Delivery Network, a collaborative effort with transportation brokers, in order to ensure accessible, cost-effective transportation in all areas of the state for TANF and Medicaid recipients.

In *Meeting the Demand: Hiring Patterns of Welfare Recipients in Four Metropolitan Areas* (Brookings Institution, May 2001), Harry J. Holzer and Michael A. Stoll report on a survey of low-income and low-skilled persons in four large metropolitan areas (Chicago, Cleveland, Milwaukee, and Los Angeles). The survey found a mismatch between the location of most of the jobs and the job seekers. Most of the opportunities for low-skilled workers were in the suburbs, while the job candidates resided primarily in the inner cities. Nonetheless, the survey found a greater readiness on the part of employers in the central city to employ welfare recipients than employers in the suburbs.

Child Support

In 2000, the Child Support Enforcement (CSE) program collected almost $18 billion for children, an increase

FIGURE 10.3

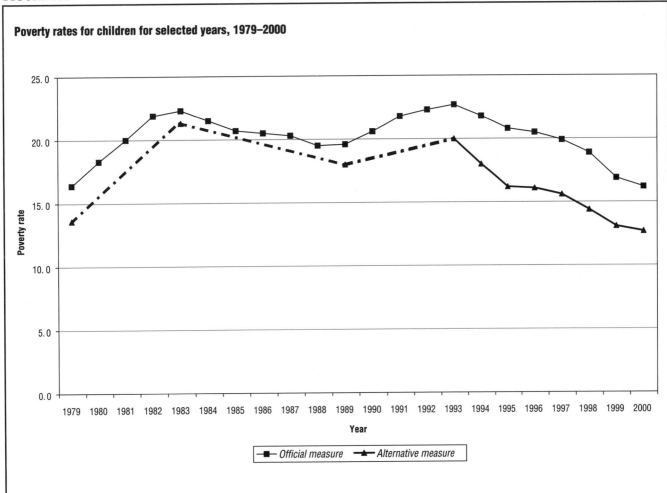

Poverty rates for children for selected years, 1979–2000

SOURCE: "Graph 9:1. Poverty Rates for All Children for Selected Years, 1979–2000," in *2001 TANF Annual Report to Congress,* U.S. Department of Health and Human Services, Administration for Children and Families, Washington, DC, 2002

of 12 percent from 1999, and a 49 percent increase since 1996.

Nearly 1.6 million paternities were established and acknowledged in 2000, an increase of seven percent in one year alone and 47 percent since 1996, when 1.1 million were established. The enhanced efforts to establish paternities and enforce child support agreements serve as a disincentive for men to father children outside of marriage. The District of Columbia, Alabama, and Michigan were awarded performance bonuses of $25 million each in 2001 for achieving the largest declines in out-of-wedlock births between 1996 and 1999.

CHILD POVERTY

Preliminary data indicate that welfare reform is having a positive effect in reducing child poverty, which declined significantly between 1993 and 2000. (See Figure 10.3.) Using the official poverty measure, rates declined from a high of 22.7 percent in 1993 to 16.2 percent in 2000. These are the lowest child poverty rates

since 1978. While poverty rates for African American and Hispanic children have declined by approximately 10 percent since 1996, one in every three African American or Hispanic children is poor, compared to one in every ten non-Hispanic white children. It remains to be seen whether these gains can be sustained in a time of economic recession.

AT-RISK SUBGROUPS

While welfare reform has been successful at reducing caseloads, more time is required to determine whether it will be successful in assisting lower-income persons become more independent and improve their situation over the long term. Two groups, the first consisting of current welfare recipients and the second of former recipients, are of particular concern.

Many of those who are left on the welfare rolls face the end of the five-year limit to TANF benefits. These are persons with multiple barriers to employment who risk the threat of even more severe poverty as their welfare benefits end. Even if intensive efforts are made to provide them with assessment, counseling, training, and educational opportunities, suitable employment opportunities may not be available, particularly as the economy slows and unemployment rates rise.

Many of those who are making the transition from welfare to work have minimal earnings. Based on an examination of the safety net in 12 states, the Urban Institute reported that income for a family with one parent and 2 children could increase dramatically when the parent moved from welfare to work, if the family received all available benefits. However, income support programs operate independently and families need help in taking full advantage of the safety net available to them as they make the transition from welfare to independence. Numerous studies indicate that former welfare recipients are not accessing all the benefits for which they are eligible. For example, most families with incomes under 130 percent of the poverty line are eligible for food stamps. Thus, many of those who leave welfare are still eligible for benefits due to low earnings.

However, a recent study, *Former Welfare Families and the Food Stamp Program: The Exodus Continues* (Sheila R. Zedlewski and Amelia Gruber, Urban Institute, 2001), indicated that only 40 percent of former welfare families were receiving food stamps. Most reported leaving the program because of the complexities of the bureaucratic process. Medicaid coverage is also low among those who leave welfare (57 percent) compared to coverage of more than 90 percent for those receiving TANF benefits. Receipt of Supplemental Security Income is also down, and many former welfare recipients report being unaware of their eligibility for the Earned Income Tax Credit. Thus, improved service coordination is required to ensure that families receive the assistance they need while they make the transition from welfare to work.

On the eve of the TANF reauthorization process, Demetra Smith Nightingale, in *Work Opportunities for People Leaving Welfare* (Urban Institute, 2002), urges that states be given the latitude to continue to develop employment programs. "Some of the more promising employment-related programs for welfare families are just beginning to mature. In the upcoming reauthorization process and in future welfare policy debates, it will be important to avoid making policy changes that might disrupt or stifle innovative programming, and to encourage more innovation where it is still needed..." Nightingale added: "Although caseloads have declined considerably since the enactment of welfare reform in 1996, recent economic weakness and the changing nature of welfare provide some justification for maintaining federal TANF funding at the current level."

IMPORTANT NAMES AND ADDRESSES

Administration for Children and Families
U.S. Department of Health and
Human Services
370 L'Enfant Promenade, SW
Washington, DC 20447
(202) 401-9200
FAX (202) 401-5770
URL: http://www.acf.dhhs.gov

American Public Human
Services Association
810 First St., NE, #500
Washington, DC 20002-4267
(202) 682-0100
FAX (202) 289-6555
URL: http://www.aphsa.org

America's Second Harvest
35 E. Wacker Drive, #2000
Chicago, IL 60601
(312) 263-2303
(800) 771-2303
URL: http://www.secondharvest.org/

Center for Law and Social Policy
1015 15th St., NW, #400
Washington, DC 20005
(202) 906-8000
FAX (202) 842-2885
URL: http://www.clasp.org

Center for the Study of Social Policy
1250 Eye St., NW, #500
Washington, DC 20005
(202) 371-1565
FAX (202) 371-1472
URL: http://www.cssp.org

Center on Budget and Policy Priorities
820 First St., NE, #510
Washington, DC 20002
(202) 408-1080
FAX (202) 408-1056
E-mail: bazie@cbpp.org
URL: http://www.cbpp.org

Child Welfare League of America
440 First St., NW
Third Floor
Washington, DC 20001-2085
(202) 638-2952
FAX (202) 638-4004
URL: http://www.cwla.org

Children's Defense Fund
25 E St., NW
Washington, DC 20001
(202) 628-8787
FAX (202) 662-3510
E-mail: cdinfo@childrensdefense.org
URL: http://www.childrensdefense.org

Food and Nutrition Service
U.S. Department of Agriculture
3101 Park Center Dr.
Alexandria, VA 22302
(703) 305-2286
FAX (703) 305-1117
E-mail: webmaster@fns.usda.gov
URL: http://www.fns.usda.gov/fns/

Food Research and Action Center
1875 Connecticut Ave., NW, #540
Washington, DC 20009-5728
(202) 986-2200
FAX (202) 986-2525
E-mail: webmaster@frac.org
URL: http://www.frac.org

Institute for Research on Poverty
University of Wisconsin-Madison
1180 Observatory Dr.
3412 Social Science Building
Madison, WI 53706-1393
(608) 262-6358
FAX (608) 265-3119
E-mail: evanson@ssc.wisc.edu
URL: http://www.ssc.wisc.edu/irp/

National Association of State
Budget Officers
444 North Capitol St., NW, #642

Washington, DC 20001-1511
(202) 624-5382
FAX (202) 624-7745
E-mail: nasbo@sso.org
URL: http://www.nasbo.org

National Center for Children in Poverty
Mailman School of Public Health of
Columbia University
154 Haven Avenue
New York, NY 10032
(212) 304-7100
FAX (212) 544-4200
URL: http://cpmcnet.columbia.edu/dept/
nccp/main1.html

National Conference of State Legislatures
444 North Capitol St., NW, #515
Washington, DC 20001
(202) 624-5400
FAX (202) 737-1069
E-mail: INFO@NCSL.ORG
URL: http://www.ncsl.org

Social Security Administration
Research and Statistics
6401 Security Blvd.
Baltimore, MD 21235-0001
FAX (410) 965-3308
(800) 772-1213
URL: http://www.ssa.gov

U.S. Census Bureau
Washington, DC 20233
(301) 763-4636
FAX (301) 457-4714
E-mail: customer.services@census.gov
URL: http://www.census.gov

U.S. General Accounting Office
441 G St., NW
Washington, D.C. 20548
(202) 512-4800
URL: http://www.gao.gov/

U.S. House of Representatives Committee on Ways and Means
1102 Longworth House Office Bldg.
Washington, DC 20515-6348
(202) 225-3625
URL: http://clerk.house.gov/committee/
index.php?comcode=HWM00

Urban Institute
2100 M St., NW
Washington, DC 20037
(202) 261-5709
E-mail: paffairs@ui.urban.org
URL: http://www.urban.org/

RESOURCES

The U.S. Social Security Administration publishes the quarterly *Social Security Bulletin* and the *Annual Statistical Supplement to the Social Security Bulletin*, which provide a statistical overview of major welfare programs. The Administration for Children and Families of the U.S. Department of Health and Human Services (HHS) publishes the *TANF Annual Report to Congress*, which describes the Temporary Assistance for Needy Families program enacted in 1996. Two additional valuable resources of the HHS are *Indicators of Welfare Dependence, Annual Report to Congress* (2001) and *Aid to Families with Dependent Children: The Baseline* (1998).

The National Center for Health Statistics (NCHS), which issues periodic reports on vital statistics such as birth rates and marital status as well as health status, is a part of the Centers for Disease Control and Prevention (CDC) of the HHS.

The U.S. Bureau of the Census of the U.S. Department of Commerce annually issues the *Statistical Abstract of the United States* and periodically publishes *Current Population Reports* that profile the U.S. population, as well as the results of the longitudinal SIPP studies based on the *Survey of Income and Program Participation*. *Current Population Reports* used in preparing this book include: *Poverty in the United States: 2000* (2001), *Money Income in the United States: 2000* (2001), *Dynamics of Economic Well-Being: Program Participation, 1993 to 1995, Who Gets Assistance?* (2001), *Child Support for Custodial Mothers and Fathers: 1997* (2000), *Households by Type and Selected Characteristics: March 2000* (2001), *America's Families and Living Arrangements 2000* (2001), *Dynamics of Economic Well-Being: Poverty 1993 to 1994: Trap Door? Revolving Door? Or Both?* (1998), and *Household Net Worth and Asset Ownership* (2001).

The monthly *Employment and Earnings* of the U.S. Bureau of Labor Statistics (BLS) provides data on wages and work patterns, while the annual *A Profile of the Working Poor* details labor information about low-income workers. Many of the BLS data are published in the *Monthly Labor Review*.

The Food and Nutrition Service of the U.S. Department of Agriculture provided detailed tables about the National School Lunch and School Breakfast Programs, the Food Stamp program and its participants, and the WIC program, as well as data from the *Survey of Household Food Security in the United States, 1999* (2000).

The U.S. General Accounting Office (GAO) in Washington, D.C., investigates topics as requested by the U.S. Congress. Some of its publications used in this book are *Federal Housing Assistance Programs: Costs and Housing Characteristics* (2001) and *Poverty Measurement: Issues in Revising and Updating the Official Definition* (1997).

The periodically published *Green Book—Background Material and Data on Programs within the Jurisdiction of the Committee on Ways and Means* (U.S. House of Representatives) provides the most complete information on the U.S. welfare system in a single source. The annual *State Expenditure Report* of the National Association of State Budget Officers shows how the states/territories spend their welfare funds.

The Congressional Research Service (CRS) is a government research agency that works exclusively for members and committees of the U.S. Congress. Some of its reports include *Welfare Reform: TANF Trends and Data* (Vee Burke, 2002), *Welfare Reform: Federal-State Financing under the Temporary Assistance for Needy Families Program* (Gene Falk, 1998), and *New Welfare Law: Role of Education and Training* (Vee Burke, 1997).

The Center on Budget and Policy Priorities (CBPP) is an advocacy organization in Washington, D.C., that releases reports, papers, updates, and studies on welfare.

Its publications include *A Hand Up: How State Earned Income Credits Helped Working Families Escape Poverty in 2001* (Nicholas Johnson, 2001) and *Failing the Unemployed: A State by State Examination of Unemployment Insurance Systems* (Maurice Emsellem, Jessica Goldberg, Rick McHugh, Wendell Primus, Rebecca Smith, and Jeffrey Wenger, 2002).

The *Annual Survey of Hunger and Homelessness* of the U.S. Conference of Mayors is a valuable source of information on the need for emergency food assistance and housing in U.S. cities.

America's Second Harvest, a charitable hunger-relief organization, and Mathematica Policy Research, Inc., collaborated on the national research study *Hunger in America, 2001, National Report Prepared for America's Second Harvest.* Findings from a study of the Job Corps conducted by the Mathematica Policy Research, Inc., for the U.S. Department of Labor, *Does Job Corps Work? Summary of the National Job Corps Study* (John Burghardt, Peter Schochet, Sheena McConnell, Terry Johnson, R. Mark Gritz, Steven Glazerman, John Homrighausen, and Russell Jackson, 2001) were also used in this book.

The Urban Institute, a nonprofit policy research and educational organization in Washington, D.C., published *Ten Things Everyone Should Know about Welfare Reform* (Alan Weil, 2002). Reports issued as part of the Urban Institute's Assessing the New Federalism project were also valuable resources, including *Work Opportunities for People Leaving Welfare* (Demetra Smith Nightingale, 2002) and *Former Welfare Families and the Food Stamp Program: The Exodus Continues* (Sheila R. Zedlewski and Amelia Gruber, 2001).

The Gallup Organization of Princeton, New Jersey, is one of the premier polling organizations in the United States. It provides numerous public opinion polls regarding welfare in the United States.

INDEX

A

Able-Bodied Adults Without Dependents (ABAWD), 15

AFDC. *See* Aid to Families with Dependent Children (AFDC)

AFDC-UP (Aid to Families with Dependent Children-Unemployed Parent), 93

African Americans. *See* Black/African Americans

Age
household income and, 45*t*, 47*t*, 49*t*, 50*t*–51*t*
income-to-poverty ratios and, 53–54
median household income and, 42, 43*t*
net worth of households and, 54
poverty and, 23–24
poverty level and, 24*t*, 30
poverty rates by, 26*f*
poverty spells and, 58–59, 58 (*f*4.4), 59*f*
poverty status and, 78*t*
program participation and, 84*t*–85*t*
Supplemental Security Income and, 107
of terminees in JTPA, 129
of welfare recipients, 82*t*–83*t*, 83
See also Elderly persons

Agricultural Research, Extension, and Education Reform Act of 1998, 109

Agriculture and Food Act of 1981, 112

Aid to Families with Dependent Children (AFDC)
background of, 92–93
caseload decline and, 12*f*
criticism of, reform for, 11
eligibility and benefit payments of, 94–96
enrollment trends of, 101 (*t*7.9)
federal expenditures for, 93–94, 95*t*
federal, state expenditures for, 93*f*
liabilities of, 91
overlapping services with, 89–90, 89 (*f*6.7)
payments, historic trends in, 98 (*f*7.6)
public opinion polls on, 91–92
recipients, change in number of, 101 (*t*7.10), 138*f*
recipients, characteristics of, 99–101, 102*t*

recipients, length of time on welfare, 101–102
recipients, number of, 98–99
state spending on, 94
states eligibility and payments for, 97*t*, 98 (*t*7.5)
survey of program dynamics and, 87
TANF block grant and, 12
teen mothers and, 102–105
workfare and, 127, 128

Aid to Families with Dependent Children-Unemployed Parent (AFDC-UP), 93

Aid to the Blind, 107

Aid to the Permanently and Totally Disabled, 107

Alaska
National School Lunch Program in, 114*t*
poverty guidelines for, 17, 18*t*

Annie E. Casey Foundation, 135

Asian and Pacific Islander Americans
family status, poverty of, 25–26
Food Stamp program and, 39*f*
Head Start program and, 122
median income of, 27, 28
Medicaid for, 119, 121 (*t*8.16)
poverty rates of, 23
poverty status of, 22*t*, 24*t*, 25*t*
TANF benefit recipients, 100

Assessing the New Federalism project, 134

Assets
food stamp eligibility and, 111
income definition and, 32
increased levels of, 142
net worth of households, 54–55, 54*t*, 55*t*, 56*f*, 56*t*
ownership rates for households, 57*t*
Supplemental Security Income eligibility and, 107

At-risk subgroups, 145–146

B

Balanced Budget Reconciliation Act of 1997
additions of, 12
effects of, 5–6
Medicaid coverage and, 116, 117
noncitizens and, 13

summary of, 15
TANF grant program and, 132

Beers, Thomas, 75, 78

Benefit programs. *See* Means-tested programs, federally administered

Benefits
AFDC eligibility and payments, 94–96
AFDC/TANF, maximum amount, 99*t*
AFDC/TANF, number of recipients, 98–99
of Food Stamp Program, 111–113
maximum combined, 97*t*–98*t*
minimum wage workers and, 72
overlapping services, 87, 89–90, 89*t*
payment per recipient, trends in, 98(*t*7.6)
program participation, median spell duration, 86*t*, 87*t*
program participation, overview of, 81, 83
program participation rates, 88*t*
program participation status of households, 82*t*–83*t*, 84*t*–85*t*
program spell length, 87*f*
Supplemental Security Income, recipients of, 108
survey of program dynamics, 87
TANF and food stamp benefits, 100*t*
use over period of time, 83, 85–87

Birth rate
of teenage mothers, decline of, 137
of unmarried teens, 102–103
of unmarried women, by age of mother, 103*f*

Black/African Americans
child poverty and, 145
employed, poverty status of, 75, 78*t*
family status, poverty, and, 25–26
family structure of, 63, 64*t*
Food Stamp program users, 39*f*
Head Start program and, 122
household income of, 46*t*–48*t*
in Job Corps program, 131
median income of, 27, 28, 42
median net worth of, 54
Medicaid recipients, 119, 121 (*t*8.16)
mothers and AFDC program, 92
percent of welfare recipients, 81, 83

size of, poverty and, 17, 18*t*

structure of, 61–63

tax relief for, 29–30

See also Low-income families

Family assistance grants, 95*t*

Family assistance payments, 3, 6*t*

Family households

median income of, 27, 42

relationships of welfare recipients, 82*t*–83*t*, 83

Family status

poverty and, 25–26, 27*t*

poverty level and, 24*t*

poverty spells and, 58 (*f*4.4), 59, 59*f*

Family Support Act of 1988, 130

Family Violence Option, 143

Farmer's Market Nutrition Program, 114

Fathers, custodial

award status of custodial parent, 67*t*

child support and, 64–69, 65*t*

Federal government

Food Stamp Program and, 111

hiring of welfare recipients by, 143

Federal housing assistance

described, 122–125

outlays administered by HUD, 124*t*, 125*t*

spending for, 123 (*f*8.4)

for very-low income renter households, 123 (*f*8.5)

Federal minimum wage

characteristics of earners, 74 (*t*5.11)

decline of, 72–74

history of rates, 74 (*t*5.10)

value of, 75*f*

Federal welfare expenditures

for AFDC and TANF, 93–94, 93*f*, 94*t*

for AFDC, EA, and JOBS, 95*t*

for food assistance programs, 113

growth of, 3*t*

for housing, 125

for JOBS program, 131

percent of total expenditures, 1, 2*t*

for TANF, 144*f*

for WIC program, 114

See also Social welfare expenditures

Federally administered programs. *See* Means-tested programs, federally administered

Female-headed households

earnings, increase of, 142

income gap and, 41

income-to-poverty ratios of, 54

median income of, 42

poverty spells of, 58

Focus: HOPE program, 143

Food assistance programs

emergency food assistance, 35–36

federal food programs, 116*t*

income eligibility guidelines for, 114*t*

National School Lunch, School Breakfast Programs, 113, 115*t*, 117*t*

Women, Infants, and Children, 113–115

Food costs, 30

Food insecurity

prevalence of, 36 (*f*3.5), 37*t*

statistics on, 33, 35

Food Research and Action Center (FRAC), 33

Food Security Act, 112–113

Food Stamp Act of 1997, 129

Food Stamp Program

AFDC payments and, 96, 97*t*, 98, 98 (*t*7.5)

average monthly benefits, increase in, 111–113

defined, 109

former welfare recipients and, 146

income eligibility for, 111*t*

maximum allotments for, 112 (*t*8.7)

maximum benefits with TANF, 100*t*

overlapping services with, 87, 89–90

participation and costs of, 112 (*t*8.6)

participation in, 109, 111

Personal Responsibility and Work Opportunity Reconciliation Act of 1996 and, 14

use of, by program type, 40 (*f*3.9)

Food stamp recipients

characteristics of, 113

employment, training program for, 15

housing for, 40 (*f*3.10)

income source for, 38*f*

number of, 81

racial background of, 39*f*

Former Welfare Families and the Food Stamp Program: The Exodus Continues, 146

FRAC (Food Research and Action Center), 33

G

Gallup public opinion polls, 91–92

GDP. *See* Gross domestic product (GDP)

Gender

program participation status of households and, 84*t*–85*t*

of welfare recipients, 81, 82*t*–83*t*

See also Men; Women

General Accounting Office (GAO), 72

Government transfer payments, 6*t*

Gross domestic product (GDP)

social welfare expenditures as percent of, 1–2, 3*t*

social welfare expenditures under public programs and, 4*t*

H

Hawaii

AFDC payments and, 96

National School Lunch Program in, 114*t*

poverty guidelines for, 17, 18*t*

Head Start

children served, costs, staffing, 123*t*

described, 119–122

potential number of children served by, 122*f*

Health care

increasing costs of, 1, 2–3

Medicaid expenditures, 4

national health expenditures by type, 5*t*

See also Medicaid; Medicare

Health insurance

State Children's Health Insurance Program, 15, 119

status of working poor parents, 119*f*

type of, coverage status, 121 (*t*8.15)

Heating bill, 122

HHS. *See* U.S. Department of Health and Human Services (HHS)

The High Price of Poverty for Children of the South, 25

High school diploma, 130

Hispanic Americans

child poverty and, 145

employed, poverty rates of, 75

family status, poverty, and, 25–26

family structure of, 63, 64*t*

Food Stamp program users, 39*f*

Head Start program and, 122

household income of, 48*t*–50*t*

in Job Corps program, 131

median income of, 27, 28, 42

median net worth of, 54

Medicaid recipients, 119, 121 (*t*8.16)

percent of welfare recipients, 83

percentage on welfare caseload, 137

poverty rates of, 23

poverty spells of, 58, 58 (*f*4.4), 59*f*

poverty status of, 21*t*–22*t*, 24*t*, 25*t*

poverty status of persons in labor force, 78*t*

program participation rates of, 88*t*

single-parent families, increase of, 62

TANF benefit recipients, 100

unemployment rate of, 72

in WIC program, 115

Holcomb, Pamela, 134

Holzer, Harry, 142, 144

Home equity, 55

Homeless

food assistance for, 35

housing for, 40 (*f*3.10)

Household Net Worth and Asset Ownership, 1995, 54

Households

asset ownership rates for, 57*t*

benefits and, 81

income by selected characteristics, 43*t*–52*t*

income gap and, 41

median household incomes, 41–42, 42*t*, 53–54

median net worth of, 54*f*, 55*t*, 56*f*, 56*t*

net worth of, 54–55

program participation status of, 82*t*–83*t*, 84*t*–85*t*

total money income, 53*t*

by type, 63*t*

use of programs over period of time, 83, 85–87

Housing assistance, federal

described, 122–125

outlays administered by HUD, 124*t*, 125*t*

spending on AFDC and TANF, 123 (*f*8.4)

for very-low income renter households, 123 (*f*8.5)

Housing, public, 101

Housing Strategies to Strengthen Welfare Policy and Support Working Families, 124

Housing vouchers, 122–123

HUD. *See* U.S. Department of Housing and Urban Development (HUD)

Human Service Transportation Delivery
Network, 144
Hunger
food insecurity, prevalence of, 36(*f*3.5)
by household characteristics, 36(*f*3.6)
poverty and, 32–33, 35
prevalence of, 37*t*
*Hunger in America, 2001 National
Report,* 35
Hunger Prevention Act of 1988, 113

I

Idaho, 142
IDAs (Individual Development
Accounts), 142
Illegal immigrants, 13
Illegitimacy, 93
Immigrants, legal, 13, 15
Income
at-risk subgroups and, 146
definition of, 32
food stamp eligibility and, 111, 111*t*
households by total money income, 53*t*
inequality, 41
poverty and, 27–28, 31*t*, 34(*t*3.8)
source of, for Food Stamp clients, 38*f*
Supplemental Security Income eligibility
and, 108 (*t*8.1)
welfare reform and, 142
Income distribution. *See* Wealth and income
distribution
Income, median household
by definition, 34 (*f*3.8)
factors of, 41–42, 53–54
statistical information on, 43*t*–52*t*
Income-to-poverty ratios, 53–54
Indicators of Welfare Dependency, 61
Individual Development Accounts
(IDAs), 142
Insurance. *See* Health insurance;
Unemployment
*Is the Unemployment Insurance System a
Safety Net for Welfare Recipients Who
Exit Welfare for Work?,* 72

J

Job Corps program
educational credentials from, 132*f*
federal appropriations, outlays, new
enrollees, 131*t*
history of, 131
Job Opportunities and Basic Skills Training
Program (JOBS)
federal expenditures, 93, 93*f*, 95*t*
history, description of, 130–131
replacement for WIN program, 129
Job training, 128*t*
See also Welfare-to-work programs
Job Training Partnership Act (JTPA),
129–130, 130*t*
JOBS. *See* Job Opportunities and Basic
Skills Training Program (JOBS)
Jobs
difficulty maintaining, 138
support services for, 134–135
for TANF recipients, finding, creating,
133–134

transportation for, 144
welfare reform, effect on, 142–143
See also Employment; Welfare-to-work
programs
Johnson, Nicholas, 26
JTPA (Job Training Partnership Act),
129–130, 130*t*

K

Kentucky, 144
Kids Count, 135
*Kids Having Kids: A Robin Hood
Foundation Special Report on the Costs
of Adolescent Childbearing,* 102, 103

L

Labor market, 78
Legislation and international treaties
1962 Public Welfare Amendments, 127
Agricultural Research, Extension, and
Education Reform Act of 1998, 109
Child Nutrition Act of 1966, 113, 114
Crude Oil Windfall Profit Tax Act of
1980, 122
Economic Opportunity Act of 1964, 119,
127–128, 131
Fair Labor Standards Act, 72
Family Support Act of 1988, 130
Food Stamp Act of 1997, 129
for Food Stamp Program, 112–113
National School Lunch Act, 113
Noncitizen Technical Amendment Act of
1998, 13
Omnibus Budget Reconciliation Act, 98,
112, 122
Personal Responsibility and Work
Opportunity Reconciliation Act of
1996, 3–4, 12–14
Social Security Act, 92
Social Security Amendments, 1967,
128, 129
Supplemental Appropriations Act, 109
Tax Reform Act of 1986, 29–30
for workfare, 129
Workforce Investment Act, 132
See also Balanced Budget Reconciliation
Act of 1997; Welfare-reform legislation
LIHEAP (Low-Income Home Energy
Assistance Program), 122
Low-cost housing, 124–125
Low-income families
child care for, 14
food insecurity of, 35
housing assistance for, 122–125,
123 (*f*8.5)
tax relief for, 29–30
See also Poverty
Low-Income Home Energy Assistance
Program (LIHEAP), 122
*The Low-Wage Labor Market: Does the
Minimum Wage Help or Hurt Low-Wage
Workers?,* 73
Low-wage workers
drop in wages, 41
unemployment compensation for, 72

M

Maintenance-of-effort (MOE) level, 94, 96*t*
Marriage
long-term welfare recipient and, 102
marital status of population, 66 (*f*5.2)
married mothers, employment status
of, 141*t*
never-married adults, 64
Massachusetts, 134, 143
Mathematica Policy Research, 35
Maynard, Rebecca, 102, 103
Means-test assistance, 81
Means-tested programs, federally
administered, 107–125
federal food programs, 116*t*
federal housing assistance,
122–125, 125*t*
Food Stamp Program, 109–113,
111*t*, 112*t*
free/reduced price meals, income
eligibility guidelines for, 114*t*
Head Start, 119–122, 122*f*
health insurance status of working poor
parents, 119*f*
health insurance type, coverage status,
121 (*t*8.15)
Low-Income Home Energy Assistance
Program, 122
Medicaid, 115–119, 118 (*f*8.13), 120*t*,
121 (*t*8.16)
National School Lunch Program,
113, 115*t*
non-cash means-tested benefits, 109
number of recipients of, 109*t*, 110*t*
School Breakfast Program, 113, 117*t*
State Child Health Insurance
Program, 119
Supplemental Security Income,
107–109, 108*t*
Women, Infants, and Children, 113–115,
118 (*t*8.12)
Medicaid
children covered by, 121 (*t*8.16)
costs, growth in, 119
expenditures for, 1, 3, 4, 5*t*
former welfare recipients, coverage
for, 146
in general, 115–116
health expenditures by type, 5*t*
income definition and, 32
JOBS program and, 131
number of people covered by, 81
recipients and payment amounts, 118
(*t*8.13), 120*t*
recipients of, 116–119
state expenditures for, 8*f*
Medical care. *See* Health care
Medicare
expenditures for, 3
income definition and, 32
*Meeting the Demand: Hiring Patterns of
Welfare Recipients in Four Metropolitan
Areas,* 142–143, 144
Men
child support and, 64–66
marital status of, 66 (*f*5.2)
median personal income of, 74, 76*t*–77*t*

as minimum-wage workers, 73
percent of welfare recipients, 81, 82t–83t
program participation status of households and, 84t–85t
working, poverty status of, 75, 78t
See also Fathers, custodial
Mickey Leland Childhood Hunger Relief Act, 113
Midwest, poverty rate of, 25
Minimum wage, federal
characteristics of earners, 74 (t5.11)
decline of, 72–74
history of, 74 (t5.10)
value of, 75f
Minneapolis (MN), 134–135
Missouri, 143
MOE (Maintenance-of-effort) level, 94, 96t
Mothers
employment increase for, 142
single/married, employment status of, 141t
teenage mothers and welfare, 102–105
teenage mothers, birth rate of, 137
unmarried women, birth rate of, 103f
See also Female-headed households
Mothers, custodial
award status of custodial parent, 67t
child support and, 64–69, 65t
Mother's Pension funds, 92

N

Naifeh, Mary, 57–58
National Governors' Association (NGA), 133, 137
National School Lunch Program (NSLP)
described, 113
income eligibility guidelines for, 114t
participation, lunches served, 115t
National Survey of American Families, 143
"near poor" group, 53, 54
Need standards, 94–96
Net worth. *See* Wealth and income distribution
Never-married adults
child support of, 67
effects on poverty, welfare use, 64
percent of population, 66 (f5.2)
New York, 99
NGA (National Governors' Association), 133, 137
Nightingale, Demetra Smith, 146
Non-cash means-tested benefits, 109
See also Means-tested programs, federally administered
"non-poor" group, 53
Noncitizen Technical Amendment Act of 1998, 13
Nonfamily households, 41, 42
Northeast region, poverty rate of, 25
NSLP. *See* National School Lunch Program (NSLP)

O

Old Age Assistance, 107
Omnibus Budget Reconciliation Act (OBRA), 98, 112, 122
Oregon, 134

Orshansky, Mollie, 17
Overlapping services, 87, 89–90, 89t

P

Panel on Poverty and Family Assistance, 32
Parents. *See* Custodial parents; Mothers
Paternity establishments, 13, 145
Pavetti, LaDonna, 11
Pennsylvania, 143
Per capita income, 27–28
Per capita spending, 3
Personal Responsibility and Work Opportunity Reconciliation Act of 1996 (PRWORA)
child support and, 68
effects of, 5–6
Food Stamp Program and, 109
growth of welfare spending under, 13f
optimism after, 137
poverty spells and, 57
reauthorization of, 15
state expenditures and, 3–4
summary of, 12–14
Supplemental Security Income and, 107
Temporary Assistance for Needy Families program and, 11, 91
welfare-to-work programs and, 127
Philadelphia (PA), 143
Poverty, 17–40
age and, 23–24, 26f
background on, 17
child poverty, 24–25, 145, 145f
education and, 26–27
emergency food assistance, demand for, 35–36
employment and, 75, 78
family size and, 17, 18t
family status and, 25–26, 27t
food security, insecurity, hunger, 37t
Food Stamp clients, housing for, 40 (f3.10)
Food Stamp clients, income source of, 38f
Food Stamp clients, racial background of, 39f
Food Stamp program, use of, 40 (f3.9)
guidelines, 17, 18t
hunger, 32–33, 35, 36f
median income and, 27–28, 31t, 34 (t3.8)
number of poor and poverty rate, 23f
poverty level, accuracy of, 30, 32
race and ethnicity and, 17, 19t–22t, 22–24
by regions, 25
by selected characteristics, 24t, 25t
state rates of, 26, 28t
status, of custodial parents, 67f
status, of persons in labor force, 78t, 79t
tax relief for poor, 29–30, 30f, 34 (t3.9)
unemployment compensation and, 72
work experience and, 26, 29t
Poverty and welfare use, factors affecting, 61–79
assistance from the government, 61
child support, 64–69
divorce, 63–64
employment, 75, 78

family structure of welfare recipients, 61–63
federal minimum wage, 72–74, 74t, 75f
never-married adults, 64
persons by total income, race, Hispanic origin, and sex, 76t–77t
poverty status of persons in labor force, 78t, 79t
total earnings trends, 74
unemployment compensation, 69, 70t–71t, 71–72
unemployment indicators, 73t
Poverty level
accuracy of, 30, 32
defined, 17
income-to-poverty ratios, 53–54
Poverty spells
chronic poverty rates, 59 (f4.5)
duration of, 58 (f4.3)
entry rates, 59 (f4.7)
exit rates, 59 (f4.6)
explained, 55, 57–59
median, 58 (f4.4)
Poverty threshold
accuracy of, 30, 32
defined, 17
Pregnant women, 116, 117
Private welfare expenditures
health expenditures by type, 5t
as percent of total private outlays, 9t
types of, 5
A Profile of the Working Poor, 75
Project Early Intervention, 143
PRWORA. *See* Personal Responsibility and Work Opportunity Reconciliation Act of 1996 (PRWORA)
Public aid, 1–3
Public housing, 101
See also Housing assistance, federal
Public opinion polls, welfare, 91–92, 91t
Public programs, 2t

R

Race and ethnicity
child poverty and, 145
children's living arrangements by, 64t
education and, 26
family status, poverty, and, 25–26
family structure and, 62, 63
food assistance and, 35
Food Stamp Program and, 39f, 111
Head Start program and, 122
income-to-poverty ratios and, 54
in Job Corps program, 131
of JTPA participants, 129
median income and, 27–28, 42
Medicaid recipients and, 119, 121 (t8.16)
poverty and, 17, 19t–22t, 22–24
poverty level and, 24t
poverty spells and, 58–59, 58 (f4.4)
poverty status of persons in labor force, 78t
program participation rates and, 88t
of TANF benefit recipients, 100
welfare caseload decline and, 137
welfare recipients, characteristics of, 81, 83
See also specific race